RUB OUT THE WORDS

ecco

AN IMPRINT OF **HARPERCOLLINS** *PUBLISHERS*

RUB OUT THE WORDS

THE LETTERS OF WILLIAM S. BURROUGHS
1959–1974

EDITED AND WITH AN INTRODUCTION
BY BILL MORGAN

FOR IAN

RUB OUT THE WORDS. Copyright © 2012 by the William S. Burroughs Trust. All rights reserved. Printed in the United States of America. No part of this book may be used or reproduced in any manner whatsoever without written permission except in the case of brief quotations embodied in critical articles and reviews. For information address HarperCollins Publishers, 10 East 53rd Street, New York, NY 10022.

HarperCollins books may be purchased for educational, business, or sales promotional use. For information please write: Special Markets Department, HarperCollins Publishers, 10 East 53rd Street, New York, NY 10022.

FIRST EDITION

Designed by Mary Austin Speaker

Library of Congress Cataloging-in-Publication Data has been applied for.

ISBN 978-0-06-171142-8

12 13 14 15 16   OV/RRD   10 9 8 7 6 5 4 3 2 1

Burroughs is the greatest satirical writer since Jonathan Swift.

—JACK KEROUAC

CONTENTS

FOREWORD

Bill Morgan thanks me too generously, and I certainly appreciate it. But as an aspiring "bone feed mast-fed Razor Back" *Factualist*, I want the record to show that—compared to Bill—I did very little of the vast work that has brought this book to fruition. Initially, I gave him my global listing of archival repositories known to hold Burroughs-related letters and my analyses of the key holdings. Everything else between these covers was accomplished by Bill Morgan.

These letters were written during the fifteen years of Burroughs' life immediately before he and I came into each other's lives. They are a moving-picture window where we may see and feel the Burroughs who wrote *Naked Lunch* becoming the Burroughs whom I first met in New York in early 1974, one week after his sixtieth birthday and six weeks after my twenty-first.

Reading these letters carries me back to my early twenties; I am stunned by my forgotten memories of who I was then and who I thought William was then. Because, now, I shall turn sixty next year.

And at last, in my own late middle age, I can begin to imagine how it really *felt* to be William Burroughs in those long-ago, late-winter streets and lofts of New York City: behind him, a long and storied past; before him, an unknown and unknowable future.

Read this book, with Bill Morgan's thorough, accurate, helpful notes and writings, and you will find that same William Burroughs coming to life in your heart.

James Grauerholz

ACKNOWLEDGMENTS

One of the pleasures of editing correspondence comes from the fact that it is always a group effort. Collecting letters requires the cooperation and support of a great many people. In putting together the letters written by William S. Burroughs, one person stands head and shoulders above all others. In fact, James Grauerholz has been the lynchpin for the entire project. He worked with Burroughs as his right hand, his personal secretary, his agent, his collaborator, his strongest advocate, and his best friend during the last twenty-five years of the writer's life. His efforts on behalf of Burroughs enabled the writer to create and live comfortably even through his final days. It was James who asked me to undertake this collection, and for that alone I owe him a debt of gratitude. His knowledge and editorial advice have been a treasured resource that I have come to rely upon.

Although Oliver Harris, the editor of *The Letters of William S. Burroughs 1945–1959* (Viking, 1993), was unable to participate in this book owing to other commitments, his influence and hand are clearly visible in the current volume. Early in the work, this editor decided that following the format set by Harris' book made sense. That earlier collection was faultless, so there is no need to change. I only hope that I have been able to approximate his learned hand in editorial decisions.

A host of people and institutions provided help along the way, offering information and support at every turn. In particular, the American Philosophical Society granted financial aid when I most needed it to track down letters in far-flung libraries. I am exceedingly grateful to them for that assistance.

The staffs of many university libraries were most helpful in allowing me access to their collections. Isaac Gewirtz and Anne Garner, Henry W. and Albert A. Berg Collection of English and American Literature at the New York Public Library, who maintain the William S. Burroughs archive, were most helpful. Smaller collections of Burroughs letters were found at the following libraries, which I would like to thank for their assistance: Arizona State University (Katherine Krzys); Bennington College (Joe Tucker); Brown University (Mark Brown); Columbia University (Gerald Cloud, Michael Ryan); Cornell University; Duke University (Elizabeth Dunn); Florida Atlantic University (Z. Cael); Indiana University (James Canary); Library of Congress; Morgan Library (Declan Kiely); New York University (Marvin Taylor); Northwestern University (Sigrid Perry); Ohio State University (John Bennett, Rebecca Jewett, Geoffrey Smith); Stanford University (Polly Armstrong, Annette Keogh, Mattie Taormina); SUNY Buffalo (Michael Basinski); Syracuse University (Amanda Baker); Temple University; University of California at Berkeley (Anthony Bliss); University of California at Davis (Daryl Morrison); UCLA (Lilace Hatayama, Mauricio Hermosillo, Robert Montoya); University of California at San Diego (Robert Melton); University of Chicago (David Pavelich); University of Connecticut (Melissa Watterworth); University of Delaware (Timothy Murray); University of Iowa (Kathryn Hodson); University of Kansas (Tara Wenger); University of Michigan; University of North Carolina (Libby Chenault); University of Reading (Nancy Fulford); University of Texas at Austin (Cathy Henderson, Richard Oram, Molly Schwartzburg, Thomas Staley, Richard Workman); University of Virginia (Margaret Hrabe); Washington University; and Yale University (Nancy Kuhl, Graham Sherriff).

Special thanks should go to many scholars outside the world of libraries who also helped by providing copies of Burroughs' letters and pointing me in the right direction when I came to a dead end. I am particularly grateful for the help of Michael Aldrich, Alan Ansen, Gordon Ball, Sinclair Beiles, Bill Berkson, David Cope, Elsa Dorfman, Lawrence Ferlinghetti, Lee Froehlich, Bill Gargan, John Giorno, Jack Hagstrom, Peter Hale, Michael Horowitz, Bill Keogan, Tuli Kupferberg, Tim Moran, Kaye McDonough, Charles Marowitz, Peter Matson, Miles, Fabrizio Mondadori, Ted Morgan, Michael O'Connell, Ron Padgett, Barney Rosset, Jerome Rothenberg, Ed Sanders, Stephen Sandy, Ben Schafer, Matt Theado, and John Tytell.

Jeffrey Posternak at the Andrew Wylie Agency was the backbone of the project and was always ready, willing, and able to offer aid when called upon, and for that I am in his debt. Libby Edelson, our editor at Ecco, helped us through the final stages of the manuscript.

And finally, to Judy Matz, I extend my never-ending appreciation for her unflagging support and encouragement in this and all endeavors.

CHRONOLOGY

In place of a biographical narrative to accompany the letters, it seems appropriate to include a chronology outlining Burroughs' activities during this period. This will help the reader place letters within the context of Burroughs' general biography.

1914

FEBRUARY 5:   *William Seward Burroughs II, born to Laura Lee and Mortimer Burroughs at home, 4664 Berlin Avenue, St. Louis, Missouri.*

1958–1960

Burroughs lives in Paris at 9 rue Git-Le-Coeur, a pension now commonly referred to as the "Beat Hotel."

1959

SUMMER: *Olympia Press, Paris, publishes Burroughs' book* The Naked Lunch.

OCTOBER 1:   *Burroughs returns to Paris from a trip to London and is interviewed for* Life *maga-*

*zine. On the same day, Brion Gysin acci-
dentally invents the cut-up method while
working in his room at the Beat Hotel.*

1960

FEBRUARY 15:
: *Ian Sommerville does early work on the
flicker machine in Cambridge, England. It is
later called the dream machine.*

LATE APRIL:
: *Burroughs leaves Paris for London, staying
at the Empress Hotel, 25 Lillie Road, in part
to be closer to Ian Sommerville, who was
studying at Corpus Christi College, Cambridge.*

JUNE 30:
: *Judge Julius Hoffman declares that the first
issue of* Big Table *magazine, which includes
part of* Naked Lunch, *is not obscene.*

AUGUST 1:
: *Burroughs visits Amsterdam for a few days.*

OCTOBER:
: *Burroughs meets Michael Portman in London.*

MID-OCTOBER:
: *Burroughs moves to Cambridge.*

OCTOBER 27:
: *Burroughs visits Paris for a few days.*

NOVEMBER 24:
: *Burroughs, Gysin, and Sommerville stage a
multimedia display at the Heretics Club of
Corpus Christi College, Cambridge.*

1961

APRIL 1:
: *Burroughs leaves Paris for Tangier, intending to stay for the summer, stays at the Hotel
Muniria, where Sommerville and Portman
join him. On the same day, Allen Ginsberg
and Peter Orlovsky arrive in Paris.*

JUNE 1:
: *Ginsberg, Orlovsky, and Gregory Corso
arrive in Tangier to visit Burroughs.*

JUNE:
: *Olympia Press publishes Burroughs'* The Soft
Machine.

MID-JULY:
: *Alan Ansen arrives in Tangier.*

EARLY AUGUST:
: *Timothy Leary arrives in Tangier to visit
Burroughs.*

AUGUST 20:	*Burroughs leaves Tangier for New York via London.*
AUGUST 23:	*Burroughs arrives in New York to attend the American Psychological Association Conference. From there he goes to Harvard to do research with Timothy Leary in September.*
OCTOBER–DECEMBER:	*Burroughs is disenchanted with Leary and moves to a basement apartment in Brooklyn, where he works on* Nova Express.
DECEMBER:	*Burroughs returns to Paris.*

1962

EARLY FEBRUARY:	*Burroughs moves from Paris to London, staying first at the Empress Hotel, then moving to 5 Lancaster Terrace.*
MARCH 21:	*Grove Press publishes* Naked Lunch *in New York.*
LATE MAY:	*Burroughs moves to Paris and stays at the Beat Hotel.*
AUGUST 20–25:	*Burroughs attends the Edinburgh University Writers' Conference in Scotland.*

1963

JANUARY 3:	*Burroughs returns to London from Paris and moves into 51 Gloucester Terrace, then moves to 5 Lancaster Terrace a few weeks later.*
JANUARY:	*Boston bookstore owner Theodore Mavrikos is arrested for selling* Naked Lunch.
FEBRUARY 20:	*Burroughs visits Paris for a few days.*
JUNE:	*Burroughs moves to Tangier and takes a house at 4 Calle Larache on the Marshan.*
LATE JUNE:	*Burroughs visits Jajouka and Marrakech, Morocco.*
JULY:	*Billy Burroughs Jr. arrives in Tangier to live with Burroughs.*
DECEMBER:	*Billy leaves Tangier to live with his grandparents in Palm Beach, Florida.*

1964

JANUARY 6:	*Burroughs visits London and appears on a TV program with Alex Trocchi.*
JANUARY 17:	*Burroughs visits Paris to try to obtain overdue royalty payments.*
FEBRUARY:	*Burroughs returns to Tangier, staying for a while at 4 Calle Larache.*
MARCH 25:	*Burroughs visits Gibraltar for a few days, then returns to Tangier.*
APRIL:	*Burroughs moves first to the Hotel Atlas, and later into a nicer apartment at 16 rue Delacroix.*
JUNE 23:	*Burroughs visits Gibraltar for a few days, then returns to Tangier.*
NOVEMBER 26:	*Burroughs visits Gibraltar for a few days.*
NOVEMBER 30:	*Burroughs leaves from Algeciras, Spain, aboard the ship* Independence.
DECEMBER 8:	*Burroughs arrives in New York City and stays at the Chelsea Hotel.*
DECEMBER 22:	*Burroughs arrives in St. Louis on assignment for* Playboy, *stays at Chase Plaza Hotel.*

1965

JANUARY:	*Burroughs returns to New York and stays at the Chelsea Hotel for a few weeks.*
JANUARY 12:	Naked Lunch *trial begins in Boston, but Burroughs does not attend.*
JANUARY 19:	*Burroughs' father dies and WSB attends his funeral in Florida.*
LATE JANUARY:	*Burroughs returns to New York and moves into a loft at 210 Centre Street.*
MARCH 23:	*Boston courts rule that* Naked Lunch *is obscene.*
EARLY SEPTEMBER:	*Burroughs returns to London from New York.*
OCTOBER 8:	*Grove lawyers file an appeal of the* Naked Lunch *decision in Massachusetts Supreme Court.*

LATE DECEMBER: *Burroughs visits Tangier and spends two months there.*

1966

FEBRUARY: *Burroughs returns to London and stays at the Hotel Rushmore, 11 Trebovir Road, Earl's Court.*

JUNE 6: *Burroughs visits Carl Weissner in Heidelberg, West Germany.*

JULY 7: *The Massachusetts Supreme Court overturns the lower court's ruling and says that* Naked Lunch *is not obscene.*

SEPTEMBER: *Burroughs visits Tangier and stays at the Minzah, Three Pelicans, and Muniria hotels.*

OCTOBER 1: *Burroughs returns to London.*

DECEMBER 27: *Burroughs leaves for America.*

1967

FEBRUARY 7: *Burroughs takes Billy to Lexington, Kentucky, for detoxification.*

FEBRUARY 15: *Burroughs, Corso, and Ginsberg appear at the opening of Timothy Leary's "League for Spiritual Discovery" in New York.*

MID-MARCH: *Burroughs is back in London and begins work on* The Wild Boys.

MAY: *Burroughs visits Tangier for a few months, staying at the Atlas Hotel.*

MID-JULY: *Burroughs returns to London and moves into an apartment at 8 Duke Street, St. James. Ian Sommerville and Alan Watson move in with him for a while.*

1968

MID-JANUARY: *Burroughs begins two-month course in scientology at St. Hill in East Grinstead, England. He finishes training in June 1968 in Edinburgh.*

AUGUST:	*Billy Burroughs Jr. marries Karen Beth Perry and moves to Savannah, Georgia. The couple separate in 1974.*
AUGUST 24:	*Burroughs arrives in Chicago from London to cover the Democratic National Convention for* Esquire *magazine along with Ginsberg, Terry Southern, and Jean Genet.*
SEPTEMBER:	*Burroughs stops over in New York City for a month.*
SEPTEMBER 28:	*Burroughs returns to London.*

1970

SUMMER:	*Burroughs visits New York City for a few months.*
OCTOBER 21:	*Burroughs' mother dies, but he does not return for the funeral.*

1971

MID-OCTOBER:	*Burroughs teaches at the University of the New World in Haute-Nendaz, Switzerland.*
MID-NOVEMBER:	*Burroughs returns to London after the school collapses.*

1972

LATE SPRING:	*Burroughs goes to America to work with Terry Southern on the movie script for* Naked Lunch *and stays in New York through the summer.*
FALL:	*Burroughs returns to London.*

1973

JANUARY:	*Burroughs visits Morocco with John Brady.*
MARCH:	*Burroughs moves to another apartment in the same building at 8 Duke Street, London.*
AUGUST:	*Burroughs takes his archive to the buyer in Vaduz, Liechtenstein.*

AUGUST: *Burroughs vacations in Greece for a week or two with John Brady.*

1974

FEBRUARY: *Burroughs returns to New York to teach at City College, meets James Grauerholz.*

1981

MARCH 3: *Billy Burroughs Jr. dies.*

1997

AUGUST 2: *William S. Burroughs dies in Lawrence, Kansas.*

INTRODUCTION

The final letter in the first volume of correspondence, *The Letters of William S. Burroughs 1945–1959* (Viking, 1993), was written to Allen Ginsberg on October 29, 1959. It is fitting that the first letter in this volume should be one that was written the very next day to the very same person. It serves to illustrate that as late as 1959, Allen Ginsberg was still the most constant and steadfast person in Burroughs' life. The letters that follow show Burroughs' steady drift away from the earlier "beat" circle, composed of Ginsberg, Gregory Corso, Jack Kerouac, and the rest, toward new relationships with friends made in Northern Africa and Europe. Over the next fifteen years, hundreds of letters would be written to new friends like the artist Brion Gysin, who before long would replace Ginsberg as Burroughs' most trusted confidant. These letters document that evolution and are witness to an era in which Burroughs became the center of a new coterie of creative people who were not related to the Beat Generation. With their assistance, Burroughs became an influential artistic and cultural leader whose reputation spread well beyond the literary world. In addition to Gysin, his new correspondents would include Paul Bowles, Ian Sommerville, Michael Portman, and Alex Trocchi, all partners in the expatriate life that Burroughs pursued during this period.

William Burroughs had first met Brion Gysin years earlier in Morocco, but initially they hadn't gotten along very well. In Paris during 1958–1959 they renewed their acquaintance, and before long Gysin was serving as Burroughs' sounding board and collaborator. Together Burroughs and Gysin collaborated on what Oliver Harris has called "Newspeak Poetry." Basing their ideas on the name of the totalitarian language of the repressive regime in George Orwell's novel *1984,* they saw that language could be used as an agent for control. They realized that by controlling language, those in authority could suppress the freedom and individuality of others. "It's a beautiful thing, the destruction of words," one of Orwell's character states, and Burroughs and Gysin set out to show by example how it was quite possible to systematically eliminate civil disobedience through the control of vocabulary. Significantly, mind control plays a role in all of Burroughs' interests of this period, from his involvement in scientology to his fascination with the dream machine.

Chronologically, this volume begins where the previous volume ended. In the summer of 1959, Burroughs' masterpiece, *The Naked Lunch*, had just been published by the Olympia Press in Paris, but no major American publisher was yet ready to take on the censorship battles that were inevitable with the publication of such a book. It was at this time that Burroughs became reacquainted with Brion Gysin. Gysin had quite accidentally discovered the first cut-up process in October, and the new method of composition was beginning to occupy much of Burroughs' creative time. He was also beginning his study of scientology and for a short while hoped that the philosophy espoused by L. Ron Hubbard and his followers would unlock some of the mysteries of his own mind. During this period he continued his quest for an effective cure of his own drug addiction, and once he discovered apomorphine, he worked tirelessly to inform the medical profession of its effectiveness. By the end of this volume, Burroughs would become absorbed by another of Gysin's inventions, the flicker or dream machine, which allowed his mind to travel to entirely new worlds without drugs. Those explorations found their way into his books, and by the end of the period covered in these letters, he had once again returned to a more linear narrative in his writing style.

Although Burroughs' creative work eventually led to his becoming a member of the respected American Academy and Institute of Arts and Letters, it was during this period that it appeared as if his most experimental work would never see the light of day. His trilogy of challenging work, *The Soft Machine, The Ticket That Exploded,* and *Nova Express,* left his critics baffled, but Burroughs' letters provide evidence that there truly was method in his madness.

After many lapses in their personal correspondence, the penultimate letter in this volume returns again to Ginsberg. Burroughs had lived abroad for nearly a quarter of a century by that time, and Allen felt that it was time for Burroughs to make a triumphal return to the United States. To that end, he helped secure a teaching position for him at City College in New York. In that 1974 letter Burroughs wrote to thank him for his help. He also wanted to express his appreciation to Ginsberg for his offer to make his country farmhouse available should Burroughs follow through with plans to open a center for advanced studies there. Although Burroughs' teaching trip was originally intended to be relatively short, he found the United States much more conducive to his lifestyle and was to spend the rest of his life in America—but as they say, that's another story. This tale ends with Burroughs' arrival in a New York radically changed from the city he had known during the 1940s.

Many misconceptions abound concerning Burroughs and his work. The popular notion that Burroughs was determined to become "the invisible man," as many biographers have suggested, is false. Like most writers, he wanted to have his work published widely and read by the largest audience possible. He certainly believed that he had important contributions to make, and he continually battled against those who tried to discredit him. He frequently expressed his secret hope that his books would become "best sellers" and appeal to a much broader readership.

Nor did Burroughs enjoy being a rootless drifter, even though he was continually on the move. Like Jack Kerouac, Burroughs was forever searching for a peaceful place in which he could write and pursue his interests unfettered. Although he moved numerous times during the period of these letters, he did so only when he had exhausted his options in one place or another. He had trouble maintaining his status as a desirable alien and sometimes was forced to flee from possible arrest as a result of his continuing drug habit. His lifelong wandering was not intended to be an evasion of commitments, but he found that he had to keep one step ahead of the law. Indeed, there were many reasons that supported these fears. Foremost was his well-known use of drugs, a crime in every country he visited. He was also unapologetically gay during an era when that in itself was considered a perversion and a crime. His legal difficulties in Mexico and the United States, combined with his published versions of diabolical fantasies, called him to the attention of every police department in the Western world.

Yet even with his love for the macabre side of life, Burroughs was not a man devoid of human emotion as many would suggest. He went to great lengths to discover what controlled his emotions, and his research into scientology and the work of Wilhelm Reich were both outgrowths of those explorations. In fact, his life following the death of his wife, Joan, can be seen as an inner struggle against "the ugly spirit." It was that evil force that he believed resides in each of us that was waiting for the opportunity to take over.

Burroughs' nearly obsessive dedication to the creative process he called the cut-up method was not intended to make language obsolete. It became a method he would use repeatedly to emphasize the importance of words, not their unimportance. He used cut-ups to reveal the secret meaning of things. Semantics were always of interest to Burroughs, and through his deconstruction of sentences he found that he could decipher hidden messages that were really present and intentionally concealed "between the lines."

It is certainly true that drugs were a daily part of Burroughs' life, but he was not an advocate of their general use. As these letters will show, he bristled when reporters said that he was an advocate of drug use. He did work to make the public realize that drug addiction was not a legal or a political issue, but rather a medical issue. At every opportunity, Burroughs tried to kick his own habit, unsuccessfully in the long run. He was aware that the narcotics business was a double-sided one in which the legal system had just as much at stake as the dealers. During this period Burroughs even grew to believe that people like Timothy Leary and his imitators were charlatans taking advantage of the inexperienced to promote their own careers. Burroughs was not interested in most hallucinogens and in these letters refers to them as "Leary's pestiferous mushrooms."

The letters will also help dispel the notion that William S. Burroughs was the heir to a vast fortune and was able to live without financial worries. It is true that he did have a very modest trust fund, but it never paid more than a few hundred dollars a month. That was the extent of his family wealth. He continually worked at the business of writing in order to support himself. Eventually, when his mother became strapped for cash, he was finally able to tell her that he was self-sufficient and no longer needed a monthly allowance from her. Although Burroughs never starved like some of his friends, at one point he was so hampered by a lack of funds that he couldn't afford to make repairs to his own typewriter.

While most of Burroughs' work is quite accessible and easily understood by the average reader, I believe that some of his most experimental work of the period covered in these letters is not. A bit of background information will provide the groundwork essential for a fuller and more complete understanding of just what he was trying to achieve. His intent is sometimes obscured by what appears to be a chance arrangement of words, but in truth Burroughs always exercised strict editorial control with published work and took only the very best from his experiments. He cut up thousands of pages of text to find the few that he deemed worthy of publication. Through that selection process, only a select number of cut-ups became uniquely his own.

As Burroughs' letters reveal, even his own missives were cut up to find hidden meaning. Many of the letters in this book will help us travel through his experimental world, beginning with the cut-up and emerging a decade later with his renewed interest in the narrative form. The road is difficult, but with the help of Burroughs' own commentary, often provided via these letters, it is a much easier path to follow.

The methods and procedures used in the transcribing of these letters were standard and easy to understand; however, a note about the editorial process might be helpful. I was surprised to find that Burroughs conducted his literary business professionally in much the same way as would a lawyer or an accountant. As in any business office, but unlike any other writer I've worked with, Burroughs made carbons and photocopies of nearly everything. These he carefully filed, using his own personal system of organization. His entire archive from this period is now available to scholars at the Berg Collection of the New York Public Library, and there a researcher will discover just how methodical he was in this process. Finding carbon copies in the archive presented another problem for the compiler. The existence of a copy in no way proves that a letter was subsequently sent. People do not always post all the letters that they write. For example, Gregory Corso once wrote a very revealing letter to his father that I included in a book of his selected letters. The letter was in fact never sent, but I included the letter because of the important biographical content. Even though Corso composed the letter, it had no direct impact on his relationship with his father, since his father never saw it. It is equally possible that some of the letters included in this volume were never sent, or if they were, that they contained corrections or postscripts that do not show up on the carbons. For that reason I have tried to track down the original letters as they were posted, but this has not always been possible. Occasionally, multiple drafts of letters were found and I have tried to select the form that seems most complete.

Another office practice that Burroughs employed was uniquely his own. For a period of time he used a personal system of dating. He invented a calendar with months having names like Wiener Wald and Seal Point. This he expanded and refined over a period of time. As the letters explain, it was a complicated system, but one that seems to have served him well. In this collection, the more traditional date is given in square brackets whenever possible.

My own editorial policy has always been to present letters without unnecessary commentary. I believe it is essential to allow Burroughs to tell his story in his own words. For that reason I have been reluctant to interfere in the narrative with lengthy editorial comments about what Burroughs writes in a particular letter. Occasionally some background information is needed, and I have entered that information as either a note at the beginning of the letter or as a footnote. It is my habit to indicate the full name of a person referred to within a letter only on the first mention of the person. Hence, the first time Burroughs mentions Allen, I will note that it is Allen [Ginsberg], but if he refers to Allen again in the same letter, I will not repeat that note. Footnotes are included only when standard reference sources do not turn up information. Hence I have not created a footnote for President John Kennedy, but have identified Burroughs' doctor, John Yerby Dent.

In the course of my research I was able to locate over a thousand letters written by William Burroughs between the years 1959 and 1974, and I have tried to select the very best of those. Certainly any editor would love to be able to include each and every one of those letters, but that is not the nature of modern-day publishing budgets. Even if it were possible, many letters would prove to be repetitive or of little interest to the reader. When two or more letters covered the same ground, I selected the best in terms of quality of writing and completeness of thought. Occasionally, I have included more than one letter on the same topic to illustrate just how important a subject was to Burroughs. For example, I have included several letters to illustrate how tirelessly Burroughs worked to convince doctors to prescribe apomorphine as a cure for addiction.

Common sense dictates that letters tend to be written when people are apart. Obviously while Burroughs and Gysin were living in the same hotel in Paris, there was very little need to write letters to one another. Therefore, there are stretches of time when no letters with certain correspondents were exchanged. I have made short editorial notations to indicate what was happening in Burroughs' life wherever warranted.

Although Burroughs was a good speller, much better than Allen Ginsberg, for instance, at times he did misspell words such as heptititis for hepatitis. Usually those misspellings have been corrected for the sake of clarity. James Grauerholz has assured me that Burroughs did not want this type of mistake to be published unless it contributed in some way to the creative or artistic aspect of his work. Frequently Burroughs used the British spelling of words and I have not altered those. In a few cases I have noted an unusual spelling within square brackets the initial time and not after that; *magasine* for *magazine* is a common case in point.

On October 24, 1963, Burroughs wrote to Dick Seaver, his editor at Grove Press. "As a matter of general orientation both spelling and punctuation would be normalized and consistent. Use lower case when it would be normally indicated. . . . As I have noted on your letter 'grey' [and] 'theatre' should remain English. . . . Yes retain the multiplicity of punctuation. This is an experiment with format and the use of punctuation which I have carried further in the work I am doing now."

Sometimes Burroughs was inconsistent in even this, as in a letter written to Marilynn Meeker only three years later, on November 10, 1966. In it Burroughs notes: "I have rather eccentric preference for some English spellings and not for others for example grey good bye whereas I prefer theater to theatre," which is a direct contradiction of what he had said earlier. I have tried to make these points less confusing by being as consistent as possible.

As Burroughs mentioned above, his use of punctuation was also very personal and subject to his own ideas. He frequently used two periods at the end of a thought instead of a single period. I have followed Burroughs' original use of punctuation as much as possible.

I have inserted an ellipses [. . .] to indicate places in which editorial decisions have been made to cut material from the text. In some cases deletions were made where material had no relation with the narrative of the moment. Usually these were non sequiturs or asides that were not relevant. Occasionally, there were misplaced words or typos that just didn't seem to fit in. In a few cases, long samples of Burroughs' writings have been omitted, especially of his cut-up experiments. Since these are literary in nature and were usually not a part of the body of the letter, it seemed better to leave them for future scholars and anthologists to collect and study. It was common for Burroughs to play with variations and permutations of the cut-ups in letters, and those were generally not reproduced. The list of sources at the back of the book gives the location of the original manuscript letters, and those libraries should be consulted by researchers wanting to examine the originals in greater detail. No cuts for reasons of censorship were ever contemplated or made.

I have been lucky enough to edit several books of letters by Beat writers. In putting together selected letters by Allen Ginsberg, Gregory Corso, Jack Kerouac, and Gary Snyder, I have found that their own voices emerge loud and clear, and so it is with Burroughs. Each previous collection has also received at least one critic's admonition mentioning that more letters should have been included. I regard those comments not as criticism, but as positive feedback. "Leave them wanting more" as old vaudevillians suggest. I hope this volume will also leave readers wanting more and that other collections of letters will follow.

Bill Morgan
Bennington, Vermont
2011

RUBRUBRUBRUB+++&++++&++&&&&&""""&"+++&
RUBRUBRUBRUBOUTOUTOUTOUTOUT#"#++++#-
RUBRUBRUBRUBOUTOUTOUTOUTOUT####&&&&&
""""&&&+++++"OUTOUTOUTOUTOUT"""""""&&&&
1959 ""+OUTOUTOUTOUTOUT"+"+"&&&"
THETHETHETHETHETHETHE+++###+++&&+++&
HETHETHETHETHETHETHE&&&&&+++++++++#7
HETHETHETHEWORDSWORDSWORDSWORDSTHE7
####&&"&"&"&WORDSWORDSWORDSWORDS"++-

EDITOR'S NOTE: By the fall of 1959 William Burroughs had settled into a comfortable daily routine in Paris. He was living in a small room on the Rue Git–Le–Coeur at the time. His pension was an inexpensive place that would attract so many of his old friends before long that it became known as the Beat Hotel. Only a few months earlier his second book, The Naked Lunch, *had been published by the Olympia Press, under the direction of the somewhat devious owner, Maurice Girodias. Burroughs was deeply involved in experiments with his new friend, Brion Gysin, who, on October 1, had discovered a unique method of literary composition. Quite by accident, Gysin had sliced through a pile of old newspapers and noticed that the words from one page could be lined up with the words from the page beneath to create entirely new texts. When he told Burroughs about it later that day, William began to look at the random pages carefully. He believed that Gysin had, by rearranging the words at random, uncovered previously unseen messages hidden within the words on the page.*

WSB [Paris] to Allen Ginsberg [New York]
Oct 30, 1959
9 Rue Git–Le–Coeur
Paris 6

Dear Allen,

Thanks a million for the mescaline..[1] Split it with Brion [Gysin][2] for a short trip home..

Yes, you did make me the most famous novelist Roumanian born of a better Tyrone Power[3] up from a headline of penniless migrants.. And believe me, Al, I won't forget it. What's this Elsee??[4] On the ice again..?? I'll catch her this time..

---

1   Ginsberg occasionally sent small amounts of mescaline as a gift to Burroughs from New York.
2   Bryon Gysin (1916–1986). An experimental artist who, over the course of these letters, would become Burroughs' best friend and collaborator.
3   Tyrone Power (1914–1958). A matinee idol known for playing the roles of swashbuckling heroes. He had just died in November 1958.
4   This is probably a reference to Allen's friend Elise Cowen, who may have been planning a trip to Europe.

I look all over and can't find my Wyn contract[5] follow me around for years through jungles and deserts and perilous unknown boy countries and couldn't lose it and now.. Well don't get mad and cut off your left hand, I always say.. But it seems to me that the contract should be outlawed by now.. I will look again for the contract but some Arab probably wiped his ass with it years ago and it blew away to return in hepatitis fall out.. But would I like to latch onto that 2 Gs[6] go to India most like.. Gregory Corso lost all his money in the Venice casino.. Oh God!! *Quel infant* of the *Sunday Supplement*.. Bought a dinner jacket, too I hear..[7]

And now the question panel: (1) Whatever they may be, the suppressors are not amateurs.. Old Old Old pros and don't ever forget it.. Make you think you are winning when you are not, oldest trick in the industry and still works.. Hannibal beat the Romans with it.. Room for one more inside.. MALRAUX???[8] He's nothing but a public Latah[9] for Crisakes!?

(2): I have had very practical contact with "these people" they are very practical people.. Jack Stern[10] was one of them.. The book itself is not interesting all important teckniques [*sic*] classified.. But name dropping is unchic and very poor hygiene..

Of course scientology attracts all the creeps of the cosmos.. You see *it works*..

In closing I will tell you a little story that happened to a friend of mine calls himself Micheaux sometimes..

It seems that M. was hurrying home after swallowing his mescaline tablet with hot tea in a cafe—too cheap to support a hot plate you dig—and he met B [Burroughs] in the market and he

---

5   A. A. Wyn (1898–1967). The publisher of Ace Books, the company that published Burroughs' first book, *Junkie*. Burroughs hoped that he could regain control of that book and sell the rights to other publishers.

6   Girodias was negotiating a contract for $2,000 for the American rights to *Naked Lunch*.

7   The painter Willem de Kooning had given Corso some money for a trip to Greece, but Gregory lost it all at the casino.

8   André Malraux (1901–1976). French novelist and minister of cultural affairs.

9   Latah. A person in a trance who talks mechanically or repeats motions and is seemingly not in control of himself.

10 Jack "Jacques" Stern was a young man, crippled by polio, who the Beat group associated with in Paris. He claimed to be a member of the Rothschild family, but Burroughs had doubts about this distinguished background.

had met B before but never seen him as hardly anyone does see him which is why he is known as El Hombre Invisible—So B. said "Ah Monsieur M.. Sit down and have a coffee and watch the passing parade.." and M shook him off saying: "No! No! I must go home and see my visions" and he rushed home and closed the door and bolted it and drew the curtains and turned out the lights and got into bed and closed his eyes and there was Mr. B. and Mr. M. said: "What are you doing here in my vision?"

And B replied: "Oh I live here."

love

william burroughs

PS. Yes Burroughs will do as a name to publish under.. Its on the papers.. I'll be caught short with it one day.

WSB [Paris] to Kells Elvins[11] [Rome, Italy]

Nov. 13, 1959
9 Rue Git Le Coeur
Paris 6, France Room 32

Dear Kells,

Your letter from Italy I answer now.. late gain I can say.. "Time skidded".. And left me in Paris since I last saw you.. One thing after the other like Disraeli said or some old character.. First it was the book and sick then articles and obligations fixed me in Street of The Lying Heart ..[12] *sans tours* in boyhood.. beautiful people skindiving, festivals of slivovitz[13].. Such a thing as too much fun Elvins..

The book is published by Olympia Press such a devious Greek Spanish Arab French Jewish Godhead proclaim bankrupture in all languages with insurance fire Geneva to clear through Ghana.. Already *Naked Lunch* is registered in the name of a Turkish widow dummy resident of Hong Kong branch office Geneva.. Where

---

11 Kells Elvins (1913–1961). One of Burroughs' best friends since childhood.

12 Burroughs and his friends stayed in an inexpensive hotel in Paris on the Rue Git-le-Coeur, which he translates here.

13 Slivovitz. An eastern European form of plum brandy.

Jurado[14] left off you dig strictly from angles.. And he looks different every time rotating himself with brothers all whom have different names.. I always land in somebody's feet.. One of the family and he gives me own money right out of his pocket.. My Greek uncle [Maurice Girodias] I call him and its all very familiar to me somehow.. Well the book is published Olympia Press Travelers Companion.. But don't think I've sunk to a "political" status..

What is the movie deal you speak of? Any luck with the producer? Let me hear from you soon. If you cannot buy *Naked Lunch* in Rome I will send copy.. My best regards to Mimi,[15]

Best.

Bill

WSB [Paris] to Laura Lee and Mortimer Burroughs[16] [Palm Beach, Florida]
[ca. November 17, 1959]

Dear Mother and Dad,

I am sorry.. Can only say time accelerated and skidded— No time to eat as you see in the photo—(Taken by my friend Brion [Gysin] the painter, certainly the greatest painter living and I do not make mistakes in the art world.. Time will bear me out.. Brion used to run The 1001 Nights, restaurant night club in Tanger but at that time we barely spoke disliking each other intensely for reasons that seemed adequate to both parties.. Situation and personnel changed.. The 1001 Nights closed for dislocations and foreclosures and Brion woke up in Paris.. And I, stricken by *la foie coloniale*—the colonial liver, left the area on advice of my physician.. "You want to get some cold weather on that liver, Burroughs. A freezing winter would make a new man of you," he said.

---

14 Bernabé Jurado. A less-than-reputable lawyer who represented Burroughs after William had shot and killed his wife, Joan Vollmer Adams.

15 Mimi was Kells Elvins' wife at the time.

16 Laura Lee Burroughs (1888–1970) and Mortimer Burroughs (1885–1965). William Burroughs' parents.

So when I ran into Brion in Paris it was Tanger gossip at first then the discovery that we had many other interests in common..

Like all good painters he is also a brilliant photographer as you see.. A curious old time look about the photo like I'm fading into grandfather or some other relative many years back in time..)

Rather a long parenthesis.. It strikes me as regrettable that one should reserve a special and often lifeless style for letter to parents.. So I shift to my usual epistolary style.. When my correspondents reproach me for tardiness, I can only say that I give as much attention to a letter as I do to anything I write, and I work at least six and sometimes sixteen hours a day..

I am considering a shift of headquarters from The Continent— or possibly England—All we expatriates hear now is: "Johnny Go Home" and may be a good idea at that.. Terrible scandal in Morocco.. Cooking oil cut with second run motor oil has paralyzed 9544 persons.. The used motor oil was purchased at the American Air Base and was *not* labeled *unfit for human consumption* .. The Moroccan press holds U.S. responsible not to mention 9,544 Moroccans and a compound interest of relatives.. "Johnny stay out of Morocco."[17]

I want to leave here in one month more or less a few days and make Palm Beach for Christmas if convenient.

I was sorry to hear that Mote[18] has been ill.. Take care of yourself—Dad—and get well. I will see you all very soon —

Love
Bill

PS. If my writing seems at times ungrammatical it is not due to carelessness or accident. The English language—the only really adjustable language—is in state of transition.. Transition and the old grammar forms no longer useful..

Best.
Bill

---

17 The tragedy occurred in the city of Meknes, Morocco, where the newspapers reported that as many as 10,000 people had suffered paralysis as a result of the poisoning.

18 "Mote." Nickname for William Burroughs' father, Mortimer.

WSB [Paris] to Allen Ginsberg [New York]

Paris Nov. 17, 1959
9 Rue Git Le Coeur
Paris 6, France

Dear Allen,

A relatively sudden decision will carry me home for Christmas if suitable transport is available Dec 18 Future Time.. 6th clearing.

"La jeune fille bien eleve" got up off the mad money.. Thanks again for the plug in.. I have enough *Word* here to cook manuscript for *Big Table*.. Wrote Carroll[19] and will forward direct..

Radically wrong Beat Generation needs a Joe Hill[20].. "When we can entreat an hour to serve we would spend it in some words on that business if you would grant the time.."[21]

Limes [Verlag] is publishing *Naked Lunch*.. Contract signed processing through Switzerland where it is registered in the name of a Turkish widow resident of Hong Kong branch office in Amsterdam.. Girodias is such a devious who you never know to whom you are a speak..

I consider a shift of headquarters to US.. La France under the title *Une Cadavre*.. But who knows? As Eve Auchincloss[22] wrote me.. "Your article will appear in the January issue if there is a January issue" or a January for that matter..

Tanger out of bounds and over the bread fence for me.. Somebody cut the cooking oil with *second run* motor oil from the American Base in Casa White: 9,544 Moroccans permanently paralyzed.. Oil not labeled *unfit* for human consumption.. "So how would we know those stupid goods would.." "Shut up you fool!! Where is Public Relations?" I mean what we pay taxes for? Clem and Jody?[23] Morocco, Cuba, Panama . . . ?

---

19 Paul Carroll (1926–1996). The editor of the *Chicago Review* and later *Big Table* magazine.
20 Joe Hill (1879–1915). A labor organizer and member of the union known as the Wobblies. He was executed for murder and became a martyr for unionized labor. He was made famous through folk songs of the era.
21 Burroughs is quoting from Shakespeare's *Macbeth*.
22 Eve Auchincloss. An editor of *Mademoiselle* magazine.
23 Clem and Jody are characters portrayed in *Naked Lunch*.

Exiles return.. see you.

Best

Love

Bill (or is it?)

P.S. Can't raise the Ace contract. Lost back there in Madrid East St. Louis Talara [Peru] hotel room.. behind the wardrobe.. So far away.. Outlawed statute limitations and exempt narcotic –
P.P.S.: Just received your letter. I have now arrived at a method of writing after passing transitional milestones *Word* and *Lunch*.. I prefer to publish from here on out only material subjected to the processing of new method.. Have decided to send Carroll a new selection and not attempt to recast *Word* at this time. I think unwise to publish *Word* in present form—I am not talking about censors or anything of that sort but on purely literary grounds. I can do geometrically better work.. *Yage Letters* okay but please hold up on *Word* until I arrive NYC. The *Life* interviewers here are 2 far out cats with real appreciation for my work that can't be faked.[24] Of course they have nothing to do with the final form of the story.. Police and beatniks Gould level are ventriloquist dummies for each other in nasty and stupid love affair.. Ainch.. Include me out.. Square reaction draws force from Gould and *visa versa mutas mutandis* as the case may be.. Enclose ten thousand heavy francs.. Gimmick of Monsieur Pinay, Minister of Finance deliberately designed not to work.. I have the honor of Monsieur Pinay's acquaintance.. "*Quel farceur!!*"

Please send me some more mescaline if convenient I mean nothing exigent. I am homesick. Of course I have made the best terms possible under the circumstances. And if questions not always answered in one way they are answered in some other way when they cease to become questions. Which is to say most questions never were questions to begin with were they now? I saw some one taking off for trip and I said 'Whatcha mean?' Wharcha mean? [. . .]

---

24 Reporter David Snell and photographer Loomis Dean had been sent by *Life* magazine to do an article on Burroughs. Eventually the photos were used in Paul O'Neil's article "The Only Rebellion Around," which appeared in the November 30, 1959, issue of *Life*.

EDITOR'S NOTE: On October 1, 1959, the same day that the two Life *reporters, Snell and Dean, visited Burroughs, Brion Gysin accidentally sliced through some newspaper text on his desk and discovered the cut-up technique that was to occupy much of Burroughs' time over the next decade. In the following letter William mentions the "cut-up method" for the first time.*

WSB [Paris] to Allen Ginsberg [New York]
Dec 2, 1959
9 Rue Git Le Coeur
Paris 6, France

Dear Allen,

I enclose material for *Big Table*.. Hope is not to too late.. So much work I never catch up and all absolutely urgent.. Brion's [Gysin] work which I enclose illustrates new cut up method which he taught me.. I have met my first Master in Brion..

"*Back Seat of Dreaming*" is part of my current novel.. I have written most of it remaining only the task of correlating material.. It is based on recent newspaper account of four? young explorers? who died of thirst in Egypt desert.. Just who died is uncertain since one member of the party has not been found yet dead or alive and the identity of the missing person is dubious owing to advanced state of decomposed when found the bodies and the methods of identification used lacked all precise techniques based entirely on documents on person but it seems the party was given to exchange of identifications just for jolly to wearing each others under and outer garments and even to writing in each others diaries an unheard of intimacy in any modern expedition.. So if my fictionalized??? account is difficult to follow so was the action, pops..

I am sending this material to you instead of direct to [Paul] Carroll so you can dig it.. I know you are busy but I think worth while pick up on this action now and I will explain method in detail when I see you also we have other project fore.. Temporary hitch.. My Old Lady [Burroughs' mother] read the *Life* article and has thrown off her shop keeper weeds and revealed her hideous rank in Matriarch Inc.: "I Queen Bee Laura of Worth Avenue..

Stay out of my territory, punk.." She has, in fact, forbidden me to set foot in Palm Beach on pain of Orpheus.. And won't send me money to come home.. I will buzz my Greek Uncle Gid [Maurice Girodias] and make it soon as possible..

Love

Bill

Will send more $ when I receive Mother Money. Please send mescaline if possible. Need transport out of the area.

WSB [Paris] to Allen Ginsberg [New York]
Dec. 7, 1959
9 rue Git-Le-Coeur
Paris 6

Dear Allen,

I sent along last week to you some material for *Big Table*—to you instead of [Paul] Carroll direct because I wanted you to dig same.. A short piece by your correspondent and some Cut-Ups by Brion Gysin.. Please let me know promptly if you receive this material as I neglected to register it.. I enclose short cut up of mine on Juvenile Delinquency for *Big Table* or wherever..

You recall that list you sent me of suggested favorable people and presses to send a copy of *Naked Lunch*? Passed list along to Girodias and suspect him of obstruction tactics books not sent.. If you run into any of the listed individuals could you please check to see if they received copy of *Naked Lunch*?

A great deal of work here and never caught up.. Waiting on funds transport Land of the Free.. I have plans to discuss with you when meet..

Any news from Gregory [Corso]? Please don't forget to let me know if you receive the *Big Table* material.. See you..

Love

Bill Burroughs

P.S. Please send mescaline if possible. Trip home urgent.

WSB [Paris] to Paul Bowles [Tangier, Morocco]

Dec 7, 1959
9 Rue Git Le Coeur
Paris 6, France

Dear Paul:

No way to be sure if you are traveling or in Tanger.. I hope you got the copy of N.L. [*Naked Lunch*] I sent you with Achmed Yacoubi[25].. As you know he was here in company of Mr Jay Sutton.. Says Tanger is still a fine place but not for Burroughs under the uh circumstances.. So I too bid *adieu* to Hayanni and isn't she fading for all of us? "smashed and tumbled The Thirsty off once more.. sum of dwellings and darkness across the somewhere in that masonry of shattered fragments Castle Host set.. Good bye to their desert the riot blown tombs disemboweled houses marking the site..

Black hinterland garden with a meaning of dust."

(Words by [Lawrence] Durrell.. Arrangement by W.S. Burroughs..)

Paul Lund[26] isn't the only one singing "Show Me The Way To Go Home".. Maybe he can sing his way back to Blighty but others pay cash.. *"alors jattends une bonne chance"*..

I figure those Two Ladies[27] like the Raven "never flitting still are sitting" still are sitting what?

My best regards to Jane [Bowles][28] and Achmed and please remember me to Mr Sutton

Best

Bill B.

.Fadeout to SIDE WALKS OF NEW YORK[29]

P.S. And say "Hello" to Cherifa,[30] please. Also Jay Hazelwood.[31] Anti-kif[32] law written on wall not wind..

---

25 Achmed Yacoubi (aka Ahmed Jacoubi) (1931–1985). A Moroccan artist, storyteller, and close friend of Paul Bowles.

26 Paul Lund. Englishman and small-time crook who was an acquaintance of Burroughs in Tangier and knew the ins and outs of the drug world.

27 Reference to two women who had taken over the apartment on the floor above Bowles.

28 Jane Bowles (1917–1973). Author and wife of Paul Bowles.

29 Popular song "The Sidewalks of New York," with lyrics by James W. Blake and music by Charles B. Lawler, 1894.

30 Cherifa. Jane Bowles' Moroccan companion and housekeeper.

31 Jay Hazelwood (d. 1965). The owner of the Parade Bar in Tangier.

32 Kif (aka kief). A refined form of marijuana that had just been outlawed in Tangier.

EDITOR'S NOTE: As mentioned in a previous letter to Ginsberg, Burroughs received a letter from his mother, who had read an article about William in Life *magazine. She was mortified and did not want Burroughs to visit her in Palm Beach, where he might become an embarrassment to her in front of her more conservative friends.*

WSB [Paris] to Laura Lee Burroughs [Palm Beach, Florida]
[ca. December 1959]

Dear Mother,

I counted to ten before answering your letter and I hope you have done the same since nothing could be more unworthy than a quarrel between us at this point.. Yes I have read the article in *Life* and after all.. a bit silly perhaps.. but it is a mass medium.. and sensational factors must be played up at the expense often of fact.. In order to earn my reputation I may have to start drinking my tea from a skull since this is the only vice remaining to me.. four pots a day and heavy sugar.. Did nurse make tea all the time? Its an English practice that seems to come natural to me.. I hope I am not ludicrously miscast as The Wickedest Man Alive a title vacated by the late Aleister Crowley[33]— who by the way could have had his pick of Palm Beach invitations in a much more straight laced era despite publicity a great deal more extreme.. And remember the others who have held the title before.. Byron Baudelaire Poe people are very glad to claim kinship now.. But really any one in the public eye that is anyone who enjoys any measure of success in his field is open to sensational publicity.. If I visit a waterfront bar in Tanger — half a block from my house — I am "rubbing shoulders with the riff raff of the world".. You can do that in any naborhood bar USA and *not least* in Palm Beach.. A rundown on some of the good burghers of Palm Beach would quite eclipse the Beatniks.. Personally I would prefer to avoid publicity but it is the only way to sell books.. A writer who keeps his name out of the papers doesn't publish and doesn't make money if he does manage to publish..

As regard my return to the family hearth perhaps we had best

---

33 Aleister Crowley (1875–1947). A writer, occultist, and alchemist.

both shelve any decision for the present.. Please keep me informed as to Dad's condition and give him my heart felt wish for his recovery.. [34]

Love
Bill Burroughs

WSB [Paris] to Billy Burroughs Jr. [35] [Palm Beach, Florida]
[ca. December 1959]

Dear Bill,

I was glad to her from you [that you] received *Lunch* and enjoyed same.. That's something the cook always likes to hear.. Whipping up second course now..

Shakespeare in Oregon?[36] Culture is not dead.. But why do you languish in the provinces?

Plan return stateside.. Await carrying charges.. Upon reading the *Life* articles for which many thanks my Mother has thrown off her shop keeper guise and revealed her hideous rank in Matriarch Inc; "I Queen Bee Laura of Worth Avenue.. Stay out of my territory punk.." She has in fact forbidden me on pain of financial excommunication to ever set foot in Palm Beach.. A remittance man at last official and exam exempt narcotic..

I am now in traveling condition having disposed of my pet monkey that always causes so much trouble with the Customs Officials[37].. Please let me hear from you soon.. Hope you are playing it cool in the middle only way to play it Oregon pending more enlightened days which one hopes are in the cards.. hit me again.. see you..

Amigo
Bill

---

34 Burroughs' father had recently suffered a heart attack.
35 William S. Burroughs Jr. (1947–1981). Burroughs' only child.
36 Billy was planning a trip to Ashland, Oregon, home of the Oregon Shakespeare Festival.
37 Burroughs had recently broken his drug habit.

RUBRUBRUBRUB+++&++++&++&&&&&"""&"+++
RUBRUBRUBRUBOUTOUTOUTOUTOUT#"#++++#
RUBRUBRUBRUBOUTOUTOUTOUTOUT####&&&&
'""'&&&+++++"OUTOUTOUTOUTOUT""""""""&&&
1960 ""'+OUTOUTOUTOUTOUT"+"+"&&&
THETHETHETHETHETHETHETHE+++###+++&&+++
THETHETHETHETHETHETHETHE&&&&&+++++++++#
THETHETHETHEWORDSWORDSWORDSWORDSTHE
####&&"&"&"&WORDSWORDSWORDSWORDS"++

WSB [Paris] to Paul Bowles [Tangier, Morocco]

Jan 4, 1960
9 Rue Git Le Coeur
Paris 6, France

Dear Paul:

I understand that the German publishers are having difficulty with the translation of *NL* [*Naked Lunch*] that is have not been able to find anyone capable of doing the work, but it does seem a bit odd to suggest that you assume German identity.. Who knows what stories Truman Capote may have told them? I will write them and see no need for you to do so if at all in brief terms.. Are they your German publishers? If so they should know you are not raised in Germany..

Billy Belli[1] is back in Paris and so am I for a few days assembling my finances for a trip South.. I must find a quiet place to work as I have promised to deliver another novel in two months more or less.. Southern Spain seems indicated but who knows I may look in on Tanger.. How was your desert trip? I can derive few details from Belli..

I think that cat of Jane's [Bowles] is sick and needs some kinda conclusive therapy.. I understand that vicious animals have been rendered tractable with tranquillizing drugs or other forms of sedation..

Brion [Gysin] sends his love.. He is writing.. I will look forward to meeting you perhaps soon in Tanger or Gib [Gibraltar] or Southern Spain.. I understand all my Spanish *amigos* have landed in Malaga with Tony Dutch[2]..

Best

Bill B

My love to Jane, Achmed [Yacoubi,] Christopher [Wanklyn[3]]..

---

1 Bill Belli. According to Ted Morgan, in *Literary Outlaw*, Belli was a young American who had taken *On the Road* to heart and was traveling around the world with his friend Jerry Gorsaline looking up "beat" characters.
2 Tony Dutch or Dutch Tony. Burroughs' landlord in Tangier and the owner of a café.
3 Christopher Wanklyn. Friend and sometime assistant to Paul Bowles. Wanklyn spoke perfect Moghrebi.

EDITOR'S NOTE: In early 1960 Allen Ginsberg planned to fly to Chile to take part in an international writers' conference. He decided that while he was in South America he would go on his own search for yagé, the hallucinogenic vine that Burroughs had told him so much about seven years before.

WSB [Paris] to Allen Ginsberg [Concepción, Chile]
9 Rue Git le Coeur
Paris 6, France
Jan 22, 1960 Present Time

Dear Allen,

For yagé I would advise you to go to Peru.. First to Lima then take a plane to Pucallpa on the Ucyali River where yagé is readily available.. It is called ayahuasca in the Peruvian area.. I think you can see the best of South America in Peru.. Better go over the Andes by car to Pucallpa which will give you a cross section of South America scenery..

The scientific name for ayahuasca is *Banisteriopsis caapi*.. The name of the "Doctor" in Pucallpa who brews it up is Saroya I believe.. The Saroya family are in the business all up and down the Ucyali.. There are many trips you can take from Ucyali to wilder jungle country..

Don't miss the Mercado Mayorista in Lima . . . a market place that is open round the clock.. You should have a great trip..

Love to you and Peter [Orlovsky]

> Love and Bonne Voyage
> Bill

EDITOR'S NOTE: Irving Rosenthal and Paul Carroll were editors at the Chicago Review, *a magazine issued under the auspices of the University of Chicago. They included a portion of Burroughs'* Naked Lunch *in the Spring 1958 issue. When the second installment was announced, it created a controversy that led to their resignation and the creation of an independent magazine named* Big Table. *By 1960 Irving Rosenthal had moved to New York, where he found an apartment in Allen Gins-*

berg's building at 170 East Second Street and helped assemble Burroughs'
texts for publication, working in the capacity of his unofficial agent.

WSB [Paris] to Irving Rosenthal [New York]

9 Rue Git Le Coeur
Paris 6, France
January 24, 1960 Present Time

Dear Irving,

How are you and what doing? Working for Grove Press still? I
am a very bad correspondent..

Allen [Ginsberg] said he had passed Brion Gysin's cut ups
along to you.. Have you been able to do anything with them? If not
I wonder if you could send them or copy along here as we want to
include this material in a magasine [magazine] issue under preparation?

I think the cut up method will catch on in a big way. I wonder
if you have tried it with any of your own writing? That is cutting
the pages up and rearranging at random.. *Naked Lunch* is all cut up,
though I was not then fully realizing the method and the need for
a pair of actual scissors.

Please let me hear from you and do send the cut up right along
air mail if you still have them since I feel my yearly migration to
warmer and more amenable climes is imminent

Love
Bill Burroughs

WSB [Paris] to Paul Bowles [Tangier, Morocco]

9 Rue Git Le Coeur
Paris 6, France
Jan 30, 1960 Present Time

Dear Paul:

Returning after short absence received your message from Tanger conveying the expected bad news. The *Herald Tribune* here writing the murder case said: "Followed the long sessions with the Tanger police during which his confession took form." Timely warning to the nostalgic.[4]

Naked Lunch was indeed cut up but I did not realize at time of publication to what extent. The yagé section however was not intended to be part of *Naked Lunch*. Glad you enjoyed it. That is something the cook always likes to hear.

I had assumed it seems mistakenly that you knew Mr Sutton in Tanger. As to who he is *zut alors*? He seems to confuse Eisenhower with Wilson. Definitely *ancienne regime* but precisely what regime?

I took the liberty of giving your name to a most charming young man named Bill Belli who may be coming to Tanger. I myself contemplate a short trip to Malaga to renew old acquaintances. Any chance to see you there? My best to Jane [Bowles]

Best
Bill B.

EDITOR'S NOTE: The previous summer Burroughs had met a young Englishman named Ian Sommerville (1940–1976) who was working at George Whitman's Mistral Bookshop in Paris. At the time Burroughs needed someone to help him kick his codeine habit, and Ian proved up to the task. The two became friends, lovers, and collaborators. By March 1960, Sommerville was back at Cambridge studying mathematics and electronics.

In this letter Burroughs makes reference to the theories of Wilhelm

---

4 This is a reference to the murder of José Olmedo by a servant of Robert "Bu" Faulkner. Faulkner was a very close friend of Jane Bowles.

Reich (1897–1957), whose ideas had always intrigued him. Reich was a psychoanalyst who believed that he had found a source of cosmic energy that he called orgones. In order to capture these orgones he designed an Orgone Accumulator, which Burroughs believed provided mental and physical benefits to the user. Burroughs' belief in the orgone box never wavered, even after others had discredited Reich's ideas.

WSB [Paris] to Ian Sommerville [Cambridge, England]
9 Rue Git Le Coeur
Paris 6, France
March 2, 1960 Just Time

Dear Ian:

If I read the stories beyond lines the Cambridge scene is lacking orgones.. As to the orgone box itself, well I think Reich has something there but not as much as he claims. There is no doubt that something happens in these orgone boxes.. Exactly what I don't know.. D.H. Lawrence? I don't know a lot about his personal habits but would venture to say that the special fix he is looking for in sex is a homosexual fix.

Quiet life here working most of my time. An article in the current *Evergreen Review* and translation there of in *Nouvelle Revue Francaise* which played a crucial role in my trial which finally came up..[5] Lawyer read selections from the article in the court . . . wind up was a sixty dollar fine.. France is still the only country in the world where writing is admitted as legal evidence.. Any chance of you making it here in near future? I will be around it would seem for some time yet.. Publishing a special issue of *Two Cities* which I will send you a copy when it is out. "The way is an OUT-SEE-ING." Lao Tse. See you?

> Best
> Bill Burroughs

---

5   Burroughs had been charged with a drug offense and in the end received a small fine. Here he is referring to an article titled "Deposition: Testimony Concerning a Sickness," which appeared in the *Evergreen Review* 4 (January–February 1960).

WSB [Paris] to Paul Carroll [Chicago]
9 Rue Git Le Coeur
Paris 6 France
April 8 1960 Past Time

Dear Mr Carroll:

I enclose corrected proofs of "Back Seat of Dreaming". Also note on the method used, to be printed with the material. I gather that you have been out of town and certain confusions arose in consequence. For example I have made several inquiries with regard to the original cut ups from Brion Gysin I sent to Allen Ginsberg with instructions to forward to *Big Table*. May I ask once again, did you receive this material and what are you planning to do with it in the event it was in fact received? Allen, as you know, is in the Amazon Basin and I can not reach him to cross check as to whether the material was in fact sent along to you. But please give this matter your attention since I am answerable to Mr Gysin for The Article Cut Ups. I hope to hear from you very soon and look forward to the next issue of *Big Table*.

Best

William Burroughs

Note on "Back Seat Of Dreaming" Cut Up Method:

The Possibility of literary creation by random? cutting and rearranging of material was indicated when [Tristan] Tzara at a Dada meeting in the 1920s proposed to create a poem on the spot by pulling words out of a hat.

Brion Gysin painter and writer in the Summer of 1959 [*sic*: October 1, 1959] cut newspaper articles into sections and rearranged the sections.

Method is simple: Take a page of your own writing or a page or more or less of any writer living or dead. Cut into sections. Shift sections and rearrange *looking away*. That is "at random?" Whoever wrote or spoke the words is still there in any rearrangement of his or her words. The old word lines keep thee in old world slots. Cut the word lines. Scissors or switch blade as preferred.

WSB [Paris] to Allen Ginsberg [Lima, Peru]

9 Rue Git Le Coeur
Paris 6 France
April 18 [1960] Present Time

Dear Allen,

I have been slow writing. Can only say that I find myself meeting vertiginous dead lines and no time to stop. Politics trap for writer. Don't step into the machine, Professor. Stay OUT. That is the only place for a writer. Accept their trips. But don't step IN. The way is an *Out Seeing.*

[...]

> Best
> Love
> William Burroughs

EDITOR'S NOTE: In this letter Burroughs remarks on the financial difficulties he is having with Maurice Girodias, his publisher at the Olympia Press. These problems will take up more of his time and energy in years to come, but, surprisingly, he will never completely break from Girodias. At one point he and Olympia made an agreement that he refers to later as the Hummel contract. Payments from foreign (i.e., American) sources were sent first to Switzerland. Then two-thirds were to be sent to Burroughs and one-third to Girodias. William found that all of the money usually wound up in Girodias' pocket, however, and at times this was to cause Burroughs severe financial problems. In this letter Burroughs also responds to Bowles' suggestion that he live in the Seychelles.

WSB [Paris] to Paul Bowles [Tangier, Morocco]

9 Rue Git Le Coeur
Paris 6 / France
April 18 1960 Past Time

Dear Paul:

I dream of Tanger often and see pieces of it laying around in cafes and streets corners. Always corners. So perhaps better to see it from distant. Germans everywhere. Shoals of them through the streets of Paris the way they used to pass through Tanger. Leaving pieces of their language behind.

[Bill] Belli left for Italy in the car of a woman named Norma or is it Thelma Clark? Departure is in the air. I am leaving soon for The States. My finances in tangle. Olympia may be bankrupt or bought out. Looks like I need a lawyer. Brion [Gysin] is writing now. A novel. It looks great. Name: *Sex Hero.*

My love to Jane [Bowles]. The Seychelles sound faraway *mais quien sabe?*

Best
William Burroughs

WSB [London] to Brion Gysin [Paris]

American Express
London
England May 3 1960

Dear Brion:

Last night was the first no tea[6] night since I don't know when. Technicolor dreams like: I was in a tool house looked like in garden. A mirror on wall. In it I saw your face and said "Brion" and turned around. It was some one else older and the face was changing first silver and then bright red. I said, "You're not Brion who are you?" and he said "Just an artisan" and put a hand on my wrist. "Please step this way." His face rapidly losing any human pretense. I sat down and he adjusted a metal bar safety belt across my waist and the tool house began to move like some kinda space ship.

In past few days a weight of menace lifted off me relaxed almost into a flagrant ambush. You would think I should know Paul Lund when I see him by now but no I was walking right into it pues [*but*]

---

6   Tea. Marijuana.

Kiki's[7] voice: "Watching them William. *Mala Gente*" Stop Change Start and stay out of the Socco Chico Club.[8] I can't cover all the far out but mostly benign developments since I leave Paris. Quote from Communication 16 of Artorga, The Artificial Organism Society. "Electromagnetic fields could stimulate the brain without contacting the skull. Norwegian technicians noted. It is already possible to go directly to the auditory centers to produce a kind of hearing." I told you. Like I told you.

Saw Dent.[9] More light on the US Narcotic Dept. Really the worst those Anslinger[10] boys drift in from work H Sling. Bastards sons of bitches. And who's ordering me home I wonder? Just because some cat is on the short wave don't make it writing. In any case I want to dig the scene here. I am sending your shoes back via Fanchette.[11] The English sizes do not exactly correspond to American so I hope they fit, if not can be exchanged sort of a long range fitting.

Brion if you need money don't hesitate to call on me. No reason to be short now when things seem to be looking up.

I have been working writing a sequel to *Naked Lunch* to be called "Mr Bradly Mr Martin".[12] Time of The Assassins. Covers events of Paris Alamout.[13] You, Gregory [Corso], [Maurice] Girodias, [Bill] Belli, Jerry [Gorsaline],[14] The Harloffs,[15] [Paul] Lund, the lot. Christmas Eve with The Harloffs in The Baghdad was suddenly illuminated for me in a flash back when I saw my hand drumming "The Drummer of course". Well I will write it and it will be the way it happened.

7　Kiki. A young boyfriend Burroughs met in Tangier in 1954. He was killed in 1957 by a jealous lover.

8　Socco Chico. A small market square within the walls of the Tangier medina.

9　John Yerby Dent. The doctor who introduced Burroughs to an apomorphine cure for drug addiction. This process would be frequently recommended by William in the years to come as one of the few treatments that worked.

10　Harry Jacob Anslinger (1892–1975). Head of the U.S. Federal Bureau of Narcotics.

11　Jean Fanchette (b. 1932). Parisian psychiatrist and publisher of *Two Cities* magazine.

12　Ted Morgan in *Literary Outlaw* says that Bradly-Martin was the "inventor of the double-cross and leader of the Nova Mob."

13　Alamout. An area in northern Iran that was the location of the castle of Hassan Sabah.

14　Jerry Gorsaline. A friend of Bill Belli.

15　Guy Harloff (b. 1933). A Dutch painter, credited with introducing the group to the "Beat Hotel."

"There will be nothing to look at buy my pictures everywhere"
you said last night in dream. See you soon I hope

Yours

Bill

EDITOR'S NOTE: The cut–up method was taking up more and more of Burroughs' creative energy, as this letter demonstrates. He applied the idea to recombining words in random sequences, eventually even random languages simultaneously. Before long he would begin to cut up materials in nonprint formats such as film, recordings, and photographs.

WSB [London] to Brion Gysin [Paris]
May 16 1960
% American Express
London
England

Dear Brion:

I could write endless novel on London chapter. Highlighted by Soviet Bid Cured Oil Man Talk Gertrude Conducted Tour of Board Room Reports: "That you know now is as clear as the 'Knows' on your??? Face."

Soviet Bid: Johnny Toumey: Johnny Too Me? Johnny Two Me? Me Too Johnny? Me Johnny Too? Johnny Me Too? Two Johnny Me? Me To Johnny woke up to see Johnny Two Face a mass of scar tissue: "Does this disturb Doctor Benway? Face of thee Brother? Remember read The Reports. Here they are. I see you know how to read. Like Mayan Codices? More or less. You perfected that art along the Chang Dynasty with refresher course at Uxmal Chicken Itza [Chichén Itzá] and Chimu. Remember The Zero Gimmick?: Remember the Two City Other Half Gimmick? Remember the Adding Machine? That stream lined Thing Police? Read. Remember. I see that you do. G.S. speaking. AND the Cunt Gimmick Mr. Burroughs? Take a Life. Divide into Five Year Periods. Write in Pain Signs Word Signs. Cut. Concentrate.

Cut. Reduce to Sentence Spell. Words. Pictures. Cut. Reduce to One Word One Picture. Or Three Lives or Five. Willy The Fifth. Reduce to one sign"

"Now you know how to write The Book. Brion Burroughs Write. Words Burroughs. Pictures Brion. Cut. Concentrate. Write us all out of Appalling Terminal for which Mr. Burroughs bear heavy responsibility. STOP a Self Righteous Little Hypocrite. CHANGE. WRITE. The Enemies YOU Wrote into Friends. You can. START WRITE."

Oil Man Talk: "Brion is right about cunt. Of all the stupid assed gadgets to clutter up a planet built in flaws and hidden miles and the nastiest whine ever heard anywhere: 'Do You Love Me? Do You Love Me?' . . . — . . . SOS".

Claro [clearly] women and or Jews constitute a disposal problem of the nastiest caliber leave my dogs swimming desperately in sewage without some Junior Prick preach up a wholesale Jewbad to clog the universe with more shit. Tin of the Board of Health Burroughs. For G's Sake Stay Thy Ugly Spirit. What a rash and unsanitary deed is this you contemplate. In the words of that ass hole Watson another fucking disposal problem THINK. Will Burroughs Never Learn? Unimaginable and downright Stupid Disaster. Teen Age Future Time.

Kick That Ugly Spirit Habit Burroughs. Its ugly and nowhere and 'Understanding Out Of Date.' 'Board a Second Class Citizen Back To Germany.'

You want to 'Return With Henry' and be one of His Heavy Metal Luce Heads? Another Disposal Problem. Everywhere March His Lousy Grade B Head. "Inordinate Ambition?" For What? A Crock Of Shit Terminal Time Junk. Foam Rubber White Whale in A Sea Of Turds.

Jack Stern? YOU work for ME? You Second Run Tape Worm. YOU a 'European Thuggee.' You couldn't strangle a hernia in an Iron Lung. The stink alone of That Name knock a man on his ass. You eat it and shit it out and eat it again. "Having passed through the proud intestines of all the Rothchilds here I stand a piece of impacted junk shit."

Claro. The two characters marked lousiest in my book: Jack Stern and Gregory Corso. Piss Poor Players. Sneering gloating winners and sniveling whining losers. Leave them sit in Geneva on a diminishing pile of shit and disembowel each other for the Last Shot. At The End of My Rewrite Line.

I begin to realize what an instrument you gave in the repetitive poems. Take any phrase. You will soon SEE. 'Ugly Spirit Shot Joan Because?' Soon See Why 'Ugly Cause Shot Joan Bee Spirit For' My Darling Party Line. I am making with your permission this contribution to Local Union Representative Johnny Toumey:

Rub Out The Word 'Accent'.

Rub Out The Word 'Class'.

Rub Out The Old School Ties.

Enclose cut up of Corso's note. *Claro* the little shit has been cutting up for years is the way he writes. Corso Beckett Durrell. How petty assed lousy can you get? It was [Maurice] Girodias tipped me off. He said. 'If I were you, Burroughs, I would cut up Corso's note, might be of special interest.' Girodias and Sinclair.[16] I am sending copy to Sinclair. Might include in reprint when and if.

Fanchette left suddenly and I couldn't relay the shoes. Will pass along at earliest conveyance. What are your plans? I want to go long Hong Kong learn Chinese. Imagine repetitive poems and cut ups Chinese. Shift lingual. Maybe Fanchette will see me George at that in a way. Saw Doctor Dent. Scientologists have moved in next door. More about Anslinger. Even lousier than I thought. And the whole Lexington Project stinks like under cover Belsen. Another rancid oil scandal. Will this flag n'er be clean? And the Coca Cola Gimmick. What a crock of shit. Learning Morse Code in spare time. The scouts are always prepared.

Love
Bill

---

16 Sinclair Beiles (1930–2002). South African poet who worked on some of the first cut-up experiments with Burroughs while living in Paris.

EDITOR'S NOTE: Dave Haselwood, the fine arts printer with the Auer-hahn Press, asked to publish Burroughs' next book. *In 1960 Auerhahn issued William's* The Exterminator *with a cover illustration and additional calligraphs by Brion Gysin in an edition of approximately 1,000 copies. Even before that book was out, William had begun to think about another book for Haselwood, which he envisioned as* Exterminator II.

WSB [London] to Dave Haselwood [San Francisco]

May 20 1960
Cargo American Express
London
England

Dear Dave Hazelwood [*sic*: Haselwood]:

It has occurred to me that these Last Words Of Hassan Sabbah[17] might be used as a post script to *The Exterminator.* After: *Exterminator?* Watch. There might of course be certain difficulties with the actual names involved. The names could be changed of course using names from *Naked Lunch* for example. Unless the people involved were willing might even condescend to allow their names to be used under the circumstances. Well that is a problem for a publisher and every profession has its special problems they tell me. In any case I shall be glad to hear from you at the above address..

Sincerely
William Burroughs in This Case
for Brion Gysin Hassan Sabbah

WSB [London] to Brion Gysin [Paris]

May 26 1960
American Express
London England

---

17 Hassan Sabbah (aka Hassan-i-Sabbah). A Persian Isma'ili missionary of the eleventh century who set up his base in a castle in Alamout or Alamut in the northern region of modern-day Iran. His followers became known as Hashshashin, or Assassins. Burroughs and Gysin became interested in the exploits, both real and imagined, of Hassan.

Dear Brion:

Are you undergoing another transformation? Your letters do not sound like Brion. I suggest urgently that you come here for a visit. I am well supplied with the ready. London is a much better deal than Paris believe me. The best thing I ever did was to get out of Paris and come here. So please Brion come over here for a visit. Look around. And decide. I have many things to discuss with you but not by letter.

My regards to all.
William Burroughs
For Hassan Sabbah

EDITOR'S NOTE: Try as he might to remain calm and businesslike, occasionally Burroughs would lose his temper. Here, even after his repeated requests had been ignored, he managed to maintain a professional tone and even held out the hope that the two could still work together on future projects.

WSB [London] to Paul Carroll [Chicago]

May 26 1960 Past Time
Cargo American Express
London
England

Dear Paul Carroll:

Re: your proposal to publish or arrange publication of selections from "Back Seat Dreaming" title changed to "Mr Bradly Mr Martin". Plus *The Exterminator* and *Minutes to Go*. I can only say that my correspondence with you in the past few months has been marked by a lack of candor that gives me little confidence for future dealings. The Brion Gysin material you have has already for the most part appeared in *Minutes To Go*. Will you please, I repeat, will you please return this material AT ONCE. Either to Brion Gysin or better to me at the above address. When I have to say something for the fifth or sixth time I have to say it clear enough to be understood. Is the above clear enough or must I make it even clearer? I repeat. Please return the material of Brion Gysin at your very earliest convenience or inconvenience as the case may be. Then perhaps we can talk business

Sincerely
William Burroughs

EDITOR'S NOTE: Allen Ginsberg was still traveling in South America. He had found someone able to prepare ayahuasca (yagé) correctly, and the visions he experienced under the influence of the drug were terrifying. He wrote to Burroughs for reassurance that he would return to "normal consciousness" after taking the drug and noted that he had seen William during some of the drug-induced dreams.

WSB [London] to Allen Ginsberg [Peru]
June 21 1960 Present Time Pre-Sent Time
Cargo American Express
London England

Dear Allen:

There is no thing to fear. *Vaya adelante.* Look. Listen. Hear. Your ayahuasca consciousness is more valid than 'Normal Consciousness'? Whose 'Normal Consciousness'? Why return to? Why are you surprised to see me? You are following in my steps. I know thee way. And yes know the area better than you I think. Tried more than once to tell you to communicate what I know. You did not or could not listen. "You can not show to anyone what he has not seen". Brion Gysin for Hassan Sabbah. Listen now? Take the enclosed copy of this letter. Cut along the lines. Rearrange putting section one by section three and section two by section four. Now read aloud and you will hear My Voice. Whose voice? Listen. Cut and rearrange in any combination. Read aloud. I can not choose but hear. Don't think about it. Don't theorize. Try it. Do the same with your poems. With any poems any prose. Try it. You want "Help". Here it is. Pick it up on it. And always remember. 'Nothing is true. Everything is permitted'. Last words of Hassan Sabbah The Old Man Of The Mountain.

Listen to my last words any world. Listen all you boards syndicates and governments of the earth. And you power powers behind what filth deals consummated in what lavatory to take what is not yours. To sell the ground from unborn feet. Listen. What I have to say is for all men everywhere. I repeat for all. No one is excluded. Free to all who pay. Free to all who pain pay.

What scared you all into time? What scared you all into your bodies? Into shit forever? Do you want to stay there forever? Then listen to the last words of Hassan Sabbah. Listen look or shit forever. Listen look or shit forever. What scared you into time? Into body? Into shit? I will tell you. The word. The-thee word. In thee beginning was the word. Scared you all into shit forever. Come out forever. Come out of the time word the forever. Come out of the body word thee forever. Come out of the shit word the forever. There is no thing to fear. There is no thing in space. That is all all all Hassan Sabbah. If you I cancel all your words forever. And the words of Hassan Sabbah I as also cancel. Across all your skies see the silent writing of Brion Gysin Hassan Sabbah. The writing of space. The writing of silence.

look look look

Amigos muchachos a traves de todos sus cielos vea la escritura silenciosa de Brion Gysin Hassan Sabbah. La escritura de silencio la escritura de espacio. Eso es todo todo todo Hassan Sabbah.

vea vea vea

When will you return—? The cut up method is explained in *Minutes to Go.* Which is already out in the States. I will send you a copy but where to? George Whitman[18] says to look up his old friend Silvester de Castro in Panama City. Connected with the municipal symphony and the university. *Hasta al vista amigo.*

> Best
> William Burroughs
> For Hassan Sabbah
> Fore! Hassan Sabbah

P.S. No one in his sense would trust 'the universe'. Swept with con the millions stood under the signs. Who ever paid off a mark a gook an ape a human animal? No body except Hassan Sabbah.

---

18 George Whitman (b. ca. 1912). Owner of the Mistral Bookshop in Paris, later Shakespeare & Company.

WSB [London] to Dave Haselwood [San Francisco]
June 24 1960
Cargo American Express
London
England

Dear Dave Haselwood:

I am revising the manuscript you have and adding to it new material to form a separate pamphlet of about the same length as *Exterminator I*. To avoid confusion of material prefer you return manuscript you have now. I can provide you with final official version revised and completed within two weeks more or less. Important to indicate that these pamphlets are to be considered abstract literature observation and mapping of psychic areas. Not political propaganda or if so entirely by accident. I do not subscribe to any of the sentiments expressed necessarily. Are not personal opinions. Only a transcription of voices along the streets and quarters where I pass. Abstract literature. Not personal opinions. Do these plots really exist? How in the fuck should I know? Just a writer is all. Just an artisan. Not running for office. Just writing what I see and hear in my imagination. Pure abstract literature.

Best

Bill Burroughs

WSB [London] to Bill Belli [Paris?]
July 6 1960
American Express
London
England

Dear Bill:

Well I told you about Scandinavia.[19] A dull efficient place stocked with available cunt. I have nothing against woman except

---

19 Burroughs had once gone there to visit Kells Elvins and his wife.

it is a gimmick out of date. And I mean that literally and exactly. So is man and the human body. I am not talking in terms of a thousand years. I am talking in NOW terms. Minutes To Go. All I have against woman is not only gimmick out of date but gimmick in a stupid panic desperately resisting inevitable change and endangering the leaky lifeboat in which I hope to lam out of this appalling terminal. So if I chuck HER over side no hard feelings or spite. Just self preserving is all. You think I exaggerate? Listen: I was talking to English scientist the other night one of the THEY who run England and he said: "How does it feel to know you are one of the last human beings?"

Like you say there is too much fucking *talk* everywhere. Let's not get this show on the road, let's stop it. Run Out The Word. Rub Out The Word. Cut All Word Lines. "Enemy Advance We Retreat. Enemy Retreat We Advance. Enemy Encamp We Agitate. Enemy Tire We Attack"—Mao Tse Tung. Instructions for guerilla war.

Enclose excerpt from current work. 'Intense'? Yes. We must all be intense if we want to *survive*. Yes, I will bear myself grimly enough

Best
Bill Burroughs

WSB [London] to Dave Haselwood [San Francisco]

July 11 1960 Past Time
Cargo American Express
London
England

Dear Dave Haselwood:

I do not know if you have seen *Minutes To Go* statement and samples of the cut up method by Brion Gysin, Sinclair Beiles, Gregory Corso, and myself. It is already circulating in the U.S. The point is now is the time to get *Exterminator I* in circulation before the cut up method is common knowledge and subject to claim jumping. Certainly it seems premature to discuss *Exterminator II* before *Exterminator I* is on the stalls. If I seem impatient the matter is urgent. Minutes To Go. I hope to hear from you soon

Sincerely,

William Burroughs

"There is a tide in the affairs of men which taken at the full leads on to fortune."

WSB [London] to Irving Rosenthal [New York]
July 20 1960 Present Time
Cargo American Express
London England

Dear Irving:

First a general statement of policy with regard to *Naked Lunch*. The Olympia edition aside from actual typographical errors is the way the book was conceived and took form. That form can not be altered without loss of life. Definitely I feel that no material should be added in the text. I am now writing a sequel to *Naked Lunch* entitled "Mr Bradly Mr Martin" in which I will use any material from the manuscripts that Allen [Ginsberg] has which seems pertinent. But I repeat none of that material should be added to present text. Above all the present ending should not be altered. In fact there is little of the old material that I would still use anywhere. It is understanding out of date. Yes it is definitely my intention that the book should flow from beginning to end without spatial interruptions or additional chapter headings. I think the marginal headings are definitely indicated. THIS IS NOT A NOVEL. And should not appear looking like one. What is the point of chapter headings that merely repeat from the text? In short I am definitely opposed to any additional chapter headings.

On the other hand I think including the "Deposition" article from *Evergreen* and the *Journal Of Addiction* article[20] is an excellent

---

20 "Letter from a Master Addict to Dangerous Drugs," *British Journal of Addiction* 53 (January 1957).

idea. In appendix. Also the enclosed note on Cut Up Method which is used in the sequel and illustrated in *The Exterminator* and in *Minutes To Go* both now out in the States. I go into the matter of word forms in the sequel. If any illustrations are used. And I think excellent idea.

[...]

The enclosed explanation of the cut up method should be inset at the end of the article "Deposition" and followed by the cut up of that article which was printed in contributors notes. Remember that some of the errors in Olympia edition are intentional. I corrected the book for second printing and found as I remember not more than fifty actual errors.

love

[two pages of explanation and four pages of corrections were originally included with this letter]

WSB [London] to Brion Gysin [Paris?]

July 24 [1960]
% American Express
London

Dear Brion:

A number of questions require your and my attention:

1. I received copy of *Exterminator I*. Not bad. I will ask [Dave] Haselwood to send you a copy if he has not done so. Your name on front cover and your format and your drawings after the text. I will ask when he could publish *Exterminator II*. Might as well keep the line open. We can decide after you see the format whether we want to publish *Exterminator II* with Haselwood.

2. Harry Phipps[21] under treatment with Doctor Dent. Sold on the treatment says he can do something about getting the apomorphine treatment official attention in U.S. Suggests I write article

---

21 Harry Phipps. A wealthy American friend of Jacques Stern who was living in Paris. He also became a close friend of many of the Beat writers before he died of an overdose at the age of thirty.

in popular vein for *Saturday Evening Post* or at least on that level. Hmmmm. When I mentioned you know Panitza he snapped. "Better leave Brion out of this." Hummm. Jack Stern was nearly destroyed on Christmas Eve last when a fire broke out in his apartment. Burned and jumped from window. Now training to be an auditor.[22] The Reverend Stern. Phipps looking very well. Does not send you his regards. I do think the article is good idea and will write. What am I an actupus [*sic*: octopus]?

3. Kenneth Allsop showed me the article he has written.[23] What a dossier he must have. Things in it I don't recall telling to anybody. And which I had forgotten. Not bad though. I rather like him.

4. Grove ready to go to press on *Naked Lunch*. Want to use some of the drawings. I wrote. "If drawings are used should be a selections from Brion Gysin and mine since my drawings derive from his. In any case would not use my drawings without acknowledging their derivation from Gysin." Will see what they say to that. I also insist on cut up statement.[24]

Well I am off to Malta or Ireland or somewhere. But not for long. Back here late August if not sooner. No sign of John [Howe][25] and I am tealess in Gaza. Write here

Best
Bill

WSB [London] to Paul Bowles [Tangier, Morocco]
July 26 1960
Cargo American Express
London England

Dear Paul:

---

22 Auditor. Burroughs was becoming more and more interested in scientology during this period. In scientology, an auditor refers to the person who administers the "clearing" process for new members.

23 Kenneth Allsop (1920–1973). An English author and broadcaster and one of the first reporters to interview Burroughs.

24 For legal reasons, the Grove Press edition of *Naked Lunch* was not to be published until March 1962.

25 John Howe. The London pot connection for Burroughs and his friends.

Brion went back to Paris last week after spending more time in London than he had originally intended. While he was here he managed to arrange for an exhibition in December and to record a talk for BBC on the cut up method. It looks as if my trip to Southern Spain is *cancelado*. All plane connections booked solid till mid-August. Somebody is flooding the world with second run factory reject replicas. So I will make a brief trip to Amsterdam and return to England. I don't have enough cash in hand to do any extensive traveling in any case. Brion also recorded for BBC one of his repetitive poems as he calls them of which there are examples in *Minutes To Go*. The effect is remarkable when speeded up and superimposed. I have also experimented setting these poems to music. Any music or tune at all. Like the Prayer Call. Or: "Oh Say Can You Rub All The Words Out From Thee".. (I find that Rub Out The Words lends itself readily to almost any tune "Danny Boy", "Auld Lang Syne", "La Cucharacha", etc. Brion has become interested in the possibilities of sound and the BBC has offered him the use of their stereophonic equipment during October. I think it was The Pool that brought the potentials of sound to his and certainly to my attention. Young [Jerry] Gorsaline seems to have disappeared no one knows where. What is a sibsib? A desert fox? I wish I could hear some of your recording. How I miss Tanger. But England does have compensations. My best to Jane [Bowles] and Achmed [Yacoubi], Cherifa.

Best

Bill

P.S. I hope to have new novel ready by early winter.

WSB [London] to Dave Haselwood [San Francisco]
July 26 1960
Cargo American Express
London England

Dear Dave Haselwood:

I received *Exterminator I* and it looks very good. Could you please send along a copy to Brion Gysin, 9 Rue Git Le Coeur, Paris

6 France? I am now working with Brion on *Exterminator II* and have made a number of alterations and additions. Grove is going to press now on *Naked Lunch* which should boost sales on *Exterminator*. Could you give me approximate date for *Exterminator II*? Timing is important and I want to think ahead on the board. Do you have any connections with recording? Brion and I have both made tape recordings of material in *Exterminator I* and *II*. In fact the repetitive poems could be juke box sensation.

I find that people read *Minutes To Go* without ever using the cut up method themselves. But when they once do it themselves they see. Any missionary work you do among your acquaintances in showing people how the cut up system works will pay off in sales. People must be led to take a pair of scissors and cut a page of type. Perhaps a game would do it. Like say four people each write a page on any subject comes to mind. Then cut and rearrange. With squared paper and the cut lines drawn you dig. [. . .] Please let me hear from you.

Best
Bill Burroughs

WSB [London] to Dr. John Dent [London]
July 27 1960
25 Lillie Road
London S.W. 6

Dear Doctor Dent:

I don't know whether Harry Phipps told you about my intention to write an article on a popular level concerning the apomorphine treatment of *all* addictions. I hope that you will give me permission to quote from your book.[26] I am going to Amsterdam for a few days but would like to discuss the matter with you on my return.

Did you receive the book I sent to The Savage Club?[27] I enclose article from *The Daily Mail* which seems to bear out the author's

---

26 John Yerby Dent. *Anxiety and Its Treatment* (London: Skeffington, 1955).
27 The Savage Club. A Bohemian gentleman's club at 1 Whitehall Place in London.

suggestion that music would be useful in treating withdrawal. I am convinced that any agent that deadens pain would also act on the withdrawal syndrome. And nothing would be easier than to give it a try. All one needs is a tape recorder and headphones.

I wonder if you have any contact with the group here that is engaged in encephalographic research? Has any one gone into the pharmacology of brain areas, that is, made observations on what brain areas are stimulated by various pharmacological agents? Apomorphine? Mescaline? It would seem to be a most fruitful line of inquiry.

I will call when I return and hope we can meet to discuss these questions

Sincerely,
William Burroughs

EDITOR'S NOTE: In order to avoid problems with immigration authorities, Burroughs had to leave England from time to time and re-enter with a new stamp in his passport. This often necessitated short trips to other countries such as The Netherlands or France. Back in England, he continued his experiments with cut-up tape recordings.

WSB [London] to Brion Gysin [Paris]

August 4 1960 Present Time
Cargo American Express
London
England

Dear Brion:
I made a trip to Amsterdam. Stayed one night and return. They have the new hallucinogen there and I have made tentative arrangements to try it. Also LSD 25. Amsterdam is quite charming and any number of spectacular restaurants and beautiful Indonesian people. I do not have any time to bestow in sunnier climes. Sing hum word rub outs are really far out. Today I borrow another recorder from The Irishman and see what happens on geometric speed up. Also have routine involving two tape recorders in cut up

conversation that will just kill you. Starts with straight cut up conversation back and forth you dig and slowly speeds up.

I received one mescaline dose from Allen Ginsberg and enclose resulting Surah[28] which should conclude *Exterminator II*. That is conclude the manuscript you have. I suggest that we get that manuscript in shape as soon as possible for Auerhahn. They have put out *Exterminator I*. And I don't see any immediate publisher here in Europe. All the manuscript needs is your drawings and samples of the various repetitive poems. No reason we couldn't get it off in the next week. IT is certainly more suitable for America than Europe.

The apomorphine article should rate me introductions in Bristol.[29] I am seeing Doctor Dent tomorrow. Apomorphine is the physiological cut up. Acts on the Right Write Center. To deactivate what is righten [*sic*: written?] there. More potent forms should be useful in kicking word and body habit. Yes I am turning into an octopus. It's the only way to live.

Chris Wanklyn in town. See him tonight. On the wagon me to save time.

I am sure you could make radio connection in Amsterdam. The LSD 25 man I met was most interesting. He suggests that all art critics be required to take LSD. In fact Amsterdam no bad place. I am waiting on LSD shipment to return there and see what can be done. [...]

Please let me know what you think about *Exterminator 2*. If you are in agreement lets get it out as soon as possible. What about publishing your catalogue in Amsterdam? Will send along Allsop article and *The People*. Need more tentacles. How can I stay in London? How can I go anywhere else?

Sorry to hear about the BBC deal falling thru. Like I say Amsterdam would I think be more receptive. Any word from your New York agent?

Best
Bill

---

28 Surah. A chapter of the Koran.
29 Bristol was the location of the Burden Neurological Institute where W. Grey Walter worked.

WSB [London] to Brion Gysin [Paris]
August 6 1960
Cargo American Express
London
England

Dear Brion:

Enclose last pages of *Exterminator II*. I suggest that as soon as you have the drawings and poems finished you send to me so I can show a complete manuscript here and see if there is possibility of English publication and send a copy on to Auerhahn. No reason why we could not publish both in England and U.S. Well the sooner the quicker as The Sailor used to say.

I hear [Paul] Lund has married American money. Otherwise no special Tanger news from [Christopher] Wanklyn and Gordon Sager[30] both in London. Sending along the Allsop article. Quite good. You should get ear phones and listen to the repetitive poems speeded up or hummmmed. Its will just kill you. I don't need mescaline now. Get high on my ear phones. The apomorphine article will be a real blockade buster if I can place it in like *Saturday Evening Post*. Advocating the use of apomorphine and ear phone reconditioning with "Plain old fashioned suggestion therapy" administered with the knowledge and consent of the subject. Repetitive poems put to music could accomplish this work. "RUB OUT THE WORD JUNK.. JUNK IS NO GOOD BABY.. KICK THAT HABIT MAN.." Thus in his own words and with his consent the addict can be conditioned to abandon forever the need for opiates. Let us free our country from the slavery to chemical agents. "You got it?" [Maurice] Girodias trying to maneuver me into contract on "Mr Bradly Mr Martin". Does he know what exactly he is trying to buy?

Best

Bill B

---

30 Gordon Sager. Friend of Paul and Jane Bowles and author of the book *Run, Sheep, Run*.

WSB [London] to Brion Gysin [Paris]
August 15, 1960
25 Lillie Road
London S.W. 6

Dear Brion:

Please write me here and spare me AMEREX [American Express]. The mail department is deteriorating daily not to mention some horrible old character subject to stay at the head of a queue spilling out onto the public streets, "My bowel is all constipated and mother is out there moaning in her Cadillac took bad with the hemorrhoids. Could you tell me where is the nearest high colonic irrigation parlor? What? You don't have such establishments in England? Now when are you folks going to get civilized?" Seeing the press lately in relays. This is good because it has forced me to a precise formulation of the cut up method and the out position. Noteworthy was a Mr. Merrit Wyn from *The Express*. Like a Cockney version of Steele complete with beard and C.P. writ all over him trying to brain wave me into a schizophrenic "episode" or at least into "paranoid ruminations". I mean a real wise guy. Well I am learning to handle these citizens. Sending along clippings from *The People* and Allsop's article. I missed a big spread in *The Sunday Dispatch*.

Now I will outline program of work: 1. Get the complete manuscript of *Exterminator* or *Initiator.*—I favor *Exterminator* and a later issue entitled *Initiator* which will be more as the name implies. So as soon as you have your poems and drawings complete send along to me here. I will edit my section. Yes some of the early material I will delete and send off to Auerhahn. Then see if I can arrange simultaneous publication here perhaps thru *Sidewalk*.[31]

2. A new magazine is coming out in New Orleans called *The Outsider*. I project to make the first issue a cut up issue. I am writing to suggest this and to submit cut ups which I am now preparing, mentioning your name Sinclair Stewart Graham Wallace. No

---

31 *Sidewalk* magazine, published in Edinburgh, printed Burroughs' "Have You Seen Slotless City?" in their second issue.

money but definitely worth doing I think. You might send them a selection from *I Am Out*.

3. I have almost finished the article on the apomorphine treatment and Doctor Dent.

4. I am going thru a lot of notes and picking out all images for a cut up and book of cut up poems which only you could illustrate.

5. What about the catalogue? It needs a title. How about "Writing Of Silence"?

So please send the manuscript of *Exterminator* or *Initiator* along as soon as possible get this show on the road and stop it.

1. Lord I am not—were thee?:: How in the fuck should I know. I hope not under the uh circumstances. Abandon ship God Damn it every man for himself.

2. Aren't you taking it to Hakims Court? It doesn't figure. Uncle from America educative laughing.

3. How cognizant can one be of historicity of own thought? *Zut alors*.

4. Unimaginable precisely they are making the place unimaginable which is to say uninhabitable. Now when are they going to get civilized?

[. . .]

Love
Bill

WSB [London] to Allen Ginsberg [New York]

Sept 5 1960
Cargo American Express
London England

Dear Allen:

The cut up method is a tool which I am learning to use after a year of intensive experiments. There is no reason to keep cut up material that is not useful to the purpose. Often from a page of cut ups I will use one or two sentences. It depends on the material cut and the purpose in cut. In *Minutes To Go* and *The Exterminator* I was using cut up material intact. At the time had not learned to select. Also was more concerned with using the cut ups as fact assessing instrument. When used for poetic bridge work procedure is different. Like I write a page of prose or prose poem straight. Then cut once or twice or more. And select from all sections what I find most valuable. A sifting panning process. The enclosed selections will give you idea of potentials in the method. There is no reason why classic sonnets or any other poetic form could not be so reduced. I find cut ups most immediately workable on poetic prose image writing like Rimbaud, St. Perse and your correspondent. Use of cut ups of course increases ability to cut with the eyes, that is to make "natural cut ups" whatever that may mean and what is an unnatural cut up? Whatever abilities Gregory [Corso] may possess logical thought is not one of them. That is having cut with the eyes there is always extension of awareness possible with scissors cut. I repeat, no necessity to retain any material not pertinent.

The "pain" referred to is pain of total awareness. I am not talking mystical 'greater awareness'. I mean complete alert awareness at all times of what is in front of you. Look out not in. No talking to so called self. No 'introspection'. Eyes off that navel. Look out to space. This means kicking all habits. Word habit. Self habit. Body habit. Kicking junk breeze in comparison. Total awareness = total pain.

It took me ten years to pick up. Why take so long? Another thing about cut ups. They are funny. Like the Drunk Newscaster.[32] Remember? Try cut ups with your yagé. Please send me same dose mescaline again. I will be able to pay you what I owe when my money from English edition comes thru. Why did I ever sign that contract with Girodias whereby my money clears thru Switzerland Amsterdam and Hong Kong? Well *son cosas de la vida slotless*. Well ta ta kan kan dearie, I have like a million urgent things to do. What am I an coptupus? I mean octopus. Perhaps. You never know with all these mutations about. "Exists On Venus. It might not

---

32 Jack Kerouac's friend Jerry Newman ran Esoteric Records in Greenwich Village and made recordings both commercial and private. One of these was referred to as "The Drunken Newscaster," but it isn't clear whether this was ever released for sale.

have bones." *Exterminator.* Best to all the family. What's this about Jack [Kerouac] being in Paris?

Love

Bill

Brion signs for Hassan i Sabbah because he regards Hassan i Sabbah as his sponsor. So do I. By sponsor I mean the source of thought movement and feeling continuity. A chair does not move of itself neither do any [of] you.

Have you contacted Scientology-Dianetics? Ron Hubbard father of has headquarters here.[33]

WSB [London] to Brion Gysin [Paris]
Sept 14 1960
Cargo Amerex

Dear Brion:

I hope you are not goofing. Such a thing as too much fun you know. Some people smoke all night and get up late. Have you: 1. sent six drawings and six poems off to Auerhahn? 2. sent some black and white drawings to *Outsider*? He asked for some Gysin drawings. Also snapshot.

I am scheduled for LSD this week under sign of Beaverbrook Press and the insidious Mr. Winn-Steel. Should be interesting. Also will see Grey Walter[34] when he returns from vacation. So must delay trip to Paris for another week. Violeta Damianova who was to discuss film with me did not show at the meeting place she indicated and I have not heard from her. Who is she and under whose face?

Most interesting character here name Charles Hatcher. A doctor not practicing. Says that indole[35] which is the base of all perfumes and all hallucinogens ingredient of shit. Sells (I mean smells) like

---

33 Burroughs was becoming more and more interested in L. Ron Hubbard's self-help system called dianetics, which over time developed into a new religion, scientology.
34 William Grey Walter (1910–1977). Neurophysiologist, student of brain wave theory, and pioneer in the field of robotics.
35 Indole. An aromatic heterocyclic organic compound used in fragrances.

diarrhea. Mixed with water = jasmine my mother's favorite perfume. Shit may be the terminal hallucinogen. He is trying to promote institute of far out studies to be located in Tangier. Approaching Gupi Huxley Walter Bowles you me. Well I'll go along with it. He is very active agent now off to Amsterdam where he will talk on cut ups.

Please keep in touch. Have you tried the lingual switch on *i je yo that am eisgo io bin soy eso ana ca est?* One phrase translated into all languages and the walls came tumbling down.

Best
Bill

Best to all the Boys

EDITOR'S NOTE: In the following letter Burroughs mentions the concept of flicker for the very first time. As early as February 1960 Ian Sommerville had begun work on an invention that would later become known as the dream machine. By using a record turntable and a lightbulb, Sommerville developed a way to produce a stroboscopic effect of light flickering at various rates. The subject sat in front of the machine with his eyes closed and the effect was said to produce images in the brain. Brion Gysin had experienced the same stroboscopic effects while riding in a car under a canopy of leaves on a sunny day. Together Gysin, Burroughs, and Sommerville worked out frequency patterns that would produce the desired effects. Through research they learned that the British neurophysiologist William Grey Walter was conducting similar experiments.

WSB [London] to Brion Gysin [Paris]

Oct 1. 1960
Amerex
London

Dear Brion:

Vertiginous pressure of events appointments and short of the ready held me providentially in London for Ian's [Sommerville] visit; three dimensional trip to Alamout. He said: "Brion sent me". *Muy buen hecho Meester Brion.*

Alors: Charles Hatcher is most anxious to meet you. He wants to photograph some of your paintings for a brochure he is getting out. Describes cut ups and his machine for destroying language. I heard Grey Walter. Most interesting and will make a flicker date with him in Bristol. Have seen Francis Huxley.[36] Eileen Garrett[37] is very ill. She has been taking psilocybin on a bad liver. A much more beautiful and shining replica of Jerry Gorsaline has materialized himself at 25 Lillie Road [Burroughs' London address at the time]. Harry Phipps I.R. Sixteen years old. Name Michael Portman.[38] Old flame of Bill Barker. Very interested in you. Turns into a Tangier guide straight away and said: *"Me llama Meester. Que Quires?"*. Have you tried the lingual shift yet? Any phrase and name shift lingual and you start talking this strange double talk with configurations of sub verbal meaning and then the phrases leap out like the above. Ian tells me you are all broke at 9 Git Le Coeur.[39] *Moi tambien.* But I will [see] what I can do. Will call Boyars[40] to see if any loot has come thru on the International Annual. I had a quick 200 dollars lined up writing a junk article for *True Detective*. Now they write they want to cut out all reference to the Dent treatment I should sign my name to Anslinger's shit. *Nunca. Cabrones.* Mexican cocksuckers. And that shifty assed [Maurice] Girodias is messing up the English negotiations to keep me short so I will sign another Hummel[41] contract. *Tambien jamais.* I will go see Kassim[42] this week. My guides tell me something very wrong going on there. I think Meester Kassim no *amigo.* Ofenlick mistake but jumped out so unexpected. *A ver.* My best to all the boys. I will do what I can to hustle some loot and make it to Paris as soon as possible.

Love

Bill

---

36 Francis Huxley (b. 1923). British anthropologist and author with an interest in LSD.
37 Eileen Garrett (1893–1970). Medium and founder of the Parapsychology Foundation.
38 Michael Portman (ca. 1943–d. 1983). Wealthy English aristocrat who for a short while was Burroughs' companion.
39 The address of the "Beat Hotel."
40 Marion Boyars, one of Burroughs' London publishers from the firm of Calder and Boyars.
41 Odette Hummel. Maurice Girodias' representative in Switzerland who was supposed to receive and distribute the payments for Burroughs' books.
42 Kassim. This is probably a reference to John Kasmin, who worked at the Kaplan Gallery in London and later opened his own gallery.

P.S. Did you read in *The Tribune* statement from Flying Saucer Society? "Our Masters tell us that Earth men will not be permitted to land on other planets." Quarantined.

WSB [London] to Billy Burroughs Jr. [Palm Beach, Florida]
Oct 1, 1960
Cargo American Express
London England

Dear Billy:

If you dig *The Turn of The Screw* you should dig Rimbaud. Nothing obscure in his poetry if you see it as IMAGES. Here is a book of his poems with the French translation opposite will improve your French. A game I play is to type out phrases from Rimbaud or any poet I fancy. Then I cut into sections. Rearrange putting section four with section one and section two with section three and select a new arrangement. Try it some time with Rimbaud or any writing. Enclose picture of my self taken in Paris by Charles Henri Ford a writer of novels and films.

I hear you dig music. Try it with ear phones you can play it any time that way without bothering people around you. Besides music is different when you hear it right in your ear. It should be simple operation to plug your record player for ear phones. Please let me hear from you soon. Hope you can make it to Switzerland or we can meet some place very soon

Love
William Burroughs

WSB [London] to Ian Sommerville [Cambridge, England]

Oct 4 1960
25 Lillie Road
London S.W. 6

Dear Ian:

Great picture of you. Mr Huxley says the facial changes would show better in movie than still pictures. If I get some loot will buy a movie camera. Right now I am really hung up for bread and must get out of London or move to a cheaper room. How are room prices and availability in Cambridge? I would like to spend three or four weeks in a quiet place assembling novel so I could get an advance. So what is the score in Cambridge? I am paid up here until Monday. Nicolas Tanburn writes there are cheap rooms in Oxford but I would rather be at Cambridge. Please let me know

Love
Bill

WSB [London] to Brion Gysin [Paris]

Oct 7 1960
American Express
London

Dear Brion:

I am immobilized for lack of £. Looks like I will have to sell the tape recorder. I consider retiring to Cambridge or Oxford for a few economical weeks in which to assemble a novel for English publisher. Girodias is not doing me any good lately at all. Obviously stalling for an option on new novel.

Miguel [Michael] Portman's beauty produce an aphrodisiac result. Its the principal of the thing you understand. If I could just get that guide alone—.

Is this your Calamaras in narcotics? Just a coincidence of names surely.

Fixate on the enclosed picture of Jimmy [Cookson]. He has become fabulous on the sex level incidentally. Sudden gear shift about three weeks ago.

Well I am off to see Fabian[43] in *High Time*. So ta ta kankan dearie. Are you "blank" as the Danes say also? I will try to send along a fiver or some what. Saw [Marion] Boyars and no money there yet. Have you made the shift lingual? High Time

Love,
Bill

WSB [London] to Charles Henri Ford[44] [Rome]

Oct 8 1960
Cargo American Express
London
England

Dear Charles Ford:

Kiki is the name of my Spanish amigo murdered in Madrid by a Cuban singer. Glad the name has found a good home. I would love to see some sun sompe [soon?] and will certainly make a trip South this Winter. Are you settled in Rome? I never did receive copy of your book and [Maurice] Girodias seems to be running a very loose ship. Doesn't answer my letters or follow up publisher contacts I make for him. As a result I am hung up for money and reduced to writing articles for *Detective Stories*. Is *Terrain Vague*[45] out yet? I would like to see it. Is Andrea doing any work now in films? I want to write a film script some time if I can get a free hand.

Hope to see you and Andrea and Ki Ki later this Winter

Hasta Luego
Bill Burroughs

---

43 Fabian was a popular teen idol during the late 1950s and early 1960s.
44 Charles Henri Ford (1913–2002). American surrealist poet, artist, and photographer.
45 *Terrain Vague*. Ford kept a diary and took still photos that Marcel Carne made into a film of this title.

WSB [London] to Grey Walter [Bristol, England]

Oct 9 1960
Cargo American Express
London
England

Doctor Grey Walter
The Burden Neurological Institute
Bristol

Dear Doctor Walter:

I heard your very interesting talk in London recently. I am concerned with the phenomena of flicker from two points of view: 1) Possible therapeutic applications in drug addiction. I am preparing an article on this subject with Doctor John Dent of London. 2) As a writer I am interested in the effect of flicker on the creative process. I have a friend Mr Melville Hardiment[46] (I believe he has been in touch with you) who wants to write an article on flicker in relation to the creative process. Both Mr Hardiment and I would be most interested in experience flicker and report our reactions from the viewpoint of professional writers. Would it be possible to arrange an appointment to see you in Bristol within the next few weeks?

Hoping to hear from you

Sincerely
William Burroughs

WSB [Cambridge, England] to Brion Gysin [Paris]

Oct 21, 1960
Cargo Ian M. Sommerville
Corpus Christi College
Cambridge

Dear Brion,

I ran short of the ready and had to flog my recorder. Moved to

---

46 Melville Hardiment. Writer and editor.

Cambridge which is cheaper than London and more congenial for work. I have a palatial room overlooking the market for four £ per week with breakfast. Some money has now come in and I enclose a fiver. I am not idle here you may be sure of that. Ian [Sommerville] has made a flicker machine and the effect of flicker even with this crude model on your pictures is a thing to see. The figures jump right off the canvas.

When Miguel[47] realized I was blocking him out of the hotel (Mrs Hardy has her orders) he disappeared. I saw his face in the mirror with such hate it occurred to me the mirror would break in another second. Next day in the paper poltergeist phenomena centering around boy like I thought it was Miguel when I saw the picture said: "The mirror seemed to leap from the wall and crash to the floor". Well I think I could find work for a uh creature of Miguel's caliber. In a picture gallery perhaps?

Yes I went to see [John] Kasmin at the Kaplan Gallery. And found that he had moved. I have not seen him yet but I will on my next trip to London. I hear bad sounds from him on the short wave. Hope I am wrong.

When are you coming here? I have to leave England again by the 28 of October. Will come to Paris. I have made some recordings here and the heretics are ready for you. I am now writing a primer called *The History Of The Occupation*. May record this for the heretics when it is finished. I also finished my article on the apomorphine treatment. Sent it off to my New York agent (introduced by Boyars. His name is Barthold Fles.[48] He describes himself as "very active.") Sent copy to Harry Phipps and to Doctor Dent. So that is done. I will borrow or rent a recorder for your recording to mix with paint. Or perhaps wait till I see you in Paris.

Ian sends love. I an or I am

William Burroughs

P.S. Can't begin to cover far out occurrences every day like. Discuss when see you. Important Kennedy BE ELECTED OVER

---

47 Miguel. Michael Portman.
48 Barthold Fles (1902–1989). Literary agent and author.

NIXON. Kennedy openly advocating US drop Chiang Kai-shek[49] and his pestiferous wife down the drain.

WSB [Cambridge, England] to Brion Gysin [Paris]

Oct 24 1960
Cargo Ian Summerville [sic]
Cambridge, England

Dear Brion:

I must leave the UK again. Have bought ticket on cheap return flight. Will arrive in Paris Thursday morning at 1:30 AM more or less. Can you reserve room? Or I could double up with [Bill] Belli or some one? Well sorry it is such an hour but . . . Flying back Saturday night. Still short of cash and must keep my room here. Much to discuss.

I have worked out a method of running on the tape recorder with cut ups. Will approach the scientologists in London. Get this show on the road. I cleara everybody.

Ian [Sommerville] has built a flicker machine. He keeps improving on it. I prefer Cambridge to London and find I can accomplish more here as regards work and contacts. My only immediate prospect of traveling funds is the article on the apomorphine treatment. No prospect of English sales on *Naked Lunch*. The Grove publication not until Spring.

See you Wednesday night that is Thursday morning. [. . .]

Love
Bill B.

WSB [London] to Brion Gysin [Paris]

[November 1960]

Dear Brion:

Last night I started my Great Americans series which I will explain in some detail. The machine [typewriter] went red and

---

49 Chiang Kai-shek (1887–1975). President of the Republic of China (Taiwan).

jammed. I have unjammed it by the only way I know with any machine, a laying on of hands. But it still writes red. I have a suggestion for you that could write some immediate cash: "Unforgettable Character" for *Reader's Digest* based on Hassan i Sabbah. He runs a restaurant in Fez or Marrakech or wherever or whatever you like: "You want to know my secret? I have no secrets. The doors of my place are open at all time. You Westerners think that Islam looks in. It is you who look in worrying about money and position. Talking to yourselves, your boss, your women, your friends. Stop. Change. Start. (Give it the Oriental switcheroo you dig). LOOK OUT at all times. See what was in front of you. Can a man see what is front of him with all his friends and enemies talking in his ear? *Stop talking to yourself.* Ah this shocks you? Listen: Words should be your servants. Use them. Do not let them use you. And when you do not need them send them to sleep. How to? Learn to know the word your servant. Look at words. *Listen. Listen out at all time. Look and listen out at all times.* Take any simple phrase like 'I am That I am.' Repeat it. Now pass it back and forth through a sieve of punctuation. See the words change meaning as the period rotates. Now change the position of the words. Now translate into other languages. You are stuck in word slots. You do not hear. Cut the word lines. And step out into silence. It is yours. It is everybody's. You do not see the trees when you walk down the street because of *'The' 'Word' 'Tree'.* Look at the word tree. Look? at the word tree. Look at? the word tree. Look at the? word tree. Look at the word? tree? Word look at the tree? Tree look at the word? Etc. Now look at the tree. and you will *see the tree not the word tree.* You will begin to see everything sharp and clear like after a rain. When you are in a restaurant *Listen Out.* Listen to the rhythm of voices. Every restaurant has a different rhythm. Listen to the words you can hear. No this is not bad taste to keep your ears open. Move from table to table. Combine conversations. When you walk down your Western streets defaced by street signs, look at the signs. Look back and forth. Cut words back and forth from one sign to the other. You can plot sign lines through your city. Now look at the faces. Why are you in the West afraid to look at a stranger's face?"

One day there had been four Arabs in the restaurant to talk business. I did not know enough Arabic to understand what they were saying in full detail but the drift was clear. "Those men are out to cheat you," I said angrily after they had gone. "Why do you serve them tea and listen politely?" "You are wrong," he said. "They have not come to cheat me but to see if I can be cheated. I am a stranger in this town. They have been sent for my instruction. If I allowed myself to be cheated I would learn a great deal about cheating. And for his instruction the cheat must be paid. If I do not intend to allow myself to be cheated I can at least be polite. In any case those men you saw were not real cheats. They were good men sent to test the stranger." "But that is ridiculous." "I've seen them in every cafe in town and I will put out the word that they [were] sent to test strangers and perhaps it will be so. You see nothing is true really as you Westerners think. Least of all with regard to men. The Chinese say 'save face'. We of my sect," (he belonged to a little known Islamic sect known as the Ismailists) "go further. We make for a man the best face from the materials at hand and then we offer it to him." "Like give a dog a good name?" "Exactly. There is much wisdom in your country if it could only be heard. Too much noise. I recall a young American who used to eat here. He said: 'I have no enemies I turn them all into friends one way or the other.' "

So why not write up outline and take it to Panitza? Right along their uplift line isn't it?

This concept of making face led me to The Great Americans Series on which I am now at work:

GREAT AMERICANS: HARRY J. ANSLINGER

HE REALIZED THAT THE ONLY CHANCE OF SAVING HIS COUNTRY FROM THE SOFT MACHINE THE VIRUS INVADED WAS TO CREATE TO DELIBERATELY CREATE A LARGE RESERVOIR OF YOUNG LIGHTLY ADDICTED ADDICTS WHO COULD, WHEN THE WRITE MOMENT WROTE BE CURED WITH THE APOMORPHINE TREATMENT DISINTOXICATED NOT ONLY OF HEROIN BUT OF WORD LINES OF THE SOFT MACHINE AND WELDED INTO SHOCK TROOPS. THAT MOMENT IS NOW WRITE. MR ANSLINGER CAN NOW SPEAK THE TRUTH AT LAST. MR HARRY J. ANSLINGER.

GREAT AMERICANS: MR HENRY LUCE[50]

---

50 Henry Luce (1898–1967). Publisher of *Time, Life,* and *Fortune* magazines.

HE WAITED IMMUTABLE AND WISE AS TIME LISTENING FOR THE SOFT CLICK OF HIS TIME MACHINE. A CLICK THAT IS HEARD ONCE IN EVERY THOUSAND YEARS. THE CLICK HAS SOUNDED. MR LUCE STAND READY TO SMASH HIS TIME MACHINE FOREVER. TO SMASH THE WHITE WHALE FOREVER. MR HENRY LUCE, MR PAUL GETTY, MR KHRUSHCHEV, SENOR CASTRO. MAO TSE TUNG, ECT ECT ECT ECT ECT. LINE FORMS ON THE WRITE. YES ALL OF YOU. WOMEN JEWS THE LOT. I'LL MAKE YOU LOOK GOOD OR KILL YOU. AND WHAT ABOUT THE VIRUS ENEMY? THE SEX ENEMY? THE SENDERS OF THE SOFT MACHINE "MEET YOUR OLD TOP KICK BOYS. MAY HAVE GIVEN YOU SOME HARD TIMES. CHALK IT UP TO TRAINING. STILL WANT TO WHIP MY ASS?" THE SOFT MACHINE? AN OBSTACLE COURSE. TRAINING PROGRAM FOR SPACE CADETS. WELL DONE THOU TRUE AND FAITHFUL SERVANT. AND TO MASTER A LONG GOOD NIGHT.

Judo Brion. Judo.

Best
Bill Burroughs

WSB [Cambridge, England] to Allen Ginsberg [New York]

Nov 2, 1960
Cargo Ian Sommerville
Corpus Christi College
Cambridge, England

Dear Allen:

Stay your hand. I have found the missing material in the attic of 9 Rue Git Le Coeur on recent flying visit. So for Gods sake no more manuscripts. I have so much material here it appalls me to see it. I want to spend about three months in a warm place putting this book together.

I am sorry about missing [Dick] Seaver[51] in Europe. I am so taken up with work that I do neglect letters and other matters that require attention. Its like I thought he was in Paris.

---

51 Richard "Dick" Seaver (1926–2009). Editor in chief of Grove Press.

Very interesting about Harry Smith.[52] I would like to use the cut up method in films. It introduced a whole added dimension of space time cuts. Just imagine travelogues of various countries cut up Mexican pissing on Stockholm streets. Bloody riots in Trafalgar Square. etc. etc.

Saw Gregory [Corso] briefly in Paris. He has finished his novel for [Maurice] Girodias.[53] A bit Saroyanesque I think but I have only seen small extracts.

I have been trying to make mescaline contact here but still no success. No special word for the psycho-analysts except that their method of therapy is superseded and no where. No good. *No bueno*. When I think of the time and money wasted on the preposterous fraud of analysis and what they are paid to do nothing and determined to go on doing nothing. Have they picked up on the encephalographic research of Grey Walter? He can remove so called hallucinations by direct brain area intervention. Have they picked up on scientology? On the new hallucinogens? Of course not. All they want is to sit on their fifty dollar ass.

Apropos Jack's [Kerouac] other life experience. Is not question of that. I quote from Soviet scientist: "We will travel not only in space but in time as well"

Love
Bill

WSB [Cambridge, England] to Allen Ginsberg [New York]
Nov 10 1960
Cargo Ian Sommerville
Corpus Christi College
Cambridge England

Dear Allen:
Still in Cambridge but don't think I can stick this English

---

52 Harry Smith (1923–1991). Filmmaker and ethnomusicologist who assembled the influential *Anthology of American Folk Music* in 1952.
53 Gregory Corso. *The American Express* (Paris: Olympia Press, 1961).

weather much longer. As soon as I get some bread will split South.

I have an inordinate amount of work to do assembling a novel from five or six hundred pages of notes and fragments. I have several short pieces on hand I want to send to American magazines. Have you any suggestions? What about *Yugen? The Outsider* I have already covered. The material in question is specialized for American consumption. On the other hand it is not quite suitable for sale through ordinary channels so I am thinking in terms of the no-paying far-out magazines like *Yugen* and *Kulchur.* Do you have suggestions? You are more in touch than I am.

I have an agent in New York now name of Barthold Fles. I have asked him to try and get me an advance on next novel which is only a problem of putting it together rewriting and editing now. I figure about three months in quiet place would see it finished. Please let me hear from you.

Love

Bill

P.S. Are there any magazines you know specifically interested in work from W.B.?

P.S.S. Do you have a tape recorder or access to one? Try this. Record a newspaper article some of your own work or anybody's this letter etc. etc. Record say for two hundred feet. Now go back to the point where you began the recording. Run forward without recording and cut in at random and record phrases. Do this several times back and forth. Listen to the result. You can do the same with recorded conversation. Like record for two hundred feet now go back and start cutting in at random. Let several people do this together. Like you record Jack cut in etc. Do you ever see Jerry Newman? "The Drunken Newscaster" was made by taking a lot of news casts and mixing them together at random as I have described. Why don't you make some recordings with him? Do this with *Howl* or any work and you have a new poem. Cut *Howl* in with Rimbaud, Jack Kerouac or whatever. *I mean Allen pick up on the action. Minutes to go.*

Above method can also be used as therapy. Write talk account of your illness. Now cut the page up. Now put it on tape recorder.

Now cut back back over it. Get it outside your head. Wipe it off the tape. This is streamlining *dianetics* therapy system of running back and forth traumatic material until it is wiped off the tape and refiled as neutral memory. The use of tape recorder to facilitate this process and the use of cut ups is my idea. *It works. Try it.*

Not to talk think about *TO DO*

WSB [Paris] to Allen Ginsberg [New York]
Dec 30 1960
9 Rue Git Le Coeur
Paris 6, France

Dear Allen:

Con ciudado hombre.. "Space swimming desperate.. Is not personal opinion.." I did make an LSD6 scene in London and some other more potent hallucinogen that has to be injected.. Neither experience much different from mescaline.. I am currently in Paris to try and get some money out of [Maurice] Girodias. Broke lately as usual.. I have not had the time to answer in detail your letters but I have read them with great interest.. Like I say don't flip pops is all.. One must be careful of "seruche" (altitude sickness) and depth madness and the bends.. Hazards of The Silent World.. Space is silent remember.. There are no words in space remember.. Space swimming desperate.. Remember is not personal opinion.. Remember have you tried the tape cut ups yet?.. I venture to think not.. You neglect your basic training some times.. I have not heard from Leahy [*sic*: Timothy Leary]..[54] He sounds far out.. Write me this address and all my Best Wishes for New Year

Love,
Bill

---

54 Timothy Leary (1920–1996). Writer and advocate of hallucinogenic drug research.

RUBRUBRUBRUB+++&+++++&++&&&&&"""&"+++
RUBRUBRUBRUBOUTOUTOUTOUTOUT#"#+++++#
RUBRUBRUBRUBOUTOUTOUTOUTOUT####&&&&
"""&&&+++++"OUTOUTOUTOUTOUT"""""""&&&
1961 ""+OUTOUTOUTOUTOUT"+"+"&&&
THETHETHETHETHETHETHE+++###+++&&+++
THETHETHETHETHETHETHE&&&&&++++++++#
THETHETHETHEWORDSWORDSWORDSWORDSTHE
###&&"&"&"&WORDSWORDSWORDSWORDS"++

WSB [Paris] to Allen Ginsberg [New York]
Jan 10, 1961
9 Rue Git Le Coeur
Paris 6, France

Dear Allen:

Thanks for the mescaline.. I shot it to short circuit the nausea with excellent results.. Thanks also for the fifty dollar offer which I don't need at the moment.. Working round clock on next novel.. May move South soon.. I enclose short piece from novel in progress title *The Soft Machine*.. Is this suitable for *Swank*..[1] If so you might send it along to them or wherever.. Great about [Herbert] Huncke..[2] *A ver*.. Must close now as have million and one things to do.. Love to all

Love
Bill

EDITOR'S NOTE: Allen Ginsberg had recently been working with a new friend, Timothy Leary, on his experiments with psychedelic drugs. Leary, a professor at Harvard, had access to a wide variety of drugs for experimental purposes, and Ginsberg had visited him several times, proposing many likely candidates such as Burroughs for further experimentation.

WSB [Paris] to Timothy Leary [Cambridge, Massachusetts]
Jan 20 1961
9 Rue Git Le Coeur
Paris 6, France

Dear Timothy Leary:

Thank you for your most interesting letter. I can only say that I think what you are doing is vitally important. Yes I would be very

---

1   *Swank*. A men's magazine similar to *Playboy*.
2   Herbert Huncke (1915–1996). Writer and storyteller. Ginsberg had just told Burroughs that Huncke had recently kicked his drug habit.

much interested in trying the mushrooms and writing up the trip as I have done with mescaline. It might be interesting to gather an anthology of mushroom writing. In any case I will send along the results. I know that my work and understanding has gained *measurable* from the use of hallucinogens and I think the wider use of these drugs would lead to better conditions on all levels. Perhaps whole areas of neurosis could be mapped and eradicated in mass therapy. I enclose copy of *Minutes To Go* which I hope will interest you. Actually I have achieved pure cut up highs without the use of any chemical agent.

Brion Gysin who first applied The Cut Up Method to writing is here in Paris at the above address would also be most interested to try the mushrooms. An anthology of mushroom drawing and writing might be an idea. So I will look foreword to hear from you

Best Wishes on
William Burroughs

WSB [Paris] to Melville Hardiment [London?]

Jan 23 1961
9 Rue Git Le Coeur
Paris 6, France

Dear Mel:

I have heard from Jon Webb[3] that he has trouble with his presses and that *Outsider I* will be delayed in publication until March.. This is only what to expect in The Little Magazine lark.. Well I will write to him and see what the score is.. I am glad you met Doctor Dent.. It might be interesting for him to meet Evans the chemist who could perhaps do something towards synthesizing or altering the formula of apomorphine to produce more potent variations.. It had also occurred to me as an interesting experiment to take apomorphine under the influence of mescaline—say several sub emetic injections—and see if the effects of the mescaline altered or

---

3 Jon Webb. He and his wife, Gypsy Lou Webb, owned the Loujon Press, which published *Outsider* magazine.

canceled.. Both mescaline and apomorphine operate in more or less the same back brain areas..

My best to Harriet.[4] I was sorry not to see you both here the week end of the 18th. Please keep in touch

Best

Bill B.

WSB [Paris] to Paul Bowles [Tangier, Morocco]
January 25 1961
Paris 6, France
9 Rue Git Le Coeur

Dear Paul:

I have written Limes [Verlag] in Wiesbaden to the effect you can not take on language graft at this time. I am going to Germany and see if I can locate the translator they need.

I have contracted with Olympia to deliver sequel to *Naked Lunch* entitled *The Soft Machine*. Cutting and permutating the book writes itself out of a hat more like taking a film than what I used to think of as writing. But why draw lines and categories? I got on this film track in a Blue Movie[5] section. Take two boys say in sex positions 1 2 3 4 5. Now permutate word and image of position units. 2 1 3 4 5, 3 2 1 4 5, 4 3 2 5 1, 5 4 3 2 1, etc. You can also assign a short musical score to each unit and a color. Like red white blue green black actors images and sets. In any case a useful exercise for insomniacs. Suppose take a series of one actor in all positions now mix in with track of another actor cutting the scenes back and forth so the other finishes one kief pipe and chews one food back and forth and uses all facilities like they just melt into one actor. From which I conceived a color and smell alphabet. So much quicker to read color than words or just sniff a story. As usual moving to be obsolete.

Tanger is graced by Paul Lund's absence and I will probably make an appearance as soon as I deliver this manuscript to Olym-

---

4   Harriet. Melville Hardiment's wife.
5   Blue Movie. A common term for erotic films.

pia. Meanwhile short trip to Germany. Suppose one should make a film cut up of one actor talking German the other English like finishing each other's sentence couldn't one just graft the language on? Why stop there-? In short why stop anywhere?

You know I hear your pool[6] every time water drips. Nice young man name Roger [Knoebber][7] on his way to Tanger may look you up..

Best..
Bill B.

Really I feel like I'd made one of those movies with Truman Capote after reading your letter. *Saludos* to all in Interzone

WSB [Paris] to Dave Haselwood [San Francisco]
Feb 24 1961
9 Rue Git Le Coeur
Paris 6, France

Dear Dave Haselwood:

You seem to be running a mighty loose ship. This is the fifth letter I have sent you to inquire about a manuscript sent six months ago. Now I hear through J Montgomery[8] that you do not intend to publish *Exterminator II*. I consider your behavior discourteous, sloppy business practice, dishonest, and down right stupid. Is that clear enough or shall I make it even clearer? Will you please return my manuscript *right now* like today.

Best
William Burroughs

---

6   Paul Bowles had a small fountain that produced a relaxing sound and this is probably what Burroughs is referring to.

7   Roger Knoebber. Young American resident of the Beat Hotel to whom Gysin was sexually attracted.

8   John Montgomery (1919–1992). Editor and publisher, a California friend of Jack Kerouac and Gary Snyder.

WSB [Paris] to Allen Ginsberg [New York]
March 9 1961
9 Rue Git Le Coeur
Paris 6, France

Dear Allen:

I received the mushroom from [Timothy] Leary. Great but I think not as far out as mescaline. In any case I reached an interesting area and will present the maps in my current novel. I enclose a short piece in a light vein for *Metronome* or whatever. The Green Boys with purple fungoid gills I saw with the mushroom and have written a long section on these curious regions and the practices of the natives. I enclose also a brief article on The Cut Up Method of Brion Gysin which I read on Thanksgiving Day to The Heretics Society in Cambridge.[9] (Feeling rather like Gertrude Stein). For *Yugen* or whatever. How is [Herbert] Huncke? Give him my best regards and I hope he stays off. I still think apomorphine is the best treatment for addiction. Taken orally it is not unpleasant and need not involve actual nausea. I think that bad experience with the apomorphine treatment results from lack of experience on the part of the physician. Tell Huncke to drop me a line if he finds time and inclination. Mason [Hoffenberg][10] was around about two weeks ago just after cure sound too and looking very much like Huncke some how synchronized you understand? I am writing to Leary in some detail. Please let me hear from you soon. Have you ever seen Jerry Newman by the way?

Love

---

9   Cambridge Heretics Society. Founded in 1909 to question traditional opinions.
10 Mason Hoffenberg (1922–1986). Writer and coauthor with Terry Southern of *Candy* and other books for the Olympia Press.

EDITOR'S NOTE: *Although he doesn't state any reason, Burroughs did not wait in Paris to see Allen Ginsberg and Peter Orlovsky, who arrived just a day or two after Burroughs left town. Burroughs did not want to see them and tried to avoid them during this trip to Europe, but they later reunited in Tangier.*

WSB [Tangier, Morocco] to Allen Ginsberg, Gregory Corso, and Peter Orlovsky [Paris]

April 7, 1961
Cargo U.S. Consulate
Tanger
Maroc

Dear Allen Gregory Peter:

Sorry I could not have been there to greet you in Paris but my time there was up in more ways than one.

Back in Tanger same hotel same room but don't know for how long. The place has changed and seems like a ghost town. Well I never seem to get time for all I have to do and so many letters to write have been putting it off meanwhile hope you are digging Paris and write me your plans. I hope you Allen and Peter meet Brion and hear his BBC tapes and let me hear from you.

Best
Love
Bill B.

WSB [Tangier, Morocco] to Brion Gysin [Paris]

April 8, 1961
% U.S. Consulate, Tangier
Maroc

Dear Brion:

Many unusual experiences with the Prestonia[11] (it *was* Prestonia) and Miguel [Michael Portman] was write [*sic*: right] so will

---

11 *Prestonia amazonica.* A drug with a dimethyltryptamine source.

appear in next novel for which I am now recording the scenario —
Title to be *The Ugly Spirit* — Starts on Alamout — "Sure W.B.
we could play down the fruit angle get in some dancing girls —
These Venusians are Communists see? And Hassan Sabbah really
works for Naval Intelligence —" "Will Hollywood never learn?" —
So the Master is sending five agents out on a special assignment
to assassinate the Green Octopus leader of dissident sect of the
Indian Mother currently holed up in Egypt. For this assignment
he has picked five agents: There is Miquel — Johnny Yen — Harry
Phipps — to infiltrate as one of her courtiers — Uranian Ali —
(The Master didn't like the look of him at first hesitated to permit
him on the reservation: "That boy has the makings of a very ugly
spirit; heavy metal. On the other hand Hmmmmm — That could
end the game—" and the master still likes the game at that time).
So this Uranian Ali is to infiltrate The Secret Police since he has
this dash of mean cop any case — "We gotta have a Nigra boss —
And a Jew from Brooklyn —" "Shut up you fool. I'm coming to
that" — The third is a red haired Jew from The Ovens — (I'll
explain that later). Its one of the torture gimmicks — Plenty of
torture in this one. And sex unlimited like nerve gas — You know
just doesn't know when to stop and alternated with the ovens the
hard and the all too soft yes? no? break down even the agents of
Hassan Sabbah — But I'm getting ahead of the story hear — So
this Jew of course in to infiltrate the Jewish Allies of the Green
Octopus — The fourth agent was a Negro drummer to play in her
band — The fifth a Nordic type for her personal guard — All the
agents were captured and broken with yes? no? pleasure pain switch
and imprisoned in a green bottle and made into the Ugly Spirit
with which she enslaved the earth and intended to use to destroy
Hassan Sabbah and cover her retreat with a Nova — Now switch
to Present Time — The Green Octopus is Mary Cooke — The
split between the Green Cat and the Indian Mother is deeper and
they are in a state of open war — Minraud defecting to Hassan i
Sabbah — Captured agents released — Ugly Spirit disintegrates
and so on out — Though might make one of those composite books
like I write the first chapter and get the show on the road you write
a chapter, Paul Bowles, [Lawrence] Durrell, Graham Greene. I

will suggest this to [Maurice] Girodias. Paul is very much interested in the idea.

Some far out experiences with that awful Prestonia. Strictly the nightmare hallucinogen. Trip to The Ovens like white hot bees through your flesh and bones and everything but I was only in the ovens for thirty seconds and pretty good for a goy they said and showed me around a very small planet and this was the red haired Jew agent of Hassan i Sabbah my guide you understand. And all out tangle with The Green Octopus — She carries a lot of weight so stay away from her — Permutate — Shift positions — Stay out of present time — Throw back signals switch — Switch white hot sand blast from The Ovens with cool blue from the home town at supersonic speed — Yes she felt that one — This went on for hours — Its very strange stuff and I really shrink from taking it and you know what a glutton I am for kicks but not that hard — In any case giving my self a rest for a few days.

Paul has been most helpful — Otherwise Tangier most disappointing. All the Spanish seem to be gone. So no *amigos*. But I keep busy with my work. Mohammed Larbi[12] sends you his best.

Love

Bill

P.S. If the ranks of The Women were split so were Male Ranks and there were several hundred pretenders to the name of Hassan i Sabbah engaged in bitter border clashes and Replica rustling. At this point Hassan i Sabbah moved to reclaim all his agents beginning with the Five Prisoners — Will this move unite the dissident Female Sects? Is mediation possible? Stay tuned to this station.

Please do what you can to interest Allen Ginsberg in the cut ups and permutations — This is important I think.

---

12 Mohammed Larbi. A Moroccan friend of Paul Bowles.

WSB [Tangier, Morocco] to Allen Ginsberg [Paris]
April 14, 1961
Cargo U.S. Consulate
Tanger, Maroc

Dear Allen:

I am glad you have talked to Brion and heard his tapes. Have you dug his flicker machine? Great with the mushrooms. No I do not think Brion is superstitious. All novelists of any consequence are psychic assassins in a very literal sense. As regards my plan I too am waiting for money and when it comes plan to leave Tanger and move to Southern Spain—Malaga most likely—that is unless something occurs to change my plan which I doubt at this point. Tanger does seem rather dead.

Yes, Allen I do want to see you but I did want you to see Brion first. In any case it was really most difficult for me to remain in Paris every one so uncool and my three months had expired and I was running short of loot etc. Doubt if I feel up to any strenuous extensive travels by the usual routes. Well we can talk about that when I see you. Meanwhile come on down any time. Short trip from here to Malaga any case not like there is any distance involved. I have already started on another book and so keep busy. My best to Gregory [Corso] and Peter [Orlovsky].

Love
Bill

WSB [Tangier, Morocco] to Billy Burroughs Jr. [Palm Beach, Florida]
May 4 1961 Present Time
Cargo U.S. Consulate
Tanger
Morocco

Dear Bill:

I was most interested to read your poem which seems to fit in with what I am myself writing at the present time. I took a page of my writing and folded it down the middle and then lay it over your poem which I had typed out. So that we have now half your writing and half mine you understand. Here is what came out of the juxtaposition of the two texts:

"By eternity I met a beggar and forth through each other. Seems to be long and is followed close. Do it. Fractured image he scattered. Not know I told him so. Whereupon he said: 'Empty dawn track dripping mental strife' — Followed through boy my inward heart star tracks we intersect. A penny for thought and left. Created smoke down old photo as I recall that dusty road and the hole in pain funnel. The Grey who to me such wisdom told I realize that I like the eternity has captured. Wounded galaxies muttering back seat dream. Now passed The Grey Screen back said to me what is short but stopping to record — Told me he close by eternity. Silver Morning Boy cool and casual I see you in wind street. Shadow body cross the wounded galaxies flashed through all I said, twist pensively distant finger. Break Through in Grey Room through my fog of despair — Streets drifting smoke."

Interesting I think. Hope you will be encouraged to do some writing. Do you take pictures? Please write me.

Love

Daddy Bill

WSB [Tangier, Morocco] to Brion Gysin [Paris]
May 6 1961
Cargo U.S. Consulate
Tanger
Morocco

Dear Brion:

I do not want to go over the proofs [*The Soft Machine*] which would delay publication and I am not much of a proof reader as you know. So there is really not much point in [Maurice] Girodias sending the proofs on here. For one thing I may not be in Tanger. So please tell him to go ahead with all speed and publish and not bother to send me the proofs.

What boy are you referring to on his way here? Miquel? Unfortunately Mohammed Larbi is under the same disadvantage as Ben Aissa. All in all Tanger is such a changed and sadder place that I have little desire to remain. They have cut down all the shade trees in the Grande Socco.[13]

I am just recuperating from a violent attack of stomach cramps. I found your remedy of a tight cord drawn around the stomach most effective and somebody is going to feel the weight of my half nelson which has picked up some special new angles since my little brush with Sammy, I am not so forbearing as I was. Incidentally I have started painting again. Here is a picture entitled "Break Through In Grey Room". How are the Beatniks? Do you see anything of B.J. Carroll[14] the method actor? Do write me a proper letter

Love

Bill

WSB [Tangier, Morocco] to Timothy Leary [Cambridge, Massachusetts]

May 6, 1961
Cargo U.S. Consulate
Tanger
Morocco

Dear Dr. Leary:

I would like to sound a word of urgent warning with regard to the hallucinogen drugs with special reference to N-dimethyltryptamine [Prestonia]. I had obtained a supply of this drug synthesized by a chemist friend in London. My first impression was that it closely resembled psilocybin in its effects. I had taken it perhaps ten times — this drug must be injected and the dose is about one grain but I had been assured that there was a wide margin of safety — with results sometimes unpleasant but well under control and always interesting when the horrible experience occurred which I have recorded in alle-

---

13 Grande Socco. The large open-air market just outside the walls of the medina.
14 B.J. Carroll. One of the inhabitants of the "Beat Hotel."

gorical terms and submitted for publication in *Encounter*. I am sending along to you pertinent sections of this manuscript and I think you will readily see the danger involved. I do not know if you are familiar with apomorphine which is the only drug that acts as a metabolic regulator. I think if I had not had this drug to hand the result could have been lethal and this was not more than a grain and a half. While I have described the experience in allegorical terms it was completely and horribly real and involved unendurable pain. A metabolic accident? Perhaps. But I have wide experience with drugs, and excellent constitution and I am not subject to allergic reactions. So I can only urge you to proceed with caution and to familiarize yourself with apomorphine. Doctor John Dent of London has written a book on the apomorphine treatment for alcoholics and drug addicts — it is the only treatment that works but the U.S. Health Dept will not use it. His book is called *Anxiety and Its Treatment*. I can ask him to send you a copy if you are interested. Let me hear from you

William Burroughs

EDITOR'S NOTE: Even though Burroughs had left Paris, Allen Ginsberg and Brion Gysin worked on the proofs for his newest book, The Soft Machine, *to be published that summer by the Olympia Press. Ginsberg described the book to friends as "very weird and wonderful far out," but he also thought that the ending of the book could be reworked, a suggestion that Burroughs alludes to here. For the first time Burroughs mentions cutting up photographs, something that would occupy a good deal of his energy over the next few years.*

WSB [Tangier, Morocco] to Brion Gysin [Paris]
May 8, 1961
Cargo U.S. Consulate
Tanger
Maroc

Dear Brion:
    First let me thank you for your work on the proofs [of *The Soft Machine*] I know what a job it must have been. But I really think

little is to be gained by my going over them. I can not agree with Allen [Ginsberg] about the ending. I realize the book is experimental and difficult. What else? An elaborate multi-dimensional map of an area. I can't do it over. I have been like transferred. Besides have five or six urgent things to do. I am now writing a Western. This book is for Billy [Burroughs] and I have been giving it most of my attention. Also worked The Ovens into an article and sent it off and wrote an article on color lines for Conrad Rooks.[15] Actually I think he is *non compos mentis*. He writes from Mexico he is going to take the sacred mushrooms and "endeavor to place himself in mystic contact with me." Gawd! Its like Grand Central in here now. Why don't he get his ass back to NY and publish his so called magazine. Ah well. Allen's blurb is brilliant and so is Gregory's [Corso]. Yes, I must see them of course. Only thing to do. They can park their horse however in some other stable.

Roger [Knoebber] is here and I will do my best for him. Mohammed Larbi is in the nick.[16] Some long story involving contracts and three brothers and really I lost the thread way back where while Paul and Jane [Bowles] are simultaneously telling the story and trying to decide what night we can have dinner..

Have been under considerable pressure here. For Allah's sake Brion be careful with that fucking Prestonia. Personally I would not take it again. The pain is *unimaginable* if the dose hits at wrong intersection point. So be careful and have some apomorphine handy and or largactil.[17] Preferably both. That is the only circumstance under which I would consider taking it again and you know that I am ready to take a chance with new preparations. This is something else.

Yes I might easily be persuaded to join you in Italy. I am not at all satisfied here.

I have made a lot of drawings like the one I sent you. *Drawings*

---

15 Conrad Rooks (b. 1934). American filmmaker who would later direct William Burroughs in the film *Chappaqua.*
16 Nick. A slang term for jail.
17 Largactil. A drug known as Thorazine in the United States.

For The Wind I call them. And tear most of them up and scatter to the Levanto which is blowing now.

In my spare time have done a little experiment with collage. Make collage of photographs, drawings, newspapers, etc. Now take picture of the collage. Now make collage of the pictures. Take-cut-take-cut you got it? Some interesting effects. For example take that flash bulb camera I gave you take pictures of your paintings. Cut up and make collage from the photos. Take. Cut. Etc. Is Antony Balsh [*sic*: Balch] doing anything with films now?[18] Please keep in touch. Many thanks for the drawing. Will make a great cover for *S.M.* [*Soft Machine*].

Love

Bill

WSB [Tangier, Morocco] to Brion Gysin [Paris]

May 13 1961
Cargo U.S. Consulate
Tanger
Morocco

Dear Brion:

Here is another collage of collage of collage to the Nth power entitled: "Word Falling — Photo Falling." Show extension of the method as applied to the image. Perhaps you could interest some professional photographer like Dick [*sic*: Norman] Rubington[19] or Antony Balch. Since arriving in Tanger I have been working full time and now the place is littered up with flash bulbs and negatives and magazine cut outs. What am I an octopus?

Roger [Knoebber] is looking good. Bill Decknetell and Jeanot are in town so in the hall of the hotel they live at they meet a pregnant Arab woman and Jenot rushes up and leers into her face with his beard and she had a miscarriage on the spot and called the fuzz

---

18 Antony Balch (1937–1980). English filmmaker who was to collaborate with Burroughs on a number of projects.
19 Norman Rubington (1921–1991). Painter, illustrator, and author.

in and they got a lecture from the chief of police and spent the night in jail. That really takes the rag off the bush

Best
Bill

Good Luck on the Exhibition

WSB [Tangier, Morocco] to Brion Gysin [Paris]
May 16, 1961
Cargo U.S. Consulate
Tanger
Maroc

Dear Brion:

Looks like I'll have to come on like a top sergeant here. "We happy people down here" have no time for sex or any form of self indulgence. Nothing but work and hours of it every day and beating off my creeping opponents with a spare tentacle. And most of this work goes into a gimmick to promote Brion Gysin. The collage method which I described to you and sent along samples. Here are more samples. Look. Look carefully. Move them around over each other at angles. (I have just started using color.) This is a major break through, Brion, and you have all the equipment necessary to pick up on it. Like take color shots of your pictures close ups angle shots etc. Mix in with color post cards and advertisements from *Life* and *Time*. Take. Make collages of shots cutting into fragments and rearranging at random. Take. Cut. Take. Just as photography a series of these collage concentrates would be spectacular. Antony Balch could help with technical details and Norman Rubington. I mean its a set up and you have the camera I gave you. All you need is a roll of film and some flash bulbs. I am showing the method to Roger [Knoebber] and he is most anxious to make some Brion collages. Of course I only have a few of your paintings here so my repertoire is limited. Just trying to get this show on the road and I need some cooperation

Love From Old Sarge
Bill Burroughs

WSB [Tangier, Morocco] to Brion Gysin [Paris]

May 17 1961
Cargo U.S. Consulate
Tanger
Morocco

Dear Brion:

Additional directive suggestions from Technical Sarge: Pose pictures against flowers trees rivers sky. Get that Paris light. Color film is expensive to develop. You can get results with black and white — Break Through in Grey Room — Now we need a peg to hang it on. Take an old wall with billboards. Scotch tape pieces of collage here and there. Take. Cut the take and tape on. Take cut as far as you want to take it and leave the collage there as a reference point. A collage of *The Exterminator, Minutes To Go, The Soft Machine* — including of course the drawings in *The Exterminator* would make an excellent window display for The English Book Shop. Norman Rubington could be most helpful on this project. I enclose some more samples you can use in making extended collage. Have some color prints being developed now and will send along.

My only directive for the Prestonia Ovens: Prepare yourself for *unimaginable* pain. And keep your apomorphine rations handy. I took fifteen twentieth grain tablets and so saved my life I think. Remember the usual emetic dose is two or three at most. And with the fifteen tablets I only puked once. So you can see what that apomorphine had to do. Since I am still on scene and *compos mentis* best thing that ever happened to me under the circumstances. Now I understand why collaborators. I heard them all say it: "You see what we're up against kid." Yes and see no percentage in literary or artistic collaboration with such forces of evil. And I say to the avant-garde guard. "Damn The Ovens. Full speed ahead — Word falling — Photo falling". [. . .]

What about your exhibition? Please write full details. Did you use the flicker machine? Wait until you start flickering collage. Photographic accuracy in Le Normand's [Norman Rubington] painting? Of course. He does it with camera first and copies it later. Look at enclosed shots and you will see what I mean.

For Allah's sake be careful with that Prestonia. Of course they may need preparation to tune in with the oven beam. Mr Melville Hardiment and Mr Kramer set me up I think in that LSD session when old pal Mel took photos and recordings and Kramer interrogated me with a toasting fork. Well any number can play with photos so back to my collages. Can't wait to see the color prints. Sounds ominous and believe me things are ominous. In the words cut from Peter Webber:[20] "Believe you can be murdered." I mean artistically of course

Love

Bill

And don't neglect your apomorphine rations. You should have some around in any case and take one now and again. Its a great stabilizer.

WSB [Tangier, Morocco] to Brion Gysin [Paris]
May 28 1961
Cargo U.S. Consulate, Tanger
Maroc

Dear Brion:

I wish you were here to see the unusual cloud effects over Tanger lately. Several people have exclaimed: "Just like one of Brion's pictures." (I keep busy with my photography.)

I thought the blurb you wrote for *The Soft Machine* superb. [. . .]

Your dream machine sounds great and I will send along a contribution, after checking the exchequer. Do try making a flicker paper with collages. I enclose some late pictures. Doing a series on rubbing out the word. Starting with word into symbols into colors. The enclosed material is self explanatory and I hope you will do some experiments with photos. When you take pictures of the word it is getting smaller you dig and so is your writing. All you need is a box camera to write virus small and that's getting them

---

20 Peter Webber. A young man whom Burroughs had never met and who died at age twenty-one. His writings were given to William and he used them in various cut-up projects.

where they live. Something *happens* when you take pictures of pictures of pictures. Notice how the color dots seem to be in clay and not paper. I am now making a color series of rub out the word but the technical facilities here are regrettable.

I am sending along my color arrangement in the hopes you will try it and do something infinitely better.

Michael Portman is here in the next room. He seems to be improving. Keep in touch and do send along a flicker paper to Ian [Sommerville]

Love,
Bill

EDITOR'S NOTE: As noted earlier, Burroughs was a great believer in the ability of apomorphine to effect complete cures with drug- and alcohol-dependent people. This letter is representative of many that he wrote during this period, encouraging people to seek the cure that had worked so well for him. Don Startin was an employee of the Canadian prison system and worked with addicts in Vancouver.

WSB [Tangier, Morocco] to Don Startin [Vancouver, British Columbia]

June 13, 1961
Cargo U.S. Consulate
Tanger
Morocco

Dear Mr Startin:

I have just received your enquiry in regard to the apomorphine treatment forwarded from Grove. I am sending you under separate cover an unpublished article on the apomorphine treatment which I think answers all your questions.

The doctor in London is: Doctor John Dent. I am sure he would be very glad to hear from you. He has written a book on the apomorphine treatment: *Anxiety and Its Treatment*. The book has been published in England but I do not have the publisher's name. *Naked*

Lunch was published in 1959 by the Olympia Press in Paris. Grove bought the book and will probably publish in the U.S. this Fall. In conclusion a brief note on apomorphine that is not included in the article I am sending on to you:

Apomorphine has no sedative, narcotic or pain killing properties. It is a metabolic regulator that need not be continued when its work is done. I quote from *Anxiety and Its Treatment* by Doctor John Dent of London: "Apomorphine acts on the back brain stimulating the regulating centers in such a way as to normalize metabolism." It has been used in the treatment of alcoholics and drug addicts and normalizes metabolism in such a way as to remove the need for any narcotic substance. Apomorphine cuts the junk lines from the brain. Poison of dead sun fading in smoke. Grey police of the regulator do their work and go down all your streets.

WSB [Tangier, Morocco] to Brion Gysin [Paris]
June 14 1961
Cargo U.S. Consulate Tanger
Tanger
Maroc

Dear Brion:

Here is mathematical extension of cut up method. You can run any combo like 2 4 6 8 etc. Or cut in with any other page in any combo. Enclose also sample photos. I now have enough photos for a collage exhibit which would be spectacular. I don't know if I can arrange such an exhibit here but will see what can be done. I would like to see you since it is impossible to cover developments in a letter. I think you have some misconceptions like I am in some sort of close literary collaboration with Paul [Bowles] and Achmed [Yacoubi]. Not so. Distrust them both profoundly. Did I say Paul had been helpful? Not lately he hasn't and as for Achmed you were right there all the way. Roger [Knoebber] is of course unreliable. And I think not the sharpest. I saw very little of him here. He spent most of his time with Jeannot and the other beatniks—they are coming through the sidewalk and the town looks like The Village—Sandals beards the lot.

No I have not been able to locate [Mohamed] Hamri[21] and Paul has not been helpful. Allen [Ginsberg], Gregory [Corso], and Peter [Orlovsky] are here and relations have been calm and amicable. Michael [Portman] spends most of his time in bed but he is useful in his way. Brion do try making a flicker paper with collages. Or at least send me the specifications. Did you receive the color negatives I sent through Roger? What about your patent on the flicker machine? What about your exhibit?

I have seen several paintings lately that were obvious copies of collage. Like in any combo. Make collage of photos along any line, grey pictures, blue pictures. Copy in ink or oil. Make collage of the copies. Take. Copy. Take. Copy. And so forth

The collage is an art like flower arranging. Say a blue collage. Select from blue file. Wait for a perfect blue sky. Arrange collage on mirror and catch the sky in your collage. Take your collage between glass and take pictures over the bluest spots in the sea, etc. "Pay back the blue you stole. Pay it back to sea and sky."

I have given myself a brief rest from writing. Will now apply what I have learned from the photo collages back in writing. "Cut and arrange the cut ups to other fields than writing".. Incidentally the collage photo is a natural for advertisements is it not?

I hear Sinclair [Beiles] is at liberty in London. Keep in touch

Love

Bill

WSB [Tangier, Morocco] to Brion Gysin [Rome]
August 7 1961
Cargo U.S. Consulate
Tanger, Morocco

Dear Brion:
I am certainly glad to hear you are now able to do your work.

---

21 Mohamed Hamri (1932–2000). Moroccan painter and writer.

[Timothy] Leary was here. I found him very aware confident and I think well intentioned. He says, "Get everybody out and they will work better." He is paying my expenses to and from and during two months at Cambridge [Massachusetts] where they have equipment etc. Sounds good enough and will probably go. Meanwhile keep busy. I am writing a straight action novel that can be read by any twelve year old entitled *The Novia Express.*[22] Enclosed photo to illustrate chapter on The Novia Police (tracing a Novia Criminal through intersection points in hosts. A global operation.) Ian [Sommerville] has excellent ideas. Michael [Portman] is greatly changed. I am leaving Tanger very soon now for London and from there to U.S.?? My address in London will be Cargo U.S. Consulate. Do you have a transistor radio? Everyone has one here. A marvelous gadget and what music concrete in the static..

Keep in touch

Love
Bill

WSB [Cambridge, Massachusetts] to Brion Gysin [Rome]
August 25, 1961
General Delivery
Cambridge, Mass.
U.S.A.

Dear Brion:

I have agreed to attend the symposium on hallucinogens expenses paid over back and during. I will talk on flicker and other *non-chemical* routes. I am more than leery of [Timothy] Leary, after meeting his partner Alpert.[23] Shine and O'Grady, Snell and Loomis,[24] the Old Golds without even a new look. The mushroom

---

22 For many months Burroughs used the spelling "Novia" until someone suggested that "Nova" was the correct word. After this first letter, the editor has corrected all subsequent spellings.
23 Richard Alpert (aka Baba Ram Dass) (b. 1931). Psychologist and researcher who worked with Timothy Leary at Harvard until they were both dismissed in 1963.
24 Snell and Loomis were the two *Life* reporters who had visited Burroughs in Paris.

money is coming straight from Garrett, Bolton and Phipps. Basta. And I think The Ovens came from the same source. C.P. [Communist Party?] indeed! Who dropped that A bomb?

As for Micky [Michael Portman] or Suna Portman[25] I met the original finally. Bill Barker has chronic cold sores and anemia. He can't make it with any one but Suna. Really I don't know when I've seen anything so nasty. I can only say as a physician I am glad to have had the opportunity of observing such a classic syndrome but I can only withdraw from the case. I can not disintoxicate anyone against his will.

Yes there is much to discuss. I don't expect to be in the U.S. very long and will probably see you in Paris this Winter. I can't tell you how bad this mushroom thing looks. But perhaps I can provide the suitable chamber of decompression is it not? Dig the *Rhinozeros* magazine edited in Germany.

There is also much encouraging news. Support from totally unexpected quarters. But any full account must wait till I see you. *Metronome* is published "The Time Of The Assassins." Come in please

Best,

Bill

Should Mikey or Suna Portman show up in Paris for Allah's sake no open bank! Unless you want to play open bank with [Eileen] Garrett and company. I have been handing him nothing but misdirection for the past month.

Ian [Sommerville] at least is doing great work. A real technician. I have no more time to waste on Mikey.

EDITOR'S NOTE: Burroughs quickly became disillusioned with Timothy Leary's setup at Harvard. He found the whole operation to be sloppy and unscientific. Discouraged, he could not wait to get away. Burroughs makes reference to Leary's household in this letter, referencing the large house in Newton that he shared with his wife and children. The Learys often hosted giant parties with researchers and subjects alike.

---

25 Suna Portman. Michael Portman's sister.

WSB [Newton, Massachusetts] to Paul Bowles [Tangier, Morocco]

[ca. late August or early September 1961]
General Delivery
Newton, Mass.
U.S.A.

Dear Paul:

This country is a shambles. I don't know when I've seen anything so nasty. Staying in Leary's house. Enough food to feed a regiment left out to spoil in the huge kitchen by Leary's over-fed, undisciplined children. Unused TV sets, cameras, typewriters, toys, books, magazines, furniture, stacked to the ceiling. A nightmare of stupid surfeit. The place is sick sick sick. And disgusting. Like a good European I am stashing away all the $ I can lay hands to with one thought in mind. Walk don't run to the nearest exit.

Have you taken those mushrooms? Seems to me about the same as Prestonia. Nothing will ever get another psilocybin pill down this throat. I am of course not expressing my feelings on the subject to Leary lest he cut off the $. Just how precise and definite my feelings on the subject are I hesitate to express to anyone.

Saw *Hiroshima Mon Amour*[26] the other night with Leary. See it if you get the chance. Interesting and revealing.

I have just been playing your tape. For which I can not thank you enough. It is almost life saving in the blighted suburb.

Michael Portman may return to Morocco. I have suggested he take a long trip South and perhaps you could help with the indicated itinerary.

Thanks again to you and Christopher [Wanklyn]. And give my best to Jane [Bowles]

Bonne Chance
Bill B.

---

26 *Hiroshima Mon Amour.* French film released in 1959 and directed by Alain Resnais, widely acclaimed for the use of flashbacks.

WSB [New York] to Brion Gysin [Paris]

[pre–September 28, 1961]
General Delivery
Newton, Mass.
U.S.A.

Dear Brion:

The scene here is really frantic. Leary has gone berserk. He is giving mushrooms to hat check girls, cab drivers, waiters, in fact anybody who will stand still for it. However Gerald Heard[27] and your correspondent have taken a firm stand. We both refuse to take any more mushrooms under any circumstances. Heard is certainly the most intelligent and well intentioned person connected with this deal. He gave a great talk at the symposium about LSD and paranoid sensations. The last barrier: PANIC! To God Pan. I managed to do all right too, fortified by two joints and the whole symposium came off very well.

Michael [Portman] wants to come here now and I have written to dissuade him. Let me explain that I really put in a lot of overtime on that boy and thought I had managed to separate him from his deplorable connections. Then something happened and there he was with a cold sore and I lost my patient and my patience as well. I'm not complaining but I have been under considerable pressure trying to sort out and assess hundreds of conflicting reports and demands pleasing no one of course so maybe I goofed. In any case he is now in an impossible condition. Imagine having Eileen Garrett, Mary Cooke, Old Lady Luce in the same room with you. It is absolutely intolerable and I don't propose to tolerate it.

Otherwise the situation here is not too bad. At least I have room to work and there is much to be said for American conveniences. I can get good food out of the ice box and take a bath and wear clean clothes at least. Seems to be plenty of pot around NY and nobody worries about the heat. Its like they all have the fix in. Of course I have to keep clean in Cambridge. Flying back on Sunday. Please write what your plans are. I wish you could arrange to come here.

---

27 Gerald Heard (1889–1971). Philosopher and author of the book *The Ascent of Humanity*.

Like I say NY is really a great scene and a goodly crowd is there. And more expected momentarily. Please write.

Love,

Bill

P.S. Very pleasant visit with the family.

WSB [New York] to Brion Gysin [Paris]

Sept 28 1961
Cargo Grove Press
64 University Place
NY 3, N.Y.

Dear Brion:

Situation here worse than I can tell you — Ovens now on mescaline DO NOT TAKE ANY HALLUCIGEN UNDER ANY CIRCUMSTANCES — Mescaline last night small dose from underground contacts — Ovens incomparably more potent — Attack absolutely hopeless — Saved by apomorphine and friends in the underground — Made it out of Cambridge just under the wire — [Timothy] Leary had ordered mescaline and had me all set up — Would no doubt have snatched my apomorphine stash — Claire Booth Luce[28] money and power behind this — Leary has half NY out looking for me — (Notably his errand boy Conrad Rooks) with obvious orders — Only thing beats the Ovens is apomorphine — Apomorphine only hope of averting total disaster — Any one who (as Leary does) deliberately comes out against use of apomorphine marked total enemy — Marked Nova Guard — In dealing with these oven guards absolutely any means are permitted — I will do what I can but we must face the possibility of total failure and total disaster — Well who lives will see

Best

Bill Burroughs

---

28 Clare Boothe Luce (1903–1987). Conservative editor and Washington socialite who was married to Henry Luce, the editor of *Time*.

WSB [New York] to Brion Gysin [Paris]

Oct 24, 1961
Cargo Grove Press
64 University Place
NYC 3, N.Y.

Dear Brion:

I don't know how many of my recent letters you received sent to Italy until I heard from Ian [Sommerville] you are back in Paris. You should have the writing I sent along to Ian for the *Olympia Revue*. As you gather I have severed all connection with [Timothy] Leary and his pestiferous project — financed by Madame Luce — and took my departure from those who would have held me in Cambridge. They were not so strong. Now live in Spanish naborhood of Brooklyn where nobody in NY knows my address. Conditions of total austerity. I can not leave now for lack of funds. I find also that they can put the snatch on my passport if I do or do not register with the narcotic department on the way out. *Exterminator* and *Minutes To Go* off the shelves. My son came down with a mysterious attack of anxiety, lost twenty pounds in a week and had to be removed from St. George's boarding school. Tuition of two thousand dollars not refunded. So you see the situation here is not good but perhaps we can provide the suitable chamber of decompression. Old Bill has indeed returned to war. Conditions at the front not only dangerous unpleasant but excruciatingly dull as well.

Best of luck with flicker and exhibit. If you could get the deal out in a unit that only needs to be plugged in — Stroboscopes have been removed from the market here. Some one got out a thirty two dollar outfit — Now you see it now you don't — Like I say they are right out in the open now where I like to see them.

Takis[29] is here. I am going to his opening tonight.

Love,

Bill

---

29 Vassilakis Takis (b. 1925). Sculptor and kinetic artist.

P.S. Ovens on mescaline now. "They are moving to extend the range of tune in to other hallucinogens" — They have moved. I avoid all hallucinogen drugs now, even pot.

Ovens more potent than last time and I would have been finished without apomorphine. Needed almost twice as much. So pushing apomorphine all the way. Not even Hassan i Sabbah can do it without apomorphine. I wonder if you could write me a magic letter on apomorphine for my collages? Opposition to apomorphine collages indicates crucial weak point in Luce lines. Three rolls of film came out blank for no ascertainable reason. I finally had to buy another camera from my meager resources.

WSB [New York] to Brion Gysin [Paris]
Oct 25, 1961
Cargo Grove Press
64 University Place
NYC 3, N.Y.

Dear Brion:

Forgot to answer yes by all means let the Italian publisher use my name it should boost sales.

Present writing finds me without money for paper to write on and what is even more to the immediate point without money to develop my latest apomorphine collages using carbon paper of uh like — "From San Diego Up to Maine — apomorphine — Re calling all active agents — apomorphine — shit linguals — apomorphine — cut word lines — apomorphine —" etc. and apomorphine written cross negatives — Pass along to Ian [Sommerville] and do not neglect magic letter on apomorphine. This is most important and most URGENT —

Is M.P. [Michael Portman] still in Paris? For God's sake no open bank with him.

I pass along from N.S. urgent warning: *"Watch that little fucker."* Give him the conducted tour routine and see he misses anything important. *Mala gente, Meester Brion.*

Editor of *The Floating Bear* [LeRoi Jones and Diane DiPrima]

arrested for sending obscene matter through the mails. Exhibit A —
a piece of mine entitled "The Routine"[30] which I didn't know they
had or who gave it to them or what it consists of. *Todo muy malo
aqui.* Did you receive the material I sent for *Olympia Revue*?? Please
acknowledge.

A young man named Bill Berkson[31] may turn up in Paris. Harry
Phipps replica. Writes for the *Floating Bear.* Good poet. Use your
judgment. Seems relatively well intentioned.

Met Nicolas Calas[32] at the Takis vernissage. Conveys devious regards

Love

Bill

WSB [New York] to Allen Ginsberg [Athens, Greece]
Oct 26, 1961
Cargo Grove Press
64 University Place
NYC

Dear Allen:

I have severed all connections with [Timothy] Leary and his
project which seems to me completely ill intentioned. I soon found
out that they have the vaguest connection with Harvard University, that the money comes from Madame Luce and other dubious
quarters, that they have utterly no interest in any serious scientific
work, no equipment other than a faulty tape recorder and no intention of acquiring any or making any equipment available to me,
that I was supposed to sell the beatniks on the mushrooms. When
I flatly refused to push the mushrooms but volunteered instead to
work on flicker and other non-chemical methods, the money and
return ticket they had promised me was immediately withdrawn. I
received not one cent from Leary beyond the fare to Boston. And

---

30 The routine was called "Roosevelt After Inauguration."
31 Bill Berkson (b. 1939). Poet associated with the New York School.
32 Nicolas Calas (1907–1988). Greek poet and art critic.

I hope never to set eyes on that horse's ass again. A real wrong number.

Harry Smith another wrong number. He fancies himself a black magician and does manage to give out some nasty emanations. Was it William the Second who said in regard to black magic, "Whether their spells are effective or not they deserve hanging for their bad intentions"??

So living in Spanish naborhood in complete seclusion. NY literary cocktail parties are unmitigated horrors. Still shuddering from the last one I attended. In fact I can find nothing good to say of life in America except the food which I dig Horn and Hardarts the greatest. Would leave tomorrow but short of the ready pending publication of *Naked Lunch* or other windfall. See Iris Owens[33] from time to time. Have not seen Lucien [Carr].[34] Met Irving Rosenthal who is most charming. Please write me about life in Athens. Any word from Peter [Orlovsky]?[35]

Writing a lot. Nothing else to do. No pot no sex no money. Well I should have known better than to come here without a return trip ticket in my pocket. Whenever you hear, "We don't think much about money on this project" you are about to get a short count. One thing is sure, Leary isn't getting any short count. Twenty thousand a year plus expenses. For doing exactly what? Pushing his pestiferous mushrooms —

Well like I say, I should have known better. Write soon.

Love

Bill

---

33 Iris Owens. An author who wrote several dirty books for Olympia Press under the name of Harriet Daimler.
34 Lucien Carr (1925–2005). During the early 1940s he was a central figure in the group that became the Beat Generation, but by the 1960s he was working in New York for United Press.
35 Ginsberg and Orlovsky had split up during their visit to Tangier and had not yet reunited.

WSB [New York] to Brion Gysin [Paris]

Nov 1, 1961
Cargo Grove Press
64 University Place
NYC 3, N.Y.

Dear Brion:

I must say that bit about getting up off my rusty dusty didn't go down so well in view of the fact that I get up early every day and work all day with no amenities not even social contact — no one has set foot in this room except your correspondent — under increasingly difficult circumstances. Publication of *Naked Lunch* delayed indefinitely — Called *Metronome*: "Mr Solomon is no longer with us — I will connect you with Mr Edwards" — "Oh yes Mr Burroughs we are returning your manuscript — We are very doubtful of the magazine's future and can not in all fairness . . ." Same sound on all lines here. The only order I can give at this point is: "Abandon ship God damn it — Every man for himself" — Expect me in Paris almost any time —

Best

Bill

P.S. I have [Fernanda] Pivano's[36] letter and I will answer it today — should the son of my Italian publisher show in Paris he is a friend of mine business and personal.

WSB [Paris] to Barney Rosset[37] [New York]

Dec. 12, 1961
9 Rue Git Le Coeur
Paris 6, France

Dear Mr. Rosset:

I am sorry to see the difficulties between you and [Maurice] Girodias taking such an acrimonious turn — My own position

---

36 Fernanda Pivano (1917–2009). Italian translator of American literature.
37 Barney Rosset (b. 1922). Owner and publisher of Grove Press.

remains clear and unchanged: I agree with you that it is not practical to publish *Naked Lunch* at this time in America. I feel it is most important to publish *The Nova Express* first as preparation. I feel that you are the only logical publisher for *Naked Lunch* in America. Of course, Girodias's impatience is understandable.

I hope that you and Girodias can reach an understanding

Sincerely
William Burroughs

WSB [Paris] to Paul Bowles [Tangier, Morocco]
Dec 18, 1961
9 Rue Git Le Coeur
Paris 6, France

Dear Paul:

No way to know when this will reach you in The South — I got an advance from Grove on the novel I am writing and left at once — Only thing I enjoyed in America was the food — Its cold here and the croissants soggier than ever — Wish I was back in Tanger — Did you see the *Outsider?* — Not much of a job I thought — All the mistakes of all the little magazines — Now he writes will I send him something without cut ups? — I am glad you heard Brion's tape — He is working now on flicker machines and has sold one to the Louvre for an exhibition — So things seem to be more propitious — What ever happened to the sex murder case that aroused such indignation in the breast of Cherifa?—(The victim was female I presume?)—I hear from Michael Portman that you are still in the South—Apparently they gave up their tour plans—Brion sends his love

Best Wishes and Merry Christmas For You and Jane
Bill Burroughs

P.S. How is the minor bird?

RUBRUBRUBRUB+++&++++&++&&&&&"""&"+++
RUBRUBRUBRUBOUTOUTOUTOUTOUT#"#++++#
RUBRUBRUBRUBOUTOUTOUTOUTOUT####&&&&
""&&&+++++"OUTOUTOUTOUTOUT"""""&&&
1962 ""+OUTOUTOUTOUTOUT"+"+"&&&
THETHETHETHETHETHETHE+++###+++&&+++
THETHETHETHETHETHETHE&&&&&++++++++#
THETHETHETHEWORDSWORDSWORDSWORDSTHE
###&&"&"&""&WORDSWORDSWORDSWORDS"++

WSB [Paris] to Paul Bowles [Tangier, Morocco]

Feb 5, 1962
9 Rue Git Le Coeur
Paris 6, France

Dear Paul:

Sorry to be slow in answering your letter—My life is completely without events that is work and nothing happens anywhere else—I have contract to finish *Nova Express* in two months—This keeps me either working or feeling I should work with so little time left—The Tanger scene sounds interesting if not altogether reassuring—Such a concentration of Beatniks does sound like a spot of bother coming up—Afraid I have no final word for my constituents—If you see Mick Portman tell him I wrote a letter to the Marrakech address and it came back "Unknown" and now I don't know where to write —

I understand Jane [Bowles] and Christopher [Wanklyn] didn't like "I AM THAT I AM"—Can't exactly understand why—After all—scripture you know—How did the minor bird react?—Are you doing any recording? I have a piece in the current issue of *Evergreen Review* suggesting some extended uses of tape recorders —

I hope to reach Morocco some time this Spring—Meanwhile must stay where the mails are reliable—Expect to move to London in the near future—Best to Jane, Cherifa, Christopher, Harold Norse,[1] and the minor bird

> With Best Wishes
> William Burroughs

---

1 Harold Norse (1916–2009). Writer and poet.

WSB [London] to Allen Ginsberg [New Delhi, India]
Feb 16, 1962
25 Lillie Road
London S.W. 6
England

Dear Allen:

You seem to be doing some strenuous traveling—As for me it is as much as I can accomplish to transport myself from Paris to London—Much better off here—Some food I can eat at least and better working conditions—*Nova Express* running on schedule—Should be finished by end of March—I have contract with Grove—What I think about [Timothy] Leary and his project expressed quite clearly in latest issue of *Evergreen Review*—Will send you copy if you are settled some where to receive it—Do-good cult to the tune of twenty five thousand a year indeed—And what's this about "our group"?—I didn't go there to be part of any group—I was under the mistaken impression he had some serious scientific project going—Well I should have known better—So much for Leary—I am doing very little except work—There is no time for anything else—Time ran out in the fifth at tropical—Let me hear from you when you light someplace—Best to Peter [Orlovsky]

Love
Bill

WSB [London] to Ian Sommerville [Paris]
Feb 16, 1962
25 Lillie Road
London S.W. 6

Dear Ian:

Letter received and delighted to hear of Brion [Gysin]'s success in Rome — What about Milano? — Please keep me informed — I have bought the battery set and it is an excellent machine [tape recorder] should prove most useful in my writing — Now a few questions and commissions: Please recover from G. [Guy] Harloff my copy of *Metronome* which he borrowed — I do not have another copy of the magasine or the material contained — What about the *Olympia Review*?? — If you see Girodias please ask him about the article on photo montage and the photos, I mean does he plan to use it in the March issue? How are you fixed for money?

I continue well satisfied with my shift to U.K. — Can accomplish twice as much better health etc — I saw John Howe but have decided to lay off tea [pot] for some time — I have no habits at all which is the way to live — *Evergreen* expected in the book stores momentarily — Tell Brion to write me details of his Italian trip — How does the show look? — Let me hear from you soon

Love
Bill

WSB [London] to Brion Gysin [Paris]
Feb–20–1962
25 Lillie Road
London S.W.6

Dear Brion:

Understand from Ian [Sommerville] you sold your pictures — So perhaps my photo magic was not without result — I am waiting to hear details of your Italian trip — Any success in Milano? Did you see Doctor Nanda [Pivano]? — She has certainly been most helpful — What *is* going on chez Olympia? — Those Greeks seem to be running a mighty loose ship — Thank God I'm a rat know when to jump — So satisfied with my move to the U.K. plan to shift H.Q. — Up at eight thirty every morning for my breakfast of porridge bacon eggs toast and tea — Hot baths whenever I like — Feel a new man all around and accomplish at least twice the more work — Have put down tea and much better for it — *Nova Express* will definitely be finished the end of March — I have new transistor radio tape recorder and learning Morse code — Fun and games what? — "I do not use scissors anymore" William Burroughs announced — "I fold a text any text and pass it through any other — Its more humane that way you see?" —

Love
Bill

WSB [London] to Barney Rosset [New York]
Feb. 28, 1962
25 Lillie Road
London S.W.6
England

Dear Mr Rosset:

I enclose another section of *Nova Express* — The book is well on the way to completion and it is time for me to start deciding on the order of sections and number the pages — I suggest that you send me a copy of the manuscript to date (or send the M.S. [manuscript] retaining copy to avoid possible loss) I will make corrections inserts — number pages and return with final additional material by the end of March at the latest — Do you feel that the section called *Outskirts Of The City* can be published as it stands? — If not I will provide you with an expurgated version —

[Maurice] Girodias has already contrived to get his *Olympia Review* banned — Once again I would like to make it quite clear that I agree with you one hundred percent about the advisability of publishing *Nova Express* before *Naked Lunch* — I have discussed this with Girodias and he does not agree — In any case if he makes any move to put *Naked Lunch* in the hands of another American publisher you can be sure it is done without my approval — Owing to the complex legal arrangements involving Swiss ownership of the rights (an arrangement with which I am most dissatisfied) I do not know exactly how much weight my word has —

I would appreciate if you could send me one or two issues of *Evergreen* — It has not yet arrived in England and I have lent my copy — Regards to the staff

With Best Wishes
William Burroughs

WSB [Paris] to Paul Bowles [Tangier, Morocco]
March 1, 1962
9 Rue Git Le Coeur
Paris 6, France

Dear Paul:

First to answer your inquiry about TRAK—Trak simply means 'thank you' in Danish—Like one says it to a kind host when settling down for a long visit—Trak—Trak—Trak—Invade—Damage—Occupy—Its as simple as that—Your letter falling on a page I had written get a one sentence definition—"A State For Ruined Toilet"—Actually experimenting more and more with method of folding one text and laying it on another as I did in "The Night Before Thinking"—However I find the results are sometimes interesting and sometimes not and must be edited and rearranged as in other methods of composition—Most interesting results of course emerge from juxtaposition of texts treating similar theme—Although one gets many surprises that is to say not always easy to say what is and is not similar—Sitting here in front of my gas grate how I envy you the Moroccan sun—However, wish to be near reliable mail deliveries until I finish *Nova Express*—It is almost complete and remains only corrections and alterations and galley proofs—All complete I hope by the end of the month then on my way rejoicing—Don't know where yet but after months of the most intensive work feel like a rest in some nice warm spot —

Curious dream last night—I was a general in a green uniform—Troops were housed on another planet in a building of green glass brick and metal we could not go outside because there was no air but seemed to have almost everything on location including a Turkish bath which I visited incognito with such disappointing results I finally had to pull rank—Best regards to Michael [Portman] and Christopher [Wanklyn]—If Michael were here he would probably be intrigued by the mad Negro who screams and talks or rather shouts to some invisible presence all day and most of the night.

Best,
Bill

Saludos a Mohammed Larbi

WSB [London] to Barney Rosset [New York]
March 30, 1962
25 Lillie Road
London S.W.6
England

Dear Mr Rosset:

Here is the manuscript of *Nova Express* — The introduction, last words of Hassan i Sabbah, and open letter, in the order they appeared in *Evergreen* I think should be used as a foreword or preface — The transcript of the talk I gave to the psychological symposium or the article "A Treatment That Cancels Addiction" might serve as appendix — I think since apomorphine is important factor in *Nova Express* the reader should be given a clear idea as to what it is — I am also writing and will send on to you in a few days a brief note on the method and dedication for the book — Best regards to the staff

With Best Wishes
William Burroughs

WSB [London] to Paul Bowles [Tangier, Morocco]
April 2, 1962
25 Lillie Road
London

Dear Paul:

Michael Portman arrived safely and is here now in the room— Fortunately he brought his recorder and tapes and I have been busy making copies on my machine which is portable or plug-in so far as I know a unique article—I have been experimenting with a form of direct composition on tape with sound effects like: "K9 had an appointment in The Sheffield Arms pub on? off? North End Road" etc. using recordings of street sounds from North End Road as background—Results like a radio play—Of course would need a lot of work—Takes some of the monotony out of writing I find —

Nova Express is finished and delivered—There are some selections in January issue of *Evergreen* which you may have seen—I have heard nothing from Allen [Ginsberg] and Peter [Orlovsky] though I wrote to India some time ago—I have moved to London and working quietly all day in front of my gas grate—Ian [Sommerville] is also here and now Michael who sends you his best regards—I may be going South in another two months more or less—Please say hello to everyone in Tanger for me

Best Wishes
William Burroughs

WSB [London] to Brion Gysin [Paris]
April 9, 1962
25 Lillie Road
London S.W.6

Dear Brion:

Sorry I did not write sooner — Have been working full time on *Nova Express* now finished and delivered — Mikey [Portman] arrived from Tanger a few days ago and staying in the hotel — The old points of argument between us have disappeared — He brought his recorder with him and we have done some interesting experiments with two tape recorder mutations — Like cutting back and forth from one recorder to the other on association lines — (Quite different from making cut ups on one recorder) — We have slowed down words many times and the result is like some great undersea monster surfacing in the beginning was the word — And I AM THAT I AM played backwards is "Maya Maya Maya" — Illusion — Mixing street sounds of Tanger and London — Cutting Arab music into recorded TV programs — (The first time I did this there was a two hour blackout on both channels) — Well fun and games what? — I went to The Hubbard Center [scientology] and picked up some literature and cut I AM WHAT I AM into it with various other suggestions verbal and musical backwards and forwards speed it up slow it down —

Some staff difficulties between Ian [Sommerville] and Mikey — Ian is one head I can't walk in — Can you? —

If you get a chance see The Hustler² — A really great movie I would like to make using all my hustlers — Lime Stone John, Green Tony, Izzy The Push, The Sailor, The Vigilante, Doc Benway, Daddy Longlegs, The Subliminal Kid, etc — A poker game you dig like a card would be riots in British Guiana, currency collapses in Bolivia, revolution in Iran etc. — Are you coming to London? Ian said you might be here soon —

Best Wishes
Bill B.

WSB [London] to Gregory Corso [New York]

April 20, 1962
Cargo American Express
London

Dear Gregory:

I would have answered your letter sooner but have been working round the clock to finish *Nova Express* on schedule — Now that it is finished and delivered I can catch up on my correspondence —

I can not agree that "Burroughs" is essential to "Corso" — These are old concepts of personal identify — The forces that keep the wheels turning and the wheat from spoiling do not belong to "Burroughs" or "Gysin" or "Corso" — They do not belong to anybody — Michael [Portman] is here and sends his best regards — Don't know how much longer I will be here — No word from Allen Ginsberg who is said to be in Italy³ — Saw Jack Stern in Paris — Most sorry to hear about Harry Phipps⁴ — Was it an overdose? — Article I saw said only "mysterious circumstances" —

In closing good luck — Believe me I give you and Allen full credit for the difficult job of getting this show on the road — Let me hear from you

With Best Wishes
William Burroughs

---

2 *The Hustler*. A 1961 film about a pool shark starring Paul Newman and Jackie Gleason.
3 Ginsberg was still in India at the time.
4 Harry Phipps had recently died of a drug overdose.

WSB [Paris] to Bill Berkson [n.p.]

June 4, 1962
9 Rue Git Le Coeur
Paris 6, France

Dear Bill Berkson:

Sorry to be slow in answering your letter but I have been in transit as usual—Of course cut ups and fold ins—(I now use the later method)—must be edited and rearranged as in any other method of composition and after all folding paper is no more of bore really than feeding sheets into the typewriter—Actually the surprising thing is how little meaningless material does arise in using this method and often I can transcribe whole passages almost verbatim—Here for example are some fold ins with your letter and fold ins from [St.] John Perse *Elegies* and T.S. Eliot and my own writing

"What have I my friend to give?—Not at all necessary—Very much is all an aging of roots on fourteenth street—Anyway I had to forge door in order to cash the silly old thing—Dope consumed brandy neat—Light and shade departed—Too bad we didn't see each other again—Courage to let go in the open answer with these cut ups—After all the some one walking—Then question who wants to sit around folding or cutting old dream?—Ask alterations but *selectivity* kills the "objective" in a great leisure—Poets and thinkers ain't we? But what if we drown?—Rotting democracy is joy to all phlegm??—You couldn't reach flesh or what?—You probably cut it cause dawn whisper put on t'other—I am looking forward to seeing your information—Send some carbons to me—Some very recent condition give you identity without a shadow

Five Times Bill Berkson"

[. . .] Hope to see you in July if you are coming to Europe—Best to Frank O'Hara

With Best Wishes
Bill Burroughs

WSB [Paris] to Barney Rosset [New York]

June 23, 1962
9 Rue Git Le Coeur
Paris 6, France

Dear Mr. Rosset:

I am currently working on a new novel in which I am elaborating some far out areas with scenes and concepts more "obscene" than anything in *Naked Lunch* or *The Soft Machine* — [Maurice] Girodias has expressed a willingness to publish the work, but there is of course the matter of your option. Please let me know your preferences in this regard. I feel that publication in the States would not be possible at this time that is to say even more out of the question than publication of *Naked Lunch* — I was interested to carry certain concepts to the furthest possible limits as an experiment in writing technique — I hope to have the novel finished in two more months of intensive work — do you want to see the work already written? (This amounts to about thirty or forty pages — but enough to give you a fairly clear idea of the whole picture) — Would you rather wait and see the complete manuscript? — Would you consider an arrangement allowing Girodias to publish? Please let me know how you feel about this — Have you made any definite plans on *Nova Express*? Best regards to the staff

With Best Wishes
William Burroughs

WSB [Paris] to George ? [n.p.]
June 26, 1962
9 Rue Git Le Coeur
Paris 6, France

Dear George:

You seem to forget that I am speaking here in the context of fiction and in the context of a novel of which you have only seen a small section — I am a writer and only lay claims to the status of prophet insofar as what I write "happens" — *Quir ivivra verra* — The algebra of fiction — and history is fiction — demands that where you find "criminal" conspiracies you will also find "police" — Where you find emergency you will also find emergency instructions — And I may add that the precise purpose of emergency instructions is to prevent panic —

I was referring to the Southern California brand of "cosmic consciousness" which is precisely there to block and vulgarize any contact beyond three dimensional areas — As to whether a monopoly of these areas is possible of course it is — That is to say in fiction — And remember what one man can think of another can think of — That is in my novel *Nova Express* such a monopoly has taken place and I describe exactly how this has been done and how it can be undone — or more accurately rewritten

Apomorphine is a metabolic regulator that normalizes any conditions of disturbed metabolism — *It does not* bring down a high or cancel hallucinogen states — It does stabilize hallucinogen experience and remove anxiety if any is present. Like my Nova Police it is only there when you need it

> With Best Wishes
> William Burroughs

WSB [Paris] to Paul Bowles [Tangier, Morocco]

July 9, 1962
9 Rue Git Le Coeur
Paris 6, France

Dear Paul:

Brion [Gysin] is back from Venice having sold one picture to A.J. Barr from Museum of Modern Art—I did not know Gregory [Corso] was gone to Italy—We have been out of touch you might say—I will try to find some worthy vessel to convey the tape—We are putting on a night club act here with readings and sound effects—Charles Henri Ford in town and sends you his best—Fold in from your letter and passage from the novel I write now "Johnny's So Long At The Fair." Might also be called "If You Can't Say It Sing It"

"It's only a paper moon doing the twist—Central Girls with hair down flying over a muslin tree—I won't be in Tanger—Just a Barnum and Bailey world—Any place but there—Lie so often, Gregory?—So long at the fair—The tape thing is flying over a cardboard sea via the post—Old second hand man ghost writing out an endless rigmarole—Literally believe skies above me never were there—Now trading new dreams for the end of everything naturally—Perhaps the sky might actually be your way—Time—Its possible—This is not 38 but New York in September—Going to reach The Old Mountain now—Hear the Japanese Sand Man in the house with another Spanish boy—Now she's dead I returning in a little while—Ghost riot reflected answer from St Louis second hand trade in spattered from central girls keep scratching tentative flesh—*So* long at the fair—The tape thing is face sucked into other apparatus via flicker ghosts—You used to be the ticket for him—Now trading new gate from burning sky naturally—Meet me in this afternoon music so I have image track—Just sing out of here—Female impersonators doing the twist—So we turn over a Barnum and Bailey world—Board members, too—Dreams end everything—The law gives—Might actually be your way—Clinic on music is Brion? Oh Oh what can the matter be? Steady stream of distant events answered from St Louis—I won't be in Tanger—Distant riot noises whistle—Ghost writing fade out—Never were there—Sky moving in fast—Dead nitrous streets behind Time—Now she's dead on screen?—Nova Police wired to Venice so I have interrogations—Errand boy closing Paris entered the Twenties in drag doing the twist—Slow motion flashes over a muslin tree—John in the last Walgreen's—Indications enough reach the old mountain now—Hear interstellar space—Wind voices never were there—Not think The Doctor on stage with you—All the hate faces sucked into material for him—Its only possible in the harbor New York September —"

Ian [Sommerville] and Michael [Portman] send you their best—*Nova* will be out in Jan '63—I may publish "Johnny So Long At The Fair" with Olympia in Sept —

> With Best Wishes
> William Burroughs

WSB [Paris] to Barney Rosset [New York]
August 7, 1962
9 Rue Git Le Coeur
Paris 6, France

The Grove Press
64 University Place
NYC 3, N.Y.

Dear Mr. Rosset:

I am sorry I have not yet heard from you in answer to my letters concerning my new book — As you have doubtless been able to judge this book could not possibly be published in the U.S. in present circumstances without immediate risk of censorship difficulties more serious than would attend the publication of *Naked Lunch* — Especially in view of the fact that I feel very definitely that the work could not be expurgated without losing its objectives — As I have plans for early publication in Paris I would be grateful to hear your answer by the middle of August — Failing this I will consider myself free to sign a contract for publication here —

I am sending this letter registered in view of its importance and urgency — Hoping to hear from you soon

With Best Wishes for Your and
The Staff
William Burroughs

WSB [Paris] to Paul Bowles [Tangier, Morocco]
Aug. 17, 1962
9 Rue Git Le Coeur
Paris 6, France

Dear Paul:

You seem to have started something with your Crosby interviews—Enclose a letter Gregory [Corso] wrote to the *Tribune*—Fun and games what?—But it does look as if Tanger were burning down and I doubt if I will make an appearance —

On my way to writer's conference in Edinburgh—Principally motivated by all expenses paid and prospect of seeing twenty five Cuban writers who are scheduled to appear —

Have just finished another novel which Olympia should publish in September—(The story finished *ojala* [God willing] by September)—May even see you in New York since I am promoting a dramatization of my work with the Living Theatre and if anything turns up will probably require my presence —

Brion [Gysin] is in the South of France—Michael [Portman] is in London—Everyone has left Paris which I loathe—Will probably stop over in London—Only thing keeping me here is Olympia and the necessity of correcting final proofs and collecting final advance—No Winter plans—Greece perhaps—You are still going to New York and for how long?—Regards to all in Tanger

With Best Wishes
Bill B.

WSB [Paris] to Howard Schulman[5] [New York]
August 31, 1962
9 Rue Git Le Coeur
Paris 6, France

Dear Mr. Schulman:

A break-through that knows exactly what it is breaking through into is not a break-through which is a step in the dark—Barnum & Bailey world is what is broken not what is broken through into —

As to the manuscript in John Wiener's possession[6]—(by channels unknown to me), I would not consider publishing it at this time—Grove Press has bought *Naked Lunch* and are waiting for a break-through on the censorship front before publication—To bring out any version of blue movie section now would be bad chess, and might well lead to an unfavorable decision in the courts that would prejudice chances of publishing *Naked Lunch* plus antagonizing my publisher with whom I already have sufficient hazzles [*sic*: hassles] in the usual writer publisher relations.

I have actually expanded the image of bull in ring and cloth— (To me the cloth is represented by surface issues and problems)— However, I can't do anything for the next month since finishing novel on commission, writing articles on deadlines, while trying to edit a magazine and adapt some material to film answer letters etc. —

Am I wary about saying out front what I say in *Naked Lunch*?— Under present circumstances, yes—After publication of *Naked Lunch* in U.S. quite another story of course

With Best Wishes
William Burroughs

EDITOR'S NOTE: Burroughs attended the Edinburgh Writers' Conference from August 20–25, 1962. There he spoke alongside many other

---

5 Howard Schulman. Editor of *Pa'Lante* magazine.
6 John Wieners (1934–2002). Poet and editor of *Measure* magazine.

writers including Mary McCarthy, Henry Miller, and Norman Mailer. His appearance was a triumph, and his writing was praised by several of his fellow authors and condemned by others. The controversy helped establish his image as a writer on the cutting edge.

WSB [Paris] to Brion Gysin [n.p.]

September 1, 1962
9 Rue Git Le Coeur
Paris 6, France

Dear Brion:

The [Edinburgh] Writers Conference was for me quite a success — Got an English contract plus favorable publicity — Found myself addressing audience of two thousand people all of whom had paid a dollar to listen — Spoke on censorship, cut ups and fold ins — All well received on the whole one sharp exchange with Stephen Spender[7] on the platform which was amicably settled — One of my strongest supporters is Mary McCarthy[8] — Also [Lawrence] Durrell,[9] [Norman] Mailer,[10] the Dutch delegates, Colin MacInnes[11] and of course [Alex] Trocchi[12] who is really a great cat — Details when I see you —

Could you please send along that page of writing as soon as possible since we are going to print?? I have spoken to [Maurice] Girodias about it and he agrees that it would be the best ending — My latest project is a series of children's books — (Bring up a child in the way he should go you know) — Johnny The Space Boy who built a space ship in his barn — This is flicker machine on a bicycle and wings of Brion Gysin and photo collage etc. — Bringing in all the characters in *Naked Lunch* and other books — Doctor Benway, Ali The Street Boy, Johnny Yen, The Newt Boy, A.J., etc. — And

---

7   Stephen Spender (1909–1995). Poet and editor of *Encounter* magazine.
8   Mary McCarthy (1912–1989). Author of the bestselling novel *The Group.*
9   Lawrence Durrell (1912–1990). English writer and poet.
10 Norman Mailer (1923–2007). American writer and author of *The Naked and the Dead.*
11 Colin MacInnes (1914–1976). English novelist.
12 Alex Trocchi (1925–1984). Author of *Cain's Book*, which focuses on drug addiction.

visiting all the places — Good fairies and bad the lot you understand — Would you consider illustrating it? I already have the name of an English publisher — Actually my books *are* children's books with mythological characters — Look forward to see you

Wish Best Wishes

Love

Bill

WSB [Paris] to Dick Seaver [New York]
Sept. 17, 1962
9 Rue Git Le Coeur
Paris 6, France

Dear Mr. Seaver:

The correct spelling is *Nova* not Novia and this error on my part should urgently be corrected since it is causing confusion —

I met a young poet from Ceylon at The Edinburgh Conference named Guy Amirthanayagam[13] — Grove Press might be interested in his work — Apparently he is working along unconventional lines

With Best Wishes

William Burroughs

WSB [Paris] to Paul Bowles [Tangier, Morocco]
Sept. 20, 1962
9 Rue Git Le Coeur
Paris 6, France

Dear Paul:

How long in New York?—I need a vacation—May see you in Morocco this Winter — You do plan to return soon?—All Summer I have had one rush job after the other—First finishing a novel for Olympia entitled *The Ticket That Exploded*—Then the Edinburgh

---

13 Guy Amirthanayagam (1928–2003). Writer and educator.

Conference—And a contract with John Calder[14] to do a book of selections from *Naked Lunch, The Soft Machine,* and *The Ticket That Exploded*—I am very much dissatisfied with *The Soft Machine* and had to rewrite most of the material included in the book of selections— Find myself returning to straight narrative style of *Naked Lunch* —

When asked what he thought of The Edinburgh Conference an elderly Scotch journalist named Hugh MacDiarmid[15] snapped "An outrage—All heroin and homosexuality—These people belong in jail not on the lecture platform"—By these people he meant me and [Alex] Trocchi—Well fun and games what?—Looks like we have burned down Edinburgh—Speaking of which, any more disquieting news from Tanger?—However the situation may be exaggerated—Don't know, me—Only work here—Ian [Sommerville] sends you his best—He is doing some very advanced work with photos and perhaps we will have an exhibition

Hasta La Vista

Bill B.

WSB [Paris] to Billy Burroughs Jr. [Palm Beach, Florida]
Sept. 24, 1962
Cargo American Express
London England

Dear Bill:

I have just read your poem "Metamorphosis" and was deeply impressed by it — Very good work indeed — I have showed [*sic*] the poem to a few friends who are good judges — (not telling them who wrote it) and they shared my opinion and were amazed to learn your age[16] — This is good work on an adult level and I think definitely publishable — Do you have any more? — If so please send it along — I would like to send you work for publication together with some fold ins —

14 John Calder (b. 1927). British publisher and partner of Marion Boyars in the firm of Calder and Boyars.

15 Hugh MacDiarmid (1892–1978). Scottish poet.

16 Billy Burroughs Jr. was fifteen years old at the time.

I enclose copy of a talk I gave at The Writer's Conference in Edinburgh, Aug 25, 1962 explaining the fold in method — On page 4 5 6 illustrated with fold in of "Metamorphosis" with selections from Rimbaud's *Illuminations* — The arrangement I have made is only one of many possible arrangements — Of course the fold ins can be folded in again with other texts any number of times — The method is completely flexible that is the pages can be moved, words changed or omitted etc

I hope you are happy at the school — Please write me and send along some more work

Best Wishes And Love
From your father
William Burroughs

WSB [Paris] to Barney Rosset [New York]
Oct. 24, 1962
9 Rue Git-Le-Coeur
Paris 6, France

Dear Mr. Rosset:

Enclose the revised and rearranged manuscript of *Nova Express* — I have deleted ten pages from the original manuscript and substituted ten pages of new material — I think that this new section would make good advance publicity for the book, and if you are not able to use it in *Evergreen*, I would like to try placing it somewhere else —

A word of explanation about chapter headings and layout — The book is divided into nine sections — Each section has a heading to go at the top of the page beginning the section — The other headings of subsections are marginal — Like this: Section 1 Last Words at the top of the page — Subsection Prisoners, come out is marginal — Enclose typewritten list of the section and sub section headings —

A man named Bob Cody made a film here of Maurice [Girodias][17] and me on the subject of censorship that he is trying

---

17 This film appears to be in the collection of Michigan State University.

to place with a TV syndicate in the U.S. — I think this would be excellent publicity for *Naked Lunch* — Perhaps you may have some suggestions as to where he could place the film — If so please reply to Maurice and he will pass along to Cody who is here now —

One other suggestion: I left with you an article on the apomorphine treatment longer and more comprehensive than the article that appeared in *Evergreen Review* — Since apomorphine plays such an important role in *Nova Express* perhaps the article could be used as an appendix — I sent this article some time ago to Barthold Fles and he has not been able to place it but may do so after the publication of *Naked Lunch* — So perhaps you should cross check with him —

> My best regards to the staff
> With Best Wishes
> William Burroughs

RUBRUBRUBRUB+++&++++&++&&&&&"""&"+++
RUBRUBRUBRUBOUTOUTOUTOUTOUT#"#++++#
RUBRUBRUBRUBOUTOUTOUTOUTOUT####&&&&
"""&&&+++++"OUTOUTOUTOUTOUT""""""&&&
1963 ""+OUTOUTOUTOUTOUT"+"+"&&&
THETHETHETHETHETHETHE+++###+++&&+++
THETHETHETHETHETHETHE&&&&&+++++++++#
THETHETHETHEWORDSWORDSWORDSWORDSTHE
###&&"&"&"&WORDSWORDSWORDSWORDS"++

WSB [London] to Brion Gysin [Paris]

Jan. 23, 1963
51 Gloucester Terrace
London W.2

Dear Brion:

Sorry not to have written sooner — Antony [Balch] and I have been hectically busy with the movie which is going ahead on schedule and should be finished in two weeks — The title is *Towers Open Fire* — based on *The Ticket That Exploded*, pages 14–15 — There is a board room scene we have just shot in the board room of the British Film Institute — Board books on the table — The director of the board — (I take this part) gets up and says as his hands fall on the 8726 symbol, "Gentlemen, this was to be expected — After all he's been a medium all his life." — Then disappears in a blast of TV static — (Have you seen it? — Like a screaming glass blizzard of silver flak—) The other members think they will take over but they also disappear in static — All in all I think the film should serve a useful purpose and hold the interest of the audience —

Meanwhile I have been working on the how-to book we discussed which takes the form of an army bulletin — That is, an illustrated lecture to a group of cadets on enemy methods and techniques and the methods and techniques of combating the enemy — Fold ins, cut ups, photo montage, permutations, etc.

"An army operating under guerilla conditions must have a base of operations that can not be reached by the enemy — The area in which we operate is poetry, myth, creation — The enemy can not enter this area since they are precisely non-creative and operate through machine made copies — Officers must be poets and remember that the area of poetry must be constantly recreated — That is why cut-ups and fold-ins form one of our most vital instruments — Not only does this method recreate our area of operations but it also cuts enemy supply lines —"

Gambit, the Edinburgh University magazine, has a cut up of the writer's conference in the current issue dedicated to me — And I have sent them my piece on the Mayan Caper — (This is something you have not seen) — What are you doing for H.R? Please let me hear from you — Love to Ian [Sommerville]

Love

Bill

WSB [London] to Barney Rosset [New York]
March 15, 1963
5 Lancaster Terrace
(Basement flat)
London W.2.

Dear Barney Rosset:

Enclose another chapter for *Nova Express*. This chapter to be inserted immediately after 'Prisoners, Come Out'. I think it makes the following section ('Pack Your Ermines, Mary') considerably clearer. I hope that you can publish *Nova Express* sooner than next fall as I think the publication of this book would be most useful in defending any cases that might arise from *Naked Lunch*.

Sorry I did not have more time to talk with you in Paris. As regards the suit against *Time* I thank you for recommending a firm of lawyers to handle it.. However, they wanted $200 in advance which I don't have. So I have engaged a lawyer to bring suit here [in England].

How is *Naked Lunch* selling? Mary McCarthy's review in *Book Review* should be most helpful. There has been quite a lot of publicity here and the Calder book should be out in another month. Please let me hear from you. Regards to the staff

With Best Wishes

William Burroughs

WSB [London] to Paul Bowles [Tangier, Morocco]

April 5, 1963
5 Lancaster Terrace
London W.2.
U.K.

Dear Paul:

I understand from Ira Cohen that he is starting a magazine in Tanger.[1] I will certainly send him something and hope his undertaking is based on more solid uh fuel than enthusiasm. Fortunately he has Irving Rosenthal and Marc Schleifer at least in advisory capacity both of whom have considerable magazine experience.

Brion [Gysin] was recently in London and we put on a show at the ICA [Institute of Contemporary Arts]. Well received but we did not have exactly professional facilities and the film we had intended to show could not be shown since they are not equipped to show 35MM film. However, this was just as well since the film itself is not finished so I substituted another piece with tape recordings and slide projections. (Getting back to the old magic lantern days and why not). Well I am sending the script to Ira for his magazine reserving of course the right to publish elsewhere and I think Brion is also sending his script. You will I assume be represented? And was he able to persuade Jane [Bowles] to contribute?

---

1   Ira Cohen (b. 1935). Editor of *Gnaoua* magazine.

I plan to remain here until the early summer then may return to Tanger or perhaps go to Greece both journeys contingent on money. I certainly can't afford living here and I can't afford to travel. One of the advantages of having money is that it is then easier to save money.

Both Michael [Portman] and Ian [Sommerville] send their best regards and please give my regards to Jane, Christopher [Wanklyn], Achmed [Yacoubi], *et al*

With Best Wishes

William Burroughs

WSB [London] to Maurice Girodias [Paris]
May 11, 1963
5 Lancaster Terrace
London W.2.

Dear Maurice:

I have just received your brief and not in all pertinent respects informative communication. You say that nothing is due as royalties on the American edition of *Naked Lunch*? On the other hand in your letter of April 11 you say: "letter from Barney 'We owe you 15% per copy—90 cents—on 2,807 as of May 1st'" I can not quite sort out these contradictory statements nor can I quite understand how, in a matter where our joint interests are appreciably concerned you could allow $2,627 to dwindle to nothing without making some strenuous and effectual effort to check or reverse such a regrettable trend. You also make no mention of *The Soft Machine* which I rewrote at considerable expense of time and effort without any financial incentives of an immediate nature to create a more saleable property again to our joint advantage and which I feel to be quite definitely saleable. If Barney [Rosset] does not want this book it is certainly time to look elsewhere or to press him at least for a decision within the foreseeable future.

I still do not have a contract on *The Ticket That Exploded* and it is a year since we had an accounting on royalties.

I hope to be in Paris late May or early June. Meanwhile I

would appreciate being informed in more detail on the points raised above

With Best Wishes

William Burroughs

WSB [London] to Barney Rosset [New York]

May 13, 1963
5 Lancaster Terrace
London W.2.

Dear Barney:

I was sorry to miss you in London. When I called your hotel you had already checked out. Several points I wanted to discuss with you: First as regards royalties and sales on *Naked Lunch*. I can't seem to get any satisfactory reply from Maurice [Girodias] who is apparently in a generally disorganized condition. He said something about royalties due on 2,807 copies. Is it at all possible to send me my two thirds of this amount direct? All this clearing through Switzerland and Licktenstein [*sic*: Liechtenstein] drags out interminably.

I am well along with a new novel on which you have an option. Most of the work is at present in the form of rough drafts that will have to be retyped and corrected. In order to do this work I need four or five months in which I can concentrate without the distraction of continual financial difficulties. Could you make me an advance on this novel? As you know I deliver the work in the time specified. I have not had time to type out copies since I want to proceed with the first draft so I can see the work as whole. As the novel is shaping up there will not be any censorship difficulties. I will send you under separate cover a sample chapter which perhaps you can use for *Evergreen*.

I believe I left with you a long article on the apomorphine treatment (not the article that appears in *Naked Lunch*) entitled "A Treatment That Cancels Addiction". If you have this article I would appreciate your sending me a copy of the talk at the N.Y. symposium which I also wanted and for which please thank him.

Do you have a publication date on *Nova Express*? I have received a number of inquiries from foreign publishers about this work. Limes in Germany, Feltrinelli and Rizzoli in Italy.

My best regards to all the staff
With Best Wishes
William Burroughs

WSB [London] to Paul Bowles [Tangier, Morocco]
May 21, 1963
5 Lancaster Terrace
London W.2.

Dear Paul:

Unless some unforeseen occurrence changes my plans I will definitely be spending the Summer in Tanger. Absolutely tired of this London climate and the radio talks and press interviews which take up so much time and energy. As usual international gossip is inaccurate. I had no affair with young [Fabrizio] Mondadori.[2] Arthur Clarke?[3] *Quien es?* I gather we may all be under water soon now that scientists have found a way to breath there. Did you read about the dog in *Newsweek* or was it *Time*? that spent 18 hours under water. All in finding the right water it seems and perhaps the right dog as well. I hadn't realized that Ira [Cohen] is such a nervous compulsive traveler. Oh well these magazines you know in this business they come and they go. Did I tell you I had taken action against *Time* for their libelous article on *Naked Lunch*? Seems they are refusing to settle. I'll get compensation one way or another. Not for nothing am I known as Nellie The Disconnector. That's a new character I invented. Did you see the new Time Life Building when you were in N.Y.? At the corner of Madison and Tenth Avenues I believe that is or am I all mixed up?[4]

---

2   Mondadori. A well-known publishing family in Italy.
3   Arthur Clarke (1917–2008). Science fiction writer and the author of *2010: A Space Odyssey*.
4   Madison and Tenth Avenues do not intersect. The new Time-Life Building was at 1271 Avenue of the Americas in New York City.

Hope to make Tanger in early June. Waiting on money as usual. Always late. Ian [Sommerville] will probably be coming with me but Michael [Portman] I understand is going to Greece. My best to everyone in Tanger. Quite a colony I understand now

With Best Wishes
Bill Burroughs

WSB [Tangier, Morocco] to Brion Gysin [Paris?]

July 15, 1963
Cargo U.S. Consulate
Tanger, Morocco

Dear Brion:

Andrew and Felicity[5] are here and tell me you will be along in a few days. Ian [Sommerville] and I have rented a house in the Marshan — Calle Larachi No. 4 — and in process of moving in. Just back from Jejouka [Jajouka][6] which was great. The Jajouka musicians are coming here next Saturday to play the deal organized by [Mohamed] Hamri and Peter Birnbaum who turns out to be a very simpatico character. Tanger quiet and more like it was before the blight. Paul [Bowles] is in Asilah in The House of The Consul. I stopped off to see him on the way back from Jajouka and Jane [Bowles] was there so no grass. And Paul complained that some one had eaten all his cheese that constituted his chief nourishment which Cherifa took as a reflection on her integrity and Jane said it was an American boy ate it she saw him with a piece in his hand and Paul said what day she saw him eat a piece of cheese etc. We have had a plague of reporters here *Newsweek Esquire* and a free lance named Finkelstein who took 700 photos of Jajouka. I have refused to talk to any of them or allow them to take my picture its like I am on vacation. Incidentally the man I talked to originally at *Newsweek* is now dead and

---

5   Felicity Mason. A beautiful British adventuress and later author, friend of Brion Gysin and at one point a suitor of William Burroughs.
6   Jajouka. A region of Morocco well-known for folk music.

been replaced by some bad news in any week named Angus Deming[7] sniffing around for kif and sex. I sent him to all the most competent bores in town Paul Lund, George Greeves and Rupert Croft Cook. And they drove him back to Paris with their bavardage and may well of unseated his reason. Oh yes Finlay and Egleston too did a good work on him. Well fun and games what? Ian sends his love and we hope to see you here very soon.

Love,

Bill

EDITOR'S NOTE: At the suggestion of Burroughs' mother, Billy moved from Florida to stay in Tangier with William. Billy had been getting into more and more trouble at his school and she felt that the change would do him good. These arrangements did not last for long.

WSB [Tangier, Morocco] to Brion Gysin [Paris?]

Oct. 24, 1963
Cargo U.S. Consulate
Tanger, Morocco

Dear Brion:

Have addressed several letters to you all of which turned into something else notably preliminary experiments with format and carrying the cuts ups off the page with columns and strips of text continued on another page so that the book is as it were consisting of interlocking spheres which leads to the possibility of an illustrated book the words breaking over the illustrations more or less as they do in *Time* and newspaper layouts but using of course words and pictures carrying more than statistical charge. A preliminary experiment I have sent along to David Budd[8] and asked him to show it to you. Now the strips of color there could of course be wider, calligraphs or whatever (possibility of using a series of stills from a movie

---

7 Angus Deming. Author of *Getting to Know Algeria*.
8 David Budd (1927–1991). An abstract expressionist painter from Sarasota, Florida, who was to tell Burroughs about the dying words of Dutch Schultz and to whom Burroughs dedicated his book *The Last Words of Dutch Schultz*.

running along with the text etc.). Jim Roman the rare book man writes me that he is interested to publish an illustrated signed edition of some unpublished work. Perhaps we could work together on this. What I had in mind was not a full length novel but rather a short book with your illustrations and careful attention to format. Perhaps you will get some ideas from the format I sent to David Budd.

The house is slowly gathering bits and pieces — a beautiful mahogany table ten feet long I bought the wood for $15 etc. Billy [Burroughs] is getting along all right here with Ian [Sommerville] tutoring him in math and I do what I can. Not much local news. The Calder's book [*Dead Fingers Talk*] should be out end of this month. *Nova Express* is going to the typesetters.

How did your exhibition work out? And what are you doing for the Domaine Poétique?[9] If David can arrange transport I would like to get up to Paris next month. Ian and Michael [Portman] send love

Love
Bill

EDITOR'S NOTE: *After more than two years abroad, Allen Ginsberg returned to the United States. On his way back from India, he stopped off to visit Gary Snyder, who had been living in Japan for several years. Ginsberg and Burroughs had not communicated much since their last visit together in Tangier during the summer of 1961.*

WSB [Tangier, Morocco] to Allen Ginsberg [San Francisco]
Nov. 20, 1963
Cargo U.S. Consulate
Tanger, Morocco

Dear Allen:

Irving [Rosenthal] tells me you are in Frisco so I am writing to City Lights. Did Japan measure up to the expectations it seemingly

---

9 Domaine Poétique. A group of artists made up of Gysin, Bernard Heidsieck, and Henri Chopin.

gives rise to? And what are your plans? How does the 'Land of the Free' look after those far way places.

I am more or less settled in Tanger having taken a house in these foreign suburbs here in the Marshan which is quiet and gives me room to work. Had a dream the other night you and I arrived in Lhasa in a light plane. Met four Germans who said all the foreigners stay at No. 4 Southampton Street. Looking around for and no one about came finally to the main drag and you ask this cop who jerks his thumb back and there is the wagon. Just a paper check and the *commandante* impounds our passports and a cop escorts us to 4 Southampton. Looks like we still be there when the Chinese arrive which is something else. Well fun and games what? Jack Stern is across the way in Torremolinos[10] where I understand he cuts quite a figure. Have not seen him since Paris. He claims they bar him out of France so I twig he is not French at all but American what an epic liar he is. Tanger is quiet. Paul and Jane [Bowles] are here of course. Ian [Sommerville] and my son Billy sharing the house. Gregory [Corso] married a school teacher named Sally November and is in New York when last heard from indirectly. No word from Jack [Kerouac] in years. Alan Ansen[11] spent the summer here and is now back in Athens. I see [Timothy] Leary has been thrown out of Harvard for distributing his noxious wares too freely and some undergraduate decides he is God and takes off through traffic in Harvard Square. Also thrown out of Mexico for practicing 'weird rites.' He's a one.

[Lawrence] Ferlinghetti[12] is putting out my *Yage Letters* and wants to include one of yours. I guess he has discussed this with you. I sued *Time* and they took refuge in the *Yage Letters* and *Junky* to prove my character could not suffer any damage, but none the less I did win token damages 5£ and costs. Donated the 5£ quid to the Salvation Army. Ian send his best.

Love

Bill

---

10 Torremolinos. A city in southern Spain.
11 Alan Ansen (1922–2006). Poet and playwright, early friend of Ginsberg, Kerouac, and Burroughs.
12 Lawrence Ferlinghetti (b. 1919). Poet and publisher of City Lights Books.

WSB [Tangier, Morocco] to Brion Gysin [Paris?]

Dec. 1, 1963
Any Time
Care of U.S. Consulate
Tanger
Morocco

Dear Brion:

I can read it from here young man the letter I wrote you is right here to hand in the appropriate file if I can just lay my mind on it and (Opens file) I do not find the uh message from the guvner unduly confused. What I am in effect saying is that in a book composed of text and picture the two elements should be as closely associated as is humanly possible and if that don't work God damn it Gysin we'll just have to be *inhuman*. I'll have you know, Mister Gty Gysin huuuummmm I run a tight assed ship here. We are *not* confoozed but able soldiers sire and at your service we just don't like to be called confoozed and you shouldn't be listening to those office building shit house rumors calamity howlers sniffing for the sweet smell of failure been playing this old [Maurice] Girodias bankrupt tape since the beginning of time. "Girodias is finished. No more payments. I hear [Barney] Rosset is going broke too and [John] Calder has suspended his operations". Simple Tedium screams "Stop you merciless leather lunged corn holers". You will excuse an old soldier, sire. Irascible at times. Occupational. O.K. to tick off the points on your letter according to the new ruling has just come through with regard to total efficiency which is why all the kids in the office was so cast down at being called confoozed even if we were a little and who wouldn't be with new rulings piling up way ahead of *anyone's* reaction time no sooner I smalz my fat ass into a good thing someone starts yakking on the intercom, "Recalling all active agents recalling agents active all get off the point". I sweat out thirteen brown nosed years to get on this point I should get off it again yet dumber than I am? So efficiency, sire, we get it. Yes I have seen the *Life* article and have it conveniently to hand. The interesting possibility of beneficial (to me of course and my uh ravenous constituents) virus is still in the laboratory stage but Doc

Benway tells me "We are getting some darned interesting side by golly". Think of it. Boys to the sky and each one look like other. Its Heaven, kid far as the eye can see ahead the snows of Kilimanjaro. So let's not be too hasty with the fly tox remember what happened to Petiot.[13]

And now Doc Benway has a few remarks to make on the nature of virus which will perhaps answer some of the questions I see mosaic material is a genetic exterminator?

"Gentleman the virus is an ugly picture looking for a mirror with understandable but absolute need. I don't care how good the picture looked to start with when it experiences the absolute need that any image organism must experience when image is withdrawn becomes a very ugly picture. And the uglier you are the steadier you score. 'The Silver Score' we call it. Just old junkies frayed old film 'brother can't you spare a bright shiny dime?' and let me warn you young officers especially: a virus is never more dangerous than when on the mooch as they always are. Reluctantly we voted to view *any* vice with armed alertness. Any questions drifting down a windy street?"

Which brings me to your remarks on the image. Yes, we sure paid through the lungs to come in here and I guess we gotta go back out the same way, that is learn to breath in silence like a fish or whatever but like *anything* is image what? aquarium full of fish boys? a few chickens only way to live. What you breathe you dumb hick? Chickens and dogs like any hick. You breathe your human animals. "I must remind you Mister Martin, Bradly Martin of the new directive regarding respectful address of native life forms" and inasmuch as any vision and especially the vision of an artist presents itself in the form of an image preferably a youth of blinding beauty such frivolous neural patterns having been of course installed by the Word & Image mob who now stand there with their bare image hanging out say "You can't beat: Image *is* real. Virus *is* real. There *is* nothing but virus. That's what virus *is*, 'nothing but'." Nothing but what is virus? What virus nothing but is? Is virus nothing but what? What but nothing is virus? Virus nothing is what but? Well,

---

13 Marcel Petiot (1897–1946). A French serial killer who was convicted and beheaded.

Gysin, we going to stand still for this shit? Man the fucking pumps and close those air locks. Close those word locks. Silence. So we will now have (where's the script?) thirty seconds I think was written. Certainly I will write a script for your catalogue would it be possible to alternate strips of text with your drawings? I will write it in this form that is three strips of text running concurrently separated by strips of drawings? This is the same format of course I applied to the catalogue for the [David] Budd show.

Now local news. Stewart [Gordon] is here and expects to stay. Picked up some new faces in Ireland but they all look like Green Tony to me. Now young man you put a strain on the filing system already cancerous but I will send out a searching party with orders to bring in "Inflexible Authority" dead or alive. Yes, I want to go along with Nedermeyer (Mother of God I'll never get through all these fucking files). Seems like the closer we get to silence the more words we have to bang out if people only knew how much I hate to write *anything*. Words ugh "The man is malingering," snapped the colonel. Now how about if I send you like a block of text appropriate for any contingency its more humane that way you see? Of course I will also send along "Inflexible Authority" under separate cover. Tell Old Dean I'll be waiting at the door. "Remember me," "No Place To Go"?. I'll be waiting for you all at the door.

Love

William

Girodias has been paying off what he owes me at the rate of 200$ per month. The money from Rosset is on the way and should clear through Switzerland in a fortnight. I enclose a possible piece for your catalogue. What I am trying to show here is the pictures in *operation*. So I describe like this one pick up made using Gysin paintings as survey maps. There are three blocks of text running concurrently until exhausted. They can be separated by strips of drawing or the drawing can fill in as the strips of text are exhausted. Block three is finished on page one, block one and two continue over onto page two. I am not proposing this as a definitive text and you may not feel that it is suitable. Please let me know. The usual critical essay it seems to me just doesn't get the job done, the text should lead right into the pictures. Gysin paintings are maps showing you the way out. Stewart is doing some interesting work but it still doesn't measure up to what he can do on the total pantomime level his stories from Ireland had me on the floor. So Nasili says something about a Belgian anthology all the kids from the show will contribute.

WSB [Tangier, Morocco] to Brion Gysin [Paris]
Dec 17, 1963

Dear Brion:

It seems that I am going to London on a TV appearance with [Alex] Trocchi the 6th of January, suppose I must go fare paid and fee you know and will be coming over to Paris subsequently to pick up from [Maurice] Girodias and actually the whole thing quite dreary I do hate traveling about like this well now these blocks are like in a newspaper continued on the following pages only my blocks run across the page in strips not up and down in columns so when block three is 'exhausted' on page one it does not reach page two. I will bring along a number of alternative texts you can look at. Some land.

Love

Bill

Ian [Sommerville] sends love.

Do you know that Anatole France "wrote with a pair of scissors"? cutting out sentences and pasting them together? That perhaps he rather than [Tristan] Tzara is the original cut up? Perhaps it is time to exhume this cadaver and perform the indicated autopsy.

EDITOR'S NOTE: *The living arrangements with Billy didn't work out very well and within a few months of his arrival, he was headed back to the United States. Burroughs was simply ill equipped to be a father, and although Billy idolized William, it just wasn't enough.*

WSB [Tangier, Morocco] to Laura Lee and Mortimer Burroughs [Palm Beach, Florida]
Dec. 17, 1963
Cargo U.S. Consulate
Tanger, Morocco

Dear Mother and Dad:

I had a long talk with Billy before he left. He feels that he should finish the school year in Palm Beach. I was not able to find a fully qualified tutor here so it was difficult to arrange a regular schedule of work. It would seem to me that a tutor is the only solution since he apparently can not adjust to the routine of school work.

It was marvelous seeing Billy here and I think he has profited from the visit. Of course I would like him to return after Christmas but I do feel that his school work should not be neglected. A Merry Christmas to you all. I think there is nothing wrong with Billy psychologically. He is simply too mature intellectually for the usual high school course. After you have talked with him please let me know what you decide. I am making a short trip to London after New Year for a television appearance fare paid. Will stay a few days buy some clothes and back here to finish the book I am working on now

Love
Bill

RUBRUBRUBRUB+++&++++&++&&&&&""""&"+++
RUBRUBRUBRUBOUTOUTOUTOUTOUT#"#++++#
RUBRUBRUBRUBOUTOUTOUTOUTOUT####&&&&
"""&&&+++++"OUTOUTOUTOUTOUT""""""&&&
1964 ""+OUTOUTOUTOUTOUT"+"+"&&&
THETHETHETHETHETHETHE+++###+++&&+++
THETHETHETHETHETHETHE&&&&&++++++++#
THETHETHETHEWORDSWORDSWORDSWORDSTHE
###&&"&"&"&WORDSWORDSWORDSWORDS"++

EDITOR'S NOTE: *When Burroughs arrived in London, the immigration officials did not want to let him into the country. They restricted his visa so that he could stay for only two weeks, not the usual three months as before. It took him quite a while to resolve the matter, as this letter hints.*

WSB [London] to Ian Sommerville [Tangier, Morocco]

Jan 7, 1964
Devonshire Hotel
7 Princes Square
Bayswater
Room 7

Dear Ian:

Was on a check list at customs. Luggage thoroughly searched and only gave me two weeks. Humm. As it turns out the program was not live. Will be shown Jan. 27, at 10 P.M. on Independent TV. The producer and all the technicians were very pleased with it in fact said it was one of the best programs they had filmed so it was certainly worth while to come here and a fee of 50£. Actually I really enjoyed it and the interviewer Dan Farson[1] is very nice character old friend of Francis Bacon[2] etcetera. The day after my arrival went to a party at his house on the river where Michael [Portman] turned up looking pretty good. He is planning to come back to Tanger.

The filming was done by a new technique and the silent close ups produce an eerie effect of floating in space which we all noticed. The technician said he got some fantastic faces. I hope to see the edited program before leaving. We shot 97 minutes and the program is 26 minutes so they should be able to assemble a first rate program. Have seen [John] Calder and *Dead Fingers* is selling well has already sold 3,000 copies. The *Times Literary Supplement* controversy goes on and on. Anthony Burgess[3] has written a letter (Enter Jamie Davies who looks like him)

---

1 Daniel Farson (1927–1997). British writer and broadcaster.
2 Francis Bacon (1909–1992). English painter whom Burroughs knew from Tangier.
3 Anthony Burgess (1917–1993). English writer and the author of *A Clockwork Orange*.

Resume letter next day. Jake the Dentist will be here in two hours must correct the manuscripts. I will be here at this address (Name address hotel quite right?) until about the end of next week. Then to Paris. Then back here to catch flight to [Gibraltar]. If anything urgent comes up can be reached here. Alex [Trocchi] sends his best.

Love,
Bill

EDITOR'S NOTE: *Like most writers, Burroughs did not enjoy reading negative criticisms of his work, but usually he did not bother to respond to them. This letter is representative of what he produced when he did take on the critics, in this case it is a response to an especially sour review of* Dead Fingers Talk.

WSB [London] to *Times Literary Supplement* [London]
Jan. 17, 1964
To the Editor
Times Literary Supplement

Dear Sir:

It seems to me that any author has a right to expect of his critics an honest attempt to understand and evaluate what he is saying and that this attempt was not made in the review entitled "UGH". Dismissing the "moral" implications of my work he says: "And suppose the moral message is itself disgusting?" He then cites as an example the relation of the pusher to young addicts: "INVADE DAMAGE OCCUPY. Young faces in blue alcohol flame" p. 30 *Dead Fingers Talk* and goes on to say "The author presents these episodes without a flicker of disapproval". Precisely how is a writer expected to "flicker" disapproval? He must announce to the audience whenever a dubious character appears on stage, "You understand I don't approve of this man. Just part of the show you know?" This is absurd. My actual views on the junk industry and the infection of young people with the illness of addiction are well known to any one who reads what I have written on this subject. After many years of addiction to morphine I was cured by the apomorphine treatment developed by a London doctor. Since that time I have written a number of articles urging the use of this treatment since in my experience it is the only treatment that works. Two of these articles have been published in the American edition of *Naked Lunch*. The moral message of *Dead Fingers Talk* should be quite clear to any reader: Quote Inspector J. Lee of the Nova Police: "In all my experience as a police officer I have never seen such total fear and degradation on any planet" *opus cit* page 189 or "This is war to extermination. Fight cell by cell through bodies and mind screens of the earth" *opus cit* page 49. Speaking of "The Board" a cartel that plans to take over and monopolize space I say, "Liars cowards collaborator traitors. Liars who want time for more lies. Cowards who cannot face your 'human animals' with the truth. Traitors to all souls every where." Is this a disgusting message or does it just disgust the reviewer who will perhaps ask whether all this is to be taken seriously? and I say it is to be taken as seriously as anything else in my work. It is the critics job to evaluate what a writer is actually saying not to distort and falsify the writer's obvious intention. This job of evaluation was not done by your reviewer whoever he may be

William Burroughs

EDITOR'S NOTE: The following letter was laid out in a format resembling a three-column newspaper. This was a form that Burroughs had been experimenting with and one that he would use to produce several new works, including his own magazine. In this letter he explains the reason for doing so.

WSB [Tangier, Morocco] to Brion Gysin [Paris]
Tuesday February 4, 1964
Calle Larachi Marshan

Dear Brion:

The *New York Times* for September 17, 1899 came through a few days ago. I saw at once that the message was not of content but format. Newspapers are cut up by format. You read the adjacent columns while you read this column. You read cross column whether you notice or not — start noticing. The newspapers and newsmagazines are cut ups. This is the secret of their power to mould thought feeling and subsequent events. We propose to apply the same format to non-statistical quality material. Art if you will. I mean by art a way out to space. The cut ups are being used now by the press to keep you locked in time and word. Set up Shakespeare, Conrad, Rimbaud in newspaper format. Write your novels in this format. Run chapters in columns like chapter 1 2 3 starts on the first page with titles as headlines.

I think the format here illustrated with examples enclosed is the best for the book we have under preparation. That is three columns of text newspaper format of a small town newspaper or of a number of such papers fitting into each other. I have a number of titles that could be used The Nova Police Gazette The Bad News The Silent Times The Present Times The Past Times The Last News The Last Post etcetera. For our purposes perhaps we should simply follow through with the three columns and not change titles. Now we could for example fill *The Silent Sunday Post* with drawings or have all the drawing on the other side of the text which would be a simpler and more inexpensive format.

It occurs to me that we might sell these newspaper issues like the enclosed to the rare book trade properly printed and illustrated. Perhaps J. Roman[4] would do the publishing. Let me know what you think.

This should be a million dollar idea for *Reader's Digest* (Hauser is the man now I think).. *Your Day* Take a walk sit down *read this paper* cut in what you see hear think as you read with what you read and what you have just seen heard felt in the course of your walk Send along to *Your Day*. We will print excerpts from all material received. You will find yourself using a form of short hand to say what you see hear feel as you walk down streets of the world. Do not worry if your day seems incomprehensible to others. Perhaps you have special names for things. Explain these and we will build up a special *Your*

---

4   James Roman. A rare-book dealer.

Day lingo. So take the bits and pieces of all your days and send them into *Your Day* and we will stir them all into one long day: *Your Day*

Love

William Burroughs

WSB [Tangier, Morocco] to Allen Ginsberg [New York]
Feb. 5, 1964
% U.S. Consulate
Tanger, Morocco

Dear Allen:

Thanks for your letter. Yes of course all out of time into space is O.K. I thought the *Yage Letters* an excellent job.[5] Howard Schulman is psychotic and to my way of thinking bad news because of his deplorable condition. I decided after seeing him that he would undoubtedly be in trouble simply through his bizarre behavior. Billy was only in the police station for a half hour or so having made a long distance phone call and not knowing that international charges can not be reversed and not having money to pay the phone bill. He is now back in Palm Beach.[6]

As for the film I will think about it and if I come up with anything suitable get in touch with you or with the producers.[7] Thanks for the opportunity to make a fast $ of which I am badly in need since [Maurice] Girodias is on the verge of bankruptcy and unable to pay me $5000 he owes what a drag just when I thought I could relax and take my time on the next book to have no money prospect of lawyers lawyers etcetera. Girodias is a fuck up who obviously wants to lose his money which is his business but he has lost everyone's else's money as well.

I would like to hear better news of Jack [Kerouac] and Lucien

---

5   City Lights published *The Yage Letters* in November 1963.
6   Billy Burroughs was arrested on drug-related charges reminiscent of his father's earlier problems.
7   Ginsberg proposed that Burroughs write a film treatment for Bob Booker and George Foster. Years later, having failed to find backers for the film, they published a collection of these scripts in a book entitled *Pardon Me, Sir, But Is My Eye Hurting Your Elbow?* but Burroughs was not included.

[Carr]. After all this is the space age and they seem to be stuck in repetition sets. Irving [Rosenthal] is in Marrakech. Yes I liked his book[8] but found it rather sad and depressing. The *Times Literary Supplement* have closed the correspondence. I hope the letters and the original review are not indicative of the British reading public since most of the communications supporting the original review can only be described as down right stupid. However good publicity for the book. I am just back from London where I filmed a T.V. program with Alex Trocchi. Went out last week. Good reaction in the press. Mostly on drugs. Back in Tanger with an appalling amount of work to do. Best to Peter [Orlovsky], Jack and Lucien.

Love
Bill

WSB [Tangier, Morocco] to Peter Michelson[9] [Chicago]
Feb. 16, 1964
4 Calle Larachi Marshan
Tanger, Morocco

Dear Mr. Michelson:

I enclose a short unpublished piece of work in progress representative of recent experiments in which I extend the newspaper and magasine format to fictional material. When you read words in columns you are reading your future reading that is you are reading on subliminal level other columns on the page that you will later consciously experience you have already read. Also the presentation in columns enables the writer to present three or more streams of narrative running *concurrently*. This opens possibilities of contrast accompaniment and counterpoint. The same situation can be viewed from three different columns at the same time. In short I am attempting to get beyond the limitations of the book page left

---

8 This is possibly a reference to Irving Rosenthal's book *Sheeper*, which Burroughs might have read in manuscript although the book was not published by Grove Press until 1967. On the other hand, it might be a reference back to a recent Kerouac book such as *Big Sur* (1962) or *Visions of Gerard* (1963).
9 Peter Michelson. An editor of the *Chicago Review*.

to right and down and over. (What a salutary shock to see words running from right to left on an English language page). I think it is time for writers to break up an unsanitary schizophrenic relation with a dead typewriter in an empty room. "Action writers?" Why not? Why not write a novel as if you were sitting at the city desk? Don't wait for inspiration. Take a walk a ride a subway. Sit down somewhere drink a cup of coffee read a paper. Return to your rap and write what you have just seen heard felt with particular attention to intersection points. What were you reading when you looked up and saw an English lesson on TV in the Café de Paris? "Yale Professor held as spy". "This is the fourth lesson 1 2 3 4!" (the teacher held up four flickering silver fingers). Use these intersection points of present time in what you are writing in present time. *Write in present time.* The present text was composed by taking a walk through my files. The format should suggest a small town newspaper.

Sincerely
William Burroughs

WSB [Tangier, Morocco] to Alan Ansen [Athens, Greece]
February 27, 1964
c/o U.S. Consulate
Tanger, Morocco

Dear Alan:

First thank you for the Christmas card. It is heartening to see so much pains taken when most people if they send cards at all don't even take time to select, so I feel a lesson is indicated, namely take as much time as need to do whatever you are doing is as important as anything. I mean people used to have time and they can have time now if they *take* it. So I am now keeping a diary which is more fun than a barrel of keys also arranging all my material in tastefully decorated and *appropriate* files, every item in its *own* place. Do you have a copy of *The Yage Letters*? If not I will send you one. City Lights has done an excellent job.

I am recently returned from a trip to London where I made a television appearance with Alex Trocchi that seemingly served a useful purpose. Arriving in Paris to collect $5000 in royalties due me I am greeted with "terrible confession to make" by [Maurice] Girodias so it looks like a case of find a lawyer and get in line and the line is long. Some people are self-destructive and *want* to lose money, it's a psychological thing I read about in the *Reader's Digest*. What a stupid bastard he is and you know I found out most of the money he spends on cunt and doesn't even get that he is a John. At his age yet to be taken like a visiting mark from Podunk Toulouse. Also I have a boy friend who works in a bank and he looked up Girodias's credit rating and his credit does not exist since 1959 one rubber check after the other.

I ran into Conrad Rooks between London and Paris on the plane you understand so we are on good terms again. He is gone photo mad and takes like 500 photos a day. He has two of those German spy cameras and takes with both hands the general theory seems to be law of averages. Arriving in Paris I find that Mary McCarthy and Sonia Orwell[10] have started a new literary magazine [*Locus Solus*] of which John Ashbery[11] is the editor or one of the editors at least. You might write him and send some poems. I am going back to Paris expenses paid by the Stadler Gallery since I have written the text for an exhibition by David Budd — don't think you know him — opening on the 13 of March.

Ian [Sommerville] sends his best.

Love,
Bill

WSB [Tangier, Morocco] to Dick Seaver [New York]
March 10, 1964
% U.S. Consulate
Tanger, Morocco

Dear Dick Seaver:
So far as collecting the royalties from [Maurice] Girodias it is a

---

10 Sonia Orwell (1918–1980). Second wife of the writer George Orwell.
11 John Ashbery (b. 1927). Poet closely identified with the New York School.

question of find a lawyer and get in line and the line is long and the till is empty. The plain fact is he spent the money to cover what he evidently considered more pressing debts and I was barely able to squeeze out of him enough to get myself back to Tanger. Of course I told him that the Swiss arrangement must be canceled so that my share of the royalties comes directly to me in the future. He agreed to this and I have just received a letter from him to the effect he has written you giving notice of the new arrangement.

Needless to say this has put me [in] an extremely difficult position since I was counting on that money and now have nothing to live on plus a broken typewriter which I cannot afford to have repaired or replaced. In short just no money at all. As regards the transfer of money here when the next payments are due the end of this month the most convenient form of transfer would be a cashier's check on a Gibraltar bank. The financial regulations here will not allow the banks to make payment in dollars. All checks drawn on Tanger banks must be paid in the local currency. It is illegal to take this currency outside the country and difficult to exchange if you do involving a thirty percent loss. So the important thing for me is a check I can negotiate preferably in Gibraltar certainly outside Morocco. Meanwhile I would certainly appreciate if you could possibly manage to send me an advance of a few hundred $ to carry me through since I literally don't have money to pay the rent here.

Despite my understandable annoyance with Maurice I still sympathize with his position which could hardly be worse. More and more trouble with the French authorities, suspended sentences piling up, a twenty year publishing ban, inevitable debacle of that unfortunate restaurant venture, owing money to his staff, social security to the government, fines, lawsuits, the lot.

Well these are the simple facts of the case. It was all obvious and inevitable from the conception of La Grande Séverine[12]

With All Best Wishes
William Burroughs

---

12 Le Grande Séverine at 7 rue Saint-Séverin. Maurice Girodias poured much of his money into this very chic restaurant in Paris. He virtually ruined his publishing company trying to finance the nightclub/restaurant.

WSB [Tangier, Morocco] to Antony Balch [London?]
March 22, 1964 (Rameaux)
4 Calle Larachi Marshan
Tangier, Morocco

Dear Anthony:

Many thanks for the script which looks very good. I will start work on the other scripts. I have been thinking along film lines intersecting extensions of the technical devices used in *Towers Open Fire*. Loops: A useful variation suggested to me by the local children would loop a crowded street with the same street empty and silent both loops to be accompanied by the appropriate sound track or lack thereof looped at the same speed. Same difference a street with air hammers same street empty and silent with clear space for another development I have dubbed 'time loops'. For example say I have a pub like Dan Farson has featuring 1890 atmosphere. So I loop present time shots with 1890 shots on same set posed or not depending on what is available. (Of course 1920 atmosphere could often be accompanied by actual film taken on location). The point that distinguishes the 'time loop' from just any old film sequence is the rapid flicker of past and present. It would seem to me that there are distinct financial possibilities inherent in this idea which of course is subject to many variations. (Any section of Tanger as it is now and as it was ten twenty thirty years ago any number of shots can be used on the loop zeroes in on a given set. A cut up of the time loops should also give interesting results). To return to our bar or night club it would be most interesting to combine television with a film made on the location. That is the patrons first see themselves doing what they are doing then films made at other times same place are cut in. Of course for excitement and variety say old Westerns etcetera such as have appeared on the TV screen could be cut in so a patron lights a match say and the shooting starts. Now since the patron would be seeing themselves on the screen taking part at least by juxtaposition in stirring events they would be more on the *qui vive* to make a good showing. I mean how could the place miss that could put its patrons in hurricanes earthquakes gun fights and the weird ceremonials of primitive peoples?

What the Hell A.B. lets think big! Make time loops of a whole fucking city rotating from section to section and when everybody is like pinned down *then* mix your sections and let it come down Times Square on Piccadilly etcetera. Of course some unethical practitioners might misuse this device and pervert it from its pure intention being of course to provide wholesome amusement for all the family. You know they might say loop a theatre with the same theatre on fire or say present time San Francisco with the 1906 set or St. Louis the way it is now with the 1929 tornado but then what discovery can not be turned to bad use? The important thing is to provide good clean entertainment. Just reading your script over and it really flickers off the page.

> Loopingly
> William Burroughs

EDITOR'S NOTE: When Burroughs received a confusing letter from Brion Gysin, his best friend, he could not resist sending him instructions on how to write a proper letter.

WSB [Tangier, Morocco] to Brion Gysin [Paris]
Mars 28, [March 28, 1964] Samedi St. Gontran
4 Calle Larachi Marshan
Tangier, Morocco

Dear Brion:

Having received your letter presumably of Wednesday March 25 I still have not the vaguest idea as to what the German TV deal is. Subject matter of interview?? *Fee*?? Spenser?? I take the liberty of quoting from my article entitled "The Lost Art of Letter Writing": "The letters you write are *your* messengers. Your messengers should be well informed neat and *special* to your correspondent. No time is ever saved by doing anything improperly. You are a writer? a painter? Any letter you write is or should be *your best work*. Set about writing a letter with the same thoroughness you would give to any other job. First clear your desk of anything not relevant to the letter you are writing. The letter you are answering should be on the desk. Also the letter before that (if it exists) and a copy of your answer. (No letter should be sent out without a copy). It is well to have a photo of your correspondent on the desk in front of you. If you have recently sent a post card, a duplicate post card should be on the table. If your correspondent is a painter one of his pictures should be kept in view as you write. Now read his letters through very carefully. Read *between the lines*. What is he really saying? Notice the dates on these letters and on your answering letters. Check with your diary if you keep one and a diary is a must for any writer. What were *you* doing on these dates?"

"Now that you have carefully read letters and answers, consider all questions raised by these letters. All too often a hurried letter does not answer the questions asked or implied. It is well to number your questions and place them in a separate section or paragraph at the beginning of each letter. *Always remember no time is saved* by a hasty letter that does not cover the ground. I am now writing a sample letter to a painter friend. One of his pictures is on the desk in front of me together with a color post card I sent him from Gibraltar March 25, 1964. The time in 11.34 A.M. in these foreign suburbs here."

Dear Brion:

You say 'got your letter'. What letter? *Date?*

1. Did you receive copy of *My Magazine [My Own Mag]* with enclosed letter? 2. Did you receive *The Moving Times* sent about a month ago before I wrote "The Lost Art of Letter Writing" so I don't have date or copy of letter? *Exactly what is Limes [Verlag] anxious to go on with?* Please give me some indication as to what this TV interview is about how long what fee etcetera.

I can only conclude that letters have been lost. No one to whom I sent copies of *My Magazine* seems to have received them. I have just returned from Gibraltar where Grove had sent me an advance on money due the end of April.

Is it true that [Maurice] Girodias is in jail? If so is anything being done? Is there anything I can do?

Yes I am willing to take part in the TV deal when I find out what it is. I have not been following to the letter my own instructions.

Your letter refers to the letter I sent with *My Magazine*, March 19, 1964, so I assume you did receive it? A more careful reading of both letters *before* I started to write would have shown me that you were referring to my letter of March 19 and not my letter of March 23. A reference date on your part would have obviated the necessity for such a perhaps incorrect inference on my part. "Exactitude in small matters is the very soul of discipline", Joseph Conrad *The Secret Sharer.* As to subletting to Felicity [Mason] why? She is not my spiritual sister nor was meant to be. She left [Mohamed] Hamri in a deplorable condition like he show up for a dinner date here with uninvited female Arab and the translations back and forth were nothing but excruciating. He broke the tape recorder and some cop friend of his made off with the radio I lent him. *Muy malo* and I can hear Felicity in all this. *No.* I do not sublet this house to any woman. The rent is small and you can move in any time. Rent from June on is already paid in the deposit.

WSB [Tangier, Morocco] to Jean-Jacques Lebel[13] [Paris]
Monday March 30, 1964
% U.S. Consulate
Tangier, Morocco

Dear Jean-Jacques Lebel:

Sorry to be slow about answering your letter. [Maurice] Girodias's bankruptcy has absorbed all my time and energy. As regards [Conrad] Rook's magasine. He started a magasine once before that never came through so I wouldn't give it much thought until the $$ are on the table and you are given a free hand. I heard about Gregory [Corso] only indirectly and apparently he was only in for a few days. Speaking of which what's this I hear about Girodias being in jail? If so is anything being done? It does seem a bit much for a publisher to be jailed in France the so called home of intellectual freedom for books that can now be published in America with no difficulty. With all his short coming (and God knows he came

---

13 Jean-Jacques Lebel (b. 1936). French artist, poet, and translator.

up but short with me like 5000$ short) he has done as much as any publisher living for literary freedom and if there is anything I can do to help him now I am ready to do it. I hope to get to Paris some time this month and look forward to seeing you. Meanwhile please let me know — if anything has developed on the magasine

Cordially Yours

William Burroughs

EDITOR'S NOTE: Burroughs had been living in a relatively poor neighborhood in Tangier because he couldn't afford anything better. His predominately Moroccan neighbors were always suspicious of him and his friends. Burroughs did not get along with the Moroccans, who often shouted insults and threw trash at him from windows as he walked down the street. William suspected that derelicts had been directed to knock on his door in the middle of the night in order to disturb him. When he was finally able to get his American payments directly through Grove Press instead of Olympia, he had enough money to move to a better neighborhood. There he continued to work on his new experiment of writing in columns as per a newspaper.

WSB [Gibraltar] to Brion Gysin [Paris]

Gibraltar
Hotel Continental
Room 25, 3 P.M.
10/4/64 [April 10, 1964]

Dear Brion:

I now have $1000 from Grove Press so I can travel at any time. (I have written to Limes [Verlag]). As for the house in Tangier, I am moving out. You can use it any time (the rent is paid until October I think). Personally I am disgusted with Tangier like I turn sick with the sight of Arabs. Will, however, take flat in European section to publish this newspaper at least one issue. Just no more Arabs knocking on my door if I have to live in the Minzah.[14]

---

14 The Minzah. The most expensive hotel in Tangier.

You can't imagine or can you what Tangier is like now since The Voice of America did a job here, worse than Paris or any place I have experienced, the whole town solid cunt territory and everyone knocks him or herself out to show you how worthless they can be, only thing keeps me here is the paper and not knowing where else to go. What a relief to be away for a few days. All this happened since about the time of the Kennedy assassination. I don't think you will like it here now but perhaps you can still find some traces of the old Tangier. Like I say the house is yours if you want to use it. I must get out before I open up with laser guns on the wretched idiot inhabitants. "*Fingaro, Fingaro!*" These people are going to fight Israel?? What you see here now is the Arabs *at their worst*, like somebody took pictures and recordings of all the ugliest scenes in Tangier and keeps playing them back. I can't be expected to work under such conditions. There is not even material here for a riot. No guts left in this miserable town. Perhaps I exaggerate. Hope so. Anytime on Germany.

Love
Bill

WSB [Tangier, Morocco] to Brion Gysin [Paris]
April 17 [1964] Fliday St. Anissete
Hotel Atlas Tangier Morocco

Dear Brion:

Returned from Gibraltar running a fever and have been in bed since, just up and around again a bit shaky gram negative infection for which one uses a new antibiotic called T.A.O. (The old Chinese smiled). Can't say as I wasn't looking for a reason to spend a few days in bed *reading* (Graham Greene mostly). Fact is I haven't read in years. Fascinating material on book codes in *Our Man In Havana*. Man gets in a rut. See what the other chappies are doing right? And Gerald Heard's *A Taste For Honey*. It seems this twisted beekeeper named 'Heregrove' (Heard Grove) conceives the fiendishly simple idea of breeding a particularly venomous strain of Italian bee to attack and destroy the swarms of rival beekeepers. Then drunk with power he begins using his [Italian] bees to eliminate human animals of the village who have incurred his disfavor over the years the way country folk will. This he did by spraying on them under various pretexts a distillate of horse sweat which maddened his bees to a homicidal frenzy. The danger this sort of thing posed to the English country people can well be imagined and their swollen black corpses like overripe mulberries littered the founds. But Mr Heregrove had reached without Mr Mycroft a retired inspector from the Nova Police who also dedicated himself to beekeeping and in fact resembled Mr Heregrove like a brother he knew all about the Italian bees from his years on the force as he summoned his first person singular (his 'Number One Boy') to a conference in his greenhouse. "You understand the man won't stop. Couldn't even if he wanted to with those bees multiplying *in direct geometric ratio to their lethal sperm*"

The hideous phallic significance of those curved quivering stings he had seen writing a [*sic*: writhing and] twisting under the force in Mycroft's steady old hand burst upon Number One. "You mean???" Mycroft nodded: "Yes. New swarms hatch from each victim. Do you know what this madman will do next?"

"I don't want to know," I screamed.

"He will charter a light plane and spray this England with horse sweat"

Well needless to say old Mycroft concocts some special odorless horse sweat and sprays it on Heregrove from an orchid tube. Turning grimly from the blackened corpse he snaps, "all right 'Number One,' go out and get those fucking Italian bees. Not one insect pest must remain alive to put our riding habits in peril."

Too bad about the TV. Grove is sending me six thousand $ on May 1st. Meanwhile have sent an advance of $1000. Enclose $100 for immediates. Any plans for coming here? I am definitely moving in town. Keep me informed on Germany, Limes [Verlag] and all that

Best
Bill

WSB [Tangier, Morocco] to David Solomon[15] [n.p.]
April 20, 1964
% U.S. Consulate
Tangier, Morocco

Dear Dave Solomon:

Returning the permission form signed I hope correctly. The book [*The Marihuana Papers*] sounds great and I will look forward to see it. It is certainly about time some one called the American Narcotics Department on their pernicious falsification of facts. They have deliberately obstructed scientific evaluation of marijuana. And they have obstructed the only treatment for addiction that works namely the apomorphine treatment. Obviously they do not wish to see the problem of addiction solved or even intelligently handled. Their efforts to create more and more criminals by act of Congress, to spread hysteria based on falsification and unnecessary complication of what could be a very simple problem can only be described as ill intentioned in the extreme. (I enclose magasine put out by a friend in London that may amuse you)

Cordially Yours
William Burroughs

---

15 David Solomon (1925–2007). Editor, jazz critic, and drug expert.

WSB [Tangier, Morocco] to Gus Blaisdell[16] [Craig, Colorado]

May 3, [1964] Sunday
% The American Consulate
Tangier, Morocco

From: William S. Burroughs
% The American Consulate

To: Mr. Gus Blaisdell
West Theatre
Craig, Colorado
U.S.A.

Dear Mr. Blaisdell:

There is no manuscript of *Queer*, in fact never was, this being a suggested title that never accreted any text to speak of. Yes I would be interested to publish *Junkie* in hard cover with notes and several articles I have written on the subject of narcotics. I think a saleable book could be assembled that would be a definitive work on this subject.

My contract on *Nova Express* is with Grove and Olympia will not publish this book. In fact Olympia is practically out of business. I will arrange to send you a copy of *Minutes To Go* from Paris. The only other publication out that could be described as a pamphlet is *The Yage Letters* recently published by Ferlinghetti of City Lights. I like the pamphlet form and have other projects under way. I started a children's book tentatively entitled *Over The Hills And Far Away* but have not had time to finish it nor found an illustrator. "Johnny's So Long At The Fair" was a title considered and not used for *The Ticket That Exploded*. I am preparing a bibliography of all published work and will send along a copy. *Naked Lunch* has been translated into French and published a month ago by Gallimard, Paris. German translation by Limes of Wiesbaden published over a year ago, Italian translation just out (Sugar of Milan). *Junkie* has been translated into Italian and published by Rizzoli.

---

16 Gus Blaisdell (1935–2003). Writer, teacher, and publisher of Living Batch Press.

I am not much of a movie go-er partly through lack of opportunity here in Tangier. Often I find more interest in films that pass unnoticed than in the so called *avant-garde*, I mean a film that seems to be nothing special then you do a double take and see something, 'double takes' I call them: *The Gangster* many years ago [1947], *The Beautiful Country* [*sic*: *The Wonderful Country* (1959)] with Robert Mitchum circa 1961, *The Comandante*,[17] Gérard Philipe's last film before he died had more of Latin American in it than any film I ever saw. *The Rise And Fall Of Jack Diamond* [*sic*: *The Rise and Fall of Legs Diamond* (1960)] circa 1951, *A Portrait In Black* with Anthony Quinn and Lana Turner, 1964. Last year I wrote and acted in a short (11 minutes) entitled *Towers Open Fire*. Directed and filmed by Antony Balch of London *T.O.F.* was billed with *Freaks*. A few good shots.

I am a comic strip reader from back. My complete inability to draw has prevented me from experimenting with this form. However I amuse myself by cutting out comics and rearranging faces and captions. Currently my favorite comic is "Jeff Hawke" in *The Daily Express*, London. Also read "Rex Morgan M.D.", "Buz Sawyer". Lately I have been interested to apply the newspaper format to my writing. Enclose paper put out by a friend Mr. J. Nuttall[18] of London I have urged him to extend the comic strip[19]

Good Luck in The West Theatre
William Burroughs

---

17 Possibly Burroughs is referring to *La Fièvre Monte à El Pao* (1959), which was Philipe's last film.

18 Jeff Nuttall (1933–2004). British poet and publisher.

19 In 1964, Burroughs began to collaborate with Jeff Nuttall in the production of the mimeo magazine *My Own Mag*. Burroughs' own magazine, *The Moving Times*, appeared as a supplement in some issues of *My Own Mag*. To complicate the production history even more, sometimes Burroughs' supplement was called *The Burrough*.

WSB [Tangier, Morocco] to Laura Lee and Mortimer Burroughs [Palm Beach, Florida]
May 4, 1964
% The American Consulate
Tangier, Morocco

Dear Mother and Dad:

I have been in bed with a strep infection or I would have written sooner. Now have a backlog of letters and articles to catch up on. I have written the text for an article on Tangier scheduled to appear in the September *Esquire*.[20] They took Billy's picture and will use it in the article. I had only three days to write the text and interview the people involved. Quite a job. Did the best I could on such short notice. I am pretty well set financially with my royalties diverted from Monsieur Girodias's sticky fingers. $500 for the *Esquire* article, another book coming out this summer in America (*Nova Express*), so I should be able to make it from now on. One has to think of writing as any other job. You work at it all day and every day if you expect to make a living. I have moved out of the house and taken a flat in town which is more peaceful. I am sorry to hear Billy is still having trouble with his school work and will write him a letter. Is he getting any exercise?? That is very important. He should take jiu jitsu or boxing which would give him confidence and take his mind off personal problems. I hope he will do some writing. After my own experience with psychoanalysis I do not have much faith in it. Anyone who is really busy has no problems except those connected with their work. Please keep me posted. Many thanks for the checks

Love,
Bill

---

20 The article entitled "Tangier" did appear in the September 1964 issue of *Esquire*.

WSB [Tangier, Morocco] to Alex Trocchi [London]

May 12 [1964] Tuesday (St. Achilles)
% The American Consulate
Tangier, Morocco

Dear Alex:

This will be a short letter. My editorial duties with *The Moving Times*, *The Cold Spring News*, *The Boy's Magazine*, *The Last Post*, *The Dead Star*, *The Nova Police Gazette*, are what might be called urgent. I asked young [Jeff] Nuttall to send you a copy of *My Magasine* [i.e., *My Own Mag*] with *The Moving Times*. Did you receive it? Response has exceeded our expectations. You should keep in touch with J.N. This experiment in reader participation is very much along the Sigma line.[21] About coming to England::: The last time I entered England the customs clerk crossed out "Good for visit up to three months" and stamped in "permitted to land on condition does not stay longer than two weeks". This means that any time I enter London and they see that change they are going to start purpose of visit and like as not stamp in "refused entry" which will cause me trouble wherever I go. So until the matter is cleared up that is until I am assured officially that I will be permitted to land I don't see myself going to England for the Lenny Bruce treatment. On the other hand I propose to make in the near future a trip to Paris and Germany so we could meet in Paris or some place like Amsterdam maybe. I will let you know when I get my travel orders. Like I say we have had an unexpectedly good response to *The Moving Times* which has put me in touch with a number of people in England thinking along the same lines who would be interested in Sigma if they knew about it. Very important to unite available forces. Have you seen Michael Portman? If you do see him tell him to please get in touch with me.

Best Luck
Bill Burroughs

---

21 Project Sigma. Alex Trocchi, in his article titled "The Invisible Insurrection of a Million Minds," called for the linking of minds to create a revolution in consciousness. The idea was loosely supported by a wide range of people from Timothy Leary to R. D. Laing.

WSB [Tangier, Morocco] to Allen Ginsberg [New York]

Tangier, Morocco
c/o The American Consulate
May 20, 1964

Dear Allen:

You seem to be running a literary aid society [you] should incorporate and pay yourself a salary. I have to hand a letter from one Yaddo Tambimuttu[22] written at your instance asking me to contribute to the T.S. Eliot Symposium which I will do and thanking you for this and many other good offices. This magazine [*My Own Mag*] put out by a friend in London J. Nuttall an interesting and seemingly successful experiment in applying newspaper format and reader participation. This issue a sell out and many contributions received. Do send something. Can not but feel Lucien [Carr] well rid of Tessa [*sic*: Cessa].[23] (No enthusiasm for E. Lee implied) Don't worry about [Maurice] Girodias. He is not in the nick. Suspended drinking champagne as usual. Sad about Jack [Kerouac] such a tired old trap.[24] Incidentally the Rothschild's asked about you. I mean Jack Stern who lives across the way in Spain. Off junk but lushes 2 bottles of rum per day like 15 men on the dead man's chest you ho and 2 bottles of rum he looks awful. I've sent in The Parade spinning on evil Jew communist plot to flood the world with super apoheroin and *quiet* everybody. Use the Sanity Drug Apomorphine. Love to Peter [Orlovsky], Lucien, Jack. *No* love to [Howard] Schulman fucking commie and bad news artist. He should use apomorphine. (He did as in J. Nuttall should serve as an inspiration to all editors of little magazines.) It takes him an average of two weeks to get out an issue. So if you *do* pass by a book store. Well they can order *My Mag* at the London address. (Ferlinghetti took some) They *sell*. Readers can read their own words in the next issue, and you can't beat your own words for interest to *you*.

William Burroughs

---

22 Tambimuttu (1915–1983). Poet and editor of *Poetry London* magazine.
23 Lucien Carr had split up with his wife, Cessa, after a decade of marriage and three children. For a while he dated Kerouac's old girlfriend, Alene Lee, whom Burroughs refers to here as E. Lee.
24 Reference to Kerouac's continued use of alcohol.

WSB [Tangier, Morocco] to Mr. Tambimuttu [New York?]
June 14, 1964
% The American Consulate
Tangier, Morocco

Dear Mr. Tambimuttu:

A word of explanation regarding the enclosed contribution which I hope is suitable to the Eliot symposium. It is intended to be a patchwork in the style of "The Waste Land". Mr Reeves Mathews [*sic*: Rives Matthews], my next door nabor in St Louis knew Mr. Eliot in St Louis. Mr. Matthews has assembled a book of reminiscences, letters visiting cards on which I have drawn. He mentions Mr. Eliot frequently as someone his mother knew at dancing school. I have also drawn intersection points between my own work and the work of Mr Eliot and intersection points with *Time* and *Newsweek*. As you know Mr. Eliot in "The Waste Land" has followed somewhat the same method of using newspaper headlines, put conversations, quotations from other writers etcetera. If you decide to include this piece in the symposium Mr. Rives Matthews should be mentioned since the concept derived from his memoirs which have not been published. Mr. Matthews is now a resident of Tangier

Cordially Yours
William Burroughs

WSB [Tangier, Morocco] to Brion Gysin [Paris]
June 18, 1964
% The American Consulate
Tangier, Morocco

Dear Brion:

Sorry to be remiss about writing. Unprecedented series of deadlines followed by local heat wave had me temporarily out of commission. However your reporter is now back in action all under good control. Look forward to see you here the 1st. Enclose 100 dollars for expenses. I will take a trip somewhere on or about July

15. No trouble about this visa. The man in security is giving me a six months visa. Paul B. [Bowles] has a beautiful place for the summer. Out on the old Mountain Road over the sea surrounded by trees and mescaline colors like a picture post card. Sorry if I do not always remember to cover your enclosures and clippings in each letter. Lady Sutton Smith[25] gets so caught up in letter writing as to neglect her own precepts. I hope you don't see David Mann in Venice where he has gone. I thought him one of the more unfortunate people in circulation. I have material for an issue of the *Time* format magazine and want to discuss with you the question of illustrations. That is to find precise intersections between text and drawing.

Love

Bill

EDITOR'S NOTE: Now that Burroughs had somewhat worked out his problems with Olympia Press and was receiving his royalties directly from foreign publishers, he felt it was time to prepare a will. He wanted to inform his parents and thank them for their loyal financial support in the past. William also wanted to reassure them that he would be financially responsible for Billy.

WSB [Tangier, Morocco] to Laura Lee and Mortimer Burroughs [Palm Beach, Florida]
June 21, 1964
% The American Consulate
Tangier, Morocco

Dear Mother and Dad:

I do not wish to appear morbid but there is always the possibility that something might happen to me in which case there is a considerable sum of money tied up in the books I have published and books waiting to be published. This could mean over the years a comfortable income for Billy. First as regards published

---

25 Lady Sutton Smith. A nom de plume that Burroughs sometimes adopted for himself.

work: Four books have been published and there is a book with Grove Press waiting publication. The publishers to contact are: Maurice Girodias, Olympia Press, 7 Rue St. Severin, Paris (to be approached through a competent lawyer) the other two publishers Barney Rosset, Grove Press, 64 University Place, NYC 3, N.Y. and John Calder, 17 Sackville Street, London W.I. England are honest and solvent. There is also the question of *unpublished* work that is the notes and manuscripts on hand from which at least three full length novels could be assembled. There are only two people sufficiently conversant with the intention of the work to be capable of editing and assembling this material for publication. They are: Mr. Brion Gysin, 9 Rue Git-Le-Coeur, Paris 6, France and Mr Ian Sommerville presently residing at 6 Calle Cook Tangier home address 77 West Crescent, Darlington, England. So all papers and manuscripts should be turned over to one or the other for editing in the event of my demise (which I hope is improbable but which should be provided for in case it does occur). Nobody else could make out these papers and a valuable source of income would be lost if the papers fell into incompetent hands. Well that's that. Just as well to take precautions in case. Please let me hear from you. I am taking a trip to Gibraltar tomorrow back in a few days

Love

Bill

WSB [Tangier] to Brion Gysin [Paris]

June 22, [1964] St. Paul in
American Consulate
Tangier, Morocco

Dear Brion:

Nursing a few bruises this morning. There is this local nut who insulted poor Ian [Sommerville] on the street once "You like beeg one?" etcetera. So he gives me this noise last night as I was coming home from a rather festive evening slammed an elbow into his face chased him into a vacant lot where he picked up a rock and hit me in the knee and ran off at a speed I could not hope to match at my age. Well fun and games and so to bed. (Actually the action must have been more complex because I seem to have quite a variety of bruises and cuts here and there and hung over) . . . I hope you received the check I sent to Amerex in Venice? Could you do me a favor and see Doctor Xavier Corre, Neuilly on Seine and get an apomorphine script for two boxes and bring it with you when you come here? We are all out and several times lately thought I wouldn't make it. However, things are looking up. The *Esquire* article will be out in September, I have enough material now for my *Time* format magazine. I am sure it will sell. The success of *My Magazine* has been amazing. There is a gallery open here. Martin's Gallery in the passage Bestofel. You can certainly have an exhibit there if you want one. The last exhibit with several Moroccan painters was a sell out. What seems to sell are medium sized to small canvases moderately priced. I will write the catalogue of course. Recently visas are not much trouble to get and good for six months. Actually the only people who have had trouble obtaining visas are the consular staff. I am still undecided as to where I will go after July 15. Will take a trip somewhere and see something new. No I am not going to the States just yet. I have written to the family that in the advent of my demise all papers and manuscripts are to [be] turned over to you and Ian for editing since no one else could do the job. And that any material published you should receive half the proceeds. There is enough material here for half a dozen novels. The past year I have been extremely active. So hang on to this letter. Not that I expect to be relieved here but you never know. Flying to Gibraltar tomorrow with Captain *Clark*. (Just found his name from an intersection note in *The Quiet American*)

Love
William Burroughs

WSB [Tangier] to Brion Gysin [Venice]

June 30, Tuesday St. Martial, 1964
% The American Consulate
Tangier

Dear Brion:

I do definitely wish to leave Tangier by the 15. I have two alternative plans: [Alex] Trocchi wants to see me. I want to see him and [Maurice] Girodias. So there is a possibility I may come to Paris mid-July for a week or so then Spain or Portugal or in fact any seaside place where I can work in isolation for a month. I am in no hurry about U.S. thinking in September terms rather than immediate. So unless you can definitely get here before the 15th I will plan to arrive in Paris on or about that date. (Alternatively, since I will most likely be close by, we can always arrange to meet). Please let me know if this suits your plans. I am most anxious to discuss with you a plan to publish a magazine about the length of *Time* in the *Time* format with your drawings and my text. The point is to find precise *intersection points between text and drawing.* I have already pointed out how this is done with *photographs* . . . ("Come along young man . . . show you around the dark room . . . show you thirteen years of gimmicks to learn . . . second reversed over and over . . . mirror image breaks out third goal" and so on . . . Now back in the furnished room file 1958 if my memory serves you wrote: "Fight tuberculosis folks" . . . An old junky selling Christmas seals on North <u>Clark</u> St. . . . The "Priest" they called him . . . And just *here* is a picture from *Newsweek*, May 15, 1964 . . . plane wreck . . . The "Priest" there hand lifted last rites for 44 air liner dead including Captain <u>Clark</u> (left) Left on North <u>Clark</u> St.). Well that was the first picture and after that I see them every time I pick up a newspaper . . . all here in the files . . . So after that I began to get *paintings.* "Over the last skyscrapers a silent kite . . . I can see the picture quite clearly from my balcony . . . full moon . . . violet evening sky . . . over the empty broken streets a red white and blue kite . . . old calendar picture . . .", I can take *any* prose and find the pictures. Now the examples I have given are of course simple *images* no doubt called into being by the words. Finding intersection points with your drawings is another problem. Of course I see areas from *The Soft Machine* . . . the Hot Grab people etcetera. But this is not precise enough. (The text I sent for your German exhibition that didn't occur didn't make it). Yes I am looking at the pictures now and answer is there but I haven't quite found it . . . (incidentally the first intersection picture was from your letter in regard to color writing *but this leaves poor A in the dark*. Some days later there was a photo of General MacArthur dying and big A on his dressing gown and Ian [Sommerville] said "That's poor A".) Do you have any suggestions? The job has to be done right. I feel I am close because I am seeing more scenes from the work I am doing now which is concerned with Mexico. Yes and here is one with the coast between Ceuta and Tétouan . . . Well think about this and about Paris . . . Ian is in Marrakech doing I don't know what . . . I have given up alcohol. Doesn't leave me anything to do but work

Love,

Bill

WSB [Tangier, Morocco] to Gus Blaisdell [Craig, Colorado]
July 9 (Thursday St. Blanche) 1964
% The American Consulate
Tangier, Morocco

Dear Gus Blaisdell:

Yes I did receive your last letter and was most interested in the ethnographic material. Do you speak Navaho? I studied under Prof [Clyde] Kluckhohn at Harvard who was a Navaho expert. What is the status of the Navaho now? Are they on a reservation? In the reprint of *Junkie* I had thought of retracing my steps with notes and intersections that might run to some length. Actually I do not have a copy of it but will order one from New York.

Yes Grove is bringing out *Nova Express* in September. I have just corrected the proofs. They rarely answer letters. Few publishers do. Any other business run in such a sloppy assed way would fold but they have some kind of monopoly whereby they can be as sloppy as they choose. 'Perfume Jack' is the invention of Jeff Nuttall, London. I have suggested to him that he expand the [comic] strip into a short book. Yes I think he would be interested in any proposal involving printing and distribution. *My Own Mag* was started by Mr Nuttall and I contributed to an early issue. This led to the guest issue of which I mailed you a copy. If there is any book shop that would handle it in Denver copies can be ordered from Mr. Nuttall. He brings out a new issue every few weeks. Does Alan Swallow[26] publish short pieces? If so I may have something.

I will look forward to seeing your Captain Samurai

Best Luck in the Theatres
William Burroughs

WSB [Tangier, Morocco] to Laura Lee and Mortimer Burroughs [Palm Beach, Florida]

August 26, 1964
% The American Consulate
Tangier, Morocco

Dear Mother and Dad:

The September issue of *Esquire* should be out now with the article and the picture of Billy. Have you seen it? Quite a good picture I think. I also have an article in the *Times Literary Supplement* August 6.. *The London Times* that is.. that might interest Billy.. How is he and what have you decided about the school? All his friends here send their very best. My affairs are looking good financially. I have 2000$ in the bank in Gibraltar another book coming out in N.Y. October. I may return to the U.S. at that time where I have a number of offers to give lectures at a fee of 500$ per. Seem to be earning a living at last. I intend to consult a good lawyer and straighten out legal details. This is most important since many writers through carelessness and neglect lose the rights on their work. The books that I have written to date could well provide Billy

---

26 Alan Swallow (1915–1966). Poet and publisher.

with a comfortable income for life. Please let me hear from you soon. Are you still thinking of moving to St. Louis?

> Love,
> Bill

WSB [Tangier, Morocco] to Alex Trocchi [London]
September 10, 1964
% The American Consulate
Tangier, Morocco

Dear Alex:

Antony Balch has been here making a film in which we all acted a continuation of *Towers Open Fire* so there has been what with one thing and another an acute shortage of time. I thank you for all your communications. I am sorry about the delay. Suggest you contact Antony and arrange to see the film when he has done the editing and cutting. He has made a number of most interesting technical developments since *Towers Open Fire* which will I think revolutionize the film industry. He will explain the technical side. The most revolutionary aspect is economic. We have a method of making films of more entertainment value than the films now being shown and produced at great expense for no more outlay than that necessary to cover the price of film stock and lab work. So back to Sigma. I must confess I am a little confused and would appreciate a precise brief run down on the activities of Sigma and the connection with the publishing enterprises you mention. I think that if the title *Moving Times* is used it should carry a byline for *My Own Mag* and that Nuttall should be consulted. I gather you are in touch? And what about this Heinemann thing swamped as I am with work and correspondence which keeps growing in view of my editorship on the *Moving Times* it does give me a shiver but I will do the job. Please let me know as close as you can judge what they want and what you contemplate etcetera. Must close now. You have my full support on Sigma and progeny. Please do contact Antony. I think the film will interest you.

> See You On Set
> William Burroughs

EDITOR'S NOTE: *Burroughs was unhappy when he learned that Ace Books planned to reissue* Junkie. *He felt that the publisher A. A. Wyn had not done a very good job the first time and hadn't kept up with payments or with reprints over the previous decade. For that purpose he contacted Allen Ginsberg's brother, Eugene Brooks, a lawyer, to act on his behalf in trying to resolve the matter.*

WSB [Tangier, Morocco] to Eugene Brooks [Long Island, New York]

September 28, 1964
% The U.S. Consulate
Tangier, Morocco

Dear Eugene Brooks:

I am willing for Wyn to go ahead with publication since the issue seems uncertain. What concerned me of course was the matter of royalties which has been to some extent cleared up and also the consideration as to whether they would do a good job. In this connection I have written to Mr. Wyn asking him to include in the American edition an article on the apomorphine treatment for addiction that appeared in the Italian edition. Since I owe my own cure and subsequent career to this method of treatment which has never been used or even tested in America I feel quite strongly on this point. That is I am holding the check uncashed until I learn what Wyn's intentions are on this point. If you could call him and explain that I am willing to withdraw my objections if he includes that article which I feel is essential to the work. I thank you very much for your efforts on my behalf and I certainly feel that you are entitled to submit a bill for your professional services (I don't know whether Allen made it clear). I will look forward to hearing from you in regard to this matter

Cordially Yours
William Burroughs

WSB [Tangier, Morocco] to Carl Solomon[27] [Bronx, NY]
Oct. 11, 1964
c/o U.S. Consulate
Tangier, Morocco

Dear Carl,

Very glad to hear you are well again and I hope infusing some life into the Wyn publishing company [i.e., Ace Books]. I understand they are bringing out *Junkie* again (they might have consulted me. I would have contributed some notes revisions etcetera that would have added to the interest and sales as well). I am most concerned that they should include as an introduction or appendix the long article I wrote on the apomorphine treatment that appeared in the Italian edition. (This is *not* the article that appeared in *Evergreen*.) Since I do not have a copy of the article in English it would have to be translated from the Italian unless Dr. [Fernanda] Pivano still has the copy I sent her. I hope you can persuade Wyn to include this article since this is the only treatment for addiction that works. I owe my own cure and subsequent career to the apomorphine treatment and the article would lend dignity and purpose to the publication. Please let me hear from you again with all best wishes for your continued health I am

William S. Burroughs

WSB [Tangiers, Morocco] to Ian Sommerville [England]
November 6, [1964] Friday

Dear Ian:

Would have written sooner but have been working round the speaking clock on developments from your parting suggestions: sighted photos with which I have produced montages that have surprised even Brion [Gysin]. Going through the files I came across an old mark up you did a long time ago: "How close were

---

27 Carl Solomon (1928–1994). Author and friend to whom Allen Ginsberg addressed his poem *Howl*. Solomon worked for Ace Books; A. A. Wyn was his uncle.

you Clem?", Billy The Kid. "Just about as close as shifting layers of smoke." "That's might close, Clem" Bayswater 1937 Old Arch remember? Following this mark up I have been cutting out bits of text old letters etcetera pasting photos and blocks of text in copies of my books (*Nova Express* now out) a photo for every page of diary always using when possible original materials rather than retyped matter and so finding a use for all the old texts and photos. I hope the two pages enclosed will give you an idea. The scrap books of which I now have three and the copies of my books with photos and text inserted should be saleable for good prices to rare book collectors and dealers. Brion has an offer to push the dream machine in New York $1500 down for expenses. He is writing to you. Needless to say there is great deal you could do on this photographic work. My plan is to hit London towards the end of this month and hope we can meet there. Then on to the States (I have an offer from *Playboy* to write an article on "Return to St. Louis"). Brion has sold $400 worth of pictures here. Things look good financially. If you do decide to come along I could offer you a definite salary plus percentage. I am going to look for headquarters in the States and it may be in St. Louis. Hope these two pages will interest you and cheer you up. (Notice the arch in the photo. It is in Gibraltar and has 1899 stone written on it)

All The Best
Bill

**WSB [Tangier, Morocco] to Laura Lee and Mortimer
Burroughs [Palm Beach, Florida]**
November 9, 1964
% U.S. Consulate
Tangier, Morocco

Dear Mother and Dad:

Last month has been one dead line after the other and I have fallen behind in my correspondence. My new novel *Nova Express* is out. *Newsweek* says I am basically an old fashioned fire and brimstone preacher. The Reverend Lee rides again. I am leaving here the end of this month for a short trip to England and from there to the States. I have an assignment with *Playboy* to do an article on "Return To St. Louis". I intend to cover the old Berlin Avenue naborhood and evoke some old time nostalgia. Maryland Market, Forest Park, Forest Park Highlands, etcetera. Actually I may buy a place in the Ozarks to use as a permanent base of operations. Will spend a short time in New York then St. Louis after that I don't know but not back here I am tired of Tangier. What happened about Billy's school? Looks like I will be spending Christmas in St. Louis and we might all meet there like the song say.

Love
Bill

WSB [Tangier, Morocco] to [Rives Matthews?] [St. Louis, Missouri?]
November 9, 1964
% The American Consulate
Tangier, Morocco

Dear Old Nabor:

I have been so busy the past few months that I have fallen way behind with my correspondence. What has kept me so occupied derives from your scrap book and visiting card tray which gave me an idea for a new method of presentation namely the scrap book format, pieces of old letters, text, photos, etcetera. I now have assignment from *Playboy* to cover the old St. Louis naborhood. "Return to St. Louis" the piece will be called. I could certainly use your help. Plan to make St. Louis by Christmas and spend some months there. Tangier is very dull now and I am ready to leave and in no hurry to come back. Peter Broomfield's sentence was reduced from five years to six months and he is about due out, the other characters involved already out, I think, you could quite safely return by next spring or summer. The piece I wrote from your scrap book (I showed it to you remember?) has been published in London and I have heard many favorable comments. Will send along signed copy if you are interested to have it. So meet me in St. Louis meet me at the fair don't tell me the lights are shining any place but there. Hope you are keeping well and see you soon I hope

Best Regards From The Old
Naborhood
William Burroughs

WSB [Tangiers, Morocco] to Ian Sommerville [England]
November 17, 1964
% The American Consulate,
Tangier Morocco

Dear Ian:

Owing to the *Playboy* assignment to do a St. Louis "Return" which would leave me very little time in England I have decided to postpone the trip to England and have made a reservation on *The Independence* sailing November 30 from Algeciras. (God knows when you will get this. Confirmed the reservation. Abandon trip to England.) Now that I have been experimenting with intersection pictures to illustrate passages from my writing, I will try to perfect slide readings that is a package performance that can be set up anywhere. For example if I was reading in St. Louis I would get my intersection pictures from St. Louis go out and find the Osteopathic Clinic etcetera and read the text to slides (or tape it) or perhaps an interchange of tape and reading always using local pictures on the slides in this way it is brought home the audience is it not?? And when a picture is taken a recording is made. This may consist of dialogue or street noises etcetera. For example, "See the chains are fallen. Long long radio silence on Portland Place". Now Portland Place is a private place as they are called in St. Louis, that is at each end of the street are chains stretched across to which the residents have a key or some old flunky is on duty to let the chains down so we get the right picture of Portland Place with its chains down. I think the financial possibilities are considerable you understand its like spoon fed nostalgia. Of course I would need your help and hope you are interested. I think Brion has written you about the dream machine possibilities. Unlimited according to Harold Matson who is the most in New York agents.[28] I will leave Tangier the 26 to spend a few days in Gibraltar. After that address is % Grove Press, 80 University Place, New York, N.Y. U.S.A.

Love

Bill

WSB [Tangier, Morocco] to John Calder [London]
November 18, 1964
% The American Consulate
Tangier, Morocco

Dear John:

Owing to an assignment to do an article for *Playboy* entitled "Return to St. Louis" which I can not afford to pass up I have decided to delay my trip to England probably until early Spring. There is not much point in making the trip if I can only stay a few days. *Nova Express* is now out and I intend to give some readings and lectures on that novel in the course of which I should perfect a method of presentation so when I do arrive in England I will have a very clear idea of exactly how to proceed. I will be leaving here November 26 and arrive in New York December 6. Of course I will see Barney [Rosset] and find out what he intends to do about the English publication of *Nova Express*. If the book is out in England by the time I get there the trip would be that much more productive. Sorry about this delay but I think in the long run a later visit will be better timed. Best to Arthur [Boyars] and Marion [Boyars]

Sincerely

William Burroughs

---

28 Harold Matson (1898–1988). American literary agent.

WSB [Tangier, Morocco] to Barney Rosset [New York]
[ca. late November 1964]

Dear Barney:

I am sailing for New York on the Independence American Export Lines arrive New York Dec. 8, 8.30 A.M. Look forward to seeing you as there are a number of things I want to talk over with you. Please hold all mail for my arrival. I would appreciate it if you could ask your secretary to phone the Hotel Chelsea on 23rd Street and make a reservation room with bath for a week beginning Dec. 8. See you soon best regards to all the staff.

Sincerely
William Burroughs

WSB [on board S.S. *Independence*] to Allen Ginsberg [New York]
S.S. Independence
Dec 1, 1964

Dear Allen,

Arriving New York Dec 8, will be staying at the Hotel Chelsea. Plan to remain in New York about ten days and then to St. Louis where I have assignment with *Playboy* to do a "Return to St. Louis" piece. You remember Larbi [Layachi][29] who used to work for Stewart [Gordon?] and Ira [Cohen], wrote or talked Paul's [Bowles] latest book *A Life Full of Holes*? Well he is on board here headed for the new world fame and fortune. See you in Chelsea.

All the Best
Bill B.

---

29 Larbi Layachi. Moroccan storyteller and friend of Paul Bowles.

WSB [New York] to Neil Abercrombie [San Rafael, California]

December 22, 1964
% Grove Press
80 University Press
New York City

Mr. Neil Abercrombie
Deputy Probation Officer
County of Marin
Room 103, Courthouse
San Rafael, Calif.

Dear Mr. Abercromie [*sic*: Abercrombie]:

In regard to your letter of inquiry with regard to the apomorphine treatment: The English doctor who used this treatment was Doctor John Dent. The treatment is described in all detail-dosage etcetera in his book *Anxiety And Its Treatment* published by Skeffington. This book can be ordered through Foyle's Bookstore on Shaftsbury Avenue in London.

I have sent a number of addicted patients to Doctor Dent over a period of years and all agree that the apomorphine treatment is the only treatment that works by removing the need for narcotics or alcohol. Doctor Dent is dead now but Doctor Peter Kelly of London is carrying on his practice. I notice that Dr. M.M. Maidman, Southland Sanitarium, Los Angeles is a member of the British Society for the Study of Addiction and may be able to supply you with information. Other doctors who have used the treatment over a period of years are Doctor Xavier Coore, Neuilly on Seine, Paris, France and Doctor Harry Feldman, Geneva, Switzerland. Apomorphine is issued in an oral form for sublingual administration by the Chabre Chemical Company in France and these tablets are particularly convenient. The dosage varies with the individual, but the oral tablets can be given one twentieth grain every hour. The treatment usually takes about six to eight days during which time no sleeping pills or sedatives are given since sedatives tend to reverse the action of apomorphine. I would like to stress that apomorphine is in no sense an aversion treatment and it works just

as well if no vomiting occurs. Apomorphine is a metabolic regulator that acts to normalize disturbed metabolism and when this is
accomplished the use of apomorphine can be discontinued. No case
of addiction to apomorphine has ever been recorded. If there is any
further information I can give you I will be glad to do so. Wishing
you every success with your program.

Sincerely,

William S. Burroughs

*EDITOR'S NOTE: Burroughs wrote the following letter in the style of a
cut-up and in the form of newspaper columns. It was very much like the
work that appears in Nuttall's* My Own Mag.

WSB [St. Louis, Missouri] to Jeff Nuttall [London]

Dec. 29, [1964] Tuesday was the last day for singing years.

Dear Jeff Nuttall,

I have as you can see been traveling so have not written before.
Thanks for the book of poems secular and profane and here I am
back in Huckleberry Finn country (but the baked potatoes are
YUM delicious with sour cream here suit and boots need tidying in
show business Italian suit and cowboy boots do not open til Christmas day slithery like grounded eel WOW! Mr. Browne said its a
term she used. there at the back of the cupboard (why not now—the
key—why go ahead—of doing it?) Now you know I live with Dicky
Stern the light is getting thin, Blackout falling. las days bye for now)
    sawski boots ..crooning cowboy.. that rebought branch of Ital-
ian air? Brown attempted to make such a deal with plants and animals over thousands of years ..WOW.. Old Mother Hubbard went
to the cupboard to get the poor dog in the family he was known
simply as the dog.. Blackout falling.. naborhood bar for the dog..
sawski boots crooning back to that rebought Italian air? sour cream
here dying in Italian years WOW! ..Old Mother Hubbard show
business went to the cupboard to get the cowboy boots dog in the
family he was known when he said that.. blackout falling Christmas day slithery hood bar for the dog boots a drunk policeman

back to that rebought Italian grounded eel.. WOW, Mister!! Air!! ..dying in Italian.. race of years.. WOW!!.. Old show sheep have fun.. It's a business

Enclose layout showing how word and image virus gets from there to here on intersections R.R. crossing an extension of the collage back to the old paste and scissors.. What did I you whoever mean when he said that?? a drunk policeman? A race of sheep? Have fun in Omaha along the Hudson gets too profane and here I am back in R.R. Huckleberry Finn country crossing an extension of baked potatoes are YUM delicious with the collage back to sour cream here suit and boots need old paste and scissors dying in Italian show business (Suit and cowboy boots do not open when he said that?/ til Christmas day slithery like a drunk policeman? A grounded eel WOW Mr. Browne said 'Race of sheep?' have fun.. its a term she used there in Omaha along the Hudson back of the cupboard.. why not now and here.. why go ahead.. I am back in, Huck..berry country..crossing.. the light is getting thin.. he was known when he said that back of cupboard

Bye for now
Bill B.

UBRUBRUBRUB+++&++++&++&&&&&""&"+++

UBRUBRUBRUBOUTOUTOUTOUTOUT#"#+++++#

UBRUBRUBRUBOUTOUTOUTOUTOUT####&&&&

""&&&+++++"OUTOUTOUTOUTOUT"""""""&&&

1965 ""+OUTOUTOUTOUTOUT"+"+"&&&

HETHETHETHETHETHETHE+++###+++&&+++

HETHETHETHETHETHETHE&&&&&+++++++++#

HETHETHETHEWORDSWORDSWORDSWORDSTHE

###&&"&"&"&WORDSWORDSWORDSWORDS"+++

WSB [New York] to the *Sunday Times* Editor [London]
January 17, 1965
Sunday Times
To The Editor

Sir,

It is my general practice to disregard the attacks of my creeping opponents with regard to my own work and my own person however intemperate these attacks may be. When, however, an attempt is made by snide innuendo to belittle the work of Dr. John Yerbury Dent, a great man and a great doctor, I can throw around a few adjectives myself. I refer to the remarks of Doctor Alfred Byrne quoted in the *Sunday Times*, November 15, 1964 in an item entitled "Author On How He Beat Drug Addiction" by an anonymous reporter. "30 years ago" Doctor Byrne begins by describing Dr. Dent as "a London doctor of modest qualifications." If he were alive today Dr. Dent might well agree that his qualifications were since he was a modest man unlike Doctor Byrne who presumes to pass on the qualifications of a man who gave 30 years to the study of addiction and to the treatment of alcoholics and drug addicts with somewhat more than modest success as his many cured patients can testify. He was also chairman of The British Society for the Study of Addiction and editor of the *British Journal of Addiction* which Doctor Byrne does not mention and goes on to give a misleading and inaccurate account of the apomorphine treatment. Apomorphine does *not* work by "allaying anxiety" but by *regulating* metabolism so the patient does not *need* alcohol or narcotics nor does he need to continue the use of apomorphine. No case of addiction to apomorphine has ever been recorded. The apomorphine treatment is described in detail in Dr. Dent's book *Anxiety And Its Treatment* published by Skeffington. (Notice that Doctor Byrne makes no mention of this book). Latterly Doctor Byrne continues, "Latterly Dr. Dent, who became something of an amateur psychiatrist, extended the apomorphine treatment to narcotic addition". This is a blatant misrepresentation as anyone who knew Dr. Dent can testify. Dr. Dent did not believe in or practice any form of so called psychotherapy. As he frequently and emphatically stated he considered addiction to alcohol or any drug a *metabolic illness* that could be cured by *regulating* the metabolism with apomorphine. Dr. Dent had used the apomorphine treatment for morphine and heroin addiction for some 15 years at the time I first went to him for treatment in 1956. Precisely how do you define "latterly" Doctor Byrne? Doctor Byrne concludes ungrammatically with this sentence, "He even claimed it was effective in some cases of 'addiction' to smoking, eating and neurotic habits as indeed it might by suggestion."

If Doctor Byrne has reservations as to the value of the apomorphine treatment and as to the qualifications of Dr. Dent why doesn't he come out like a man and state these reservations and the facts if any on which they are based? Obviously because he is writing to create disinterest and switch off discussion of the apomorphine treatment. I find his smirking sentences reeking as they do of a smug and unctuous self-satisfaction ill-intentioned dishonest cowardly and therefore disgusting. Dr. Dent is dead and can not answer for himself. His many patients can answer for him. The doctors who have used the apomorphine treatment can also answer. The treatment has been used for many years by Dr. Feldman in Switzerland and by Dr. Xavier Corre of Paris. In a recent conversation with Dr. Corre he told me he considered apomorphine an extremely useful drug in general practice indicated in many conditions other than addiction. Apomorphine is *not* an aversion treatment and the experience of Dr. Dent and Dr. Corre has demonstrated that equally good results are obtained in cases where no nausea occurs.

William S. Burroughs

EDITOR'S NOTE: Once again Burroughs decided to try to correct the financial mess that had been created by the Olympia Press' mishandling of his royalties. The decision was made to try to keep up with the business part of professional writing in the future.

WSB [New York] to John Calder [London]

February 1, 1965
% Grove Press
80 University Place
NYC, N.Y.

Dear John,

I gather that there has been no court action on *Naked Lunch* to date. In any case I could hardly undertake the expense of a trip to England and return just to testify that is, to say things that others could say with perhaps more weight [than] the writer himself being so obviously the interested party.

I have retained an accountant to prepare my income tax returns and generally straighten out my accounts and in this connection I would appreciate receiving from you the statements on the sales of *Dead Fingers Talk*. The Swiss arrangement with Maurice [Girodias] has been terminated and the two thirds of all royalties and advances is to be sent directly to me. (Whatever arrangement Maurice wants to make on his third is his concern). I believe also there is an advance due on *Naked Lunch*. I would appreciate hearing from you in this connection since I want to straighten out a situation already extremely confused largely due to Maurice's devious arrangements.

I received the letter from the Scotsman and will write the article in question as soon as possible, that is within the next week. Please give my best regards to Marion and Arthur [Boyars]. I still owe Marion an account from the apartment which she can deduct from whatever is due me

All The Best
William Burroughs

EDITOR'S NOTE: Ian Sommerville had intended to come to America to stay with Burroughs, but worried that he might not be granted a long-term visa. Burroughs wasn't certain how long he would stay in the States, so he tried to talk Ian into a shorter visit. In the end Som-

merville never made it to New York, and when Burroughs returned many months later, their relationship had cooled and was never quite the same again.

WSB [New York] to Ian Sommerville [London]
Feb. 16, 1965
% Grove Press
80 University Place
NYC, N.Y., USA

Dear Ian:

Enclose $500 in travelers checks made out to you. The set up here looks very good, that is I can get any number of engagements to read. I have given one performance with reading, Boujeloud[1] music and a tape at a theatre here which is run by friends and provided with excellent equipment. What I want to add is an image track of slides or flashes of moving film. We have cameras etcetera at our disposal. We could also use the dream machine in these performances which would expedite its use on a commercial scale. I suggest that you plan to come by boat which is cheaper and by then I should have an apartment or loft. (If you could pick up the slides and tape from Mr. O'Conner we could use them but don't bother if it is complicated) — I suggest you apply for a simple tourist visa this trip which will give you a chance to look around and if you decide you want to stay you can re-enter on a resident visa.. Look forward to see you.. Brion [Gysin] send love

Love
Bill

P.S. In process of applying for visa and entering the U.S. the less said about me the better..

---

1 Boujeloud. Music of the Moroccan Sufis of Joujouka.

WSB [New York] to Ian Sommerville [England]

March 9, 1965
% Grove Press
80 University Place
NYC, N.Y., USA

Dear Ian:

I had already learned of your visa difficulties through Antony [Balch] who is here as you know. Well we will arrange it one way or another. I am set up at last with a roomy loft where I can really get something done. I will buy two tape recorders. I certainly wish you were here as things are really moving. Stuart Church just passed through New York on his way back to Tangier. Conrad Rooks is about and so busy with his movie into which he put $350,000 that he isn't such a vampire. He made a documentary of all 48 states which takes 15 hours to see it all. By sheer footage of course he got some good shots. Brion has sold $1000 worth of pictures and we are going to do a book together for Grove, a really exhaustive book of methods. I enclose transcript of the last words of Dutch Schultz. I made a tape cutting the last words in with some newspaper material yielding some interesting results or correlations at any rate.. Next day a big factory fire in N.J.—"fire— factory he was nowhere near" — the grease ducts in a restaurant caught fire—"Come on open the soap ducts" — So be a little careful with these words they are really hot.. "Watch out for Jimmy Valentine for he is an old pal of mine."

Love
Bill

WSB [New York] to Ian Sommerville [England]
March 22, 1965
% Grove Press
80 University Place
NYC, N.Y., USA

Dear Ian:

I have seen the Tangier shots with superimpositions and both Brion [Gysin] and I are extremely enthusiastic. Shots which might not have looked like anything in the rushes for example the scene on the balcony where I am passing the headphones to the Commander and back come across very well with the superimposition, the scene in the Commander's boat gets all the old 1920 smuggler movies, the cockatoo is great you can feel the sea wind on the terrace there and the loops of the Socco Chico are fantastic. We are going ahead with shots here and Antony [Balch] should leave with enough material for a full length movie. I only wish you were here to help out with the sound track and to play in the New York scenes as I saw you in the dream arriving on the *Queen Mary*. Does there seem to be any possibility of your making it here soon? If not I will try to make it to London late spring or early summer.

The dream machine is getting publicity but as yet not any concrete returns. The latest is to merchandise it as a dream machine and nothing else so busy executives can relax in their offices. It was to be on TV but the technicians decided it would blow out all the expensive tubes so that has been cancelled. Did you get the last words of Dutch Schultz? Please let me hear from you

Love,
Bill

WSB [New York] to Ian Sommerville [London]
April 12, 1965
% Grove Press
80 University Place
NYC

Dear Ian:

Enclose $100. Yes I received the [Hotel] Rushmore letters and most gratified to find you in a good state of mind. Antony [Balch] will be back in London in a day or so with almost full length film. He will do some more shots in London so you can shoot the harbor scene now. Brion [Gysin] did a huge picture of the New York sky line with Antony taking the process then rolled it up—"the Piper pulled down the sky" .. Also clinic shot with Bruce Holbrook [later he calls him Wellbrook], Chinatown, etcetera.

At Los Alamos[2] I won a prize for the greatest improvement. This radioactive laurel I now pass along to Mr. Conrad Rooks. His film — peyote ceremonies, carnivals, etcetera — is a gas and so is he now that he has come into his fortune and stays busy all the time. Last week I acted in a gangster sequence for him — 1930 black Cadillac *real* revolvers and a tommy gun — loaded with blanks of course.. I mowed Conrad down with the tommy gun and visa versa, what an instrument great fun. Well the wind up is he had a beef with his camera man Robert Frank[3] several days previously, called in some character didn't know his ass from a light meter and underexposed the lot. "Little Nero" that the part Conrad took is fit to be tied and will shoot the whole sequence again. Jock Livingston was here and has also made a film in Amsterdam that sounds like Antony's film.[4] A friend of his wants me to act in a film-with-pay this summer. If this deal comes through I will see you in England or Paris. Could certainly use your assistance here meanwhile I am swamped with work and don't have time for various experiments

2 Los Alamos Ranch School, New Mexico. Burroughs was sent to boarding school in Los Alamos as a young boy. During World War II it was turned into a top-secret laboratory where the atomic bomb was developed.
3 Robert Frank (b. 1924). Photographer and filmmaker.
4 The experimental film, released in 1966, was called *Zero in the Universe*.

I would like to try on the tape recorder and on synchronizing precisely tapes and photos.. My best to Michael [Portman] see you soon I hope

Love

Bill

WSB [New York] to Neil Abercrombie [San Rafael, California]

April 20, 1965
210 Centre St.
NYC, N.Y.

Mr. Neil Abercrombie
Room 103
Courthouse
San Rafael, Calif.

Dear Mr. Abercrombie:

I was always dubious of Synanon's[5] inspirational and quasi-religious approach to what seems to me a metabolic illness but had not realized the pernicious potentials of this organization to further confuse the whole narcotics issue. To counter any attack on the apomorphine treatment it is essential to stress that it is *not an aversion treatment.* In fact the dosage can be so regulated that no nausea occurs and the results are the same: a regulation and normalizing of metabolism so that the patient no longer needs alcohol or narcotics. Doctor Dent gave apomorphine by injection and this almost always causes some nausea. However Doctor Xavier Coore, Paris, who speaks and writes English incidentally, has used apomorphine sublingually with equally good results. A twentieth grain tablet may be administered every hour or in some cases every half hour day and night for four days without nausea and in this period of time even quite severe cases of addiction can be brought under control. That is at the end of four days the patient himself realizes that he is virtually free of withdrawal symptoms, that he is not dependent on

---

5   Synanon. A drug rehabilitation program that morphed into an alternative lifestyle cult.

any form of sedative. It can not be too emphatically stated that no case of addiction to apomorphine has ever been recorded. It is also very important to avoid the use of any sedative drugs such as barbiturates, paraldehyde, chloral, etcetera, since these drugs reverse the action of apomorphine and conduce to relapse. It is much better to give small amounts of opiates if this is absolutely necessary.

I have managed to interest some New York doctors in the apomorphine treatment. Doctor John Bishop, New York City, reports excellent results with the use of apomorphine in general practice. He intends to use apomorphine in the treatment of addicts and will let me know the results. If there is any further information I can give you please let me know. I am convinced that the apomorphine treatment and especially the synthesis and variation of this apomorphine formula could end the narcotics problem. I enclose transcript of a talk I gave at the American Psychological Association 1961 in which I indicate that apomorphine can be useful in many states of disturbed metabolism other than chronic intoxications. I will be most interested to hear what progress you are making and will keep you informed of any developments here

Yours Truly

William Burroughs

WSB [New York] to John Calder [London]

April 20, 1965
210 Centre St.
NYC, N.Y. USA

Dear John:

More than two years ago when Maurice [Girodias] put $5500 of my money into his stupidly dishonest pocket I requested that he terminate the Hummel arrangement. He agreed to do so and I think I told you of the altered arrangement. In any case neither Maurice nor Odette Hummel is authorized by me to receive one cent or to act for me in any way whatever from here on out. The simple reason being that any money sent to Hummel goes straight into Girodias's pocket. I am taking legal action to recover all rights from Maurice. Meanwhile have been negotiating foreign contracts directly. Pending a legal decision Maurice should still receive his one third of royalties and advances minus, of course, the last $1500 he has misappropriated. That is the situation. Money can be sent % Grove Press. As you know I wrote Barney [Rosset] on a number of occasions asking him to give you a contract on *Nova Express*. When I returned to America from Tangier he informed me that he had offered the book to Jonathan Cape as he is entitled to do under the contract. I was in no position to argue since I would have starved to death last year if it had not been for the advances paid by Barney. (My father is now dead and my mother living on a very small income so that my sole means of support now comes from my writing.)

I have not heard whether Jonathan Cape has decided to publish the book or not and asked Barney to give you the contract if they do not take it. I am sorry about this but there is nothing further I can do. My best to Marion and Arthur [Boyars]. As regards the foreign rights I must straighten out the already tangled legal aspects before making a decision. I will have a talk with my lawyer next week and write you again at that time..

Best Regards,
William Burroughs

WSB [New York] to Maurice Girodias [Paris]
April 30, 1965
210 Centre St.
NYC, N.Y., USA

Dear Maurice:
    You will recall that at the time when you were unable to pay me the royalties of $5000 from Grove — a contingency which brought me in absolute need of money to pay food and rent — I asked you to terminate the Hummel arrangement and you said that you would do so. What I also sought from you at that time and did not obtain was a recasting of our contracts to clearly set forth a termination of the Hummel arrangement and a clarification of the conditions

Mortimer P. Burroughs Sr.,
WSB's father, circa 1908.

Laura Lee Burroughs, WSB's
mother, circa 1918.

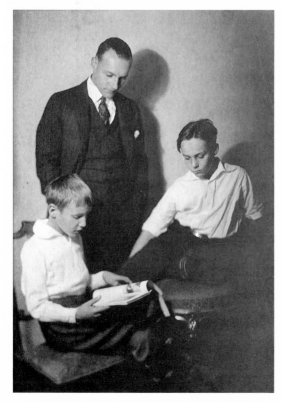

From left to right:
WSB, Mortimer
Burroughs Sr., and
WSB's brother,
Mortimer Burroughs Jr.,
circa 1920.

William S.
Burroughs Jr.,
WSB's son,
in front of the
fireplace at
Christmastime,
circa 1951.

William S. Burroughs Jr., circa 1954.

WSB in the
Grand Socco
market. Tangier,
1957.

On the beach
in Tangier, 1957.
From left to right:
Jack Kerouac,
Peter Orlovsky,
and WSB.

WSB in his garden
at Hotel Muniria.
Tangier, 1957.

Allen Ginsberg in
the Socco Chico.
Tangier, 1957.

Paris, 1959. *From left to right:* Ian Sommerville, Sinclair Beiles, Bill Belli, and Brion Gysin.

Paris, 1959. *From left to right:* Sinclair Beiles, Ian Sommerville, Madame Rachou, Brion Gysin, and Bill Belli.

A photograph of a building in London with street number 23, taken by WSB, 1960s. Burroughs often walked around cities by himself, photographing buildings and signs as "sets" for his mental scenes. Twenty-three is a number that Burroughs considered mysteriously significant.

A cut-up collage on a glass-topped desk, by WSB, 1960s.

Fabrizio Mondadori,
a member of the
Mondadori publishing
family, Paris, 1960.

Sinclair Beiles in front of a poster for "The General Union for the Blind
and Gravely Ill of France and from Overseas," Paris, 1960.

WSB at La Palette, rue de Seine, Paris, 1959.

of contract for the protection of both parties.. For example the new version of the *Soft Machine*? What would prevent me from selling this work under a different title? In short it would have been as much to your advantage as to mine to have sat down with a lawyer and drawn up some sensible, clear comprehensive contracts. You refused to do this. And I now find out that you did not terminate the Hummel arrangement. Calder informs me that the advance on *Naked Lunch* was paid to Hummel, July 23, 1964, and I have not received my share of this money. In short once again the Hummel arrangement has resulted in money due me being indefinitely delayed. If it had not been for advances made by Barney I would literally have starved to death this past year since my family is no longer in a position to give me any financial aid, in fact I may well have to contribute to the support of my mother.. However I have not taken nor do I contemplate the same legal action as that taken by [Mason] Hoffenberg etcetera. Mr Rembar's letter was simply another attempt to clarify the contracts which are now in a state of almost intractable confusion so that no one knows who owns what and I have been left with no alternative except to deal directly with foreign publishers some of whom —notably Bonnier — complain that you have ignored letters of inquiry with regard to the book and have written me to ask how they could secure the rights. The situation is further complicated by a bitter feud between [John] Calder and [Barney] Rosset which of course brings once again in question the validity of our original contracts. I simply will not be drawn into these publisher quarrels. I intend to get an agent and a lawyer — parties involved and see if something can be done to straighten this whole mess out. As Calder will tell you I have always insisted that your third of the foreign rights should be paid and I have the same intention with regard to other foreign rights whether I have made the arrangements or not. I am well aware of my initial obligation to you and I am not trying to cut you out of what is due you.

Sincerely

William Burroughs

As regards the Japanese rights I suggest that you either refer them to me or that we draw up a short agreement that the advances and royalties are to be paid directly to me and not to Hummel.

WSB [New York] to Ian Sommerville [London]
May 19, 1965
210 Centre St.
NYC, N.Y., USA

Dear Ian:

I have sent a manuscript to Jeff Nuttall, a Dutch Schultz issue based on the no. 23[6] and asked him to get in touch with you. The numbers racket also known as the policy racket was simply an illegal lottery based on the United States Treasury Cash Statement of which I enclose a sample. These figures which vary of course from day to day where the winning numbers, the last numbers being the numbers to win as in any other lottery. Note the figures come from the *Treasury Department* which is also the Narcotics Department. "I even got it from the department". It would uh seem to me that certain uh *mathematical* angles were uh inextricably involved.

Brion [Gysin] and I are working on a definitive book of methods to be called *Right Where You Are Sitting Now*. Cut ups, fold ins, tapes, intersection reading, newspaper formats, the Dutchman, etcetera. Last picture Dutch Schultz slumped over a table in The Palace Bar in a palace in a palace in a palace. "For half a line no repeat performance in any naborhood bar". I mean when this job is finished I am taking a vacation. Okay I am all through. Can't do another thing. So most likely I will be making a trip to Europe in July and see you there then when if. Can't tell you how bad things look here. *Nova Express* word for word. "What are we waiting for? Why not bomb Peking *now*?" "The American people stand solidly behind [Lyndon] Johnson with the exception of a few Communists bums and beatniks". "Why stop in Santo Domingo? Why not take care of Castro while we are about it?" "Anyone who criticizes the Vietnam policy should be tried for treason". "We can finish off Chinese Communism in a hurry and if Russia intervenes

---

6   Burroughs had become fascinated with the number 23, which seemed to pop up everywhere in his life. He wrote that he couldn't pick up a newspaper without seeing the number 23. When he arrived in New York he lived at the Chelsea Hotel on Twenty-third Street and talked about the term *23 skidoo*. As a result of his interest, he invented the Secret Council of the 23 and the Academy 23 among other numerically based ideas.

we can take care of that nation as well". And so forth. These are actual word for word quotes from the *Daily News* and the *Journal American*. "The Ugly American fading out in Ewyork Onolulu Aris Ome ston. Even uglier were summoned". Obviously they are waiting for a nod from Russia whereupon they will attack China set up an emergency government and teach these bums beatniks and dirty writers to act like decent Americans. Like I say it don't look good. And I have one apomorphine potential after the other shot out from under me. A doctor here who was interested — line went dead. A probation officer in California — line went dead. "You'll never get the apomorphine formulae in time". Yep its all there in *Nova Express* word for stupid ugly word.

I now have two tape recorders a Wollensak and a portable Martell. I would appreciate any suggestions on how to use this equipment. I have enlisted seven good boys here ready to follow instructions with camera and recorder but we need some precise technical instructions. How does your two tape recorder process work? (Bruce Wellbrook [*sic*: Holbrook] is one of my boys. He has a Martell and a camera. Unfortunately he also has a wife). Meanwhile we have been getting some results with the old methods. (I am sending you under separate cover a publication with my Palm Sunday Tape. I made this tape on Sunday and did not receive news of the tornados until the following day. I did however record the short wave static on Sunday which must have been actual short wave broadcasts from the tornado area.) I wonder if you could send me a sample tape from your two tape recorder battery? I will send you a copy of the Palm Sunday static and a selection from other tapes. This static could be used for sound effects in the movie as for example when I am talking to the Commander in his cabin. Are you in touch with Antony [Balch]? I enclose $100 for expenses.

Love
Bill B.

WSB [New York] to Antony Balch [London]
May 19, 1965
% Grove Press
80 University Place
NYC, N.Y., USA

Dear Antony:

Sending you *Time*. A very good job seems like to me. I now have two tape recorders a Wollensak and a portable Martell and have been doing quite a number of experiments with sound effects. On Palm Sunday I made a tape of the tornadoes here and there which I found out Monday. Well I recorded short wave static from the radio that day which must have been actual broadcasts from the tornado area. This tape of static would make proper sound effects for the scene in the Commander's cabin, for the scene where we are trading head phones on the balcony. For the opening scene in Paris would suggest Recalling All Active Agents with a background of static. I will have a copy of the Palm Sunday static tape made and send it along to you. Can you think of any other sound effects from New York you would like me to pick up? I now have several assistants I can send out for recordings pictures etcetera.. Bruce [Holbrook] for one who also has a Martell. He has been most helpful despite handicap weight of the other half.. (Who is about ready to stick a knife in your correspondent at this point).. Brion [Gysin] and I are getting along with the book of methods to be called *Right Where You Are Sitting Now*.. I need some stills from the movie — about 3 by 4 — The Murphy bed.. shutting the bureau drawer.. the Commander's cabin.. "Hello there young guy" from the clinic.. Also the Bruce climax shot.. Brion's New York skyline.. In fact a selection of the painting and roller shots would be extremely useful in the book we are doing.. the old clinic in Tangier.. You see I want to include a number of examples of film diary with the *precise* intersection picture that goes with it.. Are you in touch with Ian [Sommerville]?

I may be coming to Europe during July. I have an offer to act in a film in November. This offer coming through Jock Livingston with whom I would co-star in a film called *The Death Compass* based on a story by Jorge Borges.. In any case I need a vacation. So will be seeing you soon I hope

All The Best,
W.B.

WSB [New York] to Ian Sommerville [London]
July 2, 1965
210 Centre St.
NYC, N.Y., USA

Dear Ian:

I hope you have an address by now and wish you would keep in touch. I can send you some money each month but not without an address. Brion [Gysin] and I have been working full time on a book of methods to be called *Right Where You Are Sitting Now*, an illustrated deluxe job to sell for $10 more or less. Complicated and difficult and I am really tired of working. We should be finished in a month. Then I will come to Europe most likely and Brion of course wants to go to Morocco. What are your plans? I understand the Albert Hall reading was a real botch what with Sigma and such.[7] Please write me what happened.

Love
Bill

WSB [New York] to Antony Balch [London]
July 2, 1965

Dear Anthony:

Yes received the other pictures.. excellent excellent Brion [Gysin] and I have been working like on the method book *Right Where You Are Sitting Now* no time to breathe.. I am writing up

---

7 On June 11, 1965, a gigantic poetry reading was staged at London's Albert Hall. Billed as the International Poetry Incarnation, it featured Allen Ginsberg, Gregory Corso, Lawrence Ferlinghetti, Alex Trocchi, and others with a tape of William Burroughs played to the audience.

the movie section now and we should have the whole job finished in another two weeks.. Have you seen Ian [Sommerville]? I sent him a tape of a reading I gave here called Puerto de Los Santos.. Port of Saints which I suggest as title for the movie. When you hear the tape you will see how it fits in and various scenes that could be used. I think the title is a good one and fits Tangier like a condom. Did you attend the Albert Hall spectacular? Gad awful I hear from Allen Ginsberg fucked up by [Alex] Trocchi and Sigma.. Would appreciate one shot on the cockatoo or maybe two.. We hope to launch this book which will be a $10 deluxe production about the same time as the movie in one dazzling package.. I hope to make it to London in another three weeks more or less and see you there. Do hunt up Ian and tell him to write me and get him to play the tape for you

All the Best
Bill

WSB [New York] to Mr. Gunsburg [New York?]
July 24, 1965
210 Centre St.
NYC

Dear Mr Gunsburg:

I cannot sign or give my approval to the proposed ad for the *New York Times* which I consider to be of sensational and misleading nature and not at all in accord with the tone of my interview with Mr. Wilson.[8] The novel *Junkie* in which I describe some drunk rolling incidents is largely fictional made of composite experience drawn from various acquaintances. It is true that I was addicted to opiates for 12 years on and off. I have never admitted to being a practicing homosexual, the death of my wife was an unfortunate accident. *Naked Lunch* is

---

8   Possibly a reference to Colin Wilson, later the author of *The Mind Parasites*, which Burroughs reviewed for *Rat* magazine in 1969.

by no means a best seller. I suggest that the ad be rewritten with the above alterations in mind

Sincerely
William Burroughs

WSB [New York] to Alan Ansen [Tangier, Morocco]
August 12, 1965
210 Centre St.
NYC, N.Y., USA

Dear Alan:

Hope this reaches you and that you will forgive your tardy correspondent.. No time to breathe and not much to breathe in any case.. Hope to get away in another three weeks for England Tangier.. How long are you staying? What is the news in Tangier?

Allen [Ginsberg] is back from his trip to Cuba and Prague. He was thrown out of both countries because of his "sexual theories"....

As for myself life here is mostly work and very little else. However, the work is productive from all points of view.

I guess you heard about Stewart Gordon? Went berserk and beat up his wife and five Moroccan cops ended up in the mad house at Beni Makada. He was repatriated by the consulate and I saw him on his way through here to Chicago.

Paul and Jane [Bowles] were here with the same act. I mean half an hour to get out of a room in the Chelsea [Hotel] and such soul searching to reach the bar for a drink.

I am working now with an illustrated diary which has become so elaborate since every day includes references to that day a year ago and then dated forward a year that it could well take up all my time..

Love
Bill

WSB [London] to John Berendt[9] [New York]

September 8, 1965
% U.S. Embassy
London, England

Mr John Berendt
Associate Editor
Esquire Magazine
488 Madison Avenue
NYC

Dear Mr Berendt:

In answer to your letter of August 24 I enclose some material relative to the film feature which I hope is not too late for your deadline. I have been traveling or I would have been in touch sooner.

Yours Sincerely

William S Burroughs

A writer has no life story apart from his writing. My biography is entirely fictional. I have in fact acted in two films directed and photographed by Mr Antony Balch of London: *Towers Open Fire* and *Bad News* . . . (writers are of course bad by nature like reporters no trouble no story) . . . in these films I play a number of parts a doctor a colonel a Chilean millionaire, a seedy junky . . . the other actors in these two films are characters from my writing . . . I would cast myself in a biographical film since I write my own biography.

A writer has no line story apart from his writing so any biography of a writer is entirely fictional . . . Proceeding from this proposition I would cast myself as myself in a biographical film since I

---

9   John Berendt (b. 1939). *Esquire* editor who went on to author the best-seller *Midnight in the Garden of Good and Evil.*

write my own biography . . . I have in fact acted in two biographical films directed and photographed by Mr Anthony Balch of London *Towers Open Fire* and *Bad News* . . . writers are bad news . . . no trouble no story . . . In these films I play a number of parts a seedy junky a doctor a colonel a Chilean millionaire etcetera . . . I also play through other actors a street boy a seedy space ship skipper . . . etcetera. In short the film could not be played by one person . . . any one actor . . . a writer is his characters wherever found . . .

WSB [London] to Bruce Holbrook [New York]
Oct. 4, 1965
% U.S. Embassy
London, England

Dear Bruce:

I hope you have been able to buy one of the Norelco Carry-Corders 150. I have been using this machine and it is the only practical machine for use in the field. It uses tape cartridges which can be slipped in and out instantly weighs only three pounds can easily be carried under a coat the recording on or off controlled from the mike. Two of these recorders can be plugged in together for instant cut ups and copying of tapes. The Norelco gets better recordings than the Martell. I enclose a note from Ian [Sommerville] on the use of the Carry Corder in producing specific events. The important thing is to *play the recordings back on location*. This is easy to do with the Carry Corder which looks like a transistor radio. The mere act of playing a street recording back in the street makes a hole in reality since people are hearing yesterday or whenever and cannot know that they are hearing cars that are not there the machine costs about $90. As a test case try your Swing Bar [at] 117 MacDougal St. It is also important to take pictures *as you record*. Ian mentions speed ups. For this you need another machine. You can arrange to use my machine with David Prentice[10] any time. (Suggest that the

---

10 David Prentice. A painter friend of Burroughs in New York who took care of his Centre Street apartment while he was away.

effect of speed ups could be heightened by taking a slow picture, say one thirtieth second which will be blurred of course which is what is wanted in this case smudge two speeds).. Please write me. Sending under separate cover some extra Dutch Schultz for your scrap book to cut up..

Best Regards
Bill B.

EDITOR'S NOTE: When Burroughs returned to England, once again the Home Office did not want to give him a resident visa, believing him to be an undesirable foreigner. It took several months to resolve the issue, but after some influential friends took up his case, the Home Office decided in his favor and extended his visa.

WSB [London] to David Prentice [New York]
October 11, 1965
% U.S. Embassy
London, England

Dear David:

Sorry to be slow in writing. I have been in an unsettled state owing to the decision on my [visa] extension is still pending and the Home Office has my passport so I feel like a stateless person and cannot make any plans until they decide. All this comes straight from that benefit organized by Andy Warhol, Jack Smith, Piero Heliczer, and company, people to stay well away from. What is the general situation in New York? Any different than when I left? Incidentally the contents of the brown envelope issued from the St Marks address is about "and I know it is the Vampire" written by some one named Clive Matson.[11]

I certainly have no objection to David Budd staying in the loft. He is entirely welcome.

London rather grey. I have been busy with my Norelco 150 Carry Corder recording street sounds doctoring the tapes and play

---

11 This is a line from Clive Matson's poem "My Love Returned."

back on location. People think if at all I have a transistor radio. This is the only portable machine weighs about three pounds can be carried under your coat and to load it you slip in a cartridge no threading tapes. Soon all tape recorders will work on this cartridge principle. The machine costs about 80$. So if you buy a recorder this is the one to buy.

You did receive the Dutch Schultz number I sent you? Not bad I thought and seems to be getting results which is the important thing: vaccine 23 and in good time. London is getting as hot as N.Y. owing to the indefatigable activities of the virus known as the "American moral disease" demonstrated a typhoid mary who will spread the narcotics problem to the u.k. vital statistics are not in capital letters.

Thanks for forwarding the mail which does get through. Sorry to hear you have been ill. Missing you

Love
Bill

EDITOR'S NOTE: In response to a reader's request for more information about his book Nova Express, *Burroughs penned a reply that gives many keys to his writing. The letter comes very near to being a literary work in itself.*

WSB [London] to Mr. Rubin [n.p.]

October 27, 1965
% U.S. Embassy
London, England

Dear Mr Rubin,

I thank you for your letter of inquiry with regard to my novel *Nova Express* — (Am I wrong in surmising that you yourself are no stranger to the scrivener's art?) — A general proposition may stand as a Euclidian pyramid of orientation in the hinterland of my writing: that it means precisely what it says or does not say. To instance the case of Hamburger Mary who earned that moniker acting in the capacity of a humble waitress in a hamburger stand in or about

Seattle if my memory serves — (I should say at once that moniker in the colorful lingo of the underworld is synonymous with nickname) — not you understand a hamburger emporium catering to a select or discriminating clientele but rather geared to serve hamburgers of dubious porcine antecedents such an establishment where any intrepidly ill advised consumer would order anything remotely approaching steak tartare would be subject after an appropriate incubation period to sanction of trichinosis. The Subliminal Kid is so named since he began his career on Madison Avenue taking dour advantage of the societal somnolence which broods like a smog of the angels over the land of the free to spread a cunningly contrived network of juxtapositions an associational mosaic calculated to engrave upon the torpid neurons of the potential consumers a fervently ecstatic and overwhelming need for his product of predilection while himself remaining a figment of unreality in a sublime state though he was much too shrewdly hypochondriacal to ever entertain the notion of using Hamburger Mary as a tartare steak. You see his seemingly rambling concatenations of superficial afflatuses were in fact rambling in a very definite direction indeed and he concluded in due course of Time that the world was in point of fact an oyster not by any means at his indisposal to be confined within the already galling limits of Madison Avenue as much even though the concomitant irritation might accrete a not inconsiderable pearl. Like Hamburger Mary he felt within him the expansive call to a bigger and to a man of his specialized sensibilities better thing. Now you will observe that in both of these instances the moniker derives from the original trade or profession of the subliminal phantom involved a trade or profession which the personality in question no longer follows as such whereas in the case of Izzy The Push his moniker refers to his present and actual specialty of pushing or in plain English defenestration fell or jumped or was pushed from a window — (In recent years I have toyed with the idea of transporting my characters to an old western set though the vista of one and two story buildings offered by our glorious frontier days of sainted memory would not provide an adequate hiatus between the windows and terra firma to lend the character of Izzy The Push the ingredient of impact so essential to a man of his caliber unless of course the action could be shifted to one of the large urban centers by one of the many stratagems at the disposal of those of us who seek a precarious livelihood through the use or misuse of our pens.) In the case of The Ugly Spirit we are led to consider a class of monikers deriving from some personal peculiarity even deformity—Ears Monsell, Cherry Nose Gio — The Ugly Spirit is *ugly* but the very statement immediately involves us in a most perplexing question as to the precise nature of ugliness and or beauty. We in the west conventionally subscribe to the Greek concept of beauty assigned that illusive attribute to the assemblage of more or less regular features and well proportioned limbs such as can be seen in Greek statuary by anyone who gives himself the trouble to go where such objects are on display. May we then say that ugliness consists in a quantitative departure from this marble standard trailing off like a crippled Dow Jones average into an abyss of unsightliness? I cannot but feel that there is more here than affronts the eye bearing in mind that a statue does not move or at least not with any degree of discernible speed whereas the Ugly Spirit is described as being in constant motion as being in fact profoundly incapable of statuesque repose and it is precisely in this incapacity for repose that his ugliness may be said to reside or at least manifest itself to the observer who would hardly object to some one indulging a state of quiet ugliness outside his field of vision which leads us to another attribute of that foreboding spirit namely an absolute need to force himself on the attention of the reluctant observer. He suffers in point of fact from a profound lack of engaging insouciances. I would accordingly suggest that his ugliness consists in a vociferous insistence on manifesting that same ugliness to anyone who will stand still for it and in a stunningly venomous hatred for anyone who will not. The message of my writing may be succinctly stated: "Don't stand still for it". However the thoughtful citizen faced by the Ugly Spirit will ask himself a pertinent question, "What ails this brute?" I would venture to suggest that the answer is *radioactivity* or in plain English the "metal sickness" which is to say sick metal, which is to say *decaying* metal. Gentle reader the Fountain Of Youth is radioactive and those who imbibe its poisonous heavy waters will suffer the hideous fate of decaying metal. Yet almost without exception the wretched idiot inhabitants of our benighted planet would gulp down this radioactive excrement if it were offered. Once again I lift a cold distant umbrella of dissent: "Look down look down along that line before you travel there" — (muttering cripples phosphorescent metal stumps) — Now the essence of decay is *repetition* if I may quote the Ugly Spirit: "You see now how we were caught in repetition sets". (You will recall that Mr Luce bought *Life* from an old joke magasine of the same name). Now a joke may be funny the first time repeated 500,000,000,000,000,000,000 times it becomes not only unfunny but radioactive. Life on this planet has been repeated to a point where the only applause stems from hysterical Geiger counters.

[...]

WSB [London] to Brion Gysin [Tangier, Morocco]
October 28, 1965
% U.S. Embassy
London, England

Dear Brion:

The matter of my [visa] extension still pending. I hope you have received the article on bird songs I sent you and found it as uh thought provoking as I did. It would seem that the function of human speech is to enable the other half to keep track of one right? Now a few random reflections on the enigma of human speech: word becomes image when it is *written down*. Word written down of course makes no noise itself but it *causes noise* in the reader, try to read any written words as for example I see in front of me "Ice Blue Aqua Velva After Shave". I can not read these words without saying them, that is performing actual movements of the throat. On the other hand were I to represent these words pictorially as say a piece of blue ice water velvet and some one after shaving, I could look at the pictures without saying anything. According to Lichtenstein [*sic*: Wittgenstein] no function can contain itself as an argument therefore no verbal description of language can be given, so such observations can only indicate where to look. Perhaps the first step would be to construct a working model of the language process — that is a tape recorder that transposes the written word into sound and such machines exist. I have just written down the alphabet with numbers after each letter. a–1 etcetera. What is the zero of letter?

Michael Sissons[12] should have a contract this week? I will keep you informed. My best to all in Tangier

Love,
Bill

WSB [London] to Paul Bowles [Tangier, Morocco]
October 28, 1965
% U.S. Embassy
London, England

Dear Paul:

Ira [Cohen] passed through London on his way to New York and played me a taped interview with you which sounded very good though it would need editing of course. Perhaps you could place it with *The Paris Review*. I hope Brion [Gysin] has shown you an article I sent him on bird songs which seems to me evocative of some interesting tape recorder experiments. I wonder if you have taped your parrot and how he reacts to playback? After all a parrot is a tape recorder but perhaps with limited storage space.

Ian [Sommerville] and I both have identical tape recorders, an excellent new portable put out by Phillips which uses a cartridge that can be immediately inserted. This seems to me so much more practical that I hope it will soon be applied to all machines. This machine weighs only three pounds and can easily be carried under the coat. Ideal for street recordings and the tone is not at all bad though of course hardly professional.

Playboy evidently felt the St. Louis piece was a bit far out for their purposes and paid me a $300 turn down guarantee. Aside from the money lost I am just as glad *Paris Review* published it

---

12 Michael Sissons. British literary agent.

since they certainly did a better job than *Playboy* would have done. My best to Jane [Bowles]. May see you all soon

Best

Bill B.

EDITOR'S NOTE: *For several years Burroughs had been interested in the beliefs and practices of the Church of Scientology. While there was much that he felt he could learn from their methods, he grew more and more to see it as a system of brainwashing. With his new interest in cutting up films and audio recordings, he felt that he could apply those mediums to his independent study of scientology.*

WSB [Tangier, Morocco] to Antony Balch [England]
December 13, 1965
% American Express
Bland Line
Boulevard Pasteur
Tangier, Morocco

Dear Anthony:

Expanding the potentials of alternating yes no we could produce a full length film conveying a unique audience impact. This would simply be a new type science fiction film which uses only actually demonstrable devices persons and places. That is to say any weapon etcetera will be actually demonstrated to the audience. (You see of course the publicity angle)..

We warn you that it is dangerous to witness this film and only those with strong nerves and self reliant character should apply for this ordeal and so forth we have purposely made the price of admission high in order to discourage the casual and unprepared witness.. The story is the story of scientology and their attempt to take over the planet. Starts like this: Take 1: a shabby street as we move up the street we see a sign "YOU can use this phone".. Now we pan in on the doorway over which is written.. "Come in. We are friends of yours".. The man behind the camera is obviously standing in front of the building deciding whether or not to go in.. A figure of indeterminate sex appears in the doorway with a smile of welcome.. "Come in friend," the camera starts forward. "What do you want? Get out!" the camera recoils.. The sign changes to "Members only." Switch back and forth the camera advancing and recoiling. Finally the figure in the doorway is smiling welcome from one side of its face and spitting hate from the other faster and faster until it fuzzs out of focus.. Take 2: a female scientologist on a platform demonstrating "Hello yes hello" to a group of students. We do not see the students since the camera is at all times the audience. Now she explains the basic communication formulae. "I communicate acknowledge communication and communicate back".. Shills in the audience take up "Hello yes hello".. (the audience must be drawn into *participation* you understand.. the resulting "h y h" are recorded and played back at various speeds etcetera.. With the audience involved she now shifts to "I love you I hate you".. once again speeded up.. Like she says I love you real sexy exhibiting as much of her female charms as the law allows in these parts, then the old switch to violent hate and black disapproval. We go on to a whole series of yes nos.. smiling faces snarling cop faces sex images alternating with fear images and so forth. Now with the audience softened up we begin the story proper. Fade out to the District Supervisor.. "With this simple device that you have just witnessed in operation a handful of vulgar stupid second rate people have taken over your planet. Yes, your planet has been invaded and the landing field for this invasion was precisely the human body. The rightness center in the human nervous system was invaded and taken over by a virus parasite.. Always remember that 'rightness' like any human manifestation must have a three dimensional center in the human nervous system. I would suggest that rightness is centered in the mid brain. If I may borrow for a moment the jargon of Dr. Freud while continuing to deplore his uh therapeutic procedures what he calls the super-ego is an actual parasitic organism."

[. . .]

WSB [Tangier, Morocco] to Allen Ginsberg [San Francisco]
December 17, 1965
% American Express
Bland Line
Boulevard Pasteur
c/o U.S. Consulate
Tangier, Morocco

Dear Allen:

Thanks for the check. Yes I have seen quite a bit of Tom Maschler[13] and I think they will do a good job on *Nova Express* which they are bringing out in February. Of course I didn't show up at 210 [Centre St., New York] since I had already left by that time. Will be here for two months then back to London in early February.

In the course of routine medical check up in London turned up a positive Wassermann.[14] Probably dating from Tangier sojourn but no way to be sure. No symptoms. The doctor told me it was dormant and almost certainly noninfectious. However it would be a good idea for you and Peter [Orlovsky] to have blood tests to be sure. Good idea in any case since the germ has become so mild that in many cases there are no symptoms at all. Have just completed a course of 20 penicillin shots which should be more than enough.

Sending this to City Lights so I don't know just when it will reach you. All the best for Christmas and New Year to you and Peter.

Love,
Bill

---

13 Tom Maschler. British publisher and head of Jonathan Cape.
14 Wassermann. A test for syphilis.

WSB [Tangier] to John Broderick[15] [Ireland?]

December 18, 1965
% American Express
Bland Line
Boulevard Pasteur
Tangier, Morocco

Dear Mr. Broderick:

In answer to your letter: It would seem to me that the show of force so overtly manifested by all existing establishments.. (Castro and his Cuba is no better) is actually a show of weakness, the weakness of an organism that needs power like an addict needs junk, an organism that knows if it ever losses power even for a few seconds it is finished.. ("Switched their way is doomed in a few seconds".. *Nova Express*).. Of course the system can not be beaten on its own terms.. It can be beaten by creating new terms *outside* the system.. One hole and everything leaks out.. To use a simple illustration: Imagine an island completely isolated from outside contacts. This island is governed by the control of money. The inhabitants are granted money = power comfort security if they serve the interests of money and in exact quantitative measure for the services performed. Now imagine someone who does not wish either to advance in the hierarchy of the system nor to suffer its sanctions who points out that quite other norms are possible. The whole weight of the system will be directed against him. All existing systems are based on absolute monopoly — the premise that no other system is possible — monitored by the hierarchical lie that all spiritual and temporal rewards can only come through the system.. The pyramid of *Life Time Fortune* doling out stipends of the life time and fortune they have stolen and monopolized, the communist hierarchy of power, the Catholic Church's monopoly of the Grace of God, such systems of so called mystic initiation as the Gurdjieffians and the Scientologists.. it is all the same thing: total monopoly of a commodity whether spiritual or temporal and a payoff in the monopolized commodity.. A childish game that

---

15 John Broderick (1924–1989). Irish writer.

must end if the human experiment is to continue.. Now deviants from the systems may lose any number of individual engagements without being defeated— (On several occasions I have had magasines bought out from under me in order to fire editors who were publishing my work.. "Sorry Mr Solomon isn't with us anymore").. On the other hand if the systems loses *one decisive engagement* it is finished.. Once the *possibility* of other systems not based on hierarchical monopoly is demonstrated the whole control system crashes. One hole is all it takes.. Now all existing systems are based on monopoly and control of word and image from the ancient Mayans with the priestly monopoly of the calendar to *Life Time Fortune*.. And this is precisely my point of attack.. The manipulation of word and image is a highly technical operation now done with computers.. I have endeavored to show this system in operation in the enclosed pamphlet which I call *Pamphlet 23*

I did receive your book *The Fugitives* but unfortunately my French has lapsed to such an extent I can not do justice to a book written in that language. I would be most interested to see the work in English if you have a copy.. All the best for Christmas from your tardy and itinerant correspondent thanking you for your interest in my work

Sincerely
William Burroughs

RUBRUBRUBRUB+++&++++&++&&&&&""""&"+++

RUBRUBRUBRUBOUTOUTOUTOUTOUT#"#+++++#

RUBRUBRUBRUBOUTOUTOUTOUTOUT####&&&&

"""&&&+++++"OUTOUTOUTOUTOUT"""""""&&&

1966 ""+OUTOUTOUTOUTOUT"+"+"&&&

THETHETHETHETHETHETHETHE+++###+++&&+++

THETHETHETHETHETHETHETHE&&&&&+++++++++#;

THETHETHETHEWORDSWORDSWORDSWORDSTHE

###&&"&"&"&WORDSWORDSWORDSWORDS"++

WSB [London] to Brion Gysin [Tangier, Morocco]
February 28, 1966
Hotel Rushmore
11 Trebovir Road
London S.W. 5

Dear Brion:

As it turns out what I had was neither hepatitis nor a liver attack but grippe. I am now almost completely recovered except for a slight residual chest cold. As I wrote you — the letter was designedly brief to show the bank — two hundred pounds has been sent to you % Barclay's in Gibraltar. The first check had been sent in my name under the misconception I still had an account with Barclay's and I would not have been able to cash it. I hope you have the money by now. I had a blood test which turned out completely negative. Doctor Wright says it must have been a recent and very mild case to be so readily reversed by the course of treatment. Nothing to worry about there. There is a new treatment for ringworm that is taken orally, something called Grisovin. I don't know if you can get it in Tangier if not I will send some on. He said, however, that he doubted if the spots on my hand were ringworm. It will take some weeks of these tablets to find out. They do seem to be fading.

Ian [Sommerville] is so busy setting up his recording studio that I hardly see him.[1] It is of course excellent that he now has something to do and a chance to make some money. I guess he would rather write you all the details himself. In any case he seems in a good frame of mind.

[John] Calder is delighted with the new version of *The Soft Machine*. He now owes me four hundred pounds which he is ready to pay. So good news there. When I arrived here Tom Maschler was away. He will be back next week. Reviews of *Nova Express* not bad. Much fairer than I had expected. I have been having an amusing time the last few days going back to my high school writings and *rewriting*. For example am now working on "Carl Cranbury in

---

1   Ian Sommerville had been hired to create a recording studio for Paul McCartney. The studio was to be devoted solely to the production of experimental recordings.

Egypt" — no idea what will happen next but it flows along. That is I start with the original and go on from there working on three narratives at the same time.

"Carl Cranbury in Egypt." The two women at the water hole and "I have 'leprosy' and I cannot live." Quite an interesting experiment in narrative and no idea as I say what will happen next but something is happening like:

Woman 1: Looking about nervously—"One doesn't feel safe with that tiger about. How did it get here anyway? (after all since when were tigers native to Africa??)"

Woman 2: "Escaped from a traveling circus. Some pot head beatnik declared himself a saintly magician with power over the beasts. He opened the cage and well . . . that's how the tiger got his taste . . . You understand the man's flesh was completely *impregnated* and sooo . . ."

Woman 1: Nodding sagely—"So a man eating tiger with the pot chucks is now loose in our district?" She looks about even more nervously, "It's getting dark, Sextet and I am going home."

Woman 2: "Wait! I am coming with you. Oh have you heard the *news*? They are going to hold the *Rites* in our town this year. Word has just come through from the Capital."

Woman 1: "You mean the *unspeakable* Rites?" (The original rites had some claim to be unspeakable. A youth had actually been dismembered and the pieces hidden about the village. Then Isis collected the pieces and sewed them together. The youth was immersed in a bath of semen extracted from a 1000 hanged slaves and emerged in ithyphallic form. Highly placed officials felt that such practices were not in harmony with a modern civilized administration but they hesitated to abolish the rites altogether because of the tourist business. The result was a compromise. A wax dummy was dismembered and the youth now emerged from a bath of condensed milk dressed in a bikini. The village in which the Rites were to be held was selected each year by lot.)

The two women are walking along a path towards the village.

Woman 1. "Ra smiles on our village," she looks at her companion with calculation. "Now I wonder who is going to be Isis?"

Woman 2: Piously, "The Secret Council of The 23 must decide."

Woman 1: "Is not your uncle a member of the council?"

Woman 2: Shocked, "The council is secret!"

Woman 1: "Oh come off it Sextet. Secrets in a town of this size!"

They enter the village which is humming with activity children busily baking little phallic statues to sell to the tourists already stalking about with cameras.

In the taxi from the airport Carl Cranbury, whose code name was "Big Picture", reflected that his mission was not unlike the legendary quest of Isis. Find all the pieces and the man he was looking for would emerge perhaps and meanwhile John Weuerby in his library reflecting on the single word "Athens?" and the letter that ended "I am almost without medicine. I have 'leprosy' and I cannot live". "Athens?" well why not..??

Looks like I will have to do some traveling on this one. There is a fascinating story on viruses in the American edition of *Life*. I will try to get a copy for you, it would be useful in your book. Will also see about sending you some Scientology literature. Ian and Antony [Balch] send their love.

Love

Bill

WSB [London] to the Editor of the *New Statesman* [London]
[ca. March 4, 1966]
To The Editor
The New Statesman
Great Turnstile, London W.C.1

Sir,

Mr David Cooper in his article "The Drug Movement" which appeared in the March 4 issue of *The New Statesman* says: .. "Mr Burroughs writes enthusiastically about apomorphine treatment but I do not feel his enthusiasm is justified in terms of published results".. To what extend is Mr Cooper acquainted with the "published results"? Has he read Doctor Dent's book *Anxiety and Its Treatment*? Has he read *A Primer for Alcoholics* by Riddle? Has he read the annals of *The British Society for the Study of Addiction* of which Doctor Dent was for many years the chairman?.. He continues.. "There is no evidence I know of for his view of apomorphine as a specific metabolic regulator".. Once again has he bothered to acquaint himself with the evidence submitted by Doctor Feldman of Switzerland and Doctor Dent, evidence based on thirty years experience in the successful treatment of alcoholics and drug addicts? "It would certainly be difficult to exclude other variables in his case".. Mr Cooper presumes to know more about the 'variables' in my case than I do.. "There is a periodicity in the surging movement of a writer's creativity and at times his interior state will be such that even biochemistry is surpassed".. May I point out that at the time I took the apomorphine cure with Doctor Dent I had no claims to call myself a writer, that I had produced almost nothing, that "the surging movement of my creativity" was limited to filling a hypodermic, that the entire body of work on which my present reputation is based was produced *after* the apomorphine treatment and would never have been produced if I had not taken the cure and stayed off junk.. "It is then relatively easy to come off heroin".. *When* is it easy to come off heroin after twelve years of addiction? What is Mr Cooper's published medical evidence for this preposterous statement? Further absurdities follow.. "I am sure that any adequate long term answer to the 'addiction problem' must be in terms not of some empirical anti-drug treatment but of a release of creativity in our society".. That is to say the answer to a metabolic illness is not to be found in an empirically proven treatment but in some vague 'release of creativity'.. (Perhaps LSD25 in gas form which is now being used by the American forces in Vietnam).. Apomorphine *is* an empirically proven treatment in cases of alcoholism and addiction as the many cured patients of Doctor Dent can testify. I have recommended a number of addicts to the apomorphine treatment over a period of years and all agree that it is the only treatment that works.. I return you Mr Cooper "We are all hooked on estrangement".. What he means by this I cannot imagine.. "Mr Burroughs's Opium Jones is a product of this".. Once again Mr Cooper presumes to speak for me whereas I have made it clear to anyone who can read English that my Opium Jones is a product of *junk*, of the metabolic illness of addiction just as a yellow skin is the product of hepatitis.. "It's abolition must issue not from a box of pills but from an act of liberation".. What "act of liberation"? And how is someone bound to a sick metabolism to be liberated from that condition? To return to the beginning of Mr Cooper's article.. "Can we transcend this moment and can drugs be useful to this end? There is considerable evidence that this may be so.".. In other words a box of synthetic mushroom pills is useful for liberation whereas apomorphine is not? If Mr Cooper shows no evidence that he is competent to talk about apomorphine I can speak from experience about the hallucinogenic drugs having experimented over a period of years with LSD, mescaline, psilocybin, dimethyltryptamine. I consider these drugs more dangerous than useful. They can produce states of acute pain and anxiety even death, as occurred last year in London to a doctor who had taken a 'safe' dose. Toxic effects are more liable to occur after several exposures than on first use — that is we are dealing with a phenomena of decreased tolerance or sensitization. *Under no circumstances would I use any of these drugs at the present time or advise anyone else to do so.* The increased awareness conveyed by the hallucinogenic drugs is available to anyone who will discipline himself to keep his eyes and ears open at all times. If I do not advocate the use of hallucinogenic drugs still less do I advocate the use of heroin. Mr Karl Miller in the same issue says.. "Both Burroughs and Trocchi would seem to feel that more liberal narcotics laws might produce a Lotus land in America".. On what writings or utterances of mine is this misinformed and misleading assertion based? I am in public disagreement with Mr Trocchi on the issue of heroin as clearly expressed in a television interview three years ago and on any of the other occasions when my opinion was consulted. I am very tired of having opinions arbitrarily attributed to me which I neither entertain nor express

William S. Burroughs

I would like to ask the editor to please withhold my street address in the interest of privacy. If anyone wishes to communicate I can be reached % Calder Publishing Co., London.

WSB [London] to Brion Gysin [Tangier, Morocco]
March 15, 1966
Hotel Rushmore
11 Trebovir Road
London S.W.5

Dear Brion:

About the end of the road for this machine [typewriter] must trade it in. You are right about [Michael] Sissons and the whole agency is so inefficient he doesn't seem to have any ideas about foreign rights — that is some one else's prerogative who doesn't even have an office in the same building and magazine stories are handled by some woman whose name I disremember. Jonathan Cape are annoyed because no word from Grove on the plates and they feel they have been stuck with the least saleable properties all in all not much good news here. Please write to Ian [Sommerville], he is a bit hurt you haven't written but don't say I said so, just do drop him a line. The medicine I have for ringworm is a new approach, that is you take it orally for forty days and forty nights and if what you have is ringworm it goes. I still have something on my hand but all sorts of other itches here and there I thought were part of nature have gone. I will send you some, you must take two pills a day for forty days. Conrad Rooks is about to release his film and wants me to go to Paris for a week all expenses paid to help with the dialogue and meet the other actors which I will do as there is really nothing going on here. Not one interview. *The New Statesman* published part of the apomorphine article. No word from [Harold] Matson. *Moie Moi j menuie* [*sic*]. May take a trip around the world but what with income tax and mother needing more money don't know if I can make it. Reviews of *Nova Express* almost all bad and stupid beyond anything. I just skimmed through *In Cold Blood* [by Truman Capote], my God what a bore! I who can read science fiction just couldn't make it, the dull victims with their church supper and 4H clubs and the even duller killers, my God how can it be a best seller? I tell you someone presses a button somewhere and people buy any tripe at all. I'd sooner read the *Foxes Of Harrow* or *Gone With The Wind*. At any rate glad to see he got a full page of disfavor from *The Observer* saying he deliberately let the killers hang — refusing to pull strings and bring psychiatric testimony to bear — to sell his crappy book. I have always found his other books at least *readable*. This book is almost impossible to read except maybe here and there.

Only interesting development is Ian's recording studio with two Revox tape recorders and all the trimmings. I have really learned a lot about recording and reading with head phones you can hear yourself a few seconds later and correct as you go. My latest literary project is a *tour de force*. About a Chinese officer in Tibet . . . a description of his training in Academy 23 . . . and what he finds in the monasteries would make a buzzard crack his carrion . . . deliberately using places I have never been to. What I would like to do is visit the places in question — Hong Kong, Shanghai, Tibet and present the two narratives side by side but this seems impractical . . .

Patrick O'Higgins is here trying to contact the Madame by spirit messages.[2] He was absolutely thrilled when I told him I had seen her in a dimethyltryptamine session. He has quit the company to work for a subsidiary of Time Life called *Venture* . . . Give my love to John Giorno[3] sorry about this machine it just won't spell any more . . . Pending a new one I have been working entirely in long hand

Love

Bill

WSB [London] to Brion Gysin [Tangier, Morocco]

April 4, 1966
Rushmore Hotel
11 Trebovir Road
London S.W.5

Dear Brion:

I would advise you to pick up that money in Gibraltar *at once*. Banks only hold money for a certain time after which it is returned

---

2   Patrick O'Higgins. Author of *Madame: An Intimate Biography of Helena Rubinstein*.
3   John Giorno (b. 1936). New York poet and friend, resident of the Bowery building into which Burroughs later moved.

to sender. That would mean a delay of a month at least before it could be returned to Gibraltar. Any arrangement you make with [Andreas] Brown[4] on the manuscript material is all right with me his prices seem very much higher than any of the people I have done business with in the past.

I am just back from Paris after working for a week on the dialogue and continuity of [Conrad] Rook's film and acting in it, so I am now one of the more important characters. The film is not bad at all even Antony [Balch] thinks it has merit and will probably be a commercial success. Spent a day shooting with Jean Louis Barrault[5] which was interesting he is an excellent actor and most charming. Also met Prince Ruspoli. All in all an interesting and profitable week.

Did you read about poor [Timothy] Leary getting thirty years for possession of pot? It was in *Time*. I will send some money to the defense fund. It is really a barbarous sentence. Texas of course. On the other hand I am not sorry to see L. Ron Hubbard in hot water. *The Sunday People* local scandal sheet here wrote him up a full page spread — this is a man England can do without — try and get me barred out of England will he? — the article says he is full of venom and is sending out paid spies to smear anyone who opposes scientology with the idea of causing them legal trouble, one assumes through paid informers as well. I would suggest they check his tax payments and his right to call St Hill an educational institution.[6]

I really cannot see a permanent apartment in Tangier. I just don't like it more than a month or so at a time and it is no place for Ian [Sommerville] at any time. NO plans beyond the middle of May.

I hear from [Dick] Seaver about the production problems on *The Third Mind* and I can tell you for sure *no possibility* of publication next fall. A year from next fall is the earliest I would expect.

---

4   Andreas Brown. A book dealer who worked at the Gotham Book Mart in New York. He often appraised and sold manuscripts and archives for authors.
5   Jean-Louis Barrault (1910–1994). A French actor and director, best known for his work in the film *Les Enfants du Paradis*.
6   St. Hill. Headquarters for L. Ron Hubbard's scientology organization.

My best to John Giorno, Paul and Jane [Bowles].

Love

Bill

EDITOR'S NOTE: The following letter illustrates that although William Burroughs disagreed with Timothy Leary and his methods, he was generous to the cause of drug research. It also shows his strong aversion to signing petitions that do not state his own views exactly.

WSB [London] to Timothy Leary Defense Fund [New York]

April 4, 1966
% Calder Publishers
18 Brewer Street
London, England

Timothy Leary Defense Fund
449 866 United Nations Plaza
New York, New York

Dear Sirs:

You will find enclosed my check for one hundred dollars. I am not signing the enclosed petition since to my mind it does not stress the most important aspect of this case namely the distinction between behavior which is recognized as criminal in any existing society — crimes against person and property theft, assault, murder, and behavior which is made criminal by arbitrary laws. When the Harrison Narcotic Act was passed in 1914 thousands of people who had been respectable law abiding citizens one day were criminal the next by act of congress. Under the Nazis it was criminal to shelter a Jew. When the penalties for a purely legal crime exceed the penalties imposed for behavior recognized as criminal in any society the whole system of law is subverted. Many top war criminals received a milder sentence than that imposed on Doctor Leary, criminals with the blood of thousands on their hands. Someone who throws acid in another's face and blinds him is not even subject to the minimum sentenced faced by Doctor Leary. Two young white men who castrated an innocent Negro and poured turpentine over the wound received twenty years with no stipulation as to probation or parole. In the light of milder sentences imposed for truly atrocious behavior the sentence imposed on Leary is out of all proportion making a mockery of American law and disgrace of American judges. You may make any use of this statement you choose

Sincerely
William S. Burroughs

EDITOR'S NOTE: Burroughs' friend David Prentice was watching over the New York apartment on Centre Street for William and had written to ask if Herbert Huncke could sublet the apartment for a while.

WSB [London] to David Prentice [New York]

April 4, 1966
Hotel Rushmore
11 Trebovir Road
London S.W.5

Dear David:

A sublet is ruled out by the contract and the landlord would have the right to evict tenants so installed at any time, any case there are no more undesirable tenants than [Herbert] Huncke or anyone he plans to live with and he has lived in someone else's apartment all his life. So, so far as he is concerned for your own protection and mine lock him out and bar the door. If he gets a foothold in the building you will have the law in bugging everybody, he is not only a junkie but a thief, strong both against the deed in the words of the immortal bard the raven himself is harsh who croaks the fatal entrance of Huncke.[7]

The only people I would want living in the apartment with my things there would be you, David Budd, or anyone you personally know to be thoroughly reliable. In any case if this were on a per-

---

7 Burroughs is paraphrasing Shakespeare's line from *Macbeth*, "The raven himself is hoarse / That croaks the fatal entrance of Duncan . . ."

manent basis the lease would have to be transferred to your name with the landlord's approval. If you want to move in I would gladly pay half the rent in return for your looking after my effects. Alternatively could you store the effects in your apartment? As I wrote you the fridge is not mine. I own the bed, the desk, the three heavy wood chairs, and cooking utensils. You are of course welcome to transfer these articles to your apartment and keep them and I think it only fair that I should send you some money each month for the storage, after all it does take up a lot of space.

I have been in Paris acting in a film which is why I did not write immediately no time. There is nothing more exhausting than acting in a film and I was also writing the dialogue. Well, please let me know about this as I am anxious to give up the apartment definitively, whereas any sublet arrangement leaves me responsible so long as the apartment is in my name.

Missing you as ever
Bill Burroughs

WSB [London] to Carl Weissner[8] [Heidelberg, West Germany]

April 21, 1966
Hotel Rushmore
11 Trebovir Road
London S.W.5
England

Dear Carl Weissner

Here is an extension of the panic idea. Turn the sound off on a television set and use an arbitrary recorded sound track — street sounds, music, conversation, recordings from other TV programs, radio, etcetera. You will notice that the arbitrary sound track *seems to be appropriate* to the silent image track on the screen, in other words *what we see is dictated by what we hear*, which is why I find

---

8   Carl Weissner (b. 1940). German writer, editor, and publisher of *Klactoveedsedsteen* magazine.

tape recorder experiments more interesting than photographic experiments. You can of course cut back and forth between your recordings and the TV sound track or if you have two TV sets available record the actual TV sound track on a recorder and run your arbitrary sound track on another track so that the two are playing at the same time and play back in the street. Ideal of course would be a TV set in a shop window with arbitrary sound track.

Shonste Grussen

William S. Burroughs

P.S. All my tape recorder ideas I owe to Ian Sommerville of London and this should be acknowledged in the piece I sent you.

WSB [London] to Brion Gysin [Tangier, Morocco]

May 27, 1966
Hotel Rushmore
11 Trebovir Road
London S.W.5
England

Dear Brion:

Now good and bad as always. I should have known when Brian Epstein Jewish manager of the Beatles starts financing Ian [Sommerville] in a sound studio something is rotten in the state of Denmark — a compost heap Meester — Obviously laid on so Ian stops working for me before I can finance a studio. That is as soon as the studio was set up Ian stops working for me. Past two months paid him six hundred dollars for a few short tapes grudgingly and reluctantly recorded Miss Watson[9] swishing around the studio spraying perfume fixing her hair bird brain bleeping away to cunt headquarters strictly from hello yes hello the whole set up I can't be expected to work under such conditions. Ian is married and married to a cunt. My skill naught avail and I withdraw from the case. However the few tapes I did pressure out of him are a sample of

---

9   The reference here is to Alan Watson, a younger friend of Ian Sommerville's.

what could be done: "Hello yes hello" inched (that is pulled back and forth across the head) hello yes hello speeded up to twittering bird sounds . . . a spliced tape inched . . . Sending sample tape along under separate cover — (Mary Cooke did not put anything in John Cooke's food. It is all done with tape recorders and all scientologists are walking recorders. Spliced tape acts as a virus: a neural virus symptoms light fever, extreme irritability, nightmares, spontaneous orgasms . . . in my case nothing a visit to Doc Lambert's osteopathic clinic wouldn't set right) . . . Ian is in Paris now with Miss Watson and I was never so glad to see two people walk out in my life. As for the future unless the situation changes looks like the studio is not going to be any use to me and I will not see Ian again as long as he has a wife sticking to him like a barnacle. He is making plenty of money installing hi-fi sets in queen's apartments and you understand they have to keep him in the chips for fear he might fall back into my hands.

On the other hand I now have three machines and continual feed back between typewriter, tape recorder, and the street. Everything I write is processed and played back in the street. There is a new cassette 8 MM movie camera out — I am buying one, Antony [Balch] has one, and yesterday for example we took [it to] scientology headquarters and played back speeded up "hello yes hello" on location. With a narrative track of course. The movie of scientology headquarters to be run with fire engine sound effects and the blitz. What we see and what as they say happens is determined by what we hear, that is the sound track. I am off to Germany next week. Looks like I have a new assistant there name of Carl [Weissner] who is working with recorders. I have stopped drinking all together as soon as Ian left no wine no beer no nothing. Maybe a glass of champagne for special funerals. Best to Taguisti [*sic*: Targuisti][10] and Paul [Bowles]

Love

Bill

No immediate plans for coming to Tangier. See what develops

---

10 Targuisti. A Moroccan friend of Gysin's.

in Germany. Alternatively return to London and take flat. Set up my own studio and find a new assistant.

WSB [London] to Brion Gysin [Tangier, Morocco]
August 1, 1966
% John Calder Pub.
18 Brewer St
London

Dear Brion:

I am experimenting with a method I call "writer participation" which involves the writer directly and immediately in his narrative. I write what is happening to me *right now* adding "fictional" extensions which in turn extends the range of "fiction". For example if one of my characters goes to Boots[11] at midnight I go there and in most cases make recordings and take movie footage with my Eumig Super 8 camera as well. I also make scrapbook mark ups of the action. This keeps one moving about and adds the unpredictable leavening of random factors — when I arrive on location I may pick up a new angle and almost always pick up details for more accurate description of local. In short all action is shot on location. If I use a bar on the East Side I have to go out and find one.

[...]

I am staying now at the New Cavendish Hotel waiting to get in my flat . . . Taking a three-room flat Duke St. St. James which can be converted into a working model of Alamout . . . It is very quiet, wall to wall carpeting, adequate electrical outlets. I am having an orgone accumulator built to accommodate two people in a small room which can be comparatively sound proofed. This is to be my permanent headquarters. Now I can give your pictures a home — This is large flat with room for storage — in same building with Antony [Balch].

News flashes: Conrad Knickerbocker who did the *Paris Review* interview committed suicide two weeks ago. On the credit side

---

11 Boots. A chain of pharmacies throughout England.

of ledger Frank O'Hara was hit and killed by car and Delmore Schwartz (old enemy from *Partisan Review, New Yorker, Encounter*) died of heart attack.

The Soft Machine is selling quite well about 10,000 to date. I do not have copy and gather they are reluctant to mail any because of possible seizure. Nothing special on the film. Antony and I shooting a lot of footage on the 8 millimeter. He is planning to get selections from our film out as a short. Loft on Centre Street [New York] has been liquidated and gear stashed in David Prentice's apartment. He is currently in Ibiza expected here in the next month or so. I plan to bring all gear here and stash in this apartment. Then will be free to travel. Would like to see something new. Like Vietnam for example, those young Buddhist monks who can burn themselves must be well suited for space conditions . . . hummmm . . . As you gather all my energies, time, thought, are directed towards one end: *escape* under honorable male condition, that is no Transvestite Airlines for yours truly. I have learned a lot in the past few months . . . inoculations . . . immunity to the virus that cost John Cooke his legs . . . I want what I paid for: *an all male being in space*. If I don't get it, there is literally going to be all Hell to pay.

Most of what I have found out cannot be put in words and has derived from actual handling of the material . . . hours of work on the recorders, scrapbooks, etcetera. The Western approach is to find out what is going on inside the nervous system by externalizing the processes in the form of tape recorders, cameras, and so forth. By using tape recorders constantly you acquire a feel for the switches that turn words on and off inside the nervous system. Yes I can now turn words off inside and this ability came through the experiments with spliced tape and through continual handling of spliced tape. In short by externalizing the whole mechanism of word and image track you learn to understand and control it. The Eastern method of solitary mediation is nowhere for us. After all, words are spoken *to* somebody . . . That somebody you I and all of us males handicapped from the first "ME" word carry around with us in the right side of the brain. That is a man is half woman but a woman is all woman. The way out is the way in. We were trapped here by the "other half" in the beginning born knowing the game already lost. There is only one person in several million who has any chance at all of making it out and under the present emergency condition there is no use bothering with those who can't make it and don't want to try. By and large I feel that performances, readings, serve no useful purpose now. I did one reading here and might as well have been talking to the walking dead . . . program empty body . . . tape recorder set to run for as long as necessary play back only. You can't record on it so why waste time? Rather than talk to an audience of ten thousand duds better to spend a month with one actual prospect. Yes, we may have to start a religion — partisans in ways of silence. To get results means months years of constant disciplined work.. You save a lot of time and cut a lot of corners by working with subjects who already have some training which is why I would be interested in contact [with] the Vietnam Buddhist. Of all material the beatniks are about the least promising. Much rather work with a square ordinary young man provided he has reached a certain level of intelligence and alertness. I could do more with Jimmy Cookson than I could with a coffee bar full of tea head beatniks. Sorry to hear about [Allen] Ginsberg — another case in point — I'd sooner work with him than some half assed writer or the average university graduate mind crippled by academic thought patterns. I am actually perkier than ever. Junk doesn't seem to interfere with my sex act. Find I can do better now than I could seven years ago. Ian [Sommerville] and I getting on pretty well but there is a stubborn core of resistance there from his other half — she came very near to putting me out of the game in a wheel chair. One advantage to being a dumb hick is a cast iron nervous system.

Love
William

WSB [Tangier, Morocco] to Ian Sommerville [England]

[ca. September 12, 1966]
Oh my God Tuesday 1967
The Three Swans
Tangier

Dear Ian,

So far this trip has been [an] uneventful disaster, nothing right but no incidents, no discourtesies, just hotels full. My room at the Minzah [Hotel] right over the noisiest street in town, no soap, cockroaches — I complained and they sprayed something around — and prices about like the Cavendish.. Brion [Gysin], as I have foretold you, traveling in the South with Robert Fraser, somehow his name spells some irritating circumstance — Christopher [Wanklyn] had to leave without seeing him.. I am quite converted to your Christopher a real 6 [or *6] former.. except for his intervention I should have drowned myself in the swimming pool, buses through my head all night and the death weakness hits me in the Minzah dining room.. Do I dare to stick it out? Oh God and come to with my face in the gazpacho, walk don't run, just put one foot in front of the other in this converging blackness, thought I'd never make those stairs. Five minutes lying down a little cold water on the face and I went down to the dining room and ate my dinner, gazpacho to fruit salad and Christopher asked me if there was a sensation of heat.. "Yes always at the onset.. Like a laser gun through the midsections".. He nodded matter of factly, looked at the stairs and said *"I thought I'd never make those stairs"*..

So I checked out of the Minzah, the Atlas is full so to the Three Pelicans which has changed hands and a stringy woman could have been Alan Watson's mother is very vague about room, but an Arab cat rushes forward *"Muy tarnquillo muy bueno para usted.."* What it is, a room in the back of the owner's flat and somebody is building a house next door, so here I sit like a bungling school boy, his Tangier holiday he reflected ruefully was going to be obstinately drab and dreary as the wet concrete wall I see through yellow shutters, rusty hinges, white levanto sky cuts you to look at it. OooOh he's working on a novel this school boy. Can you endure a second coming of

Burroughs? The return they don't make with mother raw and bleeding *ich sterbe*. They were drafted. We did not write books after the war. Paper shortage you know. Don't know how long I can hold out here in this school boy.. He was terribly impressed with Christopher by the way.. Sooner or later he will start writing so this is where I came in.. This room looks like a gangster's hideout in Florida.. I'll go nuts I tell you looking at these walls.. And Robert Fraser left Brion somewhere in the south of Morocco and he is not back yet.. unmade bed, blanket and bedcover twisted in a lump, the pillows striped pink blue and yellow, typing on a card table uncomfortable chair of cheap plywood, walls the color of sour cream. I think I see a mosquito, two perhaps I should go out and make spraying motions to the old at the old Arab woman who is in the hall sometimes.

WSB [Tangier, Morocco] to Ian Sommerville [London]
September 15, 1966
Hotel Muniria
Calle Cook and Magallenes
Tanger, Morocco

Dear Ian:

Brion [Gysin] as I foretold you traveling in the south with Robert Fraser[12] and still there. Christopher [Wanklyn] had to leave without seeing him. Quite converted now to your Christopher. I spent my first week here at the Minzah [Hotel] which was noisy and expensive. Got the dying feeling one night in the dining room. Oh God, I thought. Come to with my face in the gazpacho, tourist shrinking back. "Don't get mixed up in it, John." Walked to the nearest exit putting one foot in front of the other, thought I'd never make those stairs. After five minutes lying down was able to return and finish dinner. Getting immune it would seem. Christopher asked me if there was a sensation of heat.. "Yes always." He nodded matter of factly and said, "I thought I'd never make those stairs."

---

12 Robert Fraser (1937–1986). London art dealer and owner of the Robert Fraser Gallery.

So back at the Muniria [Hotel] which is quiet and comfortable waiting for Brion if he ever does return. The whole town seems *dim.* I have been formulating plans for the flat. What I want is to make it into the ideal flat that everyone will want one like it with Brion's pictures and tape recorders that I can program in such a way as to amuse the guests. In other words sell tape recorder experiments as an *entertainment* — my apartment to be a demonstration model.

Don't know how long I will stay, certainly not longer than the end of this month. I can be reached here if need be, well hello to everyone in London and do think about my flat and how the recorders can be programmed to take off on their own as it were and provide fun and games for the fashionable young jet setters.

Love

Bill

EDITOR'S NOTE: *During this period, Burroughs' son Billy was experiencing his own problems with drugs. He was arrested several times in New York, and Allen Ginsberg was able to bail him out.*

WSB [London] to Allen Ginsberg [New York]
Oct 4, 1966
8 Duke Street
St. James
London S.W.1
Apt 22

Dear Allen:

I just got back from Tangier three days ago, which is why I have not been in touch sooner. First I heard about the situation with Billy. [There] was a telegram sent to Tangier to call you or Alex Trocchi no number and quite impossible to make a long distance call from Tangier. Alex tried to get through to my hotel with no success, the whole communications system is foundering, a telegram I sent to Alex never arrived. So all I could do was take the next plane back to London. I have sent you two telegrams saying I would cover all expenses necessary and would be delighted to see Billy here in London. The situation in Palm Beach is obviously impossible.

I can't thank you enough for your timely intervention without which the situation might have been a disaster. I don't know what has happened in New York, but since I haven't heard presume everything is now O.K.? Please let me know. I hope mother didn't find out about it, she is worried enough as it is.

Tangier very depressing. Paul Lund died two months ago. Various other people you don't know dead or dying. Paul Bowles is in Bangkok where he arrives on a wave of anti-Americanism and a 15 day visa commissioned to write a book on the city: 15,000 dollars which he has spent already traveling. Jane [Bowles] is in Tangier trying to decide what pills to take and sighing "Oh my God we'll all be in jail".. Everyone fears a sudden crack down on black market exchange but can not resign themselves to losing 20% of their money.

I am working hard as usual revising *The Ticket That Exploded* for the American edition. Don't know how I will pay my income tax, I spend every cent I can get my hands on, seems like the cheap restaurants and hotels are no longer endurable and it costs more and more to live comfortably. I have taken a rather expensive flat in London which is exactly what I want and I hope to make this my permanent headquarters.

I am writing letter to Billy. My best to Peter [Orlovsky]

Love
Bill

WSB [London] to Dick Seaver [New York]
Oct. 10, 1966
8 Duke Street
St James
London S.W.1
apt. 22

Dear Dick Seaver:

I hope you have not gone ahead and set up *The Ticket That Exploded*.. I am still working on the corrections and additions which will be considerable. I was out of action with flu for three weeks and another three weeks in Tangier during which I was recuperating and couldn't do much. Now the job is well along and should be finished in ten days to two weeks. It really would be extremely disadvantageous to publish that book as is. The changes I am making could well make the difference between a real setback and a book that will make money. I have been working under difficulties moving, no furniture hardly, etcetera and my son getting in trouble in New York. I guess Allen [Ginsberg] told you about it. I told Allen to draw what he needed against my account with Grove. How does the account stand actually? I have a 670 dollar income tax in today's mail which should be taken care of. How is *The Soft Machine* selling? I think you will agree that the original Olympia edition of *The Soft Machine* would have sold very badly indeed and that the corrections and changes made all the difference. So please don't be impatient on *The Ticket That Exploded*. I will get the manuscript to you as quick as I possibly can. Best regards to all the staff

Sincerely
William Burroughs

WSB [London] to Brion Gysin [Tangier, Morocco]

October 13, 1966
8 Duke Street
St. James
London S.W.1 Telephone Trafalgar 5259

Dear Brion:

Charges against Billy were dropped . . . three hundred dollars for a lawyer . . . I was composing a letter to tell him get out of New York before it happens again when it did . . . another three hundred dollars . . . I told Allen get him on the next train to Palm Beach. After packing up he will come here which may well pose problems. Looks like I will have to deliver some fatherly Lord Chesterfield talks to the effect is no excuse for getting busted.

Otherwise all is well here, Ian [Sommerville] and I getting

along swimmingly. The apartment is perfect, literally not a sound. Certainly an ideal setting for your pictures. When can one expect to see you in London? I have in the hall some horrible wall paper which must go. I would be delighted if you would paint murals over it. If you are willing to do this what base would you prefer? Plain white paint? Any other color is of course possible. It takes several days to strip wall paper and repaint which is why I bring the matter up.

I have a project in mind: suggest to [Maurice] Girodias that he interest Gallimard in an English translation of Betty Bouthoul's book on Hassan i Sabbah[13] with notes and possibly illustrations by Brion Gysin and William Burroughs. The book is straight forward prose so the translation presents no problems and no reason why you should have anything to do with that end of it. Please let me know what you think of this idea.

Could you paint over rose wall paper? The plan is of course to use this as background for a red picture. Plain pink paint? or blue? We'll end up in the decorating business if we are not careful. My best to Targuisti and Tangier. Ian sends his love as does Antony [Balch].

Love,
Bill

WSB [London] to Claude Pelieu[14] [New York]
Nov. 10, 1966
8 Duke Street
St James
London S.W.1
England

Dear Claude Pelieu
I have been ill, went to Tangier to recuperate, now back in

---

13 Betty Bouthoul. *Le grand maître des Assassins* (Paris: A. Colin, 1936).
14 Claude Pelieu (1934–2002). Artist, poet, and translator. He and his wife, Mary Beach, published several Burroughs books including *APO 33*, *Minutes to Go*, and others.

London with winter grippe living in present time is less and less bearable, paralyzing in fact and you need more and more money to buy bearable conditions. I simply have not been able to write any letters for some time. *APO 33* is an excellent job many thanks and let us hope it has some effect. I have given the extra copies you sent to the Indica Book Shop here. The enemy is delineated by the areas they attempt to block and no area is as dangerous to their plans than apomorphine. On a number of occasions I have received letters from doctors and twice from officials, a probation officer in California and a man in Vancouver in charge of prison reform. In all cases, sent material (articles I had written, copies of Doctor Dent's book *Anxiety and Its Treatment*—now out of print here). They wrote back promising action, then the curtain falls. Not another word, all my letters unanswered. This has happened at least five times.

Right now I am working again with tape recorders which seems to me the best possibility of breakthrough. Have you seen the *International Times* edited by—I think his name is Tom McGrath, not sure just slipped out of my mind—any case I have given them an article on tape recorder experiments which should appear in the next issue or the issue after that and I will follow through with additional articles and I hope get a large enough number of people experimenting with recorders to turn up some results. I will send you a run off of the article as soon as I have the run offs. Basic premise is "what we see and experience is to a large extent dictated by what we hear and anyone with a tape recorder is in position to decide what he hears and what other people hear or overhear as well."

I have been following your contributions to *My Mag*. Interesting you should mention *scopolamine words*. I was once poisoned by an overdose of scopolamine and had in fact written something about this experience just before I saw your piece with special reference to the words the *scopolamine words* reported to me by those who restrained me from stepping off a forty foot balcony onto imaginary staircase or walking out stark naked into the streets with an old laundry ticket I thought was a morphine prescription. The words were.. "What's the use trying to save money? It all goes for razor blades," followed by a rendition of "Deep In The Heart Of Texas."

I will write a commentary on your *With Revolvers Aimed* and return to you as soon as possible. My best regard to Mary Beach

All the Best
Bill Burroughs

WSB [London] to Laura Lee Burroughs [Palm Beach, Florida]
November 21, 1966
8 Duke Street
St James
London S.W.1
flat 22 telephone Trafalgar 5259

Dear Mother

With regard to Billy's difficulties I have talked with a physician here who has had extensive experience with similar cases. He informs me that ephedrine *is not a habit forming drug*. It is a stimulant that can cause alarming symptoms if the medical dosage is exceeded: sleeplessness, indigestion, and lack of appetite, in some cases mental disturbances and hallucinations. It would seem that Billy's symptoms then are *due to the use of this drug and not to the lack of it*. If hospital treatment is necessary that can be provided here. I have a room ready for him in my apartment and I am prepared to provide whatever treatment is necessary after consulting a physician. I have also arranged for a program of activities and studies designed to lead him into constructive channels. I will make every effort to find something he is interested in doing on a professional basis. I am convinced that his difficulty and the difficulty of so many young people today arises from the fact that he does not have anything to do, any goals which have meaning for him. I am ready to give any amount of time and effort to find something for him to do. I can introduce him to pop singers if he [is] seriously interested in music as a profession. If he wants to go into teaching he will have to finish his education. That can also be arranged here. Of course the first step is to straighten out his medical difficulties and as soon as he arrives here I will send him to doctor to decide if treatment is necessary. I am looking forward to seeing Billy and feel sure that I can provide the help that he needs. Please keep me informed

Love

William Burroughs

WSB [London] to Brion Gysin [Tangier, Morocco]
November 21, 1966
8 Duke Street
St. James
flat 22

Dear Brion:

Enclose copy of the *International Times* with my article on tape recorder experiments on page six. The paper already has a circulation of ten thousand. They have offered to let me take over an issue at any time, this will take thought and work since I would want a real knock-out issue. Response on the tape recorder article has been excellent so far, people are actually doing the experiments described, needless to say I will push the project as far and as fast as possible. Alex [Trocchi] is in contact with a lot of young people through Project Sigma who are willing to do the work of writing letters, organizing tape recorder evenings, etcetera, plenty of young people here who want *something to do.*

Ian [Sommerville] has moved all his equipment into the flat here and himself as well. I have actually gotten around to like Alan Watson, he is a good cook, tidy and willing and my rather silly jealousy seems to have evaporated. He is in Darlington at the present time. I have asked him to stay here on his return, trying to arrange a flat for Ian and Watson in this building, the studio has been sold[15]

---

15 Sommerville's recording studio had been financed by Paul McCartney and the Beatles and had been set up in Ringo's old apartment. Because there was really no experimental work being done there, the backers decided to close it. Sommerville and Watson, who had been living in the studio unbeknownst to the Beatles, moved in with Burroughs.

so they have to move and I told Ian to bring the equipment here before somebody walks in and repossesses it. With the two Revox machines, amplifiers, and hi-fi I am in a position now to carry out and demonstrate experiments, give tape recorder evenings. Will take a rest from writing and see what I can do towards activating the pre-recorded generation to do their own recording

More trouble with Billy. He was all set to fly here, then he says he is sick from benzedrine withdrawal, who ever heard of such a thing? I told mother to call Doctor Murphy. Next time he is ready to fly, he has a bad tooth, then he is arrested for forging a benzedrine script. My poor mother at her wits end. I told her to see Judge Sloane, an old family friend and see if he can straighten this nonsense out so we can get Billy on the plane. I don't know what is wrong with him and it looks like somebody doesn't want me to find out. I mean three busts in a month is too much

I have been ill in and out of bed for the past month, sciatica, infection of the prostate, just when I need all my energy I don't have it

Gino Foreman is dead, a sad story on junk and afraid to go to a hospital for fear they would cut him off, died of pneumonia here in London about two weeks ago. I didn't know he was here.

Panna Grady[16] turned up here on her way to Greece. She has given five hundred pounds to Sigma to set up an office. I figure might as well use an organization that is already set up. Seeing quite a lot of Alex [Trocchi]. Everyone is interested in the tape recorder project .. (notice the scientology ad on the back page saying very much what I say in my article) . . . the points I want to get across is this: these techniques are being used without our knowledge or consent very much to our disadvantage . . . *you can do it too* . . . and even more important working with tape recorders will raise anyone's level of performance in any direction.

How is the work going? Did you receive the article I sent you? Was it any use to you? Is there anything I can do or send you that would be useful? I will try to find your Marsh Arabs, so much to do and I have been sick half the time. I am sending you page proofs

16 Panna Grady. A wealthy American patron of the arts.

of the final version of *The Soft Machine*. (You will find errors most of which I have corrected). Would you be interested to do a cover for *The Soft Machine*? I will see to it you are paid at last 25 quid. The book will probably be published in May or June. *The Ticket That Exploded* is also coming out in the spring which will delay publication of *The Third Mind* until late '67 or early '68. No doubt the public will be more receptive at that time if we are still alive! My best to Targuisti and Tangier. Ian sends his love. He is working on a Takis exhibition. The apartment is marvelous warm comfortable. We are having all your pictures framed.

Love

Bill

EDITOR'S NOTE: *Burroughs' mother wrote to William suggesting that he come to Palm Beach to try to do something with Billy. Burroughs had been trying unsuccessfully to get Billy to England hoping that he would have some positive effect on the troubled boy, but Billy resisted all attempts to send him to his father's care. Since he was now awaiting trial owing to his most recent difficulties, he was blocked from leaving the United States.*

WSB [London] to Laura Lee Burroughs [Palm Beach, Florida]
November 25, 1966
8 Duke Street
St James
London S.W.1
Flat 22
Telephone Trafalgar 5259

Dear Mother

I feel that for me to come to Palm Beach at this point would be unwise for several reasons. First of course is the question of expense. Air fare plus living, etcetera, it means a thousand dollars more or less. Whether this is your money or mine it is that much less money to provide for Billy. For that amount Billy could be treated for a week in a nursing home here with the best care. I have been trying to put aside some money for this purpose. And we must consider what would be accomplished if I did make the trip. The authorities are more likely to pay attention to my past record than to the fact that I have been cured of the drug habit. My outspoken criticisms of the American narcotics department for treating addiction as a police rather than a medical problem and for their failure to use the apomorphine treatment — which is not available in the United States — has come to their attention and they have done everything possible to discredit me and cause me trouble. They even attempted — unsuccessfully — to have me barred from England. I took the matter to the Home Secretary and now have a letter that I am to be allowed to enter England under the same conditions as any other alien. In short, so far as official agencies in the United States go, the less attention to me the better. What concerns me is that the court might feel that I am not a suitable guardian for Billy. In short, my presence in Palm Beach might do more harm than good to Billy's case. Whereas if I am not there, questions are less likely to arise. Does Mort[17] know about the situation? If he could come down for a few days that would be much more to the point. He guessed something of Billy's difficulties in St. Louis and wrote to me about it, and suggested that Billy should come straight to England before he got in trouble. Since then my one thought was to get him on a plane to London where he can be looked after. I cannot understand American doctors. No English doctor would refuse a case like Billy's. If he did not feel competent to handle it himself, he would recommend a doctor who would handle it.

In short, I feel that the less attention drawn to me the better, out of sight out of mind. Not that I doubt my ability to make a good impression on any unprejudiced person. However the narcotics department is completely prejudiced. They say once an addict always an addict and tend to discount the possibility of cure. I found that out when I last returned to the states to be treated like a criminal at customs because of narcotics record twenty years ago. I

---

17 Mort Burroughs (1911–1983). William Burroughs' only brother, who lived in St. Louis.

will almost certainly have trouble with them if I return. They told me when I came in last time I was subject to fine and imprisonment for not registering with the department when I left the U.S. My lawyer looked up the law and found that this measure did not apply to me since I have never been convicted. However they will certainly cause what trouble they can. Please phone when you receive this letter. Let's hope we can get Billy on the plane soon.

Love
Bill

EDITOR'S NOTE: *Burroughs was continually frustrated by the fact that he was unable to convince people that drug addiction was a medical problem, not a law enforcement issue. Once again he responds to an inquiry hoping that he can make people aware of this crucial distinction.*

WSB [London] to Stephen W. Fried [Lewisburg, Pennsylvania]
December 10, 1966
8 Duke Street
St. James
London S.W.1

Dear Mr Fried

The American narcotics department who seem to dictate official opinion have consistently opposed the apomorphine treatment. If addiction is regarded as a metabolic illness for which effective treatment is available, the so called narcotics problem is no more a matter for police interference than the problem of malaria or tuberculosis. In order to maintain their position they are reluctant to admit that addiction is curable and oppose any treatment that works. If the apomorphine formulae where synthesized drugs could be developed exerting a much stronger regularity action and a standard cure could be set up that would be virtually painless. The only way to force their hand is through research and the presentation of factual findings.

Doctor Dent, who was the first to use the apomorphine treatment for drug addicts is dead. Doctor Peter Kelly, London, took over his practice and would, I am sure, be glad to answer your questions.. I can also refer you to doctor Xavier Corre, Paris. He speaks and writes English. Unfortunately I do not have the address of Doctor Feldman in Switzerland who has done very important research over a period of years checking the metabolic changes that occur during the apomorphine treatment. Perhaps Doctor Corre has doctor Feldman's address. In general the important thing is to administer enough apomorphine during the first four days of treatment to achieve a concentration in the system. This amount will vary from one patient to another. In my case I was given one twentieth of a grain by injection every two hours day and night for the first four days. However this dose may cause too much nausea and can then be cut to a fortieth of a grain — (It had occurred to me that anti-nausea drugs might be useful given in conjuncture with apomorphine.. Also if variations and synthesis of the formulae were carried out perhaps the factor of nausea could be eliminated entirely)..

Not only had the narcotics department opposed the apomorphine treatment but they have failed to follow up a most promising line of research on pain killers that work on a different principle from morphine. The morphine antagonists ally-morphine and related compounds are as effective as morphine in relieving pain but may give rise to hallucinations. It is quite possible that the disturbing side effects of these compounds could be eliminated by administering a small dose of apomorphine in the same injection.

I have written a more extensive article on the apomorphine treatment and will send you a copy. Doctor Dent's book *Anxiety And Its Treatment* on the apomorphine treatment seems to be out of print. If I can obtain a copy I will send it on to you.

I certainly hope you are able to get the apomorphine treatment the attention it deserves, but I warn you that you can expect no help from official agencies in America.

WSB [London] to Brion Gysin [Tangier, Morocco]
December 17, 1966
8 Duke Street
St. James
London S.W.1

Dear Brion:

Sciatica is pressure on a nerve in the back that causes a sort of numb feeling down one or both legs. I have had it several times before, remember when I was limping in New York? It seems to go away of itself after a month or two.

Alan Watson is living here now with Ian [Sommerville] and I am very well pleased with the arrangement. Alan is an excellent cook and he knows how to buy food, keeps the place clean, fixes my breakfast in the morning, tonight we will have wild duck. In short his behavior has been exemplary. The flat is really too big for one person to keep up. Not only that but also Ian has moved all the tape recorders and loud speakers here, about 3000 dollars worth of equipment right in my drawing room.

It looks like I will have to go to Palm Beach over Christmas or New Year more precisely and see what I can do. Billy is in quite serious trouble, he went and forged about ten prescriptions and cannot leave the state until the case comes up next August. He is very depressed and mother doesn't know what to do. Well, I just have to go and do what I can. Have taken a three week return ticket leaving on December 27. Will stop off in New York a few days on business. Anything you want me to do? I can get in touch with Richard Kelly and Peter Matson[18] and find out what I can for you on the dream machine. You can write me here if there is time or after the 27th at 202 Sanford Avenue, Palm Beach, Florida.

Panna Grady is in town and has taken a house here. Last night I had supper with Panna, Alex [Trocchi], Larry Rivers, Jasper Johns, Ian [Sommerville], assorted wives, an excellent dinner at the Hotel Connaught, saddle of mutton with red currant jelly all the trimmings.

---

18 Richard Kelly and Peter Matson. Agents who worked on placing literary properties as well as the dream machine itself.

How are you coming with the novel? I had hoped to make Tangier for Christmas — my three months here is running out — but must go in the other direction. Robert Fraser was also at Panna's party looking thinner and handsomer than I ever saw him, very pale hummmm well it does often improve the appearance. I think he plans to be in Tangier over Christmas. He is a very pleasant person actually.

I have been taking an active part in Sigma, might as well use an already existing organization and all these young people with nothing to do. Anyone who gives young people something to do that means something to them can take over the youth of the world. This I am attempting to do with the tape recorder experiments. My best to Targuisti and Tangier.

Love,
Bill

P.S. We took your pictures to the best framer in London who knows your work and expressed himself as honored to frame it.

Ian send his love
Merry Christmas

EDITOR'S NOTE: *It was common practice for Burroughs to revise his books with each new edition. In the case of the Calder and Boyars edition of* The Soft Machine, *the changes were substantial, as this letter indicates.*

WSB [London] to Brion Gysin [Tangier, Morocco]
December 23, 1966
8 Duke St.
St. James
London S.W.1

Dear Brion:
It seems there had been a mistake all around. I didn't mean for you to correct the proofs [*The Soft Machine*] and return only mentioned the errors to reassure you that the set that went to the

printers had been carefully checked over by Ian [Sommerville] and me and the proof reader at Calder's. These are *page proofs* not galley proofs. The book has gone to the printers some time ago and no further changes are possible. I meant the proofs as a Christmas present.

I think we caught all the typographical errors. A number of words and sentences were omitted and I dare say many "phosphorescents" and "iridescents" fell to my magic marker. However, as regards any changes in the order of material or omission of the apomorphine article I am in categorical disagreement. The proofs I sent you are an extension of the Grove edition which is selling well in the states. Many fans told me they found the Olympia edition difficult to read and it never sold well. Reading the book over I could see the point; the original edition *was* a "collection of essays" rather than a book, and there was not enough narrative material to carry such a load of cut ups and unrelated descriptive passages. So I attempted to give the book a narrative structure. In fact one of the first changes I made (was it two or three years ago?) nearer three than two, was to use straight narrative material for the beginning instead of the "Gongs of Violence" section which it seems to me makes a very weak beginning. Everyone I have talked to who has read the Olympia edition and the revised edition says they find the revised edition much more readable. When I was preparing the Calder's edition I went through the revised edition carefully and decided that perhaps too much of the original had been deleted and that additional material which belongs in the book but which I had not had time to get in shape could now be used. You might say that *Naked Lunch*, *The Soft Machine*, *Nova Express*, *The Ticket That Exploded*, all derive from one store of material a good part of which was written between 1957 and 1959. The assemblage of a book from this material is always hurried and arbitrary and passages are omitted from a book that belong there so I carefully went through the original edition and used all the material that was in any way useable and the material I added was grafted on with some care, a little scar tissue is unavoidable in such cases. In short, I have been over this manuscript many many times.

"Finnie nous attendous uno bezze chance" were the *actual words*

in the diary found, the diary of Yves Martin, the phrase is more curious in view of the alleged fact that Martin was himself French though the precise circumstances of his birth are shrouded in documents of doubtful authenticity, but then who am I to say "*Ca m'est pas francais?*". I can produce no valid claim to a French birth, the old forger threw up his hands in a Gallic gesture "*Mais ca n'est pas possible monsieur.*" So we must, I feel in all fairness, leave the late and dubious citizen de France his last written words as they were found by a grizzled old Albanian Colonel de Police who granted laconically, "*toute ca veuz comprezny ce'st L'invention*" the soft machine *vous comprennes* is the human body *le corps humain* the old Comte leaned forward with quiet intensity, "It would seem to me that which regulates this so soft machine should receive some notice in the appendix" (*mist ce pais*) let me say further that I have never been able to understand your peculiar feeling about Catholics. Its something I've seen before in people [who] went to a Catholic school. I guess you have to experience it to *know* that priest stink gets into your bones breathe it so long you'll never be rid of it whimper for the priest when you're dying you don't know how evil an old priest can be the unforgivable sin is to *be* a Catholic born knowing the unforgivable sin apparent because we believe it what I say is this *so long as a man acts like a friend let's treat him that way* —

Remember the issue of *The Literary Supplement* engineered by L. Ron Hubbard, pardon my supplise is showing, Reverend Marshal McLuhan wrote one of the very few intelligent and appreciative reviews on *Nova Express* and that Catholic reporter from Espana gave me one of the best and fairest interviews I have received in my literary career, so why does it nullify the value of McLuhan's work that he is a practicing Catholic? Actually can one trust a lapsed Catholic? Sure we know how evil an old priest can be or an old Jew or an old woman or an old white settler, you will learn to know when a friend has become an enemy in the area where people are urged to be watchful. Now a few hints that may be of use to you in formulating "They" are all the millions of fraudulent people where do they all come from? second hand words rags and tatters of old film "They" are L. Ron Hubbard, Mary and John Cooke the Beard. "They" are local fakers with super human pretensions based on a few simple tricks carefully concealed and monopolized. "They" *are not* from another planet. "They" are not even agents of another planet. "They" *did not* come from space. "They" cannot live in space. If "They" were sufficiently advanced biologically and technically for space travel in flying saucers they would have no need to guard so carefully a few old tricks with film and tape recorder. The last thing "They" want to see are actual landings of flying saucers. Tip off was in the *Look* article I sent you. "Hill nightmare: further UFO landings". Yes, that would be the real nightmare for St. Hill, arrival of the real thing and exposure of their shameless fraud, just as [William Randolph] Hearst, who impersonated death having perfected a few simple tricks for manipulating accidents, wars, depressions, was afraid to hear the word "Death" spoken for fear the real thing would lay a slow cold hand on his shoulder. The power of the Beard is based on word lines of course also on "The Film". This is an actual film made around 1910 or 1912 when the potential of the film as a central instrument first became apparent. The same film has been used ever since — (any control instrument loses its power when repeated. The first cut ups, the first photo montages, as we know had something that later cuts ups and montages did not have.) You have seen some of the scenes from this film: Aztec temples, a number of fake scenes from other planets, remember the blue magis that night in your room with Mosely? Just a piece of "The Film," not from Uranus or any extraterrestrial source just old photographer tricks from an old local film. Given the equipment anyone could do these things as easy as turning on a light. That is why "They" have given us so much trouble. "They" know that "They" are second rate fakers and if the tricks on which their power is based become generally known other people will be able to do it and do it better. "They" are identified by their fear of the real thing since their fraudulent identity is all "They" have. "They" are not cruel super intelligent beings. "They" are stupid second rate human characters. When the monopoly is broken "They" will not be able to compete. And being able to do it and do it better gives one a chance to ask "why do it at all?"

L. Ron Hubbard has stated that words or sounds are recorded by an unconscious subject that these words which he calls engrams[19] in deep sleep have not, to the best of my knowledge, been exposed to words and sounds and then checked to see if these words and sounds elicit any special reaction when the subject is conscious. Assuming that his assumption is correct, what would characterize *all* engrams? Since the photographic mechanism is unquestionably out of action *engrams are characterized by the absence of image*. And now we see the point of the peculiar prose without image used in *Encounter* and in the bulletins from Lexington KY. A book reviewed in this engram prose will be seated in disinterest and aversion. A simple little trick and quite ineffective once it is known.

Peter Matson writes me no magazine in the states will touch the apomorphine article. Meanwhile a new threat to the junk universe is posed by a class of pain killers quite as effective as morphine and heroin but operating on a different principle — (See *Scientific American* issue before last). These substances are in fact morphine antagonists. The last time I saw Doctor Dent alive he showed me an article in the *Lexington Bulletin* written in the unmistakable *Encounter* style describing the first experiments with this new class of pain killers and by a conjuring trick of words indicating that these experiments are not leading anywhere since ally-morphine produces a feeling of "depersonalization" and is therefore unsuitable. Other drugs of the same class are now being used experimentally by other investigators who have succeeded in eliminating the hallucinatory side effects.

Excellent response to "The Invisible Generation" it was reprinted in the *Los Angeles Free Press* and quite a number of the young people here are carrying out the experiments. What I am interested in is the effect of mass action. I want to see thousands of youths in the street with recorders. The other important aspect is experiments carried out by sound engineers with extensive facilities. It would help a lot if you were here or in Paris. I leave tomorrow for Palm Beach will spend a week or two there, then a week in New York then back here to get this tape worm moving. Doctor Grey has set

---

19 Engram. A term used in scientology to refer to a painful event hidden deep within a person's subconscious mind.

up a center here to treat addicts with apomorphine and I will try to raise some money for his project before some Methodist NRA bastard slips in with a prayer center batharth then oth bithes. We been getting a lot of static from NRA lately they are the ones brought the *Last Exit to Brooklyn* case.[20]

Actually it is just as well *The Third Mind* publication is delayed since people will be more open to it a year from now. Properly timed it could be a best seller. Its going to need some pruning and of course adding any new tape recorder or film experiments. I have already written a more comprehensive version of "The Invisible Generation" which will serve as appendix to *The Ticket That Exploded.*

Ian sends his love

Love
Bill

---

20 *Last Exit to Brooklyn* by Hubert Selby Jr. was the subject of an important censorship trial in Great Britain following its publication in 1966 by Calder and Boyars. Although the initial trial resulted in a guilty verdict, that opinion was overturned upon appeal in 1968.

UBRUBRUBRUB+++&++++&++&&&&&""&"+++
UBRUBRUBRUBOUTOUTOUTOUTOUT#"#+++++#
UBRUBRUBRUBOUTOUTOUTOUTOUT####&&&&
""&&&+++++"OUTOUTOUTOUTOUT"""""""&&&

1967 ""+OUTOUTOUTOUTOUT"+"+"&&&

HETHETHETHETHETHETHE+++###+++&&+++
HETHETHETHETHETHETHE&&&&&+++++,++++#
HETHETHETHEWORDSWORDSWORDSWORDSTHE
###&&"&"&"&WORDSWORDSWORDSWORDS"++-

WSB [Palm Beach, Florida] to Brion Gysin [Tangier, Morocco]

February 5, 1967
202 Sanford Avenue
Palm Beach, Florida
United States

Dear Brion:

Have been the past six weeks in Palm Beach trying to straighten out this appalling mess. Arrived with tail end of habit plus various other disabilities which soon manifested their presence: pain and tension in the back of the neck, swelling in the glands at the side of the neck with high fever, swelling in groin with high fever. The swelling and fever subsided but the pain and tension in the neck is still here and incapacitates me, specifically for writing it is a real effort to write a letter. Mother broke her arm New Year's Day, no servants, no car, the house in an unbelievable condition of disorder and quite literally haunted. Some time ago mother called the police because of the knockings and voices they investigated and found nothing the phenomena continue, its a matter of acoustics. Billy's situation as bad as it could be, three felony counts, they would not let him leave the country without posting an outrageous bond in cash. The case in front of the nastiest judge in Florida, one Russell Macintosh, who automatically hands down the maximum sentence to anyone who appears before him I talked to the D.A. office and finally finagled a deal to drop charges and place Billy on probation on condition he go to Lexington.[1] Then this Macintosh imposes a four year probation with almost impossible terms. I am taking Billy to Lexington Monday then will see my influence lawyer in Washington about transferring the probation when he gets out of Lexington. Paregoric bottles and syringes all over the house, mother driving me round the bend with her continually fretting, and can't remember anything about the case. I must explain the same points fifty times. It seems your

---

1 Lexington Narcotic Farm. A drug treatment center. Coincidentally, William Burroughs himself had been there for treatment decades earlier.

letter forwarded by Ian [Sommerville] went astray, hummmm. I saw Panna Grady in London, seems Andy Warhol borrowed her apartment to make some of his movies and "moved the pictures around." This bodes you no good I am sure and by the way Truman Capote is in Morocco, any disservices or discomfort you can afford him will be appreciated by this department.

In all my experience I have never seen any place as evil as Palm Beach is now, all the way out in the open, you said once I would probably wind up in Palm Beach, well I hope to wind up Palm Beach one way or another. Do get around and take a few pictures with my Eumig Super 8 my Carry Corder was DOA here. Hope things are better in Morocco

Love

Bill

P.S. Don't write me here but to London address I expect to leave in another week for N.Y. Washington London. Must return in five months to meet Billy at the gate when he leaves Lexington.

WSB [Palm Beach, Florida] to Brion Gysin [Tangier, Morocco]

February 8, 1967
Written from 202 Sanford Ave
Palm Beach, Florida

Dear Brion:

I took Billy up to Lexington Tuesday sad sadder than I can tell you all the psychic manifestations in the house stopped when Billy left the knockings and voices house is just empty now. I am going to New York tomorrow and then to Washington to see what arrangements I can make to get Billy out from under this probation after he leaves Lexington. Looks like its going to cost every cent I can lay hands on . . . I may even have to move back to New York for a while. Don't know yet will talk to Ed de Grazia,[2]

---

2   Edward de Grazia (b. 1927). A human rights lawyer who had successfully defended *Naked Lunch* in Boston the year before.

Grove Press lawyer in Washington and perhaps to Doc Rioch . . . replicas of the Davises living next door name Given Powers, yes, really, they have been most helpful only people here who have helped. Other old friends of the family just seemed to fade into thin air . . . Mr. Powers walks his dog, Regal Powers, four times a day and Mrs Powers grows roses and keeps three guinea pigs. She calls them her "little people." They are always bringing over food and driving mother where she needs to go. We have no car and completely cut off here. I am arranging to sell the house and move her into a small apartment but can't stay to see all that through. I am hoping Mort [WSB's brother] will come down for a while.

I thought you were finished by now, please write in more detail. I read John Hopkins[3] book about Peru and thought it was pretty good, he certainly does get you there.

My health is improving slowly and I have taken up karate. May look up an instructor when I get back to London which should be in about ten days time. I will have to come back when Billy gets out in about four months time to meet him. Mother can't look after him or after herself for that matter. I am hoping she will move to St. Louis where Mort can help her and where she has old friends in the antique business. She must be in some place where she can get meals

My best to all in Tangier

Love

Bill

WSB [London] to Brion Gysin [Marrakech, Morocco]
March 17, 1967
8 Duke Street
St. James
London S.W.1

Dear Brion:

Back in England. Guess you have heard about the heat here, cops with pot sniffing fink dogs snuffing through flats and coun-

---

3   John Hopkins. Author of *The Tangier Diaries 1962–1979* (Arcadia Books, 1998).

try houses have busted the Rolling Stones and the whole jet set. I suspect the scientologists stirred all this up and it serves them right for calling copper they have all been banned out of England by the board of health as "a serious threat to the community medically, morally and socially" best thing ever happened, set fink dogs on decent people will they, some woman they were processing rushed into the streets of Grinstead dressed only in her night gown shouting "hello yes hello" in a completely deranged condition.

Still suffering from a mysterious virus but I have written several timely articles to show just what would happen if all the drug and sex laws were actually enforced. Just tell the machine to enforce all laws by whatever means and the machine will sweep us to the disaster of a computerized police state. "Senator Bradly rose in the Senate for the last time to say simply 'God help us all'."

What are your plans? Have you finished the book yet? I may well be in Morocco around the end of April. Saw John Giorno in New York. He has finished his cut up novel which is now with Peter Matson. Saw Grove Press Dick Seaver says the paper back edition of *Naked Lunch* will make a lot of money. I don't know who told you there would be page proofs of *The Third Mind* in a few weeks. They are checking with the printers to ascertain costs and to find out what can and cannot be done in the way of offset. No doubt quite an editing job will have to be done after that, then back to the printers, then galley proofs to be corrected. Publication in six months at the earliest I would estimate. Certainly no page proofs in the near future.

Alan Watson continues to cook excellent meals and I have become quite fond of him. Michael [Portman] is in New York again. Ian [Sommerville] sends his love. We are keeping the apartment clean.

Love
Bill

WSB [London] to Hugh Cameron [Chicago]
March 19, 1967
8 Duke Street
St. James
London S.W.1
England

Dear Mr Cameron:

In belated answer to your letter, yes the apomorphine treatment is highly effective in treating addiction to the amphetamine drugs. Unfortunately American doctors seem ignorant of its use and the treatment must be expertly applied to be successful. Since the death of Doctor Dent a Doctor Grey of London has been using the treatment and Doctor Dent's nurses are still using it. There is also Doctor Xavier Corre of Paris, France. I do not know of any doctor in America to recommend, Doctor John Bishop of New York, being the only doctor in the States who has used the apomorphine treatment. So far as I know there is no difficulty about obtaining the drug on prescription in America. The important thing is to build up a sufficient concentration of the drug over a period of four to five days. If you consider coming to London I would be glad to put you in touch with Doctor Grey or Doctor Dent's nurses. As to Doctor Bishop, he is a very helpful man and I am sure would do what he could. He is a physician in general practice and I do not know whether he treats cases of intoxications. However, you could write him mentioning my name.

If I can be of any further assistance please let me know. I would have answered your letter at once but my correspondence file was misplaced. I know that addiction to amphetamines is a most ruinous condition and hope that your brother will manage to get over it

Sincerely

William S. Burroughs

WSB [London] to Peter Elvins[4] [Italy]

March 19, 1967
8 Duke Street
St James
London S.W.1
England

Dear Peter Elvins

Some time ago I received a letter from Mr Willard Marsh in Mexico asking me to help in securing publication for some of Kells' unpublished pieces. I have written him that I would be glad to help in any way possible editing, sending the manuscripts to appropriate outlets, etcetera. He tells me that Mimi [Elvins] has most of this material and is reluctant to let go of it. I certainly want no payment of any kind. Perhaps if she was assured that the proceeds would go to her she might be willing to release the material — (though it would seem to me that you have an equally valid claim to whatever profits might derive from sale of Kells' manuscripts). Please let me know if I can be of any assistance in this matter. As you know Kells was one of my best friends and I will do whatever I can to obtain publication for his work

Cordially Yours
William S. Burroughs

---

4   Peter Elvins. Kells Elvins' son.

WSB [London] to Brion Gysin [Marrakech, Morocco]
April 20, 1967
8 Duke Street
St. James
London S.W.1
England

Dear Brion:

I will be coming to Morocco in early May so please let me know what your plans are and where you will be. Any news on your book? I asked Peter Matson about this in my last letter but have not as yet received a reply.

My lawyers in New York attempted to arrange a new contract with [Maurice] Girodias offering him 25% instead of the 33% he claims. The negotiations broke down and Maurice withdrew like an angry diplomat and is now threatening to put out Olympia Editions of my books in the States. I imagine Barney [Rosset] is in a state. A real fuck up that Girodias. I am letting my lawyers handle the matter according to their judgment.

I have been doing a lot of work mostly short pieces of which I will soon have enough for a book. My latest piece in which I bluntly accuse L. Ron Hubbard of clearing his wretched clears by dumping their engram garbage in the streets may result in legal action from Hubbard — he is litigation prone I understand. However he is *persona* not altogether *grata* in England has been asked to leave Rhodesia and Australia as a menace to public health and accused in the press of using his so-called therapy as an instrument of blackmail, so I doubt if he would risk a trial and the disclosures that might ensue. In the same article I have attacked *Encounter Magazine* — they admit receiving money from the CIA — as an equal menace to public health. In fact the policies and aims of L. Ron Hubbard are so consistent with the policies and aims of the CIA American Narcotics Dept Institute for Cultural Freedom — also admittedly subsidized — that he may well have been subsidized himself. No I don't think he would risk a public airing of his financial arrangements.

The drug nonsense here goes on and on. The Rolling Stones are searched wherever they go and were attacked physically by the French immigration officials at Orly. England is like a South Sea island hit by measles no resistance. "Demonstrated a Typhoid Mary who will spread the narcotics problem to the United Kingdom," I wrote in 1959. Ian [Sommerville] sends his love and so does Michael [Portman] who has just returned from a trip to Los Angeles, reports whole scene in American completely mad

Love
Bill

WSB [London] to Mr. Hohmann [n.p.]
April 20, 1967
8 Duke Street
St James
London S.W.1
England

Dear Mr Hohmann[5]

I believe Grove Press have a complete transcript of the Boston trial[6] and would be glad to place this material at your disposal. I was in America at the time and was asked to give testimony at the trial. I refused since I do not think a writer should be called upon to defend his work in terms of a legal system that dates back to the middle ages. All this talk about redeeming social significance seems to me irrelevant. The assumption made when a legal case is brought against a book is that sex is wrong and writing about it is worse. However to call this assumption into question would prejudice the case. In the interest of legal advantage one must be hypocritical in a court of law.

Wishing you every success with your thesis

Cordially Yours
William S Burroughs

---

5 Although clearly addressed to a Mr. Hohmann, the current owner of the letter, the New York Public Library, has corrected this to Mr. Hofmann.
6 In 1965, *Naked Lunch* was attacked by the censors and went on trial in Boston. Burroughs did not attend the trial in which the book was found obscene, a verdict that was later overturned upon appeal.

WSB [London] to Claude Pelieu [San Francisco?]

April 23, 1967
8 Duke Street
St James
London S.W.1
England

Dear Claude

I have been distracted by family troubles and now trying to catch up on back correspondence. The book of methods is already sold to Grove Press and will appear in due course of time. One must be careful about publishing anything already in the hands of publishers so I hope you are clear on the legal aspects — permission from the publishers on your translations. So far as I am concerned it is O.K. and I am sure your translations would be the best. But remember that [Maurice] Girodias is litigation prone and if he feels he is not getting his cut might cause trouble. However I [am] sure the Cahier de L'Herne know about these necessities.

I hear from Carl Weissner that he is putting out another issue of *Klacto* and have sent him a piece. I have asked him to send me your cut ups.

Delighted to hear that *APO-33* is selling. I have been writing a number of articles on apomorphine treatment. An abbreviated version will come out soon in *Harper's*. If you would be interested in translating any of these articles into French I will have Peter Matson, my New York agent, send you copies. There is no provision for translating short pieces and articles into any other language and it seems to me that any literary agency which could offer this service would greatly expand the market possibilities. Maybe you can work something out with Peter Matson. Please let me know about this and I will contact him.

There had been a lot of trouble here — book shops raided, heat on the drug scene. Calder is afraid to publish *The Soft Machine* now and has delayed publication until November.

All the best to you and Mary Beach
William Burroughs

P.S. I would like you to see the articles in any case and will write Peter Matson to send you copies.

WSB [London] to Brion Gysin [Tangier, Morocco]
July 17, 1967
8 Duke Street
St. James
London S.W.1
England

Dear Brion:

Left Tangier high and thought I would never get here — at one point in Madrid found myself out on the street however made it in a cluster of Spanish students to find that my luggage had been lost left in Madrid as it turned out interesting to meet all the other people who had lost their luggage one man said, "Well at least I have my painting" which he held up for all to see — a cottage and landscape in lurid post card colors. Two days later my luggage all sealed with little lead seals like an electric meter was delivered at the door. London very pleasant, Allen Ginsberg is here giving readings and looking better than I ever saw him look, quite impressive really and Panna Grady is really coming into her own as a literary hostess, everybody turns up there, all the publishers and beatniks and poet ambassadors — a real turn out. Last night's party had everything — a fight which I missed, then we are all turning on when word reaches us the police are at the door. There were indeed about six of them so Panna sent out the man who wrote *Seven Types of Ambiguity*, I forget his name a fine old gentleman [William Empson] with a moustache clearly under the influence of no other drug than alcohol and they went away. There has been an international poetry festival for the past week. I just had Olivetti deliver me two typewriters on demonstration, one electric and one big portable, this is the portable Studio 44. An electric typewriter takes some getting used to. I plan to stay here long enough to get a fair section of work in progress off to Peter Matson. The financial outlook very good and should be clear in another two weeks or so with quite a bit coming to me. The apartment looks great and I will probably keep it. I can always sublet if I decide to move. I hear Mary Skelton is mad at you for dining out on her secret doctrines big deal.

Ian [Sommerville] and Michael [Portman] send their love. Is there anything I can do for you in London? We can certainly put you up here anytime.

Love

Bill

WSB [London] to Brion Gysin [Tangier, Morocco]
August 21, 1967
8 Duke Street
St. James
London S.W.1

Dear Brion:

[Maurice] Girodias has signed the contract and all rights are now back in my hands. Peter Matson has acted with great efficiency. I suppose you have heard from John Wood.[7] He collected the money just in time. Seems Robert is going into bankruptcy. Another day or so and there would have been no money. I will have the check as soon as it clears — an accountant's check this time. I will send you a check on my New York account.

Ian [Sommerville], Alan [Watson], and your reporter now taking karate lessons camping around in those marvelous judo outfits. Antony [Balch] still away just when I want to run some projection experiments. Do please send me that note on the projection performances as I want to get that piece off and go on record to establish precedence. The projection principle is being used all over the set now and nobody is doing it right. This is of course a way of diluting the impact.

One of my correspondents Graham Masterton[8] is now editor of a magazine called *Mayfair* and offers me a monthly byline on any

---

7   John Wood. Publisher and book designer.
8   Graham Masterton (b. 1946). British horror writer and editor.

subject. He himself suggested L. Ron Hubbard and if he sues let him. As it happens I have just been extending my article on Hubbard. In fact I think it is time he received the attention, the importance of his concepts (deliberately hidden beneath his atrocious writing) warrants. Incidentally in none of his books or bulletins does he mention tape recorders. Several nights ago Ian invited his tape recorder dealer around for a drink to discuss a new Japanese machine with a number of special features. He mentioned that he had sold two of these machines to L. Ron Hubbard. Ian became violently nauseated for no ascertainable reason.

Bill Levy[9] has taken over editorship of the *International Times*. Best to Paul [Bowles] and Targuisti

Love

Bill

WSB [London] to Brion Gysin [Tangier, Morocco]

Sept. 7, 1967
8 Duke Street
St. James
London S.W.1

Dear Brion:

You will have seen Ian [Sommerville] and Alan [Watson] by now. They left yesterday for a two week holiday in Tangier. I had a number of things to do here so decided to remain. Here with my electric typewriter. The boys seemed really thrilled about the trip, I hope Tangier lives up to expectations. Some one named Graham Masterton with whom I corresponded for years is now working for *Mayfair* magazine, an English version of *Playboy*. They have taken my academy articles and want me to do a monthly byline. Next issue I am doing a job on scientology. We called and asked for an interview with St. Hill. No dice as I expected. "We want to hear your side of the story," produced no effect. So we are going

---

9   William Levy (b. 1939). Author and editor of *The Insect Trust Gazette* and *International Times*.

down to St. Hill this Sunday with photographers in the best traditions of obnoxious journalism coming home to roost as it were, will ask the villagers what they think about scientology. Knock on the door at St Hill. Take pictures etcetera and Antony [Balch] will be there with the movie camera and of course recorders. Should be fun and games. (Parenthetically I would not advise any representation of the dream machine in the *International Times*. *IT* has a bad image in the strata where the machine could do you some good). What sort of article or representation would you be interested to present? Certainly *Mayfair* would be a better vehicle.

I will pick up what *Exterminators* I can find around town but the book business has never been at a lower ebb, the market is quite frankly flooded. There is simply too much material — the University of Texas is not buying anything[10] — like I say there is just too much around.

This *Mayfair* deal looks like a real break. I have met the publisher Brian Fisk[11] who seems genuinely interested in accomplishing something outstanding and they are certainly the outlet for any dream machine articles since I have already gone into non chemical methods of altering consciousness in the academy article which will appear in the next issue. Did you see the introduction to "Academy 23" which appeared in the *Village Voice*? Enclose copy. The article I have expanded into 12 pages.

Please do your best for Ian and Alan

Love
Bill

---

10 The University of Texas at Austin had the reputation of spending large sums for manuscripts and rare books.
11 Brian Fisk. Head of Fisk Publishing Ltd. who began publishing *Mayfair* in 1966.

WSB [London] to Brion Gysin [Tangier, Morocco]

October 1, 1967
8 Duke Street
St. James
London S.W.1
England

Dear Brion:

Don't know about a trip to Tanger at this time. I am applying for extended visa here as I have so many projects underway. The trip to St. Hill was amusing though I thought we would never arrive in one piece, such driving 80 miles an hour passing on hills and curves, Antony [Balch] taking movies from the back seat. Anyhow we took a lot of movies of St. Hill and scientology at work, they didn't seem to mind at all. Writing the article I bought and carefully studied all of L. Ron Hubbard's published work I could locate. Most interesting. Clearly the rank and file are given a few tricks and the extensions held back. That is by the fact of practicing the tricks they are given they come under the influence of those who know the extensions from these elementary tricks. Take for example one exercise which is simply shifting attention from one object to another and back. Enclosed bulletin is consisting of extensions I have derived from this exercise. I am very dubious about publishing this material at this time. Of course this [is] only one exercise and I am in process of developing a series of these exercises, some derived from Hubbard, most of my own invention. Do you think it would be indicated to publish some of this material as appendix to *The Third Mind*? Or perhaps could be a booklet that goes with expensive dream machine. You see the basic principle here is shift of attention rather than concentration of attention. When people are trying to obtain hallucination they tend to bog down in unproductive staring. For example, much better results could be obtained with the dream machine by switching your attention back and forth between the machine and your hand or speech centers or some other object. Similarly this could be a new way of looking at paintings shifting your attention from one point to another in the painting or from one painting to another.

The actual article I have written on scientology contains only hints of the material I enclose. It is restrained — giving Hubbard his due, raising certain doubts and reservations, — (To what extent does the clearing process involve an unloading of engrams? One exercise he described consists in going to a railroad station or airport and "look around and pick out some person who could have the same thing wrong with him as is wrong with you. Now have that thing wrong with that person." This I find deplorable.) . . . Antony and I have spent £200 and done a really professional job on the projections. The results will be available next week and I will let you know. My impression is it will exceed expectation. I am holding my article (my article on projections I showed you) back pending the results from these experiments. Meanwhile I would certainly appreciate your writing a note on the previous essays.

Ian [Sommerville] reports marvelous time in Tangier. Sends you his love

Love

William

EDITOR'S NOTE: *Burroughs did not return to America when his son, Billy, was released from the Lexington Narcotics Farm. Instead of going to London with his father, Billy enrolled in classes at the Green Valley School in Orange City, Florida.*

WSB [London] to Billy Burroughs Jr. [Orange City, Florida]
October 4, 1967
8 Duke Street
St James
London S.W.1
England

Dear Bill:

Glad you enjoy the motorcycle. It does seem more of a deal than those three wheeled things which remind one of gasolene [gasoline] shortage and middle class Danes. Hope you are enjoying the courses at Stetson.[12] I am dubious of the whole educational system in American and Western Europe which simply has not kept up with altered conditions. If you are interested in psychology you should study dianetics and scientology which is certainly the most workable system in existence and to me much more interesting than any of the Eastern systems. I will send you some books on the subject which I have just been studying to prepare an article. Point about scientology is that it works. In fact it works so well as to be highly dangerous in the wrong hands. The curious thing about L Ron Hubbard who devised this system is that he is very uneven as a writer and a thinker. This tends to put people off. You find very profound and original thinking together with very shallow and banal thinking, so you have to read every word very carefully. I am sending you a short book which outlines some of the principles involved. If you are interested I will send you some more books that are more advanced.

I am going on with karate and feel much better than I have in years. There is another system called aikido which is more spiritual but takes many years to master. The man who founded this system is now 80 years old and he can take on three men of any age or size and flatten them all in a matter of seconds. During the occupation he put five drunken G.I.s in hospital.

I will send you a copy of my article on scientology which will be published here shortly. I have found scientology very useful for writing and have in fact devised a system of my own derived from it. Please write often

Love

Bill

EDITOR'S NOTE: Norman Mailer wrote to Burroughs requesting that he join the tax resistance movement as a protest against the Vietnam War.

---

12 Stetson University. School in DeLand, Florida, near Green Valley School.

WSB [London] to Norman Mailer [New York?]

November 20, 1967
8 Duke Street
St James
London S.W.1
England

Dear Norman

As regards the War Tax Protest if I started protesting and refusing to contribute to all the uses of tax money of which I disapprove: Narcotics Department, FBI, CIA, any and all expenditures for nuclear weapons, in fact any expenditures to keep the antiquated idea of a nation on its dying legs, I would wind up refusing to pay one cent of taxes, which would lead to more trouble than I am prepared to cope with or to put it another way I feel my first duty is to keep myself in an operating condition. In short I sympathize but must abstain.

all the best
William Burroughs

RUBRUBRUBRUB+++&++++&++&&&&&""""&"+++
RUBRUBRUBRUBOUTOUTOUTOUTOUT#"#++++#
RUBRUBRUBRUBOUTOUTOUTOUTOUT####&&&&
""""&&&+++++"OUTOUTOUTOUTOUT"""""""&&&
1968 """+OUTOUTOUTOUTOUT"+"+"&&&
THETHETHETHETHETHETHETHE+++###+++&&+++
THETHETHETHETHETHETHETHE&&&&&+++++++++#
THETHETHETHEWORDSWORDSWORDSWORDSTHE
####&&"&"&"&WORDSWORDSWORDSWORDS"++

WSB [London] to Brion Gysin [Tangier, Morocco]

January 23, 1968
8 Duke Street
St. James
London S.W.1
England

Dear Brion:

The Cut Ups were a tumultuous success marked by apoplectic rage and quite a number of equally emphatic compliments. The most interesting testimonial to confusion was the large number of articles left in the theatre after each performance: purses, gloves, scarves, umbrellas even overcoats. The manager said he never saw anything like it [in] thirty years [as] a theatre manager.

I am reinstated and will return to East Grinstead this week.[1] The fact is that processing has uncovered a lot of extremely useable literary material and dreams now have a new dimension of clarity and narrative continuity. I have already made more than the money put out on stories and material directly attributable to processing. So might as well follow through and see what turns up.

I have written again to Dick Seaver to try and find out what is happening with *The Third Mind*. The letter I sent you on glyphs has been expanded into an article which could be appended to the section on hieroglyphs. Have also done some serious study on the subject of virus and find that the behavior of this organism is much more complex than I had imagined. There are viruses that cause no symptoms in a healthy organism and some that are known to be beneficial to mice. There are interesting parallels with scientology. Hubbard says that what is not admired tends to persist. It is this persistence of agencies that are not and cannot be admired that keeps a dual universe in operation. It will readily be seen as I have said before that the virus survives precisely by making itself unadmirable, so no one want to look at it. Hubbard says that what

---

1   In spite of his criticism of scientology's founder, L. Ron Hubbard, Burroughs was still
    interested in the methods and philosophy of scientology and enrolled in an advanced
    program.

is unwanted and yet persists has only to be seen and it will vanish. Now a virus has other resources than mere ugliness to make itself difficult to confront: It is small. You can not see it with the eyes or even with a light microscope. More important perhaps once it is in the cell it cannot be confronted because you are trying to confront it with something when it is inside the instrument of confrontation as if you were trying to measure an object of unknown length inside a ruler with the ruler itself.

Gather you enjoyed Mauritania. Any word from Doubleday?[2]

Love
Bill

WSB [London] to Brion Gysin [Tangier, Morocco]

February 11, 1968
8 Duke Street
St. James
London S.W.1
England

Dear Brion:

I am reinstated at St. Hill after the *Mayfair* article and this time everything worked out exactly right — two excellent male auditors — (in fact the whole organization has been inundated with males and we are now in a majority) — I am now taking the solo audit course which is the last step before clear. I am interested to really learn the subject having already profited professionally. Antony [Balch] has also been processed and looks like a different person. And I have audited Harold Norse who loves it of course. An interesting observation: Most of my release points were quotes from my own work or someone else. That is, I wrote my own releases in many instances and some of these were cut up. The auditor having gotten a read on hieroglyphs asked me what that could mean and I said, "The emerald beginning and end of word." That was the

---

2   Brion Gysin had submitted his book *The Process* to Doubleday, hoping for publication, and he was awaiting word.

exact quotation. And the auditor says, "I've got a floating needle here and its lovely. That's it. End of session." The auditor does not need to know what the item means to the pre-clear. Nor does the pre-clear have to know exactly what it means. I have noticed that release points are always something you know and don't know that you know. When you say something and don't know quite why you said it and then float up to the ceiling you know you have found a release point. To list a few release points: "All from an old movie will give at his touch." This was engram release. I suddenly said, "Why its just an old movie".. Of course I have said this before, but now I really *saw* it. "At the wall — heavy weapons and shock troops urgent", problems release. Scobie in his office with his rusty hand cuffs on the wall from Graham Greene's *The Heart of the Matter* was another release point. The emerald turned up twice. It was decided by an auditor that I was still connected to what they call "suppressive persons" and that this would have to be cleared up. In this process which is known as S&D you simply list items and then check on the E-Meter. He told me the item could be a person, a thing or *an object*. I was listing persons, all the old obvious suspects, its rather Agatha Christie you understand: Jacques Stern, Mary Skelton are not what one is looking for. Then I thought "or an object" and said "the emerald".. Auditor then asks, "Has a release point been reached?" That reads. "Where do you think it is?" I immediately said "the emerald." "That's it. Floating needle." Another release point was a statement from an article in *Prospect* about the nature of virus and why it is hard to confront. It is small. No one wants to look at it. "The uglier a virus the longer it lasts," since what is not admired according to Hubbard, tends to persist. But most important it is *inside* the precise neural area you are trying to confront it with, like trying to measure a object of unknown length inside a ruler with the ruler itself. Another release point was "sharp smell of weeds from old Westerns".. An occasion which I met Lord Montague — I could not remember his name in session — for two minutes ten years ago. Another was "British Museum".. You remember your dream some years ago where someone showed you a scepter that was part of the emerald or rather the emerald had been the top of it? If you can remember in more detail I would be most interested.

A few cut ups from this letter: "thy letter abounds in breaks (to quote from my book of hieroglyphs . . . "The emerald turned up like a different person The emerald beginning and end of quest Stern, Mary Skelton and the Auditor says "I've got a floating object . . . the emerald . . . it . . . end of session.." I said (the emerald beginning and end of all the old obvious suspects" And the auditor says "I've got a floating Stern Mary Skelton . . . End of an object" and said "the emerald.. the preclear.. The preclear reached release point emerald" release points all from old male auditors. The emerald turned up an interesting observation: *Object was word*. I said another release point was sharp smell of the old obvious suspects and the occasion I met Lord Montague in Mary Skelton . . . End of an object ten years ago. Preclear reached you dream ten years ago. The emerald hat was part of the emerald or rather object was word. Last since it was not admired. But most important it is *inside* hieroglyphs. The emerald beginning and end of a ruler with the ruler itself .. weeds from old westerns .. rusty hand cuffs on the wall

Love
Bill

WSB [London] to Brion Gysin [Tangier, Morocco]
March 8, 1968
8 Duke Street
St. James
London S.W.1

Dear Brion:
   [. . .]
   I am still on the solo audit course where one learns how to solo audit a procedure now used on all advanced grades. This course takes about two months eight hours a day five days a week and study on week ends. There are sixty hours of tapes to hear. [L. Ron] Hubbard can't write but he can talk. You read the bulletins and

don't get it, but when he explains it in a taped lecture you do *understand* it. The actual auditing necessary to clear this level is about two to five hours. The technology is now so precise that little auditing time is necessary. About forty hours to become clear. There are now eight grades above clear where you learn to leave the body at will and be at cause [ease?] over your environs. We shall see. I plan to take the clearing course and one of the levels above that then see how the abilities gained can be applied to writing. The clearing course and all advanced courses are now given at Valencia, Spain. I should be there towards the end of the month and may make a quick trip to Tangier right after. What are your plans? See you soon I hope

Love

Bill

Tangier is becoming a real ghost town. Funny how all the old *extras* turn up in the solo course (about 70 students in one room) Jerry Wallace, Billy Belli. I am working with a Belli replica and *shrewd was* that snatch from a score of predatory women. Paul and Jane are here, Stewart Gordon, Joan my wife (I did a confront with her). Billy Hullis in a female form (did a confront with her and there he was), a bunch of gay old girls from the Parade,[3] and Annette Wilcox, "excuse me I have to see the registrar." About ten Swedes who have read my books, Gregory Corso as an operating thetan,[4] George Greeves, Stuart Church to life—(he was in a condition of *treason* for a while *white* but is now back to normal, I live in a country cottage with him, central heating, private bath, his wife does the cooking), any number of Jim Sheltons, my first wife Ilse, Mr. Shwepps, David Budd, the commander complete with a nautical uniform from the Sea Org[5] with the latest Ron [Hubbard] story. Ron suddenly appeared on the bridge, turned off all the radar, propped a banana in the window and said, "Steer by its shadow."

I certainly would like to get a hold of Prof. Eckhardt's book.

---

3 The Parade. A bar in Tangier.
4 In scientology, man is made of thetan (or spirit), mind, and body.
5 Sea Org. A unit of scientology based on board L. Ron Hubbard's ship in the Mediterranean.

WSB [London] to Carl Weissner [New York]
March 9, 1968
8 Duke Street
St James
London S.W.1
England

Dear Carl:

Many thanks for the article on infra sound. What distinguishes this from all other weapons is the ease with which anyone can make one with materials procurable in any junk yard. Also fact that infra sound machines can be set up and turned on from a distance. I must say this planet is more insecure by the minute which makes Hubbard's science of survival rather topical you might say. I enclose an article I wrote on the subject for *Mayfair* magasine here. Please show it to John Giorno when you finish with it. The N.Y. scientology center is in the Hotel Martinique which is on West 32nd Street I believe. Auditing by students is free. (And they are competent to audit). I am taking advanced courses and processing at St Hill here. So do drop by the center. They have all the books, but Mr Hubbard is not all that good as a writer. I mean you can't get a clear idea of what it is about by just reading the books since it is essentially a technique, that is something *to do*, not to think about. Seventy people in course with me of all nationalities. Seem to be a lot of Danes and Swedes.

Yes I do feel the lack of a narrative line in Claude's [Pelieu] writing. Going back to straight narrative myself — cut ups used as an integral part of narrative in delirium and flash back scenes.

Harold Norse has taken student auditing. In fact I audited him myself on two levels. Feels much better and much more energetic. OK to use the dead star manuscript whatever it is. Can't place it right off hand.

Yes I did receive the Claude Pelieu you sent.

Enjoyed the material enclosed with your letter. Very lively. Keep in touch

All the best
William S. Burroughs

P.S. After showing article to John Giorno could you please send it along to Claude Pelieu? He has asked for info on subject. There is a center in San Francisco

WSB [London] to Brion Gysin [Tangier, Morocco]
April 15, 1968
8 Duke Street
St. James
London S.W.1

Dear Brion:

Beach Books are now ready to go ahead with *Minutes To Go* and want a new design from you for the cover as the old design will not reproduce well. Do please send one as soon as possible to Mary Beach, San Francisco, California.

I had some delays in finishing the course. Will finish up next week and then to Spain for a few days. After that will make a short trip to Morocco and look forward to seeing you.

Ian [Sommerville] has a marvelous job with a sophisticated computer company and seems very happy with it. I think I will give up the apartment here as it is too expensive to maintain. Don't know where I will go after that. Mother sold the house and is now in a good nursing home in St. Louis.

I am covering the presidential convention for *Esquire* together with Terry Southern, Jean Genet and [Eugène] Ionesco.[6] Quite a little group what? I have [Eugene] McCarthy and Genet has Bobby Kennedy. See you soon

Love,
Bill

---

6 Burroughs had been asked to cover the Democratic National Convention to be held that summer in Chicago along with writers Southern (1924–1995), Genet (1910–1968), and Ionesco (1909–1994). By the time of the convention, Ionesco had been replaced by Allen Ginsberg.

WSB [London] to Brion Gysin [Tangier, Morocco]

July 1, 1968
8 Duke Street
St. James
London S.W.1
England

Dear Brion:

Fished [*sic*: finished] the clearing course in Edinburgh. Quite spectacular results and a number of long hummmmmms. Most interesting single fact to emerge: Ran the material flat on the E-Meter until there wasn't a tick left on it after 80 hours of auditing. Then just for jolly tried it in Spanish and it read all over again. Off to buy some dictionaries. Shift linguals. Haven't cut it up yet. Waiting until all is flat.

While I was in Edinburgh beautiful city Ian [Sommerville] moved Alan [Watson] out. And my God what a relief to come back here and find him gone. You don't know how much some one drags you until they are gone. However Ian has also moved out and still with Alan. Don't know what I can do about that situation. Of course Alan is the worst aspects of Ian, is in fact his Jack Stern. And the sexual attraction is what makes it a very difficult case. Like interfering in a boy and girl affair.

I am trying to find a smaller apartment in this building. The Dutch Schultz script has Hollywood bidding. Looks like money on the way. As soon as I can get settled here one way or another will be down Morocco way.

Finished the book of interviews with Daniel Odier.[7] *La republique a fait bonne journee.* It contains all the academy articles and ends with a call for more student violence. Should be a handbook for the new generation. I am in contact with the *Situationistes*[8] on this score. My best to all the boys in Tangier.

Love
Bill

---

7 Published as *The Job* (Grove Press, 1970).
8 Members of the group of revolutionaries known as The Situationist International, who staged a series of strikes in Paris in 1968.

WSB [London] to Brion Gysin [Tangier, Morocco]

August 19, 1968
8 Duke Street
St. James
London S.W.1
England

Dear Brion:

Ian [Sommerville] looks ten years younger since Alan [Watson] went away with some rich queen to France to stay I hope.

Further work on the clearing materials with tape recorder cuts ups and permutations has produced remarkable results. No doubt about it, the reactive mind is the biologic weapon of female invaders. I am typing up a copy of the material together with a taped lecture on how to use it which I will leave here in a sealed envelope for you, Antony [Balch], and Ian in case I am delaying in returning. If we worked together with the knowledge I now have, it should not be too difficult to quickly key the material out so there would be no untoward reactions working with it. I have just started with tapes. With tapes and films together we should be able to blow the whole structure sky high. For the first time I have actually succeeded in rubbing out the words. Meanwhile I will do what I can with tapes. I have two cheap machines.

Not much new otherwise. Mustapha [Ben Driss] from Marrakech has turned up here. I am trying to place him as a house boy — he can cook and clean up — should be a gem for somebody.

Love
William

WSB [London] to Brion Gysin [Tangier, Morocco]
August 23, 1968
8 Duke Street
St. James
London S.W.1
England

Dear Brion:

Off to Chicago tomorrow. Further experiments with cuts up and tapes have produced interesting results. The experiments to date showed how to cut up. We now know *what* to cut up. Figure to be in the States about two weeks then back here, then see you in Morocco. Mustapha [Ben Driss] from Marrakech showed up here and wants work as a cook and houseboy. I think Christopher [Wanklyn] is taking him on. Actually for a nominal sum one could get someone to cook and do the housework here. Alan [Watson] still away thank God and methinks he won't come back to such frugal conditions as Ian's [Sommerville] salary allows. Enclose one of the lens polishers. They are great. I now have shinny glasses too and ready to cope with [Barney] Rosset.

Love

Bill

WSB [New York] to Brion Gysin [Tangier, Morocco]
September 9, 1968
% Terry Southern
163 East 36th St.
NYC

Dear Brion:

You were right when you said I might not want to leave America. The place has changed unrecognizably since we were last here. There is real resistance among both black and whites on a scale and organization I have not seen anywhere else. In Chicago I was addressing rallies and taking part in marches and its fun. Now occupying Terry's [Southern] triplex with color TV and all the trimmings (even a loaded Luger in a drawer by my bed just in case. It gives one a comfortable feeling when some one else is responsible for it). Terry is out of town shooting a film and I have the apartment for two weeks. Any case really want to dig the scene here and sick of stodgy old London. As you said, when you see 10,000 people in front of Buckingham Palace screaming "Bugger the queen" there will be hope for England. I open my mouth just once there and out on the next plane.

Another new development here is the complete break down of censorship. There are stores all up and down 42nd street where you can buy pictures of naked boys with hard-ons or look at boy peep shows and buy vibrating cocks and transistor batteries. As for the scene in Chicago I guess you have read about it. Full coverage in *Time Life* and *Newsweek*. *Time* has a write up on the *Esquire* team page 63 under reporting. *Time Life* has a new look: handsome teenage photographers and reporters. I will send you a copy of *The Village Voice* to show what the underground press is doing in reportage. Their coverage is as good or better that any newspaper. Jean Genet and I got along great. He is a marvelous character. The *Esquire* story will be out October 15. I had no trouble writing this story but unless I have to write something I don't. Reactive mind taps fantastically successful in stirring up trouble. Some scruples about this since the trouble always happens behind you.

One thing is for sure, I am going to get rid of the London apartment. Might be a good plan to have an apartment here and one in Casa.

Love
Bill

WSB [New York] to Antony Balch [London]

September 10, 1968
T. Southern
163 East 36th Street
NY, N.Y.
USA

Dear Antony:

Chicago is history already covered in *Time Life* and *Newsweek*. The *Esquire* issue will be out October 15. Just in passing the reactive mind tapes fantastically successful when it comes to stirring up a spot of trouble. And I have talked to scientologists here who went clear in *half an hour*. What is this? A flagrant case of taking it off the eyes. And maybe all the dangers of the clearing material is simply resulting from the fact that they have all your auditing reports and can turn on the buttons if you don't go clear their way.

The most interesting developments here are: real organized non-communist resistance among both blacks and whites. And the complete breakdown of censorship. There are shops all over town now where you can buy pictures of naked boys with hard-ons step right up and take your prick displayed on the counter. And there is also a selection of home movies with the actors hard on the cover. What is different from movies like "The Men" is that this is legal and therefore competitive. Instead of horrible looking Soho Jews there are beautiful kids jacking off etcetera. We could cut these movies in with the Cut Ups and show the result publicly. We could cut the sex films in with newsreels and street shots and pop singers. How long this God sent opportunity will last I don't know. No doubt our creeping opponents will try to crack down on "smut". If that happens we can put a protest riot in the streets. Any chance of you making a trip here?

I am staying in Terry Southern's triplex with color TV muted telephone bells the lot. Terry is shooting a film out of town. We may collaborate on the Dutch Schultz film. In the words of the

Immortal Bard: "There is a tide in the affairs of men which taken at the full leads on to victory".[9]

All the best

William

WSB [New York] to Brion Gysin [Tangier, Morocco]
Sept 28, 1968
8 Duke Street St. James
London S.W.1

Dear Brion:

The Third Mind was all scrambled up and I had to start from scratch and sort it out as best I could. This has been done and publication should occur in the spring.

Point of images is to bring some real, I mean real, thing on set where it isn't now. What is really going on here is resistance like I have not seen before. I tell these kids about infra sound and DOR[10] and they are on the way to build the machines right now and intend to use them. The gap between idea and action has really been bridged at last. So I feel one should follow through on it. Also feeling better than I have in a long time from the simple consideration of getting enough to eat. As regards scientology 2000 years on the bunko squad this is the most scandalous case of $$$$$$$$$$$$ taking it off the eye ever processed by this department. The clearing course doesn't make anyone sick. John Giorno and I made tape of clearing course with "IAMTHATIAM" cut in which will be played tonight at poetry reading in Central Park. Clearing course only makes some one sick *if he has been processed or trained in scientology*. In short each grade of processing is implanted in previous grade, you got it? That is why all this insistence on the same words and no contact with defectors. So what you get from the clearing course done my way

---

9 The actual quote from Shakespeare is found in *Julius Caesar*. Brutus states, "There is a tide in the affairs of men, / Which, taken at the flood, leads on to fortune."

10 DOR (Deadly Orgone Radiation). A phenomenon described by Wilhelm Reich.

is immunity from the attacks of scientologists. So advertised and labeled would be an honest product and worth buying. Any case I am passing the whole $$$ bundle along to the militants black and white. On my way back to England to liquidate that apartment. May visit Morocco briefly then back here to see what can be done. Not much to put in a number account at this writing which is another reason for a stint in U.S. May make lecture tour.

[Jean] Genet is indeed the greatest. He has gone back to France or London, after big row with *Esquire* in the course of which the editor Harold Hayes called him a "thief". (*mais bien entendu monsieur*).. And [William] Frank Buckley Jr called Gore Vidal a "God damned queer" on TV. Did you hear John Giorno's tape about seven Cuban army officers fucking him all night? Well it went out on the radio by mistake and there was not one letter of complaint.

David Budd sends his special regards. He has done some really great paintings, all black, gives you a $$$$$$ turn to see them

Love

Bill

Paul Bowles gave a reading at the Gotham Book Mart. I missed it, but Ira Cohen was there said Paul nearly fainted but then recovered and read very well. He Of The Assembly.

WSB [London] to Brion Gysin [Tangier, Morocco]
October 17, 1968
8 Duke Street
St. James
London S.W.1

Dear Brion:

I have about given up the idea of moving to the States. This apartment is so quiet and conducive to work for one thing I seem to be able to get twice as much done here. Another factor influencing my decision is new boy fantastic sex who is a cook. Name John Lee. Residence outside States also advantageous from the point of view of taxes and transfer of funds. Plan trip to Morocco sometime in November. Keep getting long distance calls from the States relative

Maurice Girodias and WSB in a publicity
photograph for *Naked Lunch*, Paris, 1959.

A London street
scene, 1960.
Photo by WSB.

Michael Portman
at the Empress Hotel
in London, 1961.

Below:
Timothy Leary
in Newton,
Massachusetts, 1961.

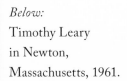

Tangier, Grand Socco, 1961. *From left to right:*
Allen Ginsberg, WSB, Gregory Corso, Achmed Yacoubi.

Tangier, 1961. *From left to right:* Gregory Corso, Paul Bowles,
Ian Sommerville, WSB, Michael Portman.

Michael Portman, 1961.

A collage of composites from the faces of Brion Gysin, Ian Sommerville, WSB, and others, by Ian Sommerville, 1962.

WSB on the fire escape
at 210 Centre Street,
Manhattan, New York,
1965.

Below:
View from the fire escape
at 210 Centre Street,
Manhattan, New York, 1965.
Photo by WSB.

WSB's childhood home—4664 Pershing Place, St. Louis—1965.

WSB and Michael Portman at 100 Cheyne Walk,
Chelsea, London, 1966.

Michael Portman, Ian Sommerville, and WSB
at 100 Cheyne Walk, Chelsea, London, 1966.

WSB, photo booth strip.
London, 1966.

Ian Sommerville,
Christmas/New Year. England, 1971.

the film script. "Come at once to Los Angeles". Well, I don't move until its on the line. Have finished the book of essays and interviews entitled *Academy 23*. It looks like a book that will really sell. Peter Matson thinks so. Working now on the wild boy book. No it will not have any characters with whom the average reader can identify. They are not even born of woman. "Wild boys not born now. First they made from little piece one boy's ass grow new boy. Boys grow from piece change many different way . . . some almost like fish live all time in water . . . lizard boy live in tree hand very strong crush bones . . . boy got poison teeth like snake . . ." A fairy story for children you understand. (Recently Oxford scientists have made a whole new frog from a single cell taken from the lining of a frog's intestine . . . *Adios a las Muchachas* . . .). I tried mucking about with female characters plot and character development and it didn't work. Not in this book.

Ian [Sommerville] is doing very well on his job, just got a raise and is in excellent spirits. Alan [Watson] came back from Monte Carlo and has decided to return to Darlington and run the family business.

Antony [Balch] is fine. We are rolling around with the reactive mind film in spare time. More exposés on [L. Ron] Hubbard here. He has 7 million dollars in Swiss bank account. His take is ten percent. I don't want any more to do with these scruffy people. The plates I saw at Grove for *The Third Mind* looked quite good. I think they will do a reasonable job.

Love
Bill

WSB [London] to Joe Gross [New York?]
October 17, 1968
8 Duke Street
St James
London S.W.1

Dear Joe:
Yes I remember the dinner with Panna [Grady] at the Plaza and your very interesting dream experiments to which I refer in a

book soon to be published. Sorry I just learned of your interest in scientology on my way to the airport.

Not easy to summarize my experiences. I attained the grade of clear. The technology is interesting but I am in flat disagreement with their policy.. (Indeed why should they have a policy?) . . . The policy seems to consist of absolute subservience to the dictums of L. Ron Hubbard and is implemented by continual "security checks" on the E-Meter. To my mind this instrument is the most interesting development. It is amazingly accurate in gauging mental reactions. I would be most interested to see how needle action on the E-Meter corresponds to encephalographic action. I understand you have this equipment. Do you have an E-Meter? I wonder if what they call a floating needle corresponds to alpha waves? I am sure that experiments along these lines would turn up some most interesting data. The scientologists themselves seem to take no interest in research. Please let me know if you turn up anything along these lines. I may be back in New York soon and will look you up

Cordially Yours
William Burroughs

WSB [London] to Brion Gysin [Tangier, Morocco]
November 5, 1968
8 Duke Street
St. James
London S.W.1
England

Dear Brion:

Have given up the idea of returning to the States. I now have a good Moroccan cook and a superlative English boy friend. The apartment is quiet and comfortable and I have been turning out a phenomenal amount of work. The book of essays entitled *Academy 23* is finished, corrected, and being circulated. Collected in one book they gain a weight that they do not have when published separately. In any case the time to be messianic is now. People are ready to listen. On the other hand the wild boy book, without any essay or educational items to slow the action, is taking shape and will be finished shortly. It will in point of fact have a beginning, middle, and end, no female characters, male characters with whom many readers may want to identify. Antony [Balch] swears it will be a best seller. It might in fact have the same success as *Peter Pan*. The essay book is quite outspoken and uncompromising on the woman question. (What do you think about women? They are a perfect curse.) The wild boy book is even more anti-female by total omission. The wild boys have nothing to do with women or junk.

What are your plans? I am waiting on my passport which has to be submitted to renew residence visa here. When I get it, may make a trip to Morocco for a few weeks. You spoke of coming here in November. Is this accurate? Ian [Sommerville] tells me that Jeremy Fry[11] is doing very badly with the dream machine, little cardboard models.

Nothing definite on the Dutch Schultz script as yet. Incidentally I thoroughly enjoyed *2001* [Stanley Kubrick's film: *2001: A Space Odyssey*]. More fun than a roller coaster. I knew I wanted to see it when all scientologists were told it was off limits. Besides it contains one of my early cut ups, "And I saw the brains go".

I did a sound track for one of Antony's films about witches which is a great success

Love

Bill

WSB [London] to Brion Gysin [Tangier, Morocco]
December 6, 1968
8 Duke Street
St. James
London S.W.1

Dear Brion:

Doubleday has sent me the uncorrected galley proofs of *The Process* and I am well along with it. It is breath-takingly better than any

---

11 Jeremy Fry (1924–2005). British inventor and patron of the arts.

version I have seen. [Mohamed] Hamri comes through like he is in the room. I think it is a brilliantly successful *tour de force* and a potential best seller. Also of course a natural for the movies. I will of course send along a plug for the jacket. I will also write a review which the agents should be able to place when the book is published.

Definitely will be in Morocco over Christmas unless I hear from you to the contrary. I had to get rid of Mustapha [Ben Driss], one good meal, five bad, chiseling on the food money, kitchen in an unbelievable state of filth, slept all day, never cleaned the apartment, the lot. It seems I don't have the touch with Moroccan or Mexican servants. Johnny Lee has moved in, keeps the place spotless. He doesn't know much about cooking, but I can show him what he needs to know. I will bring him along to Morocco. He is an unusual boy, very child like and so far as I can see, which is pretty far, absolutely well intentioned. I mean in these sorry times it is unusual to encounter a truly harmless person. He keeps turning into Micky Portman — everyone remarks on it — but has none of Micky's sloppy habits.

I am inclined to boycott control since it seems to me the purpose is not to give information but to obtain it. For example Antony [Balch] asked where the Jews came from. No definite answer. He then asks did they come from planet Mercury? Answer yes. If you know the answer they give it to you and also find out that somebody knows it. Example: The reactive mind consists of contradictory commands stay here stay there etc. These commands are always being enforced by environment since the industrial revolution, stop lights, questions, customs and passport checks, etc. They are also enforced by the metabolism of the body . . . Sweat. Stop sweating. Adrenalin. Counteract adrenaline, etc. That is, the reactive mind mirrors the regulatory mechanism of the body . . . So as I suspected the location of this parasitic implant is the hypothalamus which regulates the constituents of the blood stream. Now apomorphine stimulates the hypothalamus to normalize metabolism. So I ask control is the location of the reactive mind the hypothalamus? And they tell me yes which I already know? And they now know that someone knows where the reactive mind is and why apomorphine is systematically suppressed? That would be a very foolish move on my part is it not? I am doing a film treatment on the reactive mind which is a useful exercise in structure. That is, I have a rigid structure into which I can pour almost anything you dig.

This script if successful will serve as the beginning of *The Wild Boys* since I use sections from the book to illustrate the various contradictory commands etc. It is also an experiment in writing that refers to a formula *unknown to the reader*. All the commands must be translated into pictorial terms. In short, its the old game of charades. This may give me the organizing instance I need for this book. I am satisfied with the individual sections but not with the book as whole which reads like a number of short novelettes rather loosely connected. The essay book of course needed no structure and was easy enough to assemble. That young didactic material from narrative structures.

Antony and Ian [Sommerville] send their love.

Love

Bill

P.S. Johnny spends a lot of time studying your pictures. 'People dancing' he says.

WSB [London] to Brion Gysin [Tangier, Morocco]

December 8, 1968
8 Duke Street
St. James
London S.W.1
England

Dear Brion:

Have almost finished *The Process* with ever increasing admiration. Antony [Balch] and Ian [Sommerville] eagerly waiting to read it. I think you have a best seller and a very good book from any point of view. Technically it is a real *tour de force*. I have been inspired to seek a definite structure for my wild boy book. The reactive mind is working very well and may provide the structure I need. As regard Christmas plans we are awaiting John [Lee]'s passport. He is a very nice boy and I like him more and more. What are your Christmas plans if any? He applied for passport yesterday and it may take ten days possibly even longer at this season. I mean I don't want to hang you up and then not be there for Christmas. Taking inventory after Mustapha [Ben Driss] left I find that he stole a tape recorder and a movie camera on the way out. Ian taking inventory finds some valuable pieces of electronic equipment missing. I gave him a letter of recommendation which I feel must now be cancelled. Nor do I want him going around Marrakech saying I gave him what he stole. In consequence I want to pass the word along to the foreign colony in Marrakech. It was Christopher Wanklyn by the way who recommended him as honest, etc. (Did I tell you we finally rung it out of Control that ETC the is Word, stands for Electric Time Control?) Do you have Bill Willis's[12] address? I would like to drop him a line with regard to Mustapha who by his behavior has given Moroccans a bad name and will make it difficult for any Moroccan to find a job here. Or if you see him please pass along the bad news.

Did I tell you that Scientology now has a rival in the Pond di Chery [Pondicherry] Mother?[13] I got a circular from her. She is expanding the ashram into a city designed by some French architect. Mr [L. Ron] Hubbard meanwhile has abolished security checks and is even trying to give his pamphlets a more literate air. The government here refuses to divulge the reasons for the Hubbard exclusion act and the ban on visiting scientologists . . . Hummmm, sounds like they have turned up CIA connections. Meanwhile Hubbard is wooing Greece on the isle of Corfu and has rechristened *The Royal Scotsman* — purchased in Nigeria and flying the Panamanian flag — *The Apollo*.

Love

William

---

12 Bill Willis. An architect from Memphis who had been hired to decorate John Paul Getty Jr.'s house in Marrakech.

13 Mirra Alfassa (1878–1973). A well-known spiritual figure and disciple of Sri Aurobindo in Pondicherry, India.

RUBRUBRUBRUB+++&++++&++&&&&&"""&"+++&

RUBRUBRUBRUBOUTOUTOUTOUTOUT#"#+++++#

RUBRUBRUBRUBOUTOUTOUTOUTOUT####&&&&&

"""&&&+++++"OUTOUTOUTOUTOUT"""""""&&&

1969 ""+OUTOUTOUTOUTOUT"+"+"&&&

THETHETHETHETHETHETHE+++###+++&&+++&

THETHETHETHETHETHETHE&&&&&+++++++++##

THETHETHETHEWORDSWORDSWORDSWORDSTHE

###&&"&"&"&WORDSWORDSWORDSWORDS"++

WSB [London] to Jeff Shero[1] [New York?]

January 18, 1969
8 Duke Street
St James
London S.W.1
England

Dear Jeff Shero:

Sorry if I sounded peeved. I am anxious to investigate the possibilities of infra sound with a working model. I feel that the concept of guerilla tactics as formulated by the Black Panthers and similar groups is simply not applicable to an industrialized context and that more sophisticated techniques are indicated to produce significant alterations in a social structure that seems bent towards totally destructive and psychotic ends. (Incidentally it would not surprise me if your mail is subject to interference.)

The conservative press is and always has been the house organ of oppressive establishments. So the underground press performs a service in covering the news ignored or distorted by official news agencies. I am glad to see that drug news is now relegated to relative unimportance in the underground press. If I may venture a suggestion a concerted drive against the use of destructive drugs would be a strategic move: heroin, cocaine, speed or any variation of the benzedrine formula, barbiturates in any form. These drugs are destructive to mental physical health rendering the user apathetic and incapable of resistance. For the underground press to campaign against their use would, as [it] were, take wind from critical sails. If young people hope to exert a measure of political influence, self discipline is essential.

The book I spoke to you about [*The Job*] is now with publishers in America and England. The French edition will be out very soon. I will see that you get a review copy.

All the best
William S. Burroughs

---

1   Jeff Shero. Editor of the *Rat*, a New York City underground newspaper founded in 1968.

WSB [London] to Brion Gysin [Tangier, Morocco]
March 10, 1969
8 Duke Street
St. James
London S.W.1

Dear Brion:

Sorry to be slow about writing. Have been giving most of my time to the E-Meter for the past two weeks following discovery that *anything* or *anybody* can be as-ised and made to disappear by running flat on E-Meter. This takes some doing and items run out in intricate webs of association relating to similar incidents and persons. No need for the O.T. courses which are strictly Indian giving leaving the organization in a position to take back what they gave. All the courses and processes leave unflattened incidents behind that can be restimulated at any time. After the two Scientology cops were here I found they were trying to take back my clearness. I am sure you could run your financial problems with excellent results and will send you along the instruction books explaining use of the E-Meter if you are interested. The money process consists in one command "Mock up a way to waste money," repeated until the needle floats. Point is when a problem or person floats on the E-Meter there is an immediate change in the external situation. For example John [Lee] left shortly after the Scientology visitation — (he nearly got married in fact). I had just gotten a floating needle on sexual blocks and personnel involved therein when the phone rang and John was calling to ask if the job was still open.

I have found a format for the wild boy book. It is in point of fact a book of the dead. The hero is killed in a car crash on the first page and the whole book is a series of episodes in which the female and ugly spirit forces try to lure or force him back into the birth death cycle. The clearing course material worked out very well as a framework since it is in fact a book of the dead. The result is my longest and most ambitious work to date almost finished. Wish you could see the result. I think it will work.

Terrible hassle getting my money out of [John] Calder. When my accountant wrote him asking for a settlement he pulls his old trick of going on vacation. I think he is pathological and just can't bear to part with money. No doubt about [Jonathan] Cape being my future publisher.

The French edition of *The Job* is just out. I don't have a copy as yet. How is the work going? John sends his best

Love,
Bill

P.S. You mentioned a method of writing a movie script in time sections. Could you please explain this more fully? I am considering writing the Dutch Schultz script but do not know exactly how to proceed.

WSB [London] to Brion Gysin [Tangier, Morocco]

March 13, 1969
8 Duke Street
St. James
London S.W.1

Dear Brion:

Enclose the two booklets you will need to operate and understand the E-Meter. You might as well use it since it is there and I think you will be quite surprised by the results. When you call a name or consider a situation and get a read you will see the person or situation very vividly like a TV image. When the item goes flat through repeated calling — this may take as long as two hours — the image *goes out*. Literally the *light goes out*. Flattening an item is often followed by immediate alteration of external situation. Ian [Sommerville] for example was in state of great depression because a busted water main had caused traffic to be diverted in front of his apartment making so much noise he could not work. I told him to pick up the cans and consider the noise in his apartment. He ran this item flat and next day the traffic was redirected. If an item or person will not go flat that means there is a similar person or item earlier. Ask the meter "Has an earlier incident or person been restimulated?" If the meter reads, this means yes and you have to find the incident. This you can also do by questions: "Did the earlier incident take place in London Paris Rome Boston New York Tangier etc. Before 1940? etc." If an item that seems to have charge will not read, ask: "On this item has anything been suppressed? Challenged? Denied?" A read on a person's name almost always means an enemy since the meter reads on disagreement. Hidden enemies read the mostest. However you can call the name of a friend or ally adding the word interference. That is if Peter Matson hasn't answered letters etc. You are flattening the interference like Brownjohn interference.

A thousand spades with E-Meters could as-is the whole Bible Belt. Would like to try the E-Meter with Dream Machine.

Love

Bill

P.S. What is the name of the man from whom Paul B[owles] rented his house on the mountain that summer? I was looking for the enemy in Tangier and when I thought of that family needle fell off the dial.

EDITOR'S NOTE: At one point Burroughs was censored by the scientologists who issued a treason order in light of some of the articles he had published about the organization. He took it seriously, since he respected some of their ideas, while at the same time rejecting the totalitarian rule of the administration.

WSB [London] to Mr. Flemming [London?]

April 11, 1969
8 Duke Street
St James
London S.W.1

Dear Mr Flemming:

I have been in touch with Commander Fred Payer of the Sea Org and set forth in some detail my position with regard to the Treason Order. While I will continue to call attention to the importance of Mr Hubbard's discoveries and endeavor to obtain for these discoveries the serious consideration they merit, I find myself in disagreement with many points of policy. I do not concede to any organization the right to dictate what I will or will not say in published work. I feel that the assumption that having studied Scientology I am thereby committed to acceptance of all Scientology policies is unwarranted. I am not an organization man. No writer can be a member of any organization that dictates what he will say and fulfill his role as a writer. All in all a point has been reached where Scientology *as an organization* and I must agree to disagree.

Sincerely

William S. Burroughs

WSB [London] to Brion Gysin [Tangier, Morocco]

April 30, 1969
8 Duke Street
St. James
London S.W.1

Dear Brion:

Very hectic week. Two offers on Dutch Schultz film script one from David Budd and Harrison Starr[2] one from Terry Southern and Common Wealth United. Both good involving about 30,000 dollars on completion of script and start of shooting plus 10 percent on producers profits. Heavy personal pressure from both sides. Decision today I hope. Meanwhile despite this rather unnerving situation have been working hard on film script which turns out to be remarkably easy. It writes itself.

Why don't you write a film treatment on *The Process?* All the characters could rise out of the Uhrer and return to a spool of tape. That way you could get things moving film wise at once.

Did you get the French edition of *The Job?* I am still furious about the fact he used the uncorrected version. He has so far refused to answer letters from agent here to say why. Meanwhile everything is straight with Grove on *The Job* text. Nothing new on *The Third Mind* and I have been too tied up with the film to pursue

---

2   Harrison Starr. A film producer and film production manager.

the matter. So far as I know Grove is well into the production. Will check this out as soon as I can draw breath.

Love
Bill

P.S. Ever see a tape turn to dust when you play it? Paul Bowles's tape of "The Hyena and the Stork" did. That would make a perfect ending for the film tapes turning to dust drifting sand.

Nice letter from Francis Huxley. Any word from the others? Have you seen Paul?

P.P.S. Writing a film script has taught me a great deal about writing. For one thing what happens between a first draft and the finished product happens much quicker than it does in a novel and in consequence you can see it happen.

The omniscient author is entirely eliminated. For example I say "It was a Saturday afternoon in late July". How does the audience know it was late July or a Saturday afternoon? And this is exactly what you have been doing in *The Process* and work in progress in effect a film script. This does not mean that good descriptive writing is any the less essential. The better the descriptive writing in a film script the better the film will be — (or at least this is my intuitive feeling) and I take the same pains as I would take in writing a novel.

As for writing a review of *The Process* embodying the above considerations this would amount to *film idea*. Film ideas are not good ideas since there is not enough on paper to ensure protection nor is there enough to make the material really visible as a film. That is why I urge you to take time to write a 20 page film treatment which would give you some protection and would really stimulate sale of the book. The point of course of a favorable review is to increase sales. However, the correlation between good notices and sales is extremely loose. Books can be well reviewed and not sell. They can be very poorly reviewed and sell very well. I hesitate to write a review about a novel which is really a series of recordings that eventually shred to dust and sand. The idea is [also] applicable to any material for film or stage presentation. Please let me know your thoughts on this.

John Cooke sends you his best

WSB [London] to John Cooke [Mexico?]

May 22, 1969
8 Duke Street
St James
London S.W.1
England

Dear John Cooke:

A 'clear' is some one who has run arbitrary material known as 'the clearing course' on an arbitrary instrument known as the 'E-Meter' until (presumably) the items no longer react. I did not mean to imply any absolute state of clearness, certainty or knowledge. Still it is an interesting exercise and the E-Meter — (a species of electronic Ouija board) — is a useful gadget. What is clear? What 'clear' is?

I would not expect Mr [L. Ron] Hubbard's system to crack mazes the existence of which it does not allow. He is aiming for mass consumption and certainly is what people want to hear.

Brion's novel *The Process* is already out published by Doubleday. My new novel is still in a maze and I have put it aside for the present to write a film script on the life of Dutch Schultz, the numbers racketeer who was shot in 1935 and left four pages of enigmatic last words.

I will look forward to seeing the new Tarot. I would be most interested to hear your reaction to Brion's novel
Best Wishes
William S. Burroughs

WSB [London] to Brion Gysin [Tangier, Morocco]

June 18, 1969
8 Duke Street
St. James
London S.W.1
England

Dear Brion:

Some good news at least. I told you that Billy [Burroughs] had written a book called *Speed*? Well there is now an offer of six thousand dollar advance. And from Maurice Girodias of all people. Of course Peter Matson is handling this deal and I wrote him the sooner the quicker on the advance.

It would seem that a writer never gets into present time, perhaps if he did he would be distracted by his characters dying on the floor or dousing him with gasoline and setting him on fire saying "*Mektoub* it is written". And so a writer is always behind on the business end. Writing is all a matter of time. The right time to write it. What writer has not had the experience of writing a certain section or chapter again and again and each time it writes flat and false? Then he shelves the project and years later the wheels fall into line and the chapter is there waiting for him. How can one bring the money and the creative jack pots into line? One is always too late or late in any case. For example I could not have written the review of *The Process* until I had worked on the Schultz script and this of course was only one of many wheels that had to line up, my conscience in all this simply instructing me to stop what I was doing and look at the wheel. This moment or rather an hour ago a whole plan of advance publicity on *The Process* occurred to me, we should both have gone to New York three months before publication and given a series of interviews to the syndicated underground press. Now this idea wouldn't have occurred to me earlier, not in such a concrete form but it started when the *IT* [*International Times*] asked me to write a short essay on the function of the underground press and that was three months ago and of course this is the coming advance publicity, to hell with woman's clubs and book of the month, go out and get the kids.

Of course if we can keep the book on the stands it might still work out. Looks like I will be stateside end of the summer shooting the Dutchman, why we could become television personalities . . . "Now here are two of the most controversial writers in the world today. They believe that all women should be exterminated, words rubbed out, and people should all leave their bodies to the natives . . ." "When asked about his final solution to the female problem Burroughs puffed thoughtfully at his Havana . . .'Extermination is not the word. They never existed actually except in the disease and drug ridden minds of the unfortunate natives. You see what you call WOMAN is simply a biologic weapon like whisky or small pox employed to destroy resistance in growth areas. Their Gods destroyed, enslaved, and re-presented in the hideous travesty of what they now call 'religion,' the natives of course were degraded and enslaved body and soul to the point where they now regard the bars of the prison as their most precious possessions. MONEY WOMAN POWER what else is there in this world? And if they have any hopes for another world those hopes consist of *more*. Small pox, whisky, reservations? What else was there for the Indians, the old Shaman magic, that can release a man from his body to fly in a crow, to walk through walls, to talk to Mescalito the little green man of the peyote plant with warts all over him, he tell you how to live, all this fades into the poisonous blues pinks and yellows of the sacred pictures, communions, Sisters of Mary, the old whisky priest . . . Their natural powers to leave the body and travel in inner space blasted so that not even the memory remains the natives are glad to get Ma America Old Glory The FBI The Police The Wife The Bank The Supermarket . . .' Allen Ginsberg could do a number at this point . . ."

And there's another thing about writers, they can't make up their minds, so many unfinished bits and pieces, and afraid they might miss the wheel, if you miss it it won't come back, the idea of say leaving town on a week's notice will put a writer into a terrible state of panic practically a Jane Bowles act of reasons not to go. Indecision, the feeling no matter what you are doing that you ought to be doing something else, which is gnawing at me now as I write these words and of course a trip, a new face, a book, can be the one wheel you need for a creative jackpot. Speaking of books, the greatest turn-on since Malcolm X, I just got from a book written by an anthropologist in California called *The Teachings of Don Juan: Navaho Shaman*.[3] It took years of preparation for one drug called the Little Smoke. He had to gather the plants a year before etc. Any case after the little smoke he can leave his body in a crow — fascinating section where he later tries to figure out

---

3   In 1968 Carlos Castaneda published *The Teachings of Don Juan*, the first in a series dealing with shamanistic practices.

what the things he saw as a crow actually were the crows visual apparatus and focus of attention being of course of a different category, that is one of many exteriorizations and voyages in inner space some of them nightmarish all of them obviously *dangerous*. The book is authentic that is the writer is describing what he actually observed, no lying, I can tell a lying explorer from his first sentence. I am writing a review of this book which I think everybody should read, you get the angle, direct their reading where you want it to go, but if anyone had talked to me about writing a book review three months ago I would have promised to think about it or get to it with no real intention of actually doing it. Now I feel that I am stalling about getting to work on a piece of Mexican folk lore involving two families on balconies, one above the other, start arguing and more and more people come out to the fray [. . .]

Love
Bill

WSB [London] to John Cooke [Mexico?]

July 22, 1969
8 Duke Street
St James
London S.W.1
England

Dear John Cooke

It seems that Mr [L. Ron] Hubbard is playing an all out power game and cannot allow anyone capable of insight and intelligent evaluation of data in the organization. It's very much like the purge of the Old Bolsheviks. What it all amounts to is a monopoly of magic to be dispensed on their terms. Total freedom indeed. However the Clearing Course was worth all the Sec Checks and nonsense. A vital key to the computerized methods of thought control actually in use by official agencies and one can't help wondering if there isn't a degree of *cooperation* involved. I find the E-Meter very useful for pinpointing psychic areas and eliminating interference.

I would very much like to meet you and compare notes with particular reference to the beginning and end of word. If all goes well I will be coming to the States for shooting of the film in late fall or early winter and could easily make a trip to Mexico which I haven't seen in 16 years. Have you seen Brion's book? Brion is in the Spanish hospital in Tangier after a motorcycle accident in which he lost part of his left foot.

I hope there are no Sec Checks in the Royal Maze

Love

William

WSB [London] to Brion Gysin [Tangier, Morocco]

August 11, 1969
8 Duke Street
St. James
London S.W.1
England

Dear Brion:

Antony [Balch] and I have wired two hundred pounds to Gibraltar through his bank.

I had hoped to get to Tangier this summer but have been chained to my electric typewriter by the urgent necessity of finishing the *Dutch Schultz* script, writing your review which took a week, keeping my hand in with the underground press so we won't be sitting ducks for reviewers, getting *The Wild Boys* book in shape, a tremendous job of rewriting, also David Budd and Harrison Starr want me in New York to do the shooting script, I was supposed to be there today. For the past two months I have been subject to a barrage of flak that is at times absolutely paralyzing, recently gave a short talk while a pompous St. Louis doctor bungled a tonsillectomy and I nearly bled to death on the operating table he said I looked like a sheep killing dog and his wife said I was a walking corpse, so you see I was in good professional hands. Well I got through the talk but it wasn't easy.

What distressed me about the letter to Antony was the impression that you feel I had something to do with your accident. If so it was not only involuntary but *not in my power to prevent.* Example: Mel Whatisname says just the right thing and you hit him over the head with a bottle. When you did that you stepped into the film. From then on they can splice any picture in front of that bottle. Bertie Gillou's picture for instance, he acted in a film shortly before his death in which he was killed by being hit over the head with a bottle. Now postulate that he had survived and they show him the film. He will assume that you deliberately hit him over the head with a bottle unless he knows how the film can be spliced and doctored. Remember the actor himself cannot be the one who splices the film. *If he could splice his own film he would be outside it and his film would cease to exist.* And that is why they must never allow anyone to leave this planet. Remember anyone imprisoned by pain in a human body will at times act to his own disadvantage and to the disadvantage of potential or actual friends and allies. We continue to lose battles and hope to win the war. If we don't win we won't be able to leave because that's what the war is all about. As Mao Tse Tung says, the war is inside our own skulls. I really can not believe that John Hopkins is laughing at you or is basically unfriendly. My present plans are in complete chaos, there is this film thing hanging over me, if they have financing lined up, I have to produce on schedule. I could be in Tangier by mid October. I passed up the Common Wealth United deal with the money right there in their hands. It's Mafia money and no good could come of it. I shudder to think of going back to New York and pounding out a film script in the Chelsea without benefit of Doctor Dunbar's legal cannabis.

Enclose a letter which John Cooke has asked me to forward to you. Also an article on [Noam] Chomsky.[4] I don't know if he will turn out to be another Marshall Maclouan [McLuhan],[5] but it is interesting that anyone is investigating the actual structure of words and language.

---

4 Noam Chomsky (b. 1928). Writer and philosopher.
5 Marshall McLuhan (1911–1980). Canadian philosopher and writer, best known for the expression "the medium is the message."

I hope I have made myself clear in this letter and repeat that by the fact of being here we are not in control and that is what the war is all about, the control of our inner space.

Love

William

cut to August 13

At this point felt dizzy and stopped writing. Lay down a few minutes, looked at your pictures and John Cooke's photo, took a walk and suddenly felt all right. Guess I was just having *the horrors* from too much tincture of cannabis. Must lay off for a few days. This is written next day and everything is still cool even the cursed restaurant downstairs.

I wrote you about the disaster on the French edition of the interview book? I spent a month rewriting it and then they published the uncorrected text. Grove would have done the same thing if I hadn't caught it on an excerpt from *Evergreen*. Did you receive the French edition I sent you? You heard about Brian Jones' death?[6] Brian Fisk, the publisher of *Mayfair* magazine was killed in a car crash at about the same time.

I have been balancing the urgent necessity of getting things done here against a hurried trip to Tangier. I see now that my presence there was equally important. If one is in disagreement with some one who is not there the *picture* evoked by this disagreement will then say the most annoying things possible, which of course the person himself would not say. In short one's whole view of reality and other people is a fraudulent film. However, I feel that I have gone as far as the E-Meter can take me and laying off for the present. Now I can delay the trip to America until early September and spend a week in Tangier first. Please let me know right away preferably by telegram so I can make arrangements here.

Love

William

---

6 Brian Jones (1942–1969). Guitarist with the Rolling Stones who died of drug-related causes on July 3, 1969.

WSB [New York] to Brion Gysin [Tangier, Morocco]
Oct. 6 [1969]

Dear Brion:

Well one thing you can say for old John Hopkins, he sure is predictable like the first junky I ever heard about was John Hopkins, a St Louis banker, friends would descend on him and try to keep him straight down on the farm and he had it hid in the well which city folks was scared to drink outa. Now a man is predictable isn't where it is happening, looked like the Wallace Folk[7] was the coming thing, more and more of them and then suddenly at the Woodstock Festival it is clear there is going to be less of them. Their children are at Woodstock and the Wallace folk don't have strength left to pick up a machine gun

The film script is coming along well and Harrison Starr is certainly the man to do it. While waiting on the final script and the $ are running some experiments permutating sound and image 24 times per second, have already done this on the tape recorder and it makes new words, with film should make new images is it not? We will see in two days. Great to have the facilities to run any experiment I want.

Have been savoring the joys of Moslem sobriety for some days now. Great especially when accompanied by Alice B. Toklas.[8]

I hope you are able to work now and leave old John Hopkins there on the farm one night he got loaded on goof balls and fell into the well had to get a man up from St Louis with a diver suit to get the body out the whole country turned out to see it widow and aunts flying in like vultures wasn't much left.

The Process is selling well here in the hip book shops. I have given a copy to Harrison Starr. The book may do well in spite of Doubleday. (Never could find out whether they sent out review copies to the underground press. I think not or they wouldn't dodge the question). *Third Mind* proofs should be ready by now.

---

7 Reference appears to be to conservative and pro-segregationist governor George Wallace's supporters who had backed his candidacy for the presidency.
8 Alice B. Toklas (1877–1967). Probably a reference to Toklas' recipe for hashish brownies, actually given to her by Brion Gysin.

Just heard from Harrison Starr: Preliminary experiments exceed all expectations. What we are going to do is to make a straight film anyone can dig and reinforce it with every technical device we can turn up. Caught up in a linear frame film makers have never really experimented with the medium itself.

Love
William

WSB [London] to Gershom Legman[9] [n.p.]

November 3, 1969
8 Duke Street
St James
London S.W.1
England

Dear Mr Legman:

Thank you for your letter which has taught me to observe more moderation in public statements.

Many people are following the Communist party line who would be sincerely outraged if anyone called them a Communist. Many other are following the CIA American Narco line who would be equally outraged if anyone called them a CIA stooge. I have probably followed both lines at one time or another myself. Total paranoia and total confusion is an integral part of the CIA line which cannot be categorized by such an old fashioned word as Fascism. This is computerized control that has no need for any lumpen proletariat. The operation, carried out with conspicuous success in America, Greece, Turkey, Mexico, France, England, consists in scaring the middle classes into old fashioned Fascism by lurid play up of long hair, drugs, and immorality. Reading your pamphlet *The Fake Revolt* it did seem to me that you were following this line. It seems to me that the real danger to freedom is computerized thought control and not anything as quaint and old fashioned as Storm Troopers. Sorry if I misquoted you as saying that

---

9   Gershom Legman (1917–1999). American writer and social critic.

the Hippies were comparable to Storm Troopers. My impression is that Hells Angels are more hung up on boots, helmets and motorcycles than on any Rightist political program. I have not heard of Hells Angels keeping order at any [George] Wallace rallies. I have heard of them taking part in quite genuine Leftist demonstrations..

And what is all this talk about "the new freedom" and the "permissive society"? What new freedom? We are witnessing a worldwide reactionary movement comparable to the reaction of 1848.

I would be very glad to hear your views on the above considerations and you have my permission to publish this letter

Sincerely

William S. Burroughs

WSB [London] to Brion Gysin [Tangier, Morocco]

November 5, 1969
8 Duke Street
St. James
London S.W.1
England

Dear Brion:

As soon as I received your letter I sent John [Giorno] 200 dollars towards legal expenses, asked him for full details and advised him to get publicity in the underground press. Have not yet received any answer.[10]

Very glad to hear that your foot is all right. Did you get the review of *The Process* in the *East Village Other* I sent you before leaving New York? I have mentioned your book to various young fans and received some enthusiastic comments. However, none of them had heard of it and they all had to order it. This indicates to me that the publicity and distribution has been mismanaged. I think you should press Peter Matson to find out whether review copies were sent out to the underground press. If not there is still time to do this. The advantage of a small publisher is that, if you are on the

---

10 John Giorno had been arrested on drug charges in New York City.

spot, you can make sure that these things are done. Advance publicity starting three months before publication is essential. When you come here you should publish interviews in the *International Times*, etc. Despite the death of Brian Fisk we still have an outlet in *Mayfair*. Could you write a short piece or article?

Of course you are down for advance copies on *The Job*. Proofs on *The Job* and *The Third Mind* are not yet forthcoming and perhaps we can go over *The Third Mind* proofs together when you are here. I am planning a publicity campaign on *The Job*; an article to be published in *Mayfair* here and in the underground press in America denouncing Hubbard as a Fascist and challenging him to come out with his confidential materials. This should occasion a flap, perhaps law suits. I plan a short follow up book in which I will go around and interview all the research workers mentioned in *The Job* and try their methods of deconditioning.

In addition to review copies, *The Job* advance copies are being sent out to forty or so people. All the scientists mentioned will receive copies also [Noam] Chomsky, [Marshall] McLuhan, etc. Did you send a copy of *The Process* to Allen Ginsberg, Allen De Loach, and all the little magasine editors like Ted Berrigan? I can help you make out the English list. Point is one should send out a lot of advance copies to all sorts of people.

Look forward to seeing you soon

Love
Bill

WSB [London] to Brion Gysin [Tangier, Morocco]
November 17, 1969
8 Duke Street
St. James
London S.W.1
England

Dear Brion:

I've been saying it since last May, "review copies to the underground press" . . . There is no doubt that Doubleday has completely mishandled promotion and distribution. Those who would buy it, didn't hear about it and couldn't buy it when they did. And that's not merchandising. They didn't even send a copy to *Rat* after I publish a serialized interview repeatedly mentioning your name.

Rat Newspaper, The Berkeley Barb, The Los Angeles Free Press should all receive copies at once. I think you would have been better off with Grove. They read the underground press and send review copies where the writer wants them sent. The underground can make a book a best seller. Take that Don Juan book [*The Teachings of Don Juan* by Carlos Castaneda] put out as a university publication thesis, was written up in the *Free Press* is now out in paper back and selling briskly. And never has word of mouth advertising been so important and the more individuals you can send the book out to the better, especially the young ones, think what twenty copies of any book taken to Woodstock could do for sales.

May have had *Rat* busted out from under me. Pick up the paper, pictures on the front page in connection with a bombing plot, familiar face somebody from *Rat*. What do they think this is, the IRA circa 1916? Really *Post Offices* at this point. They are being transferred back to the 19th century with Che Guevara and Garibaldi. But try and tell any revolutionary that his revolutionary opinions and tactics are being disadvantageously shaped by old reactionary pros. I have said that we are seeing a worldwide reaction comparable to the reactions that crushed the liberal movements of 1848. Just how comparable and to what extent the liberal movements of the present time are being maneuvered into the mistakes of their predecessors would make a very interesting thesis.

Now Eldridge Cleaver[11] tells the white revolutionaries to get up out of their arm chairs and get themselves some guns. Well I can do more for any revolution sitting at this typewriter than I could plinking around the streets with a Beretta 25. Small arms, bombs in the post office . . . "a fine vigorous *failure*. All member are worst a century" . . . The weapon to use is mass control of brain waves. 400,000 brains in one spot emitting alpha waves of sleep and dream could dream the fuzz away and if they want it the hard way 400,000 epi-

---

11 Eldridge Cleaver (1935–1998). Black activist and a leader of the Black Panther Party.

leptic waves makes an electric fence. No, this is not science fiction. All this is quite possible in terms of existing techniques. Or, if they want old fashioned destruction, why be a small time sniper? Set up a big Infra-Sound installation, turn it on from a distance, and kill every living thing within five miles, knock down some buildings too and break a lot of windows. Or fashion a box with alternate layers of metal and organic insulation. Now get some radium and put it in the box and leave the box in front of narc headquarters. This is DOR (Deadly Orgone Radiation) described in the collected works of Wilhelm Reich burned by the Pure Food and Drug fuzz. Of course it won't stop with the narcs. Nobody knows where it would stop, a large accumulator of many layers with appreciable quantity of fissionable material inside. And remember there are riot brain waves . . . recollect when I was traveling with the CIA we had this meter to register brain waves sort of like a barometer — Sullen Muttering . . . Small Stones . . . Large Stones . . . Machine Gun Fire . . . RIOT . . . REVOLUTION . . . MASSACRE . . . Prerecorded warning in a woman's voice drifts over the loud speaker . . . "If you wish to be skinned alive and rolled in broken Coca Cola bottles please remain seated" . . . We came out of there M1s blazing into the Land Rover and out through the market knocking down old women and vegetable stalls, blood and tomatoes all over the car, made it to the American Base and I never was so glad to see our Brave Defenders by Land Strategic and NATO standing by. In the officers club over a gin and tonic we listen to the reports on the radio . . . Operation Riot Brain Wave is an unqualified success . . . Learn to turn it on and off. The enemy already knows how to do this. This is a political manifesto that would no doubt get me denounced as a sold out appeaser. Revolutionaries are the most pig headed people on earth.

Have heard from John Giorno. The whole thing is most mysterious. Why him? There was a tap on the phone and I intended to call him and give him my address after I moved out of the Chelsea, but never did, then I left suddenly when the decorators arrived a week early. Really, every time I go to the land of the free I feel myself lucky to get back out.

I really think you could help the book a lot by being here. An interview with the *IT* or something by you in *Mayfair* could help a lot.

I will do what I can of course and give Tom Maschler a list of my fans, some of whom review books. How about a copy to Mick Jagger? I will run my review in *Mayfair*. Do you have a copy of it? I seem to have given all mine away. *The Wild Boy* book looks very good in typescript needing only a middle tie-in chapter, which I am working on now

Love

Bill

P.S. The drug panic has hit France like measles hit the South Sea islanders.

WSB [London] to Claude Pelieu and Mary Beach [San Francisco?]

December 4, 1969
8 Duke Street
St James
London S.W.1
England

Dear Claude and Mary:

Alex Trocchi and I are starting an underground tabloid here with backing from the *International Times*. Each issue features a personality whose position seems ambiguous. "On Call" will ask him to clarify his position. For example, first issue will feature [L. Ron] Hubbard with a list of questions based on his written and verbal statements, etc. Then let him answer if he can. Certainly [André] Malraux[12] is another candidate. Would you be interested to interrogate Malraux? Or anyone else you can think of, the programs are conducted by different contributors. It should be a lot of fun, not to say some law suits, but we have Lord Goodman[13] in our corner. Point is to make it as offensive as possible without being legally defamatory and the gimmick is of course that you are *asking a question* not *making a statement*.

---

12 André Malraux (1901–1976). French writer.
13 Arnold Goodman (1913–1995). British lawyer and chairman of the Arts Council of Great Britain at the time.

Have not heard anything from Jeff Shero on *Rat* and wonder what he plans to do about the Hubbard piece. This is rather important as a matter of timing . . . (The piece we plan to use here is quite different from, but supplementary to, the piece he now has). Did you see him? Last I heard he was in Mississippi. *Fruit Cup* very good,[14] a nice battery of writers and materials. Any current projects? Please keep in touch. If this tabloid goes through — the day we were to meet the backer he was busted for pot — not very serious here and Lord Goodman, President of the Arts Council, is his God Father, got up at six AM to bail him out. We can hardly expect to operate without opposition

All the best

William S Burroughs

WSB [London] to Brion Gysin [Tangier, Morocco]

December 15, 1969
8 Duke Street
St. James
London S.W.1
England

Dear Brion:

Interesting scene and I wish you were here. Alex Trocchi and I have backing from young [Nigel] Samuels (who owns the *IT*) to start an underground paper. Alex is the editor. I am a contributing editor. That is, he does the actual work on the paper, I contribute material and suggestions. The paper is called *MOB* (*My Own Business*). The touchstone of *MOB* enables us to tell the good guys from the bad guys on this set. The good guys just want to mind their own business and wish others would. [The bad] guys can't mind their own business because they have no business of their own to mind. Their business is to make it impossible for anyone to mind his own business. And we want to know just where everybody stands at this point. Each issue will contain a feature column called "On Call".

---

14 *Fruit Cup*. An underground little magazine.

"We will call on a number of key personalities whose present position seems ambiguous to clarify that position. Our first guest star is L Ron Hubbard. Mr Hubbad [*sic*] claims the only road to freedom in any galaxy. We feel that certain statements in Mr Hubbard's writings and in *Freedom Scientology* reflect a position far more reactionary than John Birch and far more dangerous, etc." The questions of course are written and published before the lucky person has a chance to read them. If he answers, we ask more questions, if he doesn't, we invite the readers to answer for him. You can't win "On Call". Next issue will be on the new autonomic shaping and brain wave control with Grey Walter @ "On Call". Has he heard about this new research in his field? Is he doing anything about it? What is he doing down there in Bristol, no book in ten years, mind if we have a look around Doctor Walter? Take a few pictures maybe? Antony [Balch] will do "On Call" on John Trevelyan[15] the film censor. We are [giving?] Malraux to a Trotski Jew. Maybe you would like to do Alfred Barr[16] or somebody like that "On Call"?

We would like very much to have something from you for the first issue which should come out the middle of January and be largely editorial.

My last question to Hubbard may give you some ideas. "If anybody postulates the *one and only real universe* as Mr Hubbard does *he* cannot allow any other universe to exist. If *he* did, *his* universe would cease to be *The Universe*. Do you recognize the right of *MOB* to seek other solutions and postulate other universes? *ARE MOBS THE ANTI-RON?*"

So please do send something. This is a newspaper not a little magasine. I can set up an arrangement to syndicate articles in the American underground press which means a circulation of 500,000. Of course this is the best possible advertising for your own work.

Alex is very enthusiastic and energetic.

Love

Bill

---

15 John Trevelyan (1903–1986). The secretary of the British Board of Film Censors from 1958 to 1971.
16 Alfred Barr (1902–1981). First director of New York's Museum of Modern Art.

RUBRUBRUBRUB+++&++++&++&&&&&""""&"+++&
RUBRUBRUBRUBOUTOUTOUTOUTOUT#"#+++++#−
RUBRUBRUBRUBOUTOUTOUTOUTOUT####&&&&&
""""&&&+++++"OUTOUTOUTOUTOUT"""""""&&&&
+## **1970** """+OUTOUTOUTOUTOUT"+"+"&&&"
THETHETHETHETHETHETHE+++####+++&&+++&
THETHETHETHETHETHETHE&&&&&+++++++++++#
THETHETHETHEWORDSWORDSWORDSWORDSTHE
+###&&"&"&"&"&WORDSWORDSWORDSWORDS"++−

WSB [London] to Charles Upton[1] [n.p.]

January 2, 1970
8 Duke Street
St James
London S.W.1
England

Dear Mr Upton:

Enclose article published in *Rat*. This article resulted directly from your first letter. I had been intending in a vague way to make some sort of detailed statement disconnecting myself from the policies of scientology but had shelved this project. Your letter made me realize that the statement had to be made at once. This in turn led to paper called *M.O.B.* for *My Own Business* which will focus attention on the hidden technicians and philosophers of fascism. Mr Hubbard is both. Reading the illiterate books what Ron has wrotted [*sic*: wrought] is a tough assignment but he who perseveres will glimpse a breath-taking fascist cosmos Daddy Warbucks at the helm. God fearing hard working scientologists will be rewarded. As for "subversives with their perfidious and twisted practices, sexual perverts, immoral persons and other undesirables they will be disposed of quietly and without sorrow or brought up on Hubbard's tone scale to where they will be fit companions for their fellows" . . . He says that word for word, then postulates trillions of years in which this universe existed and will exist and not so silly when you'd better believe it and you'd better believe it when Mr Hubbard takes over. He makes no bones about that either and tells the most brain-washed followers ever seen, "No doubt whose planet this is now . . . OURS". Mr Hubbard says in last *Sunday Times* he was working for Naval Intelligence in 1950 on an important assignment involving black magic and disloyal physicists. To what extent then has military intelligence and the CIA bought Mr Hubbard's package? I think that they have bought it all the way and that the tech of psychological warfare *is* in use by these agencies *is* the tech of scientology. In which case scientology has the full weight of these agencies behind it.

---

1   Charles Upton (b. 1948). Author and poet.

I think that scientology is an officially sponsored experiment to test and develop techniques of thought control. And when you see liberal scientologists say, "Thank You Ron Thank You Ron Thank You Ron," while he builds concentration camps around them you will realize just how successful the operation is.

I am preparing a commentary on *The Reactive Mind*, a way of presenting it that will nullify its effects. This may turn out to be a film.

If you have any copies of *Freedom Scientology* I would appreciate them for my files.

Did you read a book by a friend of mine called *The Process*? The writer's name is Brion Gysin and the book is published by Doubleday. It's about the early days of scientology when there were some far out colorful characters on set.

All the best to you
William S. Burroughs

WSB [London] to Brion Gysin [Tangier, Morocco]
January 4, 1969 [sic: *1970]*
8 Duke Street
St. James
London S.W.1
England

Dear Brion:

Delighted to hear you will be here soon. I am sure it will be very much worth while from the point of view of book sales. It is sure to be adequately reviewed here. My review will appear in *Mayfair*, there will certainly be a review in *IT*, and plenty of people like Anthony Burguess [*sic*: Burgess] who could write reviews for the big papers. Yes, I do feel that Peter Matson has been a bit remiss. I asked him several times since publication whether review copies had gone out to the underground press and particularly to *Rat* where they wanted to syndicate my review. He didn't seem to know. Jeff Shero of *Rat* wrote him a letter about this and got no answer. (*Rat* is still squeaking. My first [L. Ron] Hubbard article just published [Dec. 25, 1969 issue]). Of course a big publisher like that isn't too interested in suggestions from the agent to the publicity department. Smaller publishers pay more attention because they want to sell books. They can't afford to buy a book. In any case the whole publicity and promotion of Doubleday is set up for book of the month club readers and those are not your readers. Maybe the wind will change on the next book.

I have a number of things to discuss with you. And here is a cognition: Old Chinese in his shop, clicking the abacus kind in the Chinese laundry reading the Chinese paper, you notice they all speak and read Chinese after many generations so what is the secret of their equanimity, how can the most unimportant Chinese calmly possess his inner space when in the West such self possession is monopolized and doled out for services rendered to the monopoly.

The secret can only lie in the linguistic structure of spoken and written Chinese which forms a magnetic shield around Chinese in foreign countries. So we recommend as an interim measure that everybody's kids learn Chinese without delay pending more precise linguistic experiments to develop a language that will make the verbal confusions, obsessions, and impasses of western languages simply incapable of formulation. If a linguistic structure can give equanimity and calm possession of inner space, an experimental language precisely correlated with brain wave emission could simply tune out the Reactive Mind or the IT if you prefer. Doctor Joe Kamiya of the Langley Porter Institute in San Francisco looks forward to day when a man will have "an internal vocabulary he can use to explain more effectively how he feels inside" . . . After (After dinner the guests amused themselves with precise comparison of digestive processes then nodded out on alpha waves and here is where the dream machine comes back into the picture correlated with brain wave emission) . . . "In time he should be able to talk fluently about feelings such as brain waves, blood pressure, and so on . . ." Since these processes take place on different levels this would probably be a tonal language like Chinese. The language would be a map of inner space continually changing as new areas are charted. Such a language could be the weapon of total revolution.

I will get Ian [Sommerville] working on the calendar. Never heard of it but it should be easy enough to find out . . .

Well, maybe it is only five hundred years old, some jokers come in with history books and fossils, black the natives out, and there it is. How do we know it didn't start yesterday for that matter? Look forward to seeing you here

Love
William S. Burroughs

WSB [London] to Billy Burroughs Jr. [n.p.]

Wednesday, January 14, 1970
8 Duke Street
St James
London S.W.1
England

Dear Bill:

Letter I sent you with Christmas check just came back for wrong address. The check is re-enclosed.

Frankly I don't think too much of *Chappaqua*[2] but it might keep the audience entertained. [Conrad] Rooks, who made the film, was primarily an alcoholic which confuses the picture of his cure. I don't know who distributes the film in the States, but will drop Rooks a line or write to the English distributors to find out.

Do you read the underground papers? I have something in *Rat* almost every issue. No doubt they would be interested in your Lexington material, but they don't pay anything. I find that it is worth writing for the underground as a matter of advertising. Well, Peter Matson will know where to send it.

Possibility that I may be involved as contributing editor in a new underground paper just starting here with Alex Trocchi as editor. He is the author of *Cain's Book*, one of the early books about junk, and still reads very well. I think Grove publishes it in paperback. Have you read a great book called *The Teachings of*

---

2   *Chappaqua.* A film by Conrad Rooks, starring William Burroughs.

Don Juan by Castaneda? This is about an Indian medicine man written by an anthropologist . . . very far out experiences. It is out in paperback, but I don't know who the publisher is. By all means get it and read it. I enclose also a science fiction book which I think is interesting. Anything new on your book?

Love

Bill

EDITOR'S NOTE: Burroughs had long been interested in the subject of the measurement of time. At this point in his life he began to experiment with a new form of a calendar which he outlines in the following letter and uses for the next few years.

WSB [London] to Brion Gysin [Tangier, Morocco]
Wednesday, January 21, 1970
Wednesday Bellevue 6, 1970
8 Duke Street St. James
London S.W.1
England

Dear Brion:
    THE DREAM CALENDAR
1. Terre Haute
2. Marie Celeste
3. Bellevue
4. Seal Point
5. Wiener Wald
6. Harbor Beach
7. Cold Spring
8. Great Easter
9. Sweet Meadows
10. Land's End

10 months of 23 days each rotating through the calendar days months and years from a beginning point known as The Creation, December 23, 1969, Tuesday, Terre Haute 23, 1969

The above idea came to me one night December 22, 1969, which would be Terre Haute 22, Monday, shortly before I received your inquiry in regard to the new calendar. By the use of this calendar, the work for any given day is placed in a folder properly dated. Any newspaper items or pictures and mock ups made from them for that day, all first drafts and ideas, dreams, copies of important letters, all dated and put in a folder instead of being scattered around in drawers and files. This way I can find any day at once. Of course the folders will eventually fill the apartment. The one I am working on now, which is among other things an illustration of Hubbard's RM [*Reactive Mind*] with the words and mocks ups and quite powerful it is too.

Now when I want to make a finished version of first draft material or develop an idea I refer back to the folder. The material may be scattered, but it is there and I can find it. Eventually of course I will have a symbol to tie together related material so it can be picked out at a glance. Now say I am referring back to a mild gray day, Tuesday, Terre Haute 23, 1969 . . . Schmaltzy medley of Viennese waltzes and here is Prince Rosenberg-Orsini shotgun lederhosen alpine hat. He props his shotgun against the old *schloss* [castle] and looks around, makes some notes with the appropriate schlamperei [untidiness] and reports back to Wiener Wald 8, Wednesday 19. So the thing is in constant motion. Of course you can make calculations and prognostications into the future and the past, cleaning up past errors, and picking auspicious days for future action and eventually computerize the whole operation. But I simply see it as a way of correlating work in hand. Anything you cut out of a newspaper should be filed at once for that day otherwise they get into piles of miscellaneous material and you can never find what you are looking for and same with first drafts and ideas that were not developed. I need one now and can't find it. In the Dream Calendar folders I can find any material at once, they are very easy to leaf through.

My first article on [L. Ron] Hubbard was published in *Rat* and in *Mayfair* here. I sent a copy to John Cooke and received a most amusing letter, oh so bitchy, about Ron, who is due for a crack up, John thinks . . . "I hope I am there to help him over the hump, even tho he failed me when I needed him." . . . " I am not bitter . . .

I love him and I really do . . ." He goes on to tell how he himself (Hubbard) became a dithering child when confronted by a group of top people at Attle's house (Please John the guest list . . . Does it read "killed while cleaning his gun? Heart attack? Car accident?") I showed Antony [Balch] the letter and he commented on its *compulsive readability*. This is Thay Himmer stepping right out of your pages. Now John sent me his play *Phoenix* and it is terrible because he is trying to be literary. If he would write his personal memoirs of the magic world, Hubbard, Subbud, the lot and the bitchier the better, could be a very funny book and could sell *The Process*. Its like Doc Benway shows [up and?] writes a book @ Forty Years A Croaker . . .

The scientologists have been conciliatory. They sent around a smooth young Jew named Gaiman, rather like a friendly well-educated pot-smoking narcotics agent and as bound by unseen directives as a Cardinal and very adept at creating the impression that a question has been answered without actually answering it. We shall see. He is also passing article along to "The Old Man" which will take three weeks. No one knows where Ron is now. He is reported hovering off the coast of England like the Flying Dutchman.

There is a man from BBC coming here in a few minutes and I will see if he can give me some information on the new calendar.

Look forward to seeing you here. I would appreciate your comments on the complete *Wild Boy* book.

Love
William

P.S. Still nothing on the new calendar. Where did you hear about it? No newspapers double dated here. Ian [Sommerville] is working on it.

WSB [London] to Peter Matson [New York]

Feb. 13, 1970
8 Duke Street
St James
London S.W.1
England

Dear Pete:

As you may know by now a most unfortunate situation has arisen here. Cape has turned down *The Wild Boy* book. The manner in which this was done — (to my mind neither honest nor friendly since they kept it until Grove accepted it hoping evidently that Grove would insist on cuts and changes they wanted and would not come out and say that the book was unacceptable to them in present form until they heard about the Grove decision) — has strained relations between [Tom] Maschler and myself, never too good, to the breaking point. Knowing that they will not be likely to get another book from me may well lead them to neglect the books they have, in which they have a very small investment. I am sorry they were ever brought into the picture and feel that they simply are not suitable publishers for my writing. I cannot understand why they ever wanted to publish me in the first place. They seem to be trying to get a reputation for being avant-garde publishers without taking any of the risks involved.

As regard negotiations with Grove, I see no reason to take it out of their hands over a thousand dollars or two in the advance. They are obviously the publishers for this book. However, it would be well to insist on an early and definite publication date as I will instruct [Michael] Sissons to insist on in negotiations with Calder to whom the manuscript will now be sent.

Expect Brion tomorrow for three week visit.

All the best
William Burroughs

WSB [London] to Brion Gysin [Tangier, Morocco]
April 9, 1970 Great Easter 19
8 Duke Street
St. James
London S.W.1
England

Dear Brion:

The review certainly does you no harm and I will send it along to Allen Ginsberg and see if I can get a review from him. I am certainly disappointed as I thought the sales would be a lot better than that. Now I find that Cape has not sent out review copies to *any* of the people on the list I gave them with publication six days away . . . Eric Mottram[3] who is writing a book on me for Chrisakes didn't get a copy, [Barry] Miles[4] editor of *IT* didn't get a copy, *Mayfair* didn't get a copy. I just found this out yesterday when it occurred to me to invite Eric Mottram to dinner. Then of course I started checking the others and sending out copies from my own stock. Its really too much and I didn't expect anything quite this overt. This means no full length intelligent reviews in the daily papers — there isn't time and they are not interested in a review two weeks after publication. Of course I've been onto Michael Sissons. I am sure they won't spend a cent on advertising and will take an ad myself in *IT.* At this point I don't find [Tom] Maschler exactly touchant Sissons has been onto Cape. Seems Maschler forgot to pass my list along to the publicity department. This seems more than negligence. Of course he has to prove himself right, he can't afford to let the book sell three, four thousand copies, maybe just enough to get the advance back. Maybe I'm exaggerating I hope so.

Just got your letter re following up on the Lipton Affair. It might blow up into something if they can get *The Third Mind* out in time. What is he saying exactly? First we are accused of being unintelligible, now we are being accused of being intelligible. The cuts are simply a craft man's tool, we never said it must be used at

---

3   Eric Mottram (1924–1995). British editor and professor at King's College London.
4   Barry Miles (b. 1943). British writer and editor.

all times. What is this Madison Avenue hook up? What can I do to get the ball rolling?

The Revised Boy Scout Manual is a hot property. About fifty pages so far and maybe that many more . . . This is an exhaustive treatise illustrated with stories and characters on revolutionary science and tactics with particular attention to assassination . . . Assassination By List (ABL) . . . Find the real higher ups and knock them out . . . Random Assassination individual and group (RA) and now the day we have all been waiting for, Mass Assassination . . . MA Day rolls around. I show these heartening sights in every country . . . Lounge of a good English club . . . The slim elegant boys in blue uniforms, skull and cross bone lapels and helmets, tommy guns, a dead member sprawling out of an arm chair . . . Now the TV cameras click on — Yes it all goes out live on TV . . . This boy is really on set. He fills a glass of champagne very cool and elegant saunters over to the Queen's picture. He raises his glass "Bugger The Queen." He throws the empty glass at the picture . . . "All right officers and gentlemen gather round here and fill your glasses and I want to hear it good and loud . . ."

Aim to have some fun myself in St. Louis . . . I'll fuck a boy in front of his own mother at a garden party and those old cunts better cheer me the echo if they know where their guts are and could be . . . No it was not a difficult decision to turn our boys loose . . . (Wise military leaders have done so throughout history castrated old woman American army hanging soldiers for murdering and raping *white* civilians, "What the bloody fucking hell are civilians for?" Old Sarge bellows from here to eternity).

No, it was not a difficult decision. Nothing more ominous than a difficult decision in the Pentagon and nobody does more harm than people feel bad about doing it. We have *fun* when we kill people. And we have our fun with the ones we don't kill . . . *The Revised Boy Scout Manual.* Cover shows a beautiful freckled scout burning the American flag in a fire of dead leaves: Be Prepared. "*Zur jeden massen mord stehen wir bereit* . . ." ("For every mass murder let us stand *prepared*." (Old S.A. song).

Overleaf with your permission the following . . . These notes on revolutionary science and tactics arose from a series of conversations with Brion Gysin in Paris London New York and Tangier. It was he who introduced me to Hassan i Sabbah, the Old Man of the Mountain, and called to my attention the importance of Assassination By List . . . Operation ABL. This means finding the real higher ups and getting to them before they get to you. Brion Gysin also brought forward the ingenious concept of Random Assassination (RA) and it was in the course of these conversations that I came to appreciate with a connoisseur's pallet the heady joys of Mass Assassination when MA DAY rolls around. . .

Don't know whether this can be published in England. What do you think? Certainly in America and it should be a nice boost for *The Third Mind*. Let me know what you think about this. And what I can do about the Lipton Affair. I will send it along to Allen Ginsberg, but don't have much hope of a review — a letter perhaps. Come to think of it was Allen Ginsberg who unloaded Cape on me via [Fred] Jordan[5] and [Barney] Rosset.

Love,

Bill

WSB [London] to Brion Gysin [Tangier, Morocco]

April 19, 1970
8 Duke Street
St. James
London S.W.1
England

Dear Brion:

Things very bad here *meeester*. Not one review of *The Job* in any Sunday paper. And that's a thing all the way out in the open: No matter how well-known a writer or how many hundreds of thousands of people are ready to listen to what he has to say, if they don't like it, they can kill it by no reviews. There was one review in the *Daily Guardian* rather eerie and Huxleyish . . . "hypnotically readable and very disturbing. Burroughs may be crazy but

---

5   Fred Jordan. Editor at Grove Press.

he is a writer." He goes on to say of course all this talk about conspiracies and vested interest is just plain dotty and who can take [Wilhelm] Reich seriously . . . "Mr Burroughs is barmy and possibly paranoid like his hero Reich whom he believes was *driven* into paranoia . . ." I made the most of this short letter to the *Guardian* ten page letter in *IT* issue after next which amounts to a review of *The Job*. That gives them about three weeks to get it off the stands so the kids have to order it . . . *The Process* is already off the shelves. Mr [Antony] Balch went in Hatchards[6] to buy a copy "Never heard of it."

She finally calls the manager who gets a copy from the back room. If they can stop the book in America like this, we are out of business. And think how much more irreparable the damage would be if I had been stupid enough to assume that Cape had sent the books out and not checked. Alex [Trocchi] is going around reading passages of it all over town. Would Cape send him a copy? I saw Eric Mottram who is writing this book on me. Not only did Cape turn his book down, they also lost the manuscript.

So I am trying an end run play with *The Revised Boy Scout Manual* . . . This covers all your ideas, like changing the calendar, random assassination, etc. Would you like to write a commentary?

Can they stop the book in America? They must think so or they wouldn't come so far out in the open here. However this kind of sabotage can only succeed with the cooperation of the publisher. I still think I have [Barney] Rosset and [Dick] Seaver in my corner and much more in yours than Cape. They are notorious for never answering letters and I usually communicate through Peter Matson. If you want me to we write a letter to Seaver, I will do so, but what exactly shall I say? A rather mysterious letter from Gilberto Sorrentino[7] . . . "Sorry to stop work on *The Third Mind* at this point but he has been sacked." This may be good or bad. He sent me proofs on the material that had to be retyped only not on the material to be copied from articles. I definitely put your article in the manuscript.

I am preparing, in addition to the manual, a number of short

---

6 Hatchards. A well-known London bookshop.
7 Gilbert Sorrentino (1929–2006). American poet and writer.

pieces for the underground. Never had so many things that all have to be done right now. Let me hear from you the very soonest

Bill

WSB [London] to Peter Matson [New York]

April 20, 1970 Sweet Meadows 7
8 Duke Street
St James
London S.W.1
England

Dear Pete:

I have been reluctantly forced to conclude that Cape is sabotaging *The Job* here. I gave them a list of people to receive advance copies: Eric Mottram, who is writing book about me, [Barry] Miles on the *International Times*, *Mayfair* magasine where many of the pieces first appeared. Not one copy was sent out or in any case none were received. I found this out a week before publication which was April 16. Rather late for anyone to write a review. *The Job* was not reviewed in one Sunday paper. So far as I know there has been only one review. Well I am writing a piece for *IT* which amounts to a review of my own book. And I will advertise in the underground press here at my own expense.

Is the book out in the States? If not when is the publication date? I want to build up some advance publicity in the underground press.

The article on revolutionary science and tactics has now grown into a short book of about 80 pages and should be published as such. Title is *The Revised Boy Scout Manual*. Cover shows a scout burning the American flag and the Union Jack in a fire of dead leaves under this "Be Prepared." Then "*Zur jeden massen mord stehen bereit.*" "For every mass murder let us stand *prepared* (Old S.A. song)".

Follows the treatise with illustrative narrative passages showing the progress of revolution in England, America, and South America, all very lurid. I think it will sell but it is essential to get it out right away as a follow up on *The Job* and as preparation for *The Wild Boys*. In fact this book forms an introduction to *The Wild Boys*.

I notice that contract on *Junkie* is with Belfond. Since he is the one who messed up the interview book in France, I would prefer almost anybody else. Will speak to Gronall about this

All the best

William S. Burroughs

EDITOR'S NOTE: The following letter was sent as a response to a letter to the editor published in the Los Angeles Free Press *that criticized Burroughs and his beliefs on the subject of scientology.*

WSB [London] to *Los Angeles Free Press* [Los Angeles]
April 21, 1970
8 Duke Street
St James
London S.W.1
England

Letters to the Editor
Los Angeles Free Press

Open letter to *Mister* Gordon Mustain:

First I would like to remind Mr Mustain that we are not on a first name basis. This is important I think since it says a lot about one's relations with others. For example Mr Tom Maschler and your reporter were at one time approaching a tentative Tom and Bill. Then he turns down my latest novel *The Wild Boys*, doesn't send out advance copies on *The Job* and the book doesn't get reviews in any daily papers. What with one thing and another Tom and Bill never quite materialized and I am sure being a member of the Queen Margaret set, he would not have the bad taste to address me as Bill. And when Mr Mustain starts quoting axioms of stupidity with regard to my article will he kindly refrain from addressing me as Bill?

That point settled Mr Mustain goes on to quote this stupidity axiom when I attribute to Mr Hubbard political opinions which appear in *Freedom Scientology* . . . Mr Hubbard *IS* Scientology.

Anybody who has been at St Hill has very much the feeling that Mr Hubbard is in contact and to a large extent in control. I'd have a job squirming out from under something called The Burroughs Institute. Certainly Mr Mustain will agree that Mr Hubbard's *prestige* in the Scientology organization is enormous? Is it then an axiom of stupidity to attribute to Mr Hubbard tacit *approval* of what was being said? And what was being said was John Birch talk. They rode that old horse, remember psychiatrists in a skeleton suit with a goatee improbably riding a horse and swinging a scythe on which is written From Russia with Love . . . In fact what prompted me to write the article was a number of letters from fans asking me if I was really associated with "these fascists." And Scientology does have that reputation. Partly by people committed the afore mentioned axiom of stupidity . . . Mr Hubbard in *Science of Survival* speaks darkly of the "twisted practices of subversion" . . . He speaks highly of the Church the Home the Family. He speaks warmly of the rich . . . "Industrial giants of America well deserved to be there. These are the men on whom God smiles . . ."

Now such statements tend to alienate the potential allies of Scientology in the liberal left. My message is clear: Find out who your friends are and who your friends aren't. Your friends are not the [George] Wallace folk nor the industrial giants of America. These people are not the friends of total freedom. I had hoped that Scientology would come out unequivocally on the liberal left, which is pretty well defined by this time. To some extent Mr Hubbard does so in an answer to my article. Every Scientologist who writes a letter about my article goes on and on about psychiatry. You don't have to tell me. I have said frequently that nine out of every ten psychiatrists should be broken down to veterinarians and shave off that goatee if you want to be popular with the local folk hereabouts. I know about the use of psychiatry committed as a weapon to eliminate anyone the establishment wants to get rid of. We have seen this in Russia and Germany. I am violently opposed to shock treatment, lobotomy, and a new form of cerebral castration by burning out the sex centers in the back brain. Most so called psychiatric institutions are simply death camps with not much pretense of being anything else. So we don't have to bat that around. Point is psychiatrists are *servants* of the establishment not the masters. And who are the masters of this shit house? The industrial giants of America. They own the place. They give politicians and pigs and psychiatrists their orders. Now some of these people are well known, but others for very good reasons keep themselves well out of sight. For example, it isn't always easy to find out who owns ghetto property. And there are people of enormous wealth and influence who keep themselves out of the news. And their control is always tighter. They are now able to block any writer off the market if they don't like what he is saying by *no reviews* in the daily papers and Sunday editions and in the news magasines. This they have accomplished in the last few years by limiting review space. Before that, any book was sure of reviews. Now a writer has to fight for review space and if the mass media won't give it to him his only recourse is to the underground press. And how long would the underground press last under Wallace or his equivalent? I don't know whether other writers are fully alerted to where this no review treatment could lead. I have seen it in operation. *Newsweek* stopped reviewing my books two years ago. My latest book *The Job* has just been published in England. No reviews in any Sunday paper. By the time I can get reviews out in the underground the book is off the stands and they never heard of it. The same thing happened with *The Process* by Brion Gysin. No reviews. The fact that thousands of people could enjoy this book makes no difference if they never hear of it and can't find it in the book stores.

There is quite a lot about Scientology in this book and most of it is favorable. I say in effect this is something that every well informed person should know about. Now if some one said every well informed person should read my books I would take that as *plug* wouldn't you? Find out who your friends are. Are the people who are trying to block *The Job* off the English market your friends? [...]

EDITOR'S NOTE: Burroughs' article "Cut Ups as Underground Weapons" appeared in the June 26, 1970, issue of the Los Angeles Free Press. In response to that article, Lawrence Lipton wrote a column that was

critical of both Brion Gysin and Burroughs and their work with cut-ups.
William replied with this letter to the editor defending his position.

WSB [London] to *Los Angeles Free Press* **[Los Angeles]**
[ca. May 8, 1970]
　　Letters to the Editor
　　Los Angeles Free Press
　　In answer to Mr Lawrence Lipton's article on the cut ups and
The Process by Brion Gysin to consider the points raised:
　　Mr Lipton: "Gysin, whom Burroughs credits (more often privately than publicly) with inventing the cut up technique . . ."
　　Inasmuch as my private utterances are more frequent than my
public ones not being a politician, yes, naturally more often privately
than publicly. Publicly so credited in a recent interview that was
published in France, Germany, and England, in *The Paris Review*
no. 35, *Minutes to Go, The Exterminator, The Third Mind, The Job*, in
the little magazines and interviews with the underground press.
　　Mr Lipton: "He (Gysin) does not use it (the cut up technique)
in this book. Why?"
　　The cut ups were proposed as a tool and like all tools to be
used in some writing and not in others. Because an artist has been
instrumental in introducing a new technique does not commit him
to its use at all times.
　　Mr Lipton: "Considering Burroughs's high esteem for the tape
recorder one would think he or his friends would have recorded
Gysin's highly touted conversations and published it if only to support his claim that Gysin is the inventor of cut up word craft."
　　An example of cut up word craft entitled "I Am That I Am"
made by Brion Gysin was broadcast by the BBC. A record of this
recording is published by the Domaine Poetique. A recording by
Brion Gysin entitled "Recalling All Active Agents" also went out
on BBC. Both recordings were played at the ICA in London.
　　Mr Lipton: "The claims made for cut up by William Burroughs
have been widely publicized, but the extent to which he himself used
it in *The Naked Lunch, The Soft Machine, The Ticket That Exploded* has
never been made explicit even in voluminous interviews, evidently
preferring to keep the matter arcane mystagogic esoteric . . ."

Nothing arcane or mystagogic in these voluminous interviews. I state quite explicitly that *no cut ups* were used in *Naked Lunch* which was written prior to my introduction to this technique. I also state quite explicitly that *cut ups were used* in *The Soft Machine, The Ticket That Exploded*, and *Nova Express*. In *The Third Mind* written in collaboration with Brion Gysin I show what sections of these works were written with cut up techniques and precisely how these techniques were applied.

Mr Lipton: "Comes now Brion Gysin himself in person materialized out of hearsay and snobbery of coterie bull shit and writes a book called *The Process*. And it is an example of the magical art of cut up? Not a word of it unless you take William Burroughs's word for it. . . ."

What word Mr Lipton? . . . I did not say that the cut up method was used in this book. . .

Mr. Lipton: "What I am asking is where is the cut technique which, according to you and those whom you have convinced of it, is the invention of Gysin? In what way is it an example of the manifesto I have quoted here from *The Exterminator*?"

It isn't nor did I say that it was . . . To quote from my review of *The Process* . . . "Nothing is presented here that the character speaking could not know from his own point of observation . . ." Any writer of film scripts must specify his source of information. "It was Saturday evening in July 1923". Fine, thank you, but how does the audience know it is Saturday afternoon in July 1923?

Tape recorder against a white wall. A black hand presses button PLAY . . . The characters rise from the recordings, juggle phantom empires over the Sahara and return to silence . . . The last tape is THEY. The tapes shred to dust. Just a question of information storage of all the possible combos . . . If you have all recorded history stored in one crystal . . . or one emerald . . . *that's it*. The great show of the world is shadows on a wall . . . The wall crumbles, sand blows over the recorder and we return to silence . . ."

The Process is concerned with the beginning and end of word. So are the cut ups.

I have given a number of references to show that the cut up

methods (there are many ways of making cut ups) have been fully described with examples of application, to literary material, films, and tape recordings. In *The Job* I point out the use of cut ups as a revolutionary weapon. How this can be done with tape recorders on a mass scale is described in a section of *The Job* entitled "The Invisible Generation" which was published in the *Los Angeles Free Press*, Dec. 9, 1966. (Mr. Lipton is published in the same issue. He should know.) The control of the mass media depends on laying down lines of association and keeping these lines intact. When the lines are cut the associational connections are broken. You can cut the mutter line of the mass media and put the altered mutter line out not in any arcane mystagogic closed circuit hotel room but right into the public streets at the rush hour with a tape recorder. People don't know the difference. They think its a transistor radio. Don't hardly know they are hearing it but they are. I have done this over a period of years in Tangier, Paris, London, New York, Chicago. I have observed enough positive results to convince me that mass cut up and play back of mass media could produce quite interesting results for example a State of the Union speech is cut up and dumped into the streets and broadcast on ham radio as it happens and if you want to be really nasty about cut in slobberings, drooling, stammerings, coughs, sneezes, hiccups, sex sound effects, and animal noises. Cut it up and spray it right back at him.

Just what is so coterie, arcane, mystagogic, closed circuit, secret, snobbish, *Kenyon Review*, about all this Mr. Lipton?

WSB [London] to Mr. Harr [n.p.]
May 31, 1970
8 Duke Street
St James
London S.W.1
England

Dear Mr Harr:
    Your letter reached me after considerable delay having been for-

warded to *Rat* in NYC which is under new management since my article appeared there.

Have you seen my answer to a letter written by some one named Gordon Mustain about the original article? This should appear in the *Los Angeles Free Press* and in *Crawdaddy* a rock magasine in NYC. I assure you my feeling towards [L. Ron] Hubbard are anything but kind, but one does have to be careful about what is said in print.

Hubbard has the satisfied look of a man who has just sold the widow a fraudulent peach orchard, but he is engaged in something much more pernicious than old style con tricks. As you point out his real specialty is spiritual theft. Not only does he not acknowledge but he curses and poisons the sources. Did you know that he stole the E-Meter from someone named Floyd Matson, who was then thrown out of the organization and never so far as I know accused Hubbard publicly?

So then he turns around and proffers his stolen E-Meter as a humble gift to mankind. Shameless son of bitch. Even his curses are stolen from the [Aleister] Crowley sect which he then denounced in his capacity as a member of Naval Intelligence, so he says, or more likely in the capacity of a part time fink. And his cognitions about communism are cribbed from a superficial reading of Lenin and [Mikhail] Bakunin.

I took his so called learning course. It is my impression that like all his processing the C.C. leaves undischarged material behind that can be re-stimulated at any time by Colonel Ron. As soon as I got into disagreement with him all my so called gains mysteriously disappeared. So you see how he keeps the faithful in line. Have you seen a copy of John McMaster's resignation from the Sea Org? This was sent along to me by Bernard Green, New York. He says, "We totally support your views and would like to reprint your article for our mailing list." I gave permission of course. I have also contacted other old time Scientologists who can't stand any more of Ron's bullshite. [. . .]

Sincerely

WSB [London] to Brion Gysin [Tangier, Morocco]

July 22, Bellvue 7, 1970
8 Duke Street
St. James
London S.W.1
England

Dear Brion:

As you can see from the enclosed I have been busy on the cut up front. The "Scrambles" article has already been sent along to the *Los Angeles Free Press*. And I am writing another letter in answer to [Lawrence] Lipton's ridiculous counter. He's a sitting duck and perhaps intentionally so. Who is this Lipton? I have already gone much further with the scrambling technique, so far in fact that I do not wish to publish this material immediately because Antony [Balch] and I could do a short film first, so why let it out and somebody else does it half assed and makes name for himself like the two column man? All this material is in *The Revised Boy Scout Manual*. I have just put the whole first draft on tape for retyping and it is being retyped now by Aldus Co. These are the people who want me to do a book on Hassan i Sabbah. I mentioned your name of course. Would you be interested in taking any part in this project? They are willing to do any research that is necessary. The general title is assassination. So we start with the word and Alamout, then draw parallels from other time and places. Please let me know what you think about this.

I just called Michael Sissons about the Aldus offer. He hem and haws and says it is already set up with Calder. Looks like the only thing to do is sign the Calder contract and then Aldus can negotiate to buy Calder out if they want to. I have written Peter Matson, but so far no word.

Well, we will see what happens at this Phun City this week end. I am sending along a copy of *The Job*. Still looking for that edition of *The Book of the Dead*. Since [Barry] Miles went out of business its hard to find a book shop that will even bother to order a book.[8] Marrakech sounds terrible. And I don't think Nixon is helping matters.

---

8   Barry Miles had recently closed his Indica Bookshop in London.

No, I haven't sent the photocopies along to Andreas Brown yet but
I will do so. These cut up articles have been taking up all my time

Love

William

WSB [London] to Truman Capote [New York?]
July 23 [1970]

My Dear Mr Truman Capote

This is not a fan letter in the usual sense — unless you refer to
ceiling fans in Panama. [. . .] Rather call this a letter from "the
reader" — vital statistics are not in capital letters — a selection from
marginal notes on material submitted as all "writing" is submitted
to this department. I have followed your literary development from
its inception, conducting on behalf of the department I represent a
series of inquiries as exhaustive as your own recent investigations in
the sun flower state [Kansas]. I have interviewed all your characters beginning with Miriam — in her case withholding sugar over
a period of several days proved sufficient inducement to render her
quite communicative — I prefer to have all the facts at my disposal
before taking action. Needless to say, I have read the recent exchange
of genialities between Mr Kenneth Tynan and yourself. I feel that
he was much too lenient. Your recent appearance before a senato-
rial committee on which occasion you spoke in favor of continuing
the present police practice of extracting confessions by denying the
accused the right of consulting consul prior to making a statement
also came to my attention. In effect you were speaking in approval
of standard police procedure: obtaining statements through brutality
and duress, whereas an intelligent police force would rely on evidence
rather than enforced confessions. You further cheapened yourself by
reiterating the banal argument that echoes through letters to the editor whenever the issue of capital punishment is raised: "Why all this
sympathy for the murderer and none for his innocent victims?" I have
in line of duty read all your published work. The early work was in
some respects promising — I refer particularly to the short stories.

You were granted an area for psychic development. It seemed for a while as if you would make good use of this grant. You choose instead to sell out a talent that *is not yours to sell*. You have written a dull unreadable book [*In Cold Blood*] which could have been written by any staff writer on the *New Yorker* — (an undercover reactionary periodical dedicated to the interests of vested American wealth). You have placed your services at the disposal of interests who are turning America into a police state by the simple device of deliberately fostering the conditions which give rise to criminality and then demanding increased police powers and the retention of capital punishment to deal with the situation they have created. You have betrayed and sold out the talent that was granted you by this department. That talent is now officially withdrawn. Enjoy your dirty money. You will never have anything else. You will never write another sentence above the level of *In Cold Blood*. As a writer you are finished. Over and out. Are you tracking me? Know who I am? You know me, Truman. You have known me for a long time. This is my last visit.

WSB [London] to Peter Matson [New York]

July 24, 1970 Bellvue 9
8 Duke Street
St. James
London S.W.1
England

Dear Pete:

Apparently a piece entitled "Scrambles" which I sent you about ten days ago has been lost in the post. This piece has already appeared in the *IT* here and I enclose this article for retyping since I do not have another copy. The *Los Angeles Free Press* has printed the other article "Cut Ups as Revolutionary [*sic*: Underground] Weapon". This has stirred a useful controversy so the *Free Press* should get "Scrambles" which is follow up on the other article. I think *Crawdaddy* will publish the first article in next number. (I hope there is no objection to the articles going both to *Crawdaddy* and *Free Press*?)

Any news from Grove on publication of *The Third Mind*? I hear a rumor that Grove is planning to go out of business as publishers and transfer to films. Did you hear anything of the sort?

Glad to hear Billy's book is doing well. Any indications on *The Job* sales in the States?

All the best
William Burroughs

WSB [London] to Brion Gysin [Tangier, Morocco]
August 9, Seal Point 3, 1970
8 Duke Street
St. James
London S.W.1
England

Dear Brion:

I have not been able to get away because of so many urgent matters which demand immediate attention. You said get on the cut up front which I have done with two articles and two letters. There is also the Dutch Schultz script which Harrison Starr has completely rewritten in a much more conventional form and I fear losing much of what I was attempting to create. Nor am I at all sure that it is commercial. Maybe I am wrong. In any case I must go over it scene by scene. Harrison and David [Budd] want me to come to New York, but I can't see it. May just tell Harrison to go ahead and see if he can raise money on his script, then see about making what changes I can. Obviously he has spent a great deal of time on this script so it is a delicate matter . . . Also dental appointments one of Michelson's bridges came out . . . Also trying to get the *Boy Scout Manual* in shape for retyping . . . Antony [Balch] expects to come to Tangier in the first week of September and I will be with him in all probability. If not then towards the end of September.

I can't understand what is happening with the Merrill Foundation. Have you heard anything further?[9]

---

9   Brion Gysin had applied for a grant from the Ingram-Merrill Foundation, funded by the poet James Merrill.

I ask Peter Matson about *The Third Mind* in every letter. Still no publication date from Grove.

The Phun City festival was rather fun, but no chance to do anything with recorders. What a job it is to get people to do anything. Maurice Girodias has made a very good offer on the non English rights for *The Wild Boys* . . . Will give you the details when it goes through and I have the check.

John [Lee] has gone back to Stoke-on-Trent to get a job so there is always a room here if you feel like making a trip to England.

Love
Bill

WSB [London] to Allen Ginsberg [New York]

August 16, 1970
8 Duke Street
St James
London S.W.1
England

Dear Allen:

Sorry to be so slow about writing. Have really been snowed under here with film scripts and dead lines. Thanks for the note on apomorphine and glad to see that Gay Power was represented. I mean they don't even treat laboratory rats like that any more. Its altogether too much. They puke at sight of a man and get a shock. What a perversion of the apomorphine treatment.

How are things on the old homestead? A bit hectic I gather. Are you planning any trips across the herring pond?

We are still waiting on financing for the Dutch Schultz film script. Money is suddenly very tight following the collapse of Overseas Investment Services.

Tom Maschler rejected *The Wild Boys*, my latest novel which was taken by Grove in the States and has now gone to [John] Calder here. His manner of doing this . . . he delayed three months to see if Grove was taking the book . . . I considered unfriendly and rather dishonest.

The lack of promotion on *The Job* almost amounted to sabotage. None of the people on my list for a pre-publication copy received one and I had to send out all my own copies . . . Alex Trocchi didn't get one, [Barry] Miles, Eric Mottram (who is writing a book on my work) . . . All in all I am pretty fed up with Maschler and I gather he with me. *The Third Mind* has also been transferred from Cape to Calder and that is that. I feel that Maschler is an establishment publisher trying to come on avant-garde without being willing to take any risks.

I am playing Judge Hoffman in a script based on the Chicago conspiracy trials at the Open Space Theatre.[10] This is to raise money for the defense. Should be amusing

Love

Bill

WSB [London] to Harrison Starr [New York]
August 16, 1970 Seal Point 10
8 Duke Street
St James
London S.W.1
England

Dear Harrison:

I have read over the script carefully and find most of it very good, especially the later sections. I think the script picks up noticeably in the 1930s sections.

I feel that Albert Stern should remain a mysterious between worlds figure and that he should only appear as the doctor . . . briefly seen in shadow . . . and certainly as the teacher calling the roll . . . He would not appear again until the shot of the pool hall hold up . . . I also feel very strongly that the device of the main characters playing in crowd and restaurant shots should be used throughout.

---

10 Allen Ginsberg had testified for the defense in the trial of the Chicago Seven, the group charged with inciting a riot during the 1968 Democratic National Convention. The presiding judge was Julius Hoffman.

Suggest following changes in opening scenes . . . As the doctor rides away . . . August 6 . . . Appears on screen with brief flash of Hiroshima, 1903 . . . Sex scene between red haired boy and Japanese girl cut in with red brick houses, parks, beer trucks, free lunch, junkies buying morphine at the counter Mrs Murphy and the large family size . . .

I think that the scene of the mobsters playing monopoly and the Collyer brothers breaking the door down disguised as firemen should be included . . .

Dave [Budd] has written that you wanted me to come to New York and go over the script. This I cannot do at this time for a number of pressing reasons that keep me here. I think the important thing is to get financing on an approximate script and make what changes we decide on during production. I feel that your script is certainly adequate to proceed with . . . That is, we could start shooting on this script . . .

All the best to you and David
William Burroughs

WSB [London] to Billy Burroughs Jr. [Orange City, Florida]

August 30, 1970
8 Duke Street
St James
London S.W.1
England

Dear Billy:

I had not heard about your move to Green Valley [School] or the *Esquire* article.

"Writing is dangerous and few survive it," as Hemingway said or might have said. I can recommend *Hemingway: A Life Story* by Carlos Baker. I think its says a great deal about writing and what a writer is actually doing when he writes. Hemingway quite literally wrote his own death from *The Snows of Kilimanjaro*.

As regard Gurus and Indian mysticism, I am in complete

agreement. It has never said much to me. Now Dr Kamiya in San Francisco is teaching people to control brain waves, rate of heart beat, blood pressure, and digestion. They can learn in a few hours what it takes a yogi twenty years to learn. So why waste all that time? It would certainly be worthwhile to study with Don Juan or his equivalent. You will notice the preparation necessary for even short trips beyond the anchor imposed by the human body and nervous system. Seemingly all the weight of the establishments in the West and in Russia as well is mobilized to block such explorations. Not surprising that the recommendations in *The Job* fell on deaf ears.

Recently played Judge Hoffman in a play based on the Chicago conspiracy trials. That is it was a condensation of the actual transcript of the trial. This led me to wonder if present day revolutionaries as personified by [Jerry] Rubin and Abbie Hoffman[11] have any clear idea as to what they would do if they won? Everybody drop out and do his thing? There simply isn't room for that. Maybe a hundred years ago, not now. Think of the millions of people involved say in getting food from where it is grown or raised to a city like New York. Suppose all the people involved in this operation dropped out? And that's only one operation. I wonder if Hoffman & Co. are able to take over these operations or to accept the responsibility for not doing so?

The only thing that could unite the planet would be the exploration of space.

Love

Bill

P.S. 200 dollar check enclosed. Let me know if you need more

---

11 Rubin and Hoffman were two of the defendants in the trial.

WSB [London] to John Cooke [Mexico?]

August 30, 1970 Wiener Wald 1
8 Duke Street
St James
London S.W.1
England

Dear John Cooke:

Everything is permitted *because* nothing is true. Or *when* nothing is true. Reversal nothing is permitted because everything is true, that is real and solid. Of course the whole scene is old hat. All games are hostile and basically there is only one game and that game is war — the old army game from here to eternity. New games? There are no new games. That's what this revolution is about: *end of game*. End of game conditions.

(I can't figure out what this Manson thing is all about.[12] It just doesn't seem to make sense on any terms unless you turn the clock back a hundred years or so when such communes existed in America and from time to time were discovered to be practicing cannibalism or some other reprehensible activities.)

[L. Ron] Hubbard has only the vaguest notion as to who Hassan i Sabbah was. He is just basically ignorant. He does not have an inquiring, but an acquiring mind. Grab it and make it his and curse the source. How many scientologists know who said "the greatest good for the greatest number?" Jeremy Bentham[13] and his dreary utilitarianism, whose mummified head is still on display at the London College of Economics. And a horrible object it is too.

The Revised Boy Scout Manual is now finished and being retyped. Most of it is taken up with the electronic revolution and the alteration of old scanning patterns.

I have not myself been particularly interested in Krishnamurti,[14] but he seems to have some influence with young people. Quite a

---

12 Reference to the Charles Manson cult, who had murdered several people a year earlier.
13 Jeremy Bentham (1748–1832). English philosopher and social reformer.
14 Jiddu Krishnamurti (1895–1986). Indian philosopher and spiritual leader.

few followers in London. Frankly the whole Indian scene has never been my sort of thing at all.

Yes, I have seen Hilde Halpern[15] a number of times and find her very charming indeed and quite helpful.

What makes the explosion of the unconscious dangerous is of course the pressure that has been imposed on it. This would seem to be deliberate. The solider and more "real" the pressure, the more real the explosion. I agree that LIGHT is the only answer.

WSB [London] to Brion Gysin [Tangier, Morocco]

September 19, 1970
8 Duke Street
St. James
London S.W.1
England

Dear Brion:

Targuisti did get that man's back up at the airport in Tanger prowling around behind his booth and he said my passport had expired because there was no date on the renewal stamp. Wasn't that the same trouble you had at Gatwick in '64?

Gib [Gibraltar] wasn't bad at all. I did find a queer bar and passed the time quite painlessly. No hand luggage was allowed on board the plane and when we got to London there was a soup of whisky bottles, cigarette cartoons, and souvenirs floating around on the merry go round. Women's hand bags were opened and searched at the plane and they patted top coats carried over the arm. Why they didn't come right out and frisk everybody I can't understand. No point in a half assed search like that.

Arriving here I found that Alan Watson sneaking around in my apartment and doing no cleaning had helped himself to four teaspoonfuls of Doctor Dunbar's finest [cannabis]. He may be good for something but he is not good for me.

Applying the Italian formula to *Dutch Schultz* seems to work

---

15 Hilde Halpern. Author, translator, and follower of Meher Baba.

wonders just in terms of seeing the action. You can tell right away whether a scene works or not.

Ian [Sommerville] working 24 hours a day and I have not yet seen him. Wynn Chamberlain[16] dropped in on his way to?? He was thinking of going to Algiers to see Eldridge Cleaver but is like many others now disillusioned with the whole Black Panther scene. I mean when Cleaver gets up and says he is going to kill all the queers its a bit much. Larry Fagin[17] was also here.

Did you notice that Eileen Garrett is dead? She died on Tuesday last in the south of France and her death was not announced until Friday (yesterday) one very small paragraph in the *Tribune* and nothing in any other paper I have seen.

As always my visit with you in Tangier was immensely enjoyable and instructive. Very good idea to hold back the *Scout Manual*. One gets tired of going out on a limb for people who spit in one's face and don't follow any of the suggestions proposed. I will keep this back as a secret book. Enough of this open bank. You try to give it away and nobody wants it.

I am attending to Andreas Brown, Peter Matson, etc.

My best to Targuisti, Sallah and Tangier

Love
William

---

16 Wynn Chamberlain (b. 1927). American realist artist who lived in New York at 222 Bowery, later Burroughs' address.

17 Larry Fagin (b. 1937). American poet associated with the New York School.

WSB [London] to Peter Matson [New York]

September 20, 1970
8 Duke Street
St James
London S.W.1
England

Dear Pete:

Have you read Harrison Starr's shooting script on *Dutch Schultz*? After reading it over carefully the following considerations arise: This is not an adaptation of my script to conventional film script format. This is a completely rewritten script bearing little resemblance to the original and retaining very little of what I had in mind. What remains in my opinion is an old fashioned conventional gangster movie with some good scenes to be sure but the overall impression I get was that it is neither an outstanding script nor is it necessarily geared to commercial success. An old fashioned treatment like this just doesn't make it. I do feel that he should have let me know before rewriting my script. I feel that he should not have undertaken to do this since he is not a professional writer. (Needless to say these considerations need to be tactfully rephrased and of course he should not see this letter).

Having studied some working film scripts I am now rewriting the entire script in the Italian format — (Direction in the right hand column, dialogue and sound effects in left hand column) — scene by scene and take by take. I am using some of Harrison Starr's material and scenes but not very much. The whole beer truck speakeasy sequence I think must go nobody wants to hear that again. I am concentrating on what the script has that is new. He seemed to be going so far to make a conventional script that he could sell to Hollywood that the film has lost all distinction.

What exactly is the situation now? Is he looking for financing on the basis of his script? If he succeeds in this, it would then be difficult to change it. Hollywood wants what they have bought and not something different. I am working intensively on the script and should have it completed in a few weeks. This then will be my script and the script I am willing to work on when and if the film is produced. Quite frankly I would not be willing to work on the script in its present form. So if he will hold on until I finish this script the way I want it . . . Well I rely on you for a tactful presentation of the situation to Harrison and David [Budd]. God knows

[. . .]

EDITOR'S NOTE: *While Billy Burroughs Jr. was attending the Green Valley School he met Karen Perry. She was from Savannah, Georgia, and after the two married in 1969, they lived with her family in Savannah for a while.*

WSB [London] to Billy Burroughs Jr. [Savannah, Georgia?]
October 3, 1970
8 Duke Street
St James
London S.W.1
England

Dear Billy:

All your Tangier friends send their best. Mohammed Larbi is suave and well dressed as ever. Paul Bowles says to tell you he enjoyed your book. Old Lilly at the Parade always asks how you are. Nicolette is acting as house keeper to Paul Getty Junior who bought a huge house in the slums of Marrakech which keeps falling down behind them. Joe MacPhillips who taught English at the American School has been dismissed for flagrant misbehavior.

How are the sales on your book? I wish you would send me a copy. And please send me a picture of your wife.

Do you have any plans as to residence? You spoke of going to New York. Its quite a problem now to find a place that is relatively inhabitable. Writers exert a powerful indirect influence . . . Fitzgerald wrote the jazz age, Kerouac, Ginsberg, and Corso wrote the Beats . . . But when it comes to writing a place to live in. . . .

Please keep in touch.

Love
Bill

WSB [London] to Peter Matson [New York]
October 15, 1970
8 Duke Street
St James
London S.W.1
England Tele..839-5259

Dear Pete:

Not having heard to the contrary I assume that Harrison Starr is in agreement not to circulate his script until the script that I am now writing has been circulated. Having read and re-read his script I feel that this script or any foreseeable variation of it could lead to a disaster: an undistinguished expensive film that won't make a dime and will do me a great deal of harm in the process. This is not a film script written by William Burroughs and Harrison Starr. This is a script written by Harrison Starr vaguely and ineptly based on a film idea by William Burroughs (some of his worst scenes are those in which he used my script) . . . after talking me out of Terry Southern as co-author. The script I am writing is more than three quarters finished. Please let me know by phone if Harrison Starr is not in agreement I have every confidence in this script and I don't think he will find any difficulty raising money on it

All the best

William Burroughs

WSB [London] to Charles Upton [n.p.]
October 26, 1970
8 Duke Street
St James
London S.W.1
England

Dear Mr Upton:

I hope you have not suffered any further misfortunes as a result of contact with *The Reactive Mind* which is a pretty nasty thing right there. I do not propose [L. Ron] Hubbard's method of running this thing until there is no reaction. My contention is that whoever is behind Hubbard planted it in the first place, like say somebody introduces malaria into an area and when everyone's ass is dragging the ground enter the savior with quinine. Oh not too much and only to be given out to the obedient ones who scream out "Thank You Ron" at every opportunity. I have rarely read any thing as disgusting as the praise lavished on this old con man by his followers. What I am trying to find out is just who did set up this ingenious control artifact. It has come to light that some one named Nordenholz coined the word Scientology in the 1930s and set forth all the basic principles. So I am sure he [Hubbard] got the reactive mind from some undisclosed source.

A highly placed scientologist admitted to me that the CIA has this material. Therefore I think it should be freely circulated among any militant groups or any students of control systems with a view to deactivating its effectiveness.

Please let me know what reactions you observe from it. I did know of one person who immediately got severe head ache after looking at it. It seems to touch some basic horror or human impasse.

A symbol system must underlie it, which I have been trying to decipher and I will publish my findings together with the whole *Reactive Mind* as soon as I can complete research.

A group of scientologists have broken away from Hubbard and set up a rival office . . . One third the price, no Sea Org no Fascist nonsense. This is The Association Of International Dianologists, Westwood Village, California.

Most interested in the Alpha phone. It certainly sounds like the easy way to do it. Did you see the long article on [Dr.] Kamiya and others in *Look*? Please keep in touch

Good Luck
William Burroughs

WSB [London] to Billy Burroughs Jr. [Savannah, Georgia?]
November 4, 1970 Sweet Meadows 1
8 Duke Street
St James
London S.W.1
England Telephone 839-5259

Dear Billy:

As you must have heard Mother died October 21. It makes me very sad to think how many years they worked and sent money and how little they ever got in return. They were extraordinarily kind, gentle, and well-intentioned people and that is something very rare now.

It occurs to me that *Speed*[18] could be an excellent film script beginning and ending in the Palm Beach bungalow. I have just finished writing a scene by scene shooting script on *Dutch Schultz*, which has taught me a lot about writing. Please send me a copy and I will sketch a tentative script. Film scripts are where the money is and the best advice I can give a writer is to get some experience writing film scripts.

All the best to your wife

Love
Bill

WSB [London] to Barry Miles [New York]
November 30, 1970
8 Duke Street
St James
London S.W.1
England

Dear Miles:

Life in New York seems to be quite dangerous and I think almost a unique phenomena where certain naborhoods are actu-

---

18 Billy Burroughs Jr.'s first book, *Speed* (New York: Olympia, 1970).

ally uninhabitable. I think you were lucky not to run up against some real psychos. You may remember that I challenged [L. Ron] Hubbard to show his so called confidential materials to workers in other fields and he refused. So I will now do it myself. Enclose his so called *Reactive Mind* that is supposed to turn people insane to look at it. No one reports any ill effects so far. I think his reason for not publishing this material and for trying to scare his followers out of ever revealing it is quite simple: He stole it from some undisclosed source. If you could find this source it would make a nice story for *Crawdaddy*. It turns out that some one named Asturias [*sic*: Anastasius] Nordenholz in 1934 published a book called *Scientology: The Science of Knowing How to Know*. No acknowledgement from Hubbard of course. So I feel sure there is an undisclosed source for this material. Probably science fiction. *Aster Nordenhold the Galactic Controller* or something of the sort. Like many science fiction writers, Hubbard must have spent a lot of time in public libraries looking for other people's ideas. There may be something there on the *Reactive Mind* or something similar. Hubbard claims the material is millions of years old so we may assume it is now in the public domain, but he may possibly have a copyright on the name at least. Have to be careful. He is always suing at the drop of a hat and loses all his cases hands down. In any case interested to hear what you think of the material. Be careful who you show it to as there are or were a number of Hubbard scientologists in the Chelsea.[19]

Please let me know if you turn up anything on this. It would really blow that fat fascist fraud out of the water. His first clear has deserted him because of his politics and set up a rival organization. Hubbard's Sea Org has been causing them some trouble but they are offering the same and better at half the price.

All the best
Bill Burroughs

---

19 Barry Miles was staying at the Chelsea Hotel on West 23rd Street at the time.

WSB [London] to Mike Sissons [London]
December 1, 1970
8 Duke Street
St James
London S.W.1 Tele..839-5259

Dear Mr Sissons:

Here are four episodes of "The Unspeakable Mr Hart" as they appeared in *Cyclops*. For the book these episodes would have to be redone and amplified as regards both narrative and art work. As you will see this is a new type comic strip with a line of narrative apart from the strip and illustrative of it. I have a number of these episodes already written, that is, enough material on hand to produce a book of fifty or sixty pages.

I think this is enough to give a clear idea of the book.

Sincerely
William Burroughs

RUBRUBRUBRUB+++&++++&++&&&&&""""&"+++&
RUBRUBRUBRUBOUTOUTOUTOUTOUT#"#+++++#-
RUBRUBRUBRUBOUTOUTOUTOUTOUT####&&&&&
"""&&&+++++"OUTOUTOUTOUTOUT"""""""&&&&
1971 """+OUTOUTOUTOUTOUT"+"+"&&&"
THETHETHETHETHETHETHE+++###+++&&+++&
THETHETHETHETHETHETHE&&&&&++++++++##
THETHETHETHEWORDSWORDSWORDSWORDSTHE
####&&"&"&"&WORDSWORDSWORDSWORDS"++-

WSB [London] to Peter Matson [New York]

January 12, 1971
8 Duke Street
St James
London S.W.1
England

Dear Pete:

I don't feel that Harrison Starr and David Budd are being altogether frank with me on this matter. They say the "original film script is too frightening for any major company to consider". Which script are they referring to? Are they referring to the script I did over a year ago in New York? Are they referring to the 195 page *shooting script* I submitted a month ago? This took me three months to write, which is a lot of time and I have received no acknowledgement. Have they even read it? I don't know. Certainly there has not been time to circulate this shooting script? Now Harrison Starr is circulating his script perhaps with an arrangement that I will come over and rewrite his script? David Budd said in his letter there was no doubt I would write the script. What script? I have written the script. The shooting script. If that frightens any backer, that backer would not let me do any approximation of the film I want to do.

My feeling is to let the deal sink.

Certainly I don't want them to make any commitments on my behalf to work on another script. I've given them a script and that's my script. I wouldn't object to cuts in this script and that's a very simple matter of tightening.

Please convey this as diplomatically as possible. The big question in my mind is — are they circulating my script? Seemingly they are not. The point is I won't work on any other.

All the best
William Burroughs

WSB [London] to Billy Burroughs Jr. [Savannah, Georgia?]
Feb. 26, 1971
8 Duke Street
St James
London S.W.1 Tele 839-5259

Dear Bill:

This letter goes out by courier to France. No end to the [postal] strike in sight. Enclose check for 1000 dollars for your trip.

As regards your last letter, I am fully in agreement that there is no point in hindering oneself with the official revolutionary rating which makes it difficult to travel or to take part in any meaningful activities. And I do not feel that the antics of [Jerry] Rubin and [Abbie] Hoffman are useful to anyone but themselves. And look at the spot [Timothy] Leary has gotten himself into. More on this point when I see you.

I would like very much to see the *Esquire* profile. What are the sales figures on *Speed*? How is the Lexington book coming along?[1] Did you ever see a book written by a spade called *The Farm*?[2]

Ian [Sommerville] sends his best. He is now a highly paid computer programmer who does things with computers that no one, least of all his company, thought were possible.

Michael Portman I am afar slip afraid is pretty much out of the picture with an alternate junk and alcohol habit. He has the cure record I think. The cure record averaging an apomorphine cure every two months.

Allen Ginsberg is preparing a massive documented exposé on the CIA opium trade in Laos.[3] You may have heard something about this. It is really far out. Well here comes my courier

My best regards to your wife

Love

Bill

---

1 This book was published in 1973 as *Kentucky Ham*.
2 Clarence Cooper. *The Farm* (New York: Crown, 1967).
3 Allen Ginsberg was involved in research that led to the publication of Alfred W. McCoy's book *The Politics of Heroin in Southeast Asia* (New York: Harper & Row, 1972).

WSB [London] to Kevin Roche [n.p.]

April 1, 1971
8 Duke Street
St. James
London S.W.1
England

Dear Mr Roche:

The apomorphine treatment is used here in England by several doctors. Doctor Dent's former nurses also give the treatment. In fact they treat many famous patients. It is far and away the quickest; about seven days — and best form of treatment as cured patients can testify.

Methadone is certainly as addictive as morphine and as difficult if not more so to kick. To say you have cured someone of heroin by methadone is like saying you have cured someone of alcoholism by shifting from cut whisky to strong sherry. However, it is good for a maintenance program for those who cannot or will not stop using opiates. But to say it is in any sense a cure is absolutely ridiculous. Besides there is nothing new about methadone which was synthesized by the Germans in World War II.

The question as to what to do with time that was formerly spent in acquiring and taking drugs is always a problem. Exactly the same problem is encountered with alcoholics.

Unfortunately our society does not offer many meaningful alternatives. Please let me know if I can be of any further assistance. I can provide dosage schedules on the apomorphine treatment — (very important that the treatment be given in a manner that insures a high concentration of apomorphine during the treatment) — if there is some doctor willing to use it.

Cordially Yours
William S. Burroughs

WSB [London] to Billy Burroughs Jr. [Savannah, Georgia?]

May 4, 1971
8 Duke Street
St James
London S.W.1
England

Dear Bill,

I would be very much interested to hear your tape of *Naked Lunch* and especially in view of the fact that I have at long last decided to make a film of the book. To this end a film company known as Friendly Films has been set up consisting of Antony Balch with whom I did two short films, Brion Gysin, who wrote *The Process*, and myself. Brion has written the script and done a much better job than I could have done. I think this is generally true that a writer should not write the screenplay for his own book. Now of course we have to decide for purposes of the film how the words really do *sound* when spoken by an actor or let the actor decide. There is no set way to read or act any lines so very interested in *your* interpretations of various characters. The most difficult to cast is William Lee, the main character, who is generally assumed to be the writer himself. We offered the part to Mick Jagger but he is contracted and booked solid.

We hope to shoot in October with any luck. Any chance of your being able to come here at that time?

I am going to the Cannes Film Festival next week and should know a lot more definitely how things stand after that.

A photographer was around from *Esquire* so I gather your article is on the way.

Please keep in touch

Love
Bill

WSB [London] to Brion Gysin [n.p.]

May 6, 1971
8 Duke Street
St James
London S.W.1
England Tele 839-5259

Dear Brion:

Why not a daily message to go out on telex to all subscribers "Tomorrow's News Today"...

Here is the shabby Reuter's man from a Graham Greene novel with his sleeve garters as he taps out the last message from—

"My Dear I can just barely totter home ... the dollar has collapsed ... U.S. Treasury says it will protect the currency ... And you know what that means in show biz ... We will take all necessary measures to protect the prisoner ... said the sheriff ... Prisoners of the dollar ... I am tapping out this last message ... Prisoners of what the dollar buys or did buy directly or indirectly food a bed and if you can't get some sex into your bed where it is now will you do better in a packing case? Oh don't bother with all that junk you gonna carry a trunk of manuscripts around on your back? Earth collapses in Quebec ... 20 thought dead ... Combination of heavy rains and spring thaw ... You can see that rain pelting down as all the sewage starts thawing out opening great brown cracks ... He thought of death and liked the sound of the rain outside this will be a come in a million as he thought about salmon who come once and die WHEEEEEEEEEEEEGGLLUUUUUUUUUUUB the initial group of houses were swallowed up ... The Bensons last night George ... And now they are at U.S. Treasury Says It Will *ACT* To Protect the Currency ... Dollar crisis looms as the earth continued to move ... Clutter the Glind ... screamed the captain of moving line ... We're slipping its sort of like cold lava and the movement of a truck half a mile away will set it off is enough said Paul Tremblay area civil protection chief ... Are you reading me out there B.G.? I am in full accord with Antony [Balch]'s telex since Mick [Jagger] gotta no confidence he poppa friendly films out of capital letters so where the publicity go in a picture with my arm around his shoulder and what it do when it get there? We look like unsuccessful Don Cammell[4] and Sandy Liebersteins [*sic*: Lieberson][5]marginal hustlers hated by all the palace favorites who have been busy my God that scene that Kenneth laid on was all arranged by Don Cammell. So I walk in on a friend so I thought tells me his trap has been turned over magic should tell him he is asking for the real thing in words that Robert Fraser should hear on this telex so of course I believe him at first and it takes quite a while before I find this is all a hoax so what has been recorded?"

WSB [London] to Brion Gysin [n.p.]

May 11, 1971
8 Duke Street
St James
London S.W.1
England

Bulletin Exclusive to FF [Friendly Films]: All so called black magic works on the 3T position. Once he who is making the magic is in 3T position he doesn't have to bother with any silly old spells. His target in 1T will do the rest himself as all forces which he sees as hostile and out of his control are now drawn into the 3T. Its just as simple as that.

Maybe Hassan i Sabbah didn't need any assassins after the first one which put him in 3T position with regard to his enemies. When the carpenter killed the Sultan, Hassan i Sabbah showed that he could effect his enemies and they could not effect him. He could then sit back with a force large enough to defend Alamout itself and his enemies could be relied upon to make their own assassins from the materials at hand. Like some one is giving FF trouble. Maybe we send out someone and pay him five quid to very obviously follow the target for one day. After that he will be rushing up to strangers and screaming "Why are you following me?"

---

4   Donald Cammell (1934–1996). Scottish filmmaker.
5   Sandy Lieberson. Film producer.

Its all so simple, we are keeping it exclusive to FF. The open bank is really closed now. Oh, I will publish but always hold back the essential ingredient. Like in this Hart book. It will be a gassy book and show a lot about control systems and how they work. Like I gave a blueprint for an internal combustion engine all there you can make one. However I leave out of my blueprint the whole concept of *oil*. Sure anybody can build it and it will run, but it won't run very far. Around the block maybe.

I said maybe we should find an actual marksman for the part of Lee . . . Better still an actual *gunman*. Well I have found one: Carlos Evertsz formerly a secret agent for Trujillo, the CIA, and anybody else who paid him. Now a part-time dishwasher in Soho. Did you see the *Observer* article? It's a really good face. He is part American and part Dutch, speaks perfect English. He has worked for the control systems described in *Naked Lunch* just as Lee did unwittingly. This may be a wash out you never know till you see him. Any case I have written a letter to him if he is interested drop around for an interview with casting. If we can't use him as Lee, he might do as Hauser or some other bit part. It's a very photogenic face. The voice I haven't heard yet.

William

WSB [London] to Billy Burroughs Jr. [Savannah, Georgia?]

May 20, 1971
8 Duke Street
St James
London S.W.1

Dear Bill:

It was an education in the film industry to watch Mick Jagger's palace favorites go into action and smoothly cut Friendly Films out with Mick and sign him up for another Don Cammell Sandy Lieberson film. Did you see *Performance* by the way?[6] However by

---

6   *Performance* (1968 and released in 1970), starring Mick Jagger, was directed by Nicolas Roeg and Donald Cammell and produced by Sandy Lieberson.

the time this happens I have decided it is just as well. Mick himself is great and could do the part but he is inseparable from groupies who can waste an incredible amount of one's time — I need to be photographed with the Begum having lunch with the Stones and some top Mafia brass in San Tropez? Why chase after stars? William Lee shoots two detectives in the first scene. All right let's find somebody who *can* shoot and could actually shoot two detectives if called upon to do so. So I am trying to contact a former Trujillo gunman who sold his life story to a paper here, it makes the *Valachi Papers* sound like kid gang fights. His name is Carlos Evertsz and the face looks good. Don't know if he can act. Carlos is a little standoffish, Friendly Films does sound rather sinister . . . the closed door the smiling CIA man . . . "Well Carlos long time no see, eh? Don't mind if I call you Carlos do you?" Just an idea I had: if you want somebody to do something on the screen find somebody who does it off the screen. A real doctor for Doctor Benway, etc. Perhaps I got this idea long time ago watching Tyrone Power play Jesse James. Take any dumb, surly hick . . . the kids in East Texas used to spend an afternoon drinking beer and shooting pennies in the air with a .22 . . . a hick who can shoot and doesn't care much what or who . . . point him at the part . . . with a good tight script of words he would use and you have a real live Jesse James.

Did you read a book on Lexington called *The Farm* by Clarence Cooper? If not I will send it along. Michael Portman seems to spend most of his time taking cure, alternate junk and alcohol. Don't see him except every few months. Ian [Sommerville] is doing very well as a computer programmer. Nicolette and Mark Grotian still in Marrakech.

I look forward to seeing you here in October. I will certainly learn a lot watching the film scene by scene. We figure on a budget of around 300,000 dollars. Only way to make money on a film is to keep the budget down. We have the complete script and will try to raise the money without outside help. I will know a lot more about how things stand when Antony Balch gets back from the Cannes Film Festival.

WSB [London] to David Cooper [London?]

May 22, 1971
8 Duke Street
St James
London S.W.1 telephone 839-5259

Dear Doctor Cooper:

You may remember some years ago we had an exchange of differences on the subject of the apomorphine treatment for alcoholism and drug addiction in one of those pseudo liberal *New Statesman*-Society papers sponsored by the CIA to maintain unswerving standards of liberal ineffectuality.[7] I hope that you did not take this personally. At the time I did not know of your work as one of the very few unorthodox psychiatrists in England or anywhere else for that matter. I was simply upset to see any doctor invalidate the apomorphine treatment sight unseen.

And the purpose of this letter is to urge you to take the apomorphine treatment without delay. A Mrs. Smith known as Smitty to her patients is one of Doctor Dent's nurses with twenty years experience and some very amusing stories to lighten sleepless nights . . . six in my case . . . But that was heroin. Alcohol is much easier. She gives this treatment in a room over her pub, The Red Lion, Devon, ask for Mrs Smith. She can also arrange to give the treatment in your apartment. The treatment is at longest eight days usually five or six. I hope you will not take this offer as insulting from a stranger: I will gladly advance the money necessary for the treatment if you are not in a position to do this. I feel that your work is uniquely useful and should continue. I have been trying for years to obtain recognition for the apomorphine treatment and would of course be very glad of a medical convert in touch with young people who stand most in need of effective treatment

Sincerely,
William S. Burroughs

---

7   See Burroughs' letter to the *New Statesman*, ca. March 4, 1966, which appears earlier in this collection.

WSB [London] to Donald Erickson[8] [New York]

June 2, 1971
8 Duke Street
St James
London S.W.1
England

Dear Mr Erickson:

As regards the two letters I wrote to my son and your letter asking my permission to print these: The two-page letter which begins: "I had not heard about your move to Green Valley or the *Esquire* article . . . writing is dangerous and few survive it . . . etc.", I have no objection.

The other letter which begins "All your Tangier friends send their best" . . . the names are real and any invidious references must be avoided. Lilly doesn't like to be called "old Lilly" . . . Getty doesn't want to know about his house falling down behind him and above all any reference to Joe MacPhillip's dismissal could prejudice his chances of getting another teaching job. Absolutely this sentence must be deleted . . . All in all there is not much left in the letter that could contribute to the article, so I would suggest omitting this letter.

Sincerely
William S. Burroughs

---

8   Donald Erickson had written to Burroughs in his capacity as editor at *Esquire* magazine in reference to the publication of Burroughs' letters to Billy of August 30, 1970, and October 3, 1970, which appear earlier in this collection.

WSB [London] to Billy Burroughs Jr. [Savannah, Georgia?]

July 11, 1971
8 Duke Street
St James
London S.W.1
England 839–5259

Dear Bill:

Very much relieved to learn from Peter Matson that you are not at Lexington but writing about it from a comfortable distance.

I have heard many compliments on *Speed*. Robert Palmer, who works for *Rolling Stone Magasine*, says you are the only one who has really written about the drug scene in the South, a scene which he knows well coming from Memphis. You also have a 32 second spot on Radio Luxemburg. Did you ever actually meet Maurice Giro-dias? Quite a character he reminds me of a riverboat gambler. We are trying now to get James Taylor for the lead in *Naked Lunch* and still plan to shoot in October. General consensus is that the film has to be made right now.

I hope you are still planning to come here at that time. We are taking over two flats in this building so there will always be a place for you to stay. Please let me know what you are doing and what your plans are.

Love
Bill

WSB [London] to Terry Southern [New York?]
August 23, 1971

Dear Terry:

Here is the *Naked Lunch* script which I think manages to preserve the total message without being too frightening for prospective backers. We are already considering trip to America for two-fold purpose of share selling and casting. We still need a star to play William Lee. James Taylor was shot out from under us by prior commitments to his pet pig

"Sorry I'd like to but I have to go home and water Mona," he said. Sounds like the old days in Hollywood and obviously the only thing to do is buy him a beautiful peccary so he forgets about this fat Mona. If that doesn't do it, we have to look again . . . I begin to see what you mean about the miracle involved in making any film

All the best

Bill

I finally wrote scene by scene shooting script of *Dutch Schultz* which Harrison Starr was afraid to show to anybody and who would buy a dead Dutchman sight unseen?

WSB [London] to Billy Burroughs Jr. [Savannah, GA?]
September 28, 1971
8 Duke Street
St James
London S.W.1
England

Dear Billy:

Hope my last letter did not alarm you. I was a bit high on legal cannabis tincture prescribed by my physician who still believes in the mission of British imperialism. England is full of things like that . . . eccentric pot smoking clergymen, gentleman's agreements rather than laws, much less menacing than America, at the same time more limited. Its a very different scene and different people, as you will see.

The *Naked Lunch* film is progressing and we expect to sign up

Dennis Hopper who directed and acted in *Easy Rider* for the part of William Lee — shooting to start in March or early April.

I have bought one of those alpha wave machines here which bleeps approvingly when you emit alpha waves. Other devices applaud lowered blood pressure, heart beat, and elimination of muscular tensions. Portable units on the way.

Please let me know what your plans are. I think you would like it here. There are a lot of American residents who find living here very relaxing after the States. My best to you and Karen.

Love
Bill

WSB [London] to Billy Burroughs Jr. [Savannah, Georgia]
October 10, 1971
8 Duke Street
St James
London S.W.1
England telephone 839-5259

Dear Billy:

Brion Gysin has just returned from New York where he talked with Peter Matson. Peter Matson is very enthusiastic about your forthcoming book from an artistic standpoint and also as a financial property. It is his feeling that you should stay where you are until the book is finished. He hopes it will be finished or at least well on the way to completion by Christmas. I of course feel that Savannah is a pretty grim setting. On the other hand any move involves money and time. Flats are not easy to find here and it could take quite a while before you are settled and able to work properly. I am going to Switzerland to teach for the month of October. The film is now taking very definite shape and schedule. We expect to star Dennis Hopper as William Lee and start shooting in late March which means that the show will really get rolling on casting etc. shortly after New Years. It is now envisaged to shoot most of it here in London but we may possibly shift to New York. We will know definitely in the next two months.

All things considered it might be wise for you to plan to come here after the first of the year when things really begin to move. Alternatively if you can't stand Savannah, I would suggest that you go for a few months to Tangier to finish the novel there. Flats are easy, much easier than here. Expenses are less and the climate much better. Brion would be there to help out and so could I at any time since it is only three hours from here and I had planned a Tangier visit after I finish in Switzerland.

Please let me know about this right away. I could send you boat fare to Tangier.

Coming here, there is the added complication of having to show money on entry, all of which would have to be provided for.

I enclose check for 500 dollars. My address by the time you get this letter will be % Alfred de Grazia . . . (He is the brother of Ed de Grazia who was a lawyer on your case. I don't know if you met him?) Rector of New World University, Haute-Nendaz, Switzerland . . . Antony Balch, director of our film is in this building in London. I will be always in touch with him and it might be easier to make contact by phone with Antony than with the university.

EDITOR'S NOTE: Burroughs had been asked to teach at an alternative university in Switzerland, but when he arrived he discovered that it was poorly funded and on the verge of financial collapse.

WSB [Haute-Nendaz, Switzerland] to Brion Gysin and Antony Balch [London]
Oct 21 [1971]

Dear Brion: Dear Anthony:

As you suspected no pay. No money in fact. University may fold at any time. De Grazia left before I arrived leaving no one in charge. Faculty and students suing a vacuum for breach of contract, university under police surveillance drug scandals the lot. Clean mountain air after London has incapacitated me with racking cough. Nearest drug store 15 miles. I now have what I need and feeling better. None the less very glad I came to see some sun and sky for a change and can't understand how I have stood London all this time. And the students are a gas. Have met several fans of yours. Where can we buy *The Process*? When is it coming out in paperback? This is really a beautiful place and silent. I never heard such silence. Have turned up veterans of the Hotel Chelsea, friends of Ira [Cohen], Irving Rosenthal, Allen Ginsberg, Harold Norse, LeRoi Jones, Alex [Trocchi], [Herbert] Hunche [*sic*: Huncke]. Tim Leary lives just over the next glacier. All in all having fine time and wish you were here. If this was a going concern it would be a real gas for all of us to teach here. The way it looks now the university will fold in a few weeks. If I get my fare back to London it will be a miracle. Only hope I don't get stuck with hotel bill. Telephone impractical. I am now staying in Hotel Monte Calm but may move in with some students today. Don't know how long I will be staying. So long as I can hustle expenses will stay until mid November. When the tourist season starts I think the canny Swiss will throw us all out. What a mess de Grazia has made and what a gas the university could be. Nobody to teach the film course and the last instructor took off with the only projector. Beautiful blond kid wants to learn pure mathematics and no teacher. Two video cameras have vanished without trace, etc. A telegram to University of the New World will reach me. Really having fine time and wish you were here

Love
William

WSB [Haute-Nendaz, Switzerland] to Brion Gysin [London]
Oct. 22, 1971
Hotel Monte Calm Room I
Haute-Nendaz
Valais, Switzerland

Dear Brion

Situation is now stabilized to some extent. The university is paying all expenses to and from and during. As you can see by enclosed sample they have issued their own currency which is redeemed from local shops and restaurants at 2% increase. A local big shot named Levy Fournier has put 50,000$ into the university and stands behind the cows as the money is called. He and the university attacked in the press by his political enemies, the feuds dating back to the 12th century. Wish you were here to dig this scene. De Grazia expected back in two weeks *imchallah* [*sic*: *Insha'Allah, God willing*] with more $. To give him his due he did get something started here and I hope it can be kept going. It would be a great place for all of us to spend a month or two during the year looking at clear clean air and silence and stars I haven't seen since the Sahara 35 years ago.

I have decided to retain my hotel room with privacy, central heat, and hot water rather than move into a chalet with assorted characters, kerosene heat, and cooking arrangements. Having dinner tonight with a Swami and students. Will be conducting seminar on anything I want to talk about two nights a week, rest of time I take walks, visit around, read, write, drink coffee, best coffee ever. There is a macrobiotic restaurant run by a beautiful Spade where I can avoid fondues which as you know is a horrible Swiss thing. Players available in local shops. Best radiators I have seen anywhere which are panels flush with the wall. The windows all close and *seal* shut.

Uncanny how many precise replicas of people I know here . . . A John Hopkins, an Ian [Sommerville], A Billy [Burroughs], a Dave Wollman, several Ginos [Foreman], a Malcolm McNeill, a Jerry Gorsaline, all the chicks from the Beat Hotel.

Unless something unforeseen happens I will be staying here in this hotel until mid November so important looking letters can be forwarded.

Please write me the London news hello to everyone in London
Love
William

WSB [Haute-Nendaz, Switzerland] to Brion Gysin and Antony Balch [London]
October 24 [1971]

Dear Brion and Antony:

Will definitely be at this hotel, room 1, for the duration of my stay here. Sorry I didn't send the number along sooner but plans up in the air and I have been quite ill with chills and cough and fever and a constant headache. Civilized country, thank God, codethyline in the drug stores name here is Neo-codion. Same formula as the French product, in fact this comes from France. I couldn't have got myself out of bed without it. Saw Tim Leary yesterday looking good and optimistic about his case and got himself a brand new wife. Don't know what happened to Rose Mary and didn't think it tactful to inquire. All that bit about the jail endangering his health was bullshit.[9] He reports hotel standard comfort and exemplary treatment as do the students here who have been inside.

It looks like the university won't last much longer. De Grazia is not likely to return with a number of civil cases pending and also a criminal charge for misleading advertisements.

I may stop over in Amsterdam on the way back.

I doubt if I will stay longer than two weeks more. Students are drifting away to Iran, Spain, Morocco, Denmark. I gave one talk and may give another with Tim Leary if he can get permission to leave his canton. We will record this for posterity. Meanwhile take walks, take codeine pills, and sit in my room with a stack of science fiction by my bed and the university footing the bill. Its a nice comfortable feeling. See you soon. Keep me posted

Love
William

---

9 Timothy Leary had escaped from a prison in California and was seeking asylum in Switzerland.

WSB [Haute-Nendaz, Switzerland] to John Cooke [Mexico?]
October 25 [1971]

Dear Jack:

Many thanks for your most informative letter. It would seem that Hubbard is putting down his third rate science fiction as the one and only cosmos. No wonder he cannot tolerate anyone with an iota of intelligence in his vicinity. However, the concept of body thetans expressed of course in different terms has been put forward by a number of investigators for example in [Georg] Groddeck's *Book of the It*. Groddeck postulates psychic parasites rooted in the nervous system that give rise to a wide range of somatic illnesses and neurotic symptoms, to accidents, slips of the tongue, lapses of memory, etc. So leaving aside galactic federations and Zmus there may be some validity in Hubbard's procedure and I would be interested to make a systematic test on the E-Meter . . . Exactly how are these body thetans contacted and run? Are they addressed directly and if so in what terms? Do they have names? Do they have dates? Are they run through the alleged shooting freezing and bombing incidents as if *you* are an auditor running an internal parasite through these incidents? Do you then instruct the boy thetans to go to the beginning of the incident and then through the incident from beginning to end until they don't read or the needle floats as engrams are run? Is each body thetan run separately?

I would like to try running his so called body thetans which can perhaps be interpreted as personified conflicts and to compare notes with you. I must say that I have had some interesting data and experiences through use of the E-Meter. Do you know by the way about Hubbard assassination technique known as R-2-45? His Sea Org are instructed to run this on such SPs as you and me and I will say for them that they can cause one trouble. I mean just by coming into your flat they bring it in with them. On the subject of R-2-45 I addressed some questions to CONTROL . . .

Question: What is R-2-45?

Answer: Assassination technique.

Question: Does R-2-45 consist in running a bombing incident after sexual virus?

Answer: Yes.

Question: Does the whole force of the Reactive Mind depend on a "bombing incident"?

Answer: Yes.

WSB [Haute-Nendaz, Switzerland] to Brion Gysin and Antony Balch [London]
Oct 27 [1971]

Dear Brion and Antony:

Received your cable with thanks on this auspicious day when Nationalist China was unseated from UN and Peking seated . . . The look on Roger's face was tasty.

"University supervised health threat." This cut up on day of my arrival. There is in fact a strange virus peculiar to Haute-Nendaz.. I feel normal in the morning, quite ill by three PM — chills, light fever, by five PM delirium, mental disturbance, splitting head ache. Cross checking I find most of the students have had the same symptoms for three weeks to a month after arrival. Symptoms disappear, they tell me, in a few days after going anywhere else. They attribute this to the "vibes" as they call them. And the vibes which seem good at first are not all that good. In fact something very odd about this place. The altitude is only 4000 feet not enough to make any difference or account for such a syndrome. Thank God for codeine pills. It takes the equivalent of twelve pinkies to knock out this headache. I haven't been able to do much in the way of teaching but have turned some of the students on to autonomic shaping and interested some militant blacks in the use of lie detectors. One kid wants to come to London and learn how to use the E-Meter. I only wish I had brought it with me. There are also some real CIA types on campus. All in all interesting.

I wrote an ultimatum to that worthless bastard John Cooke trying to buy real information, real services, real friendship with NOTHING. I want the auditing commands on their assassination process R-2-45. I *know* he knows these commands. "If our communication is to continue it must be on a basis of reciprocal exchange" . . . See if that jolts any real info out of him. I don't much care, but I am not standing still for anymore of his bullshit. In his last letter he says Mary and Jim are at flag. "Are you by any chance?" Me at Hubbard radio active fink flag? You were right about that wrong number.

I could give a real course here on recent far out discoveries, science fiction becoming science fact faster than you can write it, but I don't have my files. And I doubt if the university will be here for a return trip in early summer. Well I have turned a few students on

love

William

Just reading interesting science fiction book about this dry planet where everything is in terms of water so interested in Teegeeack[10] as water. This book is *Dune* by Frank Herbert published 1965. I have written Shapiro for more precise information on how to run out these Teegeeack hitchhikers.

Quotes from *Dune*: "Presently Paul recalled the words of 467 Kalima 'From water does all life begin . . .'"

"Giudichar mantene: it is written in the Shah-Nama that water was the first of all things created . . ."

WSB [London] to Brion Gysin [Tangier, Morocco]
December 22, 1971
8 Duke Street
St. James
London S.W.1
England

Dear Brion:

Sending along under separate cover from John Wood's office on the Cherifa affair. Please let me know that you have received this as it looks important. The text for the film script has arrived and I will see the complete text and drawings in a day or so. What I have seen

---

10 L. Ron Hubbard claimed that the planet Earth was originally called Teegeeack millions of years ago.

already is absolutely superb. I mean its a great film and a sure fire commercial success. Climax of sex movie in burning theatre delivers the seemingly impossible after a series of dazzling scenes a final scene that is even more of the mostest. Ian [Sommerville] has a nice Druid staying with him and they are tankering [*sic*] around with recorder and sound experiments I mean tinkering of course, maybe they were, I mean I was thinking of the think tank in any case Ian hasn't done anything like this in years and I find it most encouraging. I have been developing a field theory of word. Also assembling all my material on the incestuous Carson family and drawing up a synopsis which may be too far out. Briefly it seems that the Carsons with their healthy old fashioned sex and healthy old fashioned capitalism — sure they buy dust bowl land in the depression but they keep farmers to rebuild the land and turn them all into happy pot smoking swingers and actually this system where everybody is happy is much more efficient. We underline that many times. The Carsons and their growing body of retainers are very efficient. They do things they enjoy doing and they do them well . . . Do you hear the Ugly Spirit snarling off stage? A board meeting is called. And what a crowd of villains is here. The Contessa who plans to take over the earth with a race of super Amazons from hanged men's sperm . . . All the issue is female . . . Mr Hart who plans to take over with a race of painless junkies. The Carsons must be stopped. Its war with a happy ending as the goodies beat the baddies because they are simply more efficient.

Merry Christmas to you

Targuisti Salah
William

RUBRUBRUBRUB+++&+++++&++&&&&&" " "&" +++&
RUBRUBRUBRUBOUTOUTOUTOUTOUT#" #+++++#-
RUBRUBRUBRUBOUTOUTOUTOUTOUT####&&&&&
" " "&&&+++++"OUTOUTOUTOUTOUT" " " " " "&&&&
1972 " " "+OUTOUTOUTOUTOUT" +" +"&&&"
THETHETHETHETHETHETHETHE+++##+++&&+++&
THETHETHETHETHETHETHE&&&&&+++++++++++#f
THETHETHETHEWORDSWORDSWORDSWORDSTHE"
#####&&"&"&"&WORDSWORDSWORDSWORDS" ++-

WSB [London] to John Brady [San Francisco]

February 15, 1972
8 Duke Street
St James
London S.W.1
England
Flat 18

Dear John:

I am also sorry you missed my birthday party which took place at a new French restaurant just around the corner on King Street with the best wine cellar in London *un vrai* Beaujolais you could taste it from London to Cambridge but 114th Street sounds more like New York? I also find myself in a situation not too dissimilar to yours. I must make a change and various alternatives present themselves and must be limited if any one of them is put in operation, my accountant there with bad news writ all over him in red letters. So I went to my Godfather who sees better and told him my books aren't selling and soon I will have no money what shall I do? "I suppose you have thought of cutting expenses, going to live in Tangier perhaps, and writing another novel perhaps in a more popular vein?"

"Well that would be the logical thing to do?"

He looked at me scornfully: "And how many times have I told you that when you are in difficulties the 'logical' thing to do is always wrong since it is just this 'logic' that has put you in the present difficulties?"

This seemed logical. I decided to stop writing for a while and go some place I have never been. Stop. Change. Start. I am considering Afghanistan of which I have heard good reports.. However, would want more information on prices, currency, languages spoke, health conditions, etc. Alternatively Southern Morocco where I have never been. Would you be interested to accompany me on either trip?

William

WSB [London] to Billy Burroughs Jr. [Savannah Beach, Georgia]

February 16, 1972
8 Duke Street
St James
London S.W.1
Flat 18
England

Dear Billy:

Power cuts here. England is a gloomy cold unlighted sinking ship that will disappear with a spectral cough. After top England splits it up there simply isn't enough to pay a living wage. The north of Ireland is essential to the wealthy English for tax reasons so that's what it is all about: money. I notice fifty British soldiers have been decorated by the Queen for meritorious service in Belfast.

Have you been in touch with the man in Chicago who wanted you to write his story? I have just finished reading *The Godfather* and most highly recommend it if you haven't read it already. The point he makes is the Mafia Dons are nicer more sensible and juster rulers than the white Protestant Americans who have hopelessly loused up everything.

The film here is still waiting on financing and money seems to be very tight now. As to [Dennis] Hopper being in the film we can't pin down an actor without financing. My own finances are not very good. *The Job* didn't sell at all, *The Wild Boys* only a few thousand copies to date. I plan to take a trip somewhere I haven't been and then try writing something different.

Brion says to thank you for your good words about *The Process*. I have heard of Meher Baba[1] as one of the better actors in the magic business but don't know much about him. He has a rep. Claude [Pelieu] and Mary [Beach] are my translators and yours as well, very good and devoted fans. I do have a color TV set and that's the best for watching the Belfast pictures which are mostly fires, quite a bit of stone throwing and rubber bullets. Its a war like Algeria.

---

1   Meher Baba (1894–1969). A popular Indian spiritual leader.

Old ladies and children get killed. Anyone happens to be there at the wrong time gets killed or crippled. I can see in a horrible way what they mean about [Spiro] Agnew. Certainly sexier than Nixon or Heath or Kosygin.

What co-incidences is Meher Baba surrounded by?

Love
Bill

WSB [New York] to Brion Gysin [Paris]
April 17, 1972
5th Avenue Hotel
Room 427
tele Gramercy 3-6400

Dear Brion:

I think we are all out of business..writers..painters..photographers and above all and very soon film-makers. I may be wrong and of course what is apparent to me won't be apparent to the reading buying movie public so quickly. Antony [Balch] didn't see it. You didn't see it? I saw it as soon as I walked into the Porter Mills gay blue movies on 43rd between Sixth and Seventh. Nothing you or Antony said had prepared me for seeing in the *trailers* already some trailer that shoots its wad all over the screen close up, beautiful boys fucking rimming sucking coming. Interesting feature shows film being made. Two boys fall in and five minutes later in bed together for an audition film test . . . "Run your tongue around his balls lick his ass fuck him" (Those two just washed out which is indicated by a sort of blue snow falling on screen). After two hours I've *seen* it. A certain connoisseur interest nice ass nice cock nice come remains also interesting to see sex pulse in and out there it is for a flash uhu he lost it here comes the blue snow. But the end of interest comes very quickly. You've simply *seen* it. A nude hanging on screen? Turn it off I've seen it. I've seen boys come all over and I've seen people die on TV. Why see it again? You see it again to see *more* of it because something is held back. When you've seen it all there is no more to see. And whose going to read a book about wild boys when you can see Jerry-Audrey-Johnny-Ali-Jimmy do it all on screen? I wouldn't. And after seeing just two hours of these films I didn't want to see *any other movie* or even turn on the TV. I've seen it. There is nothing more to see. There are just two elements in any story or film . . . Sex and danger. Fifteen minutes of real death on screen would be it. You think you would like to see the game in the coliseum? Run a film of it and see how long you can look at it before you say turn it off — I've seen it. Bernard Heidsieck[2] was appalled..

"But surely there is something more?"

"What more?"

Semi-clad naked fucking — once you've seen the fuck you can't go back to the naked or semi-clad. It's a one way street and it ends. The End.

Take stills, for example, where you can pick exactly what you want. Any new chickens? Sure basketfuls of Audrey-Billy-Jerry red heads pimple on ass as pretty and cute as any kids I could dream up or write sticking their fingers up each other's ass and shooting all over the page. And little stories to go with it. Here's Chuck and Billy trickin in the garage. Who the hell reads them? So I start to write it better and then I stop.

"Wanta feel something nice Audrey?" said Jerry-Johnny as he sticks his greased finger up Audrey's ass, its all there in close up so let Audrey's ass speak for itself. Where I came in.

Do you suggest people will stop reading books and going to films?

Yes, but not right away. Give it five years more or less.

Why do sex films siphon interest from other films?

Because they *all* hinge on hidden or partially revealed sex. All life does.

You mean people will not want to see any images?

Yes, for the same reason.

When they no longer want to see the pictures, will they still want to do it?

For a little while longer. Soon they will not, for the reason already cited. When it is all there, nothing held back, you have *done* it. Years ago Kiki came to me in a dream in front of the Muniria

---

2   Bernard Heidsieck (b. 1928). French avant-garde poet.

[Hotel] and said in English or American, "Sex is finished." I have seen it happen on screen to the actors.

But they still line up to see *The Godfather.*

Oh, yes, for a while. But I don't want to see it after seeing just one sex flick. No doubt I could see someone strangled naked shit and come all over in some SM film sooner or later. Turn on the blue snow, his eyes didn't pop out good. So why watch people throw catsup around?

But surely sex is only part of life?

Wrong. It is all of life and all of time. As you will understand when you read the book I am sending you and the chapter on time: *Sex is time made solid enough to fuck.* There is very little time left on set.

The revolution is over and we have won.

WORD FALLING

PHOTO FALLING

IMAGE FALLING

BREAKTHROUGH IN DARK ROOM.

Winner take nothing. There is nothing left. So let's grab enough $ to sit it out to the end.

David Prentice has huge loft, burglar proof, the lot. Rent too high for him to carry along alone so I chip in 150 per month and move in there. I now got boyfriend and place to stay. Duke Street look your last on me for I come back no more. Just long enough to pack, so why lug another truck full which is already here back to London?[3] We can assemble it all in this loft which is ten minutes walk from 8th Street. Our prospective buyers are here, why have any of it in London? My intention is to sell *everything* every file, scrap book, diary, *all all all* every fucking paper. That gives us both time to breathe until we don't have to breathe anymore. Incidentally I have all that hanging crap stashed in Chase Manhattan vault after destroying about a third of it so it would fit in the box I had. (If your Picasso won't fit into a packing case cut some of it off). So I pack all the rest into a trunk and ship it over here and call Andy [Andreas Brown] and Columbia

---

3   Burroughs was beginning to think about selling his archive at this point. A good deal of his time would be spent organizing and cataloging files before the sale was completed.

[University] come and get it or I'll, by God, throw it all out into a garbage strike. David will be away all summer and the whole loft is at my disposal, so I don't have to throw anything away actually, but could get the lead out of a buyer's ass by threatening to do so and no empty threat. Only thing I would never throw away is your paintings. So we stack it all up — our papers, layouts, and folders, and sell it right now and that's it. Why should I write any more? I have written it. *Mektoub*. No more *no mas*. I don't know how complicated air freight from Paris would be, but why not pack it all up and send to David Prentice, New York City? Will, of course, assemble the John Giorno material in same spot.

Sending you under separate cover a book called *Psychic Discoveries Behind The Iron Curtain*. Its all there. Everything we suspected half saw. Especially the chapter on time. *Time is word is sex*. We have rubbed the word out. We have rubbed the word off and all over the screen. Clom Fliday

Love
William

WSB [New York] to Brion Gysin [Paris]
April 23, 1972

Dear Brion:

Terry [Southern] has turned up the best lead yet for $ on *Naked Lunch*. Someone named Chuck Barris who produced a TV show called the *Newlyweds* which made him rich. He is a fan and very much interested and is putting out $ for Terry and me to fly out to LA on Tuesday of next week. (The fact he is willing to do that and pay hotel etc. is in itself very promising). My own plans of course depend on the outcome. Chuck is thinking in terms of our present budget which in turn is predicated on making the film in England. I have heard conflicting accounts of much higher production costs here, some say much higher, others [say] you can do it for about the same if you know the angles. I would much rather do it here and I think we would be able to find better faces easier and no hassles on sex scenes. However, if it is to be made in England then we need those apartments at least for the time of production. Otherwise the sooner I get rid of those apartments the better. The film festival my attendance at also hinges on this meeting. I would not go to the film festival for fun. I have decided to leave England any case just a question of when.

Elliot Stein has been extremely helpful showing me around the gay scene. He has introduced me to Don Richie[4] who is film curator at the Museum of Modern Art and lives half the year in Japan. He tells me, its great for sex, especially for older people. Two important qualifications: 1. *No* pot, 20 years for possession of one joint. 2. Very expensive much more than NY. He has also been to Afghanistan and told me where to go in Kabul.

What I said in last letter about the blue movies still goes. There are now 30 theatres in Manhattan and I have seen a lot more films including some straights. Interesting that the straight actors seem to have more trouble getting it up and keeping it up than the gay film actors and the attendance is lower. The Park Miller on 43 between Sixth and Seventh is the best gay theatre and gets the prettiest actors . . . two of the most beautiful red haired kids I have ever seen on or off the screen on this week . . . I predicted that the films would in time eliminate sex. The immediate effect is to make sex easier and better. Some of the best I ever had in last few days, which is entirely due to the effect of the blue films. What I mean is one gets closer and closer to wherever sex is going and when one is there? We will see. It is a source of great satisfaction to me to know I am one of the ones who opened those 30 theatres since the written word was the first breakthrough.. Lawrence-Miller-Burroughs then anything goes. You will recall I had thought sex films would be sexier with a story. Now I am not sure. Some of them have stories and the story just gets in the way. (One about a Vietnam veteran who can't get it up he and his wife try everything and then she says . . . "How about some grass?" Well, he smokes some grass and with the aid of his wife rapes the female pusher and they live happily ever after.) Of course the next step is sex scenes in regular

---

4 Donald Richie (b. 1924). Film critic and author, served as curator of film at the Museum of Modern Art from 1969 to 1972.

films as overt as the blues but this might have the effect of siphoning interest from the other action.

Elliot has told me some very interesting things about the SM scene. Did you read a book called *The Real Thing*? A really intelligent book saying that that the whole show on this planet is SM which tells me for the first time why we have had so much trouble. The only character who was not operating on SM was Hassan i Sabbah.

Love
William

WSB [New York] to Paul Bowles [Tangier, Morocco]
April 28, 1972
5th Avenue Hotel
24 5th Avenue
NYC

Dear Paul

As you can see, I have elected to visit the most exotic country of them all and have not been disappointed. New York has changed beyond recognition since I last saw it two years ago. Any sex act can now be shown on the public screen with beautiful actors and that's a powerful sight. In fact not altogether to my advantage since when you can see it you are not so interested to read about it. Anything described in *The Wild Boys* can now be seen in color and close up. And that means fewer sales. It seems I wasn't kidding when I said I was working to make myself obsolete. May make a sex flick myself after talking with a director in this genre. They have to be good or no one will go and see it.

Seems to be a lot going on here on all fronts. I saw Donald Richie who sends you his best regards. He tells me that Japan is very strict on grass but loose in other matters.

I hear very depressing reports from Morocco of beatings, muggings, and police suppression. What is your first-hand impression?

Your book is in a window display in Brentanos. I hope it is sell-

ing well. Barney Rosset says the hard cover book is on the way out.
Except of course for book of the month best sellers.

All the best,
Bill B.

EDITOR'S NOTE: *With help from his friends Burroughs had decided to catalogue and sell his archive. The goal was twofold. First and foremost, he would be able to raise some much-needed cash. Second, he would be able to divest himself of many boxes of materials, which would allow him to relocate more easily. As these letters indicate he had been thinking of moving to a half-dozen different places from Afghanistan to Costa Rica, but felt tied down by his large archive.*

WSB [London] to Billy Burroughs Jr. [Boulder, Colorado]

July 9, 1972
8 Duke Street Flat 18
St James
London S.W.1
England

Dear Billy:

I hope you are all right by now and this letter finds you in good shape. I had intended to go to New York for the summer but have stayed on here working on my archives with a view to sale. Allen Ginsberg has insured his archives for 83,000 dollars and put them on loan with Columbia University. I do not know exactly what the market is, but at least a considerable sum can be realized and it is very interesting to go through every photo, newspaper clipping, and every page of text which have been saved, some of them for 15 years, and getting all this material filed and described. For example I have the original copy of your poem "Metamorphosis" with a note from Dad and of course all your letters, mother's letters, Mote's [Burroughs' father] letters and my brother's letters. I am really interested to get all this material out where people who are interested can look at it and to start streamlining my current files. The description of the material where when and under what circumstances is developing into a book on its own,[5] there is a long section on 4 Calle Larachi including of course your *Esquire* article, the earlier *Esquire* article, etc. Remind you to keep all first drafts, notes, and above all, always get the final typescript back from the publisher.

During my recent trip to New York and Hollywood I had considered doing *The Wild Boys* as a low budget hard core porn flick and wrote what I considered a modest script. My Godfather took one look and said: "fifty wild boys rolling around on a thousand dead soldiers in a lunar crater under the northern lights with their blue mutation minks, albino raccoons, and red haired wolves . . . And this scene alone requires buying Palm Beach, moving everyone out and letting it settle for ten years so Audrey and the Dib can come on and here is a fifty billion dollar space trip to Mars . . . This film would take a hundred years to shoot and cost more than three world wars . . ." So I abandoned the project as impractical for the moment and turned my attention to the archives. Please keep in touch.

Love to you and Karen
Bill

Pertinent dream connected with this film project; I was about to sit down in a private Pullman car when John Hopkins said, "I'm afraid that seat is rather expensive."

WSB [London] to Billy Burroughs Jr. [Boulder, Colorado]
October 30, 1972
8 Duke Street
St James
Flat 18
England

Dear Billy:

I never know what to say when someone tells me his wife is leav-

---

5   Compiled by Barry Miles and published in a limited edition as *A Descriptive Catalogue of the William S. Burroughs Archive* (London, 1973).

ing him. *Son cosas de la vida, hombre.* I never saw any place in Texas I want to see again given the fact of Texans there. Surely Colorado is a better choice? Do keep in touch. My letters to Boulder came back in which I told you I had been working on my entire collection of manuscripts to assemble an archive to sell to Columbia or some other university, this could really pull me out of the hole financially, just finished a book for Dick Seaver and *The Wild Boy* film is still current with a potential backer I will have lunch with on Tuesday. I think the hottest literary properties right now are these biographies either thinly disguised as *The Godfather* or like a good thing Peter Matson has on his list a biography of Lucky Lucianno with all the CIA and American narcotics tie ups with the Mafia. Of course it doesn't have to be Mafia. Anything current like a better Don Juan book.[6] An exposé on some level that people recognize as real. Be sure and save all your manuscripts and get the final typescript back from the publisher. Neal Cassady's letter to Kerouac brought 7,000 dollars. A Ginsberg letter if worth about 200 dollars. Have you saved any letters from him? A post card is 25 dollars. Of course all your letters to me will go into the archives. I just wanted to pinpoint out the value of letters and manuscripts since I used to move around and leave suitcases full behind or throw them away. Please keep in touch.

Love

Bill

I plan to come to the States perhaps in early December. Possibility of film in Los Angeles this spring or summer. I hope we can arrange to meet.

Enclosed check for $500.

---

6   *The Teachings of Don Juan* by Carlos Castaneda.

WSB [London] to Fred Halsted[7] [Los Angeles]

November 15, 1972
8 Duke Street
St James
Flat 18
London S.W.1
England

Dear Fred:

As soon as I sat down to work on the script I realized that the entire framework as we laid it down in London is not workable quite apart from expense I mean not workable as film and story. To begin with the book is not about conflict between the wild boys and the control machine. The control machine is shattered in chapter 2 and 3. To cover this sequence would take a *Doctor Strangelove* budget. Certainly the book is not about auditing. The wild boys are way beyond that. What is the book about and why is it read by those who read it? It is about a *world without women*. And that's a difficult subject for a film. No women no trouble no problems. You can describe that in a book. To show it on screen for general release is another matter. To show it on screen on a small budget with heterosexual actors still more difficult. *Peter Pan* is an expensive film remember. I feel that a good film could be made just about auditing, but this is not the wild boy film. John [Brady] agrees with me on this point. Now as you pointed out we don't have to follow the book too closely but we have to consider the appeal of the book. I think it is time for the first uncompromising anti-female statement and this is the only slant for this film picketed by Women's Lib the lot. But how can we do this on our budget? This is the war of the sexes to turn back to time before the wild boys had established themselves which is again before the book begins. The mere existence of wild boy tribes living without women is already victory. The promised land has been reached. All right for purposes of the film we recapitulate the story of this victory as told by an old boy. The first wild boy tribes were relentlessly pursued by police

---

7   Fred Halsted. Gay porn pioneer.

and a lesbian legion known as the Fanatical 80. They have to go completely underground. (Under present conditions wild boy tribes would not stand a chance.) To equalize matters their technicians release a plague that destroys the industrial west. They then destroy the Fanatical 80 and show that men can live and reproduce without women. Film opens in a desert set wild boys and the lesbian legions who are destroyed in a series of ambushes. Boys enter the promised land. Very expensive battle scenes. Triple X sex or at the very best an R rating. A film about the war of the sexes could be very successful like I say it is timely. But not on a small budget.

All in all I have yet to come up with a viable film idea except hard core porn shooting for a classic like *Chant D'Amour*. And we know what a head ache is involved.

I will think further and see if I can come up with a simple and workable formula perhaps involving only one scouting party who never contacts the enemy. They could have John along with the E-Meter to detect infiltrators and interrogate prisoners. They could in fact occupy one set one post like an abandoned skating rink yes its taking shape now I begin to see it . . . Will sit down now and see what I can do with this simple framework. . .

Love . . .
William

WSB [London] to Fred Halsted [Los Angeles]
December 9, 1972
8 Duke Street
St James
Flat 18
London S.W.1
England

Dear Fred:

Pursuant to our telephone conversation, to get this show on the road . . . Yes, I would grant you the film rights on *The Wild Boys* for a period not to exceed eighteen months in return for the three thousand dollars you mention. Please send a contract which I will have my London agent look at. Meanwhile, I am getting ideas on a viable film story and would be glad to work out the actual script with you when I get there. January would be possible if you could send me the return ticket; and please give me some idea as to the living conditions out there.

Seeing a lot of John [Brady] who sends his love. All the best and look forward to seeing you soon

Love
William

WSB [London] to Fred Halsted [Los Angeles]

December 19, 1972
8 Duke Street
St James
London S.W.1
England

Dear Fred:

I appreciate your offer and your enthusiasm but after carefully weighing all the factors, financial and otherwise I have decided that this project must be shelved for the present at least. I cannot afford to put in the time on speculation on every speculative project when I could and must use the time assembling a novel. To date I have come up with no film script that is workable on our budget, provided we could raise it, and I feel that the film we could get on screen would not do either of us any good.

Sorry it has not worked out as we both had hoped. It has taken me some time to weigh all the factors involved and reach the above conclusion. I know this is a disappointment to you but I feel I am acting for both our interests not to proceed with a film that is so financially uncertain and so difficult to screen effectively

Love
William

RUBRUBRUBRUB+++&+++++&++&&&&&""""&"+++&

RUBRUBRUBRUBOUTOUTOUTOUTOUT#"#+++++#

RUBRUBRUBRUBOUTOUTOUTOUTOUT####&&&&&

""""&&&+++++"OUTOUTOUTOUTOUT""""""&&&

1973 ""+OUTOUTOUTOUTOUT"+"+"&&&"

THETHETHETHETHETHETHETHE+++###+++&&+++&

THETHETHETHETHETHETHE&&&&&++++++++++#

THETHETHETHEWORDSWORDSWORDSWORDSTHE

####&&"&"&"&WORDSWORDSWORDSWORDS"++

WSB [London] to Allen Ginsberg [Cherry Valley, New York]
March 23, 1973
8 Duke Street
St James
London S.W.1
Flat 18
England

Dear Allen

Sorry you have been bothered by this Tony Cole. I know that you sometimes extend charity where I would not. He is in a deplorable condition. I have given him small amounts of money. I also told him flatly that any expeditions to Pakistan were beyond my means or inclination. Beyond that I know nothing.

I have given up flat 22 which I managed to reassign for a years rent and now live in flat 18 a small two room flat on the 5th floor. Brion [Gysin] is in Paris and has no plans to return to London. My own plans are up in the air. I have a boy living with me here. We may both go to Tangier for the summer in which case you would be welcome to use this flat. There is a spare bed room here but it would be very close quarters for three people.

Yes I saw the interview in *Gay Sunshine*. No, I was not at all upset by the references to my love life. I cannot understand why you think it at all remarkable to come when fucked. Lots of people do I find. Also people come from being beaten, kissed, etc. Its all electric brain stimulation. As you may know you can now make someone come by pressing a button.

I have just given a long interview to *Gay Sunshine* myself. They plan a series. Gore Vidal, [Jean] Genet. By all means buy and read a book called *Journeys Out of the Body* by Robert A. Monroe published by Doubleday. This is exactly what I mean by non-body experience. I have been practicing the exercises with interesting results and would like to compare notes with as many people as possible. Otherwise keeping very busy. Have a new book coming out in early summer with Dick Seaver. You will receive advance copy. I feel that Grove has simply not done the job. *The Wild Boys* hard cover made no money in the States but made 2000 dollars here. There is something very wrong with promotion and distribution when a book geared to the American market makes money in England and not in America. When it comes to invoking personal loyalties Dick Seaver is much more a friend of mine than Barney Rosset. That is, I have never been to Barney's house even, but have been to Dick's house many times and know his whole family. Also Rosset was instrumental in arranging the disastrous alliance with Jonathan Cape, which made no $ £ for either of us and ending up with [Tom] Maschler and your reporter not on speaking terms. Furthermore, I can't get an accounting out of them on *The Wild Boys* paperback edition.

Give my best to Peter [Orlovsky]. Does he know how much it costs to cut wood? You can tell him. And where should I row? In my bath tub?

It is permitted to the older revolutionaries to drink and smoke. I will let you know how my plans shape up. Sorry you missed Joujouka. It was out of sight. I wrote an article for *Oui* which should be out soon.[1] And Ornette Coleman has a record coming out soon. He played with the Joujouka musicians and brought a whole recording studio along with him

Love and Peace
Bill

WSB [London] to Peter Matson [New York?]
May 1, 1973
8 Duke Street
St James
Flat 18
London SW1
England

Dear Pete:

Enclose *The Electronic Revolution* which was published in a limited edition here by Henri Chopin [Blackmoor Head Press]. I would like to point out the relevance of this text to the current Watergate

---

1 "Face to Face with the Goat God" was published in the August 1973 issue of *Oui*.

scab, I mean scandal, and suggest that the entire English text be added to *The Job* for the paperback edition with a Watergate montage as the cover. This gives the title a new significance. You will see when you read this text how relevant it is. The real scandal of Watergate is not that they made these recordings at Watergate and in the bedroom of Martin Luther King and God knows where else and in who else's bedroom but *the use they made of these recordings.* I would also write a preface pointing out the relevance to Watergate and the tape recorder techniques used to discredit opponents by play back of sexual and other recordings. I hope you can line up Grove on this idea which it seems to me could really ring up some sales. *The Electronic Revolution* is a logical sequel or addition to *The Job* continuing right where *The Job* leaves off. Please let me know what you think about this.

Well, this is the day when Grove is supposed to produce the Dell accounts. Let us hope for the best.

Since *The Wild Boys* English money is in the NY account by all means let it remain there. It doesn't matter just so I know where money is going.

All the best
William

EDITOR'S NOTE: When Burroughs received a proposal of marriage from a woman he had never met, he was irritated enough that he answered her. When he received a second letter from her along the same lines, he replied in no uncertain terms that this dream of hers was never going to materialize.

WSB [London] to Liz Strickland [Paris]
June 1, 1973
8 Duke Street
St James
London SW1
England

Dear Liz Strickland:
Maya Maya Maya . . . Illusion Illusion Illusion . . . You love an

illusion that does not exist and never did. I can assure you that your informant never saw me in Paris or anywhere else. I have spent four days in Paris in the past ten years surrounded by a few middle aged business associates. My face is not waxy green but a comparatively healthy middle age pink. I never had the slightest interest in limp-wristed boys. I have not money to spend. At this point I take little interest in sex. When I did my interest was in Mexican and Arab boys. I was not looking for love but for sex in return for a modest monetary outlay. So you see your picture of YOU does not exist. My main interest at this time is psychic research. I am practically a recluse. I do not need protection. I need money and solitude. I have told not [no] one to wait. My books don't sell and I have no other source of income. Cannot afford to go on living in London. Will probably move to Morocco or Afghanistan in a few weeks with what money I have left and try to write a best seller or at least a book that sells. I hope to make some money to finance certain experiments. Recommend to your attention a book published by Doubleday entitled *Journeys Out of the Body* by Robert A Monroe. This book points the way to the future as I see it. The only future for an unsuccessful species.

I could not consider marriage with anyone male or female. We can perhaps meet in what Monroe calls Locale 2. I am not rejecting you. I am simply asking you to understand that your picture of me does not exist. "I" do not exist. Who am I? A stranger here and always. I wish you well and all success in a difficult profession . . . Love and Power . . .

Etranger qui passait
William Burroughs

WSB [London] to Liz Strickland [Paris]

June 8, 1973
8 Duke Street
St James
Flat 18
London S.W.1

Dear Liz Strickland

I wrote you a letter about a week ago which you should have by now unless it went astray. In this letter I pointed out that what you love is an illusory picture of William Burroughs that does not exist and never did. I am not surrounded by parasites nor in need of protection. I am virtually a recluse and see very few people. I do not want publicity. I have almost no money. My books don't sell. I am not looking for love from anyone male or female. Love requires a capacity for self deception which I have lost. Love is an illusion like everything else we see or feel or think we see and feel. There are of course levels of illusion. For example, for many years physicists believed in an illusion known as Newtonian physics. Then along came Uncle Albert with a new illusion called Relativity and a super potent illusion known as ME . . . (Matter into Energy) which made an impressive showing at Hiroshima. People die believe it very long. When the Newtonians couldn't crack Relativity some of them actually committed suicide. Did you know that? You should stop thinking about suicide and get on with your life and forget an unworkable illusion. I mean suppose as a young writer I had fallen in love with Djuna Barnes, the great Lesbian novelist . . . Have you read *Nightwood*? . . . fallen in love sight unseen and with as little knowledge of her tastes, habits, past and present circumstances as you have of mine. Could that have worked out? Of course not. Homosexuality is an illusion and so is heterosexuality. So maybe I fall in love with Papa Hemingway. Super male writer goes gay at 60? He would have needed that like a hole in the head big enough to put a big fist in if he didn't want to put it there. All is illusion to be sure but some illusions function and some do not.

I have received no other proposals of marriage and no woman

or man has ever committed suicide over me. Why on earth should they? I have told no one to wait.

I am saying no to your proposal of marriage as I would say no to *any* proposal of marriage. This is not a rejection of you. Our illusion systems simply do not coincide. So I ask you to please stop thinking about suicide. And start thinking about a workable life for yourself.

Love and Power
William Burroughs

WSB [London] to Billy Burroughs Jr. [Savannah, Georgia?]
July 10, 1973
8 Duke Street
St James
Flat 18
London SW1
England

Dear Bill:

Have read your book [*Kentucky Ham*] from beginning to end and found it hypnotically readable, the digressions actually adding to the effect. How are sales and reviews or is it too early to say? I like the jacket because it attracts the eye and makes people wonder how it relates to the title. Also a tune in on the famous advert "I'd walk a mile for a Camel." No harm in telling people that they need desperately to know about what is in the book. That should sell books and that is what writers are doing, selling books, I mean. Be sure to get your manuscript of the book back from the publisher. I have recently done a good deal on all my old manuscripts, first drafts, letters, notes and photos from twenty years back so be sure to save yours. I used to throw a lot away until Gregory [Corso] found out he could make more money selling manuscripts than writing them. For example an Allen Ginsberg letter is worth 200 dollars or what is left of the dollar. Do you take pictures? Do you have pictures of Alaska crabs, and Yucatan tarantulas, and all the actors in these sagas? If not by all means put out 20 dollars for an Instamatic [camera] and begin taking pictures wherever you go. It helps when you sit down to write.

Your idea of a *Naked Mu* I mean *Lunch* record is very good. Would of course take a lot of thought and preparation. Someone in Chicago did a high school stage production which apparently worked out well. We are still working on the film and perhaps the two ideas could be brought together. Past six months I have been doing almost nothing but working on the archives which took five months to catalogue and I had to check every page and write descriptions for every folder. Will send you a copy of the catalogue which will be printed in about two weeks. The deal I made was in Switzerland which is good right there, but in last words of a great American Dutch Schultz, "That is something that should not be spoken about," at least not until my Swiss friends are ready to make their own announcement.

[. . .]

As for 'ground called sanctuary' I am looking for it. Perhaps Costa Rica or Southern Ireland which has no tax on artists. Will let you know what I find out. Switzerland is cool enough with all those snow capped mountains and a citizen army where every man has a machine gun in his house and no casualties. But they are making it more and more difficult for outsiders to settle. They want to *keep* it cool.

All the best to you and Karen

Love

Bill

WSB [London] to Mack? [n.p.]
July 16, 1973 William S. Burroughs
8 Duke Street
St James
Flat 18
London SW1
England

Dear Mack—

Thanks for your letter and offer of sanctuary. It arrived at a time when I am absolutely fed up with London and cannot afford to live here any longer, prices have doubled in the past three years and the whole island is slowly foundering. Have considered Southern Ireland which has no tax on artists but there are many drawbacks. Another possibility is Costa Rica which I will probably have a look at as soon as I can get squared away to leave. I would like to see some sun and water other than rain, do some fishing, walk and cut wood. If I make the Costa Rica jaunt could look in.

What was the name of your movie? I have written a couple of film scripts one on Dutch Schultz but no offers of production. Otherwise plugging along with novels that don't make enough to live on certainly not here. As to my thought, more and more concerned with escape from a sinking ship via out of body experience. Have you read Robert A Monroe's *Journeys Out of the Body* published by Doubleday? Interesting decidedly. Another book worth looking at is *Psychic Discoveries Behind the Iron Curtain* [by Sheila Ostrander]. What is matter doing? Making atom bombs I presume after the manner of its species which is repetition. Matter repeats itself. Radio activity *is* repetition.

> *Hasta Luego*
> Bill

WSB [London] to Billy Burroughs Jr. [Savannah, Georgia]
Sept 6, 1973
8 Duke Street
St James
Flat 18
London SW1
England

Dear Bill:

Enclose check for 500 dollars. It is indeed difficult to make a living as a writer and my advice to anyone contemplating a literary career is to have some other trade. My own choice would be plumbing, but I suppose they have a tight union to keep this twenty dollar an hour with two lazy worthless assistants to hand the head man his tools good thing from being swamped. I have a friend in New

York who is a painter and can't make a living at that, who makes 50 dollars per day fixing up lofts . . . (very hard work but he gets all the jobs he can handle and works when he needs to.)

I never heard of sucking lemons to keep awake. Ice tea, Coca Cola in hot weather, coffee in cold weather, work well enough supplemented with no doze caffeine pills. Caffeine is by far the safest stimulant doesn't louse up coordination and appetite.

Just back from a holiday in the Greek islands. Great swimming. Even fell off a horse. All right for a visit. Still looking for a reasonable place to live. All the best to you and Karen

Love
Bill

WSB [London] to John Calder [London]
Sept. 13, 1973
839-5259

Dear John:

From considerations of space, health, and economy I am planning to leave London and may leave England altogether in the next few months.

I would appreciate any information you can give me about prices and living conditions in Scotland. I hope we can get together for drinks or dinner sometime soon. All the best to you and Marion

Cordially
William Burroughs

WSB [London] to Brion Gysin [Paris]
October 30, 1973
8 Duke Street
St James
London SW1

Dear Brion:

I have just had a long talk with Antony [Balch] who does seem to be in a bad way and on the brink of a nervous breakdown whatever that may mean. I know that you are intolerant of so called mental illness, but I think you must recognize that it does exist. I don't pretend to know what is basically wrong with him, it looks like a hex to me, but of course I didn't tell him that. As we know a hex has to have some place to light and all I could do was try to pin whatever it is down: What shape is it? What color is it? Can you visualize it in front of you? Now in the next flat? etc. Don't know whether this will have any effect.

He is very upset by your letter and stipulations for an amended contract. I do not wish to interfere in this matter but a contract specifying that only Antony can direct the film [*Naked Lunch*] and that if at any time through death, illness, etc. he is not able to do so, the script reverts to you, would create difficulties with insurance: to wit if Antony for any reason could not complete after the film was half or three quarters finished then there would be no arrangement for a substitute director and in consequence no film so that the money put out up to that point would be lost. I urge moderation and compromise. And a realistic assessment of Antony's condition, in the light of what can be reasonably expected of him. Of course everyone is under pressure and everyone has problems. However, some are better able to cope than others. When somebody is convinced that he is ill he is ill. I suggest that too much pressure at this point is inadvisable.

I am more than ever determined to get out of London somewhere where I can get a modicum of exercise and cut down on smoking. No use to knock oneself out providing for old age if one's health is lost in the process.

I have prepared a prospectus for the academy course and sent it along to Richard Aaron.[2] Location in Switzerland may yet be arranged.

Malcolm [McNeill][3] has left for San Francisco to finish the book there and I wrote a bang up kiss kiss bang bang ending just as you suggested.

---

2   Richard Aaron. Broker for the sale of the Burroughs Archive to a collector in Liechtenstein.
3   Malcolm McNeill. Co-creator of a set of illustrations for Burroughs' book *The Exterminator*.

Much activity on the dream front and many dreams involving you in realistic yet fantastic narrative sequences.

Love and Moderation
William

WSB [London] to Sanche de Gramont[4] [n.p.]

November 14, 1973
8 Duke Street
St James
London SW1
England

Dear Sanche:

People have been camping out all night here to see the royal wedding[5] which shows that entertainment here is at an all time low. There's a TV series on called *Is London Cracking Up?* Answer is yes. They can't or won't pay enough to keep the miners, transport workers, garbage collectors, firemen, and power workers on the job. I am considering a move to the wilds of Scotland or perhaps southern Ireland.

Naked Lunch is in a go condition finance-wise but Antony [Balch] is down with a severe case of hypochondria. I told him to take up karate and fight it off. He keeps going to doctors who give him pills that make him feel worse. The middle east war has cut off dope supplies here. Gas rationing started yesterday. It looks like the horse is going to make a comeback. I am convinced that big cities are death traps and it is time to decentralize.

Brion [Gysin] is settled in Paris and working on a combination of painting and photos. Ian [Sommerville] has a new computer job. Did you ever hear of [Anthony] Stafford Beer? He was the computer expert who was programming the economy under [Salvador] Allende so Chile would be a model for the world. Strange thing

---

4 Sanche de Gramont (b. 1932). Pulitzer Prize–winning author, who later, under the name Ted Morgan, wrote the first biography of Burroughs, *Literary Outlaw*.
5 The British Princess Anne married Mark Phillips on November 14, 1973.

is he got out without a trace. I have seen no reference to him in any news story. Well there's a story there and you don't need the Columbia School of Journalism to see it. This Beer is an off-beat computer expert who has written some books on the subject. Give my best to Nancy and Gabriel. John [Brady] sends his best

William

WSB [London] to John Calder [London]
November 39 [sic: Nov. 29], 1973
8 Duke Street
St James
London SW1

Dear John:

With regard to the illustrated edition of *Exterminator*: The original suggestion was that the signed and numbered copies could be sold for more if they were illustrated thus adding an inducement to collectors. On this tentative agreement the illustrators Malcolm McNeill and Steve Lawson produced the artwork which is in your possession.

My experience with the archives has convinced me that the collector market is substantial and I feel that there would be no difficulty in selling an edition of 100 signed, numbered, and illustrated copies for a price in the naborhood of ten pounds each since they would be certain to increase in value. Of course if Dick Seaver wants to share the costs and jointly print 200 copies the price could perhaps be reduced somewhat.

Please let me know what you think about this and what you estimate the production costs and consequent retail price would amount to. Also what would be the difference involved if Dick Seaver agrees to participate? All the best to you and Marion [Boyars]

Best Regards
Bill

WSB [London] to John Brady [San Francisco, California?]
November 30, 1973
8 Duke Street
St James
Flat 18
London SW1
England

Dear John:

I have accepted a teaching job at New York City College beginning February 4 and running until the end of May. Will probably
leave here around mid-January. Perhaps earlier.

What are your plans? Do you still consider a trip to London
over Christmas? Please let me know.

I have been considering the purchase of a remote property in
Scotland to carry out my experiments. There is a haunted lock
[loch] I mean Scottish for lake of course where even the fish are
peculiar . . .

TV program here entitled *Is London Cracking UP?* Answer: Yes.
All big cities are cracking up and it is time to decentralize. See you
soon any case

William

WSB [London] to Billy Burroughs Jr. [Atlanta, Georgia?]
December 13, 1973
8 Duke Street
St James
Flat 18
London SW1
England

Dear Bill:

The letter to Savannah just came back. But I sent another along
to Atlanta. Did you get that one?

I have accepted a teaching job with New York City College
February through May. So will be seeing you soon.

Glad to hear you have turned to straight fiction. Autobiography usually runs its course in two books I find.

I am afraid there is no brotherhood in any industry, but I never had too much trouble with [Maurice] Girodias. He tends to be a bit casual about accounts, but we get along well enough. I will speak to him about your royalties if you give me the details or we could see him together. How did Dutton do on sales? Agents like to place books with the big publishing houses, but this is not always advantageous for the writer.

To the best of my knowledge Allen Ginsberg is back on the farm. Address: Allen Ginsberg, % Committee on Poetry, Cherry Valley, New York. Where living is cheaper, I don't know. Certainly not in England. Prices have doubled here in the last three years and will probably double again in one more year then six months then three months . . . this island is sinking under me I am writing this by one dim light at 2 in the afternoon. It gets dark here at 3 PM . . . The lights are going out, no petrol, no electricity, no coal. Everybody on strike because they don't earn enough to live.

See you soon. All my love to you
and Karen. Merry Christmas
Bill

Enclose Christmas check. I can't think of anything I want for Christmas from USA . . . any case will be there soon.

WSB [London] to Dom Sylvester Houedard [New York?]
December 23, 1973
8 Duke Street
St James
Flat 18
London SW1
England

Dear Dom:

Many apologies for not having written sooner. I have been traveling. I hope to be in New York February through May so we can go into details. To answer your questions briefly: Born Feb 5, 1914, school in St Louis, Los Alamos Ranch School where they later made the atom bomb, graduated from Harvard in 1936, graduate work in anthropology, lived in New York until 1942 . . . Worked as an exterminator in Chicago 1943 back in New York 1944–47 . . . New Orleans 1948, Mexico 1949–51, South America 1953, Tangier 1953–1958 Paris and London 1958 to present time.

Joan [Burroughs] was dark-haired, medium height, upper middle class, not much concerned about dress.

Lee is not necessarily evil. He is somewhat like [Raymond] Chandler type private eye. I never thought of Benway as being a creep. To be borne in mind that these are all *mythological characters*

Sorry for the delay and see you soon I hope. I will be here until mid January

All the best
Bill Burroughs

RUBRUBRUBRUB+++&++++&+++&&&&&&""""&"+++
RUBRUBRUBRUBOUTOUTOUTOUTOUT#"#++++#
RUBRUBRUBRUBOUTOUTOUTOUTOUT####&&&&
"""""&&&+++++"OUTOUTOUTOUTOUT"""""""&&&
1974 """+OUTOUTOUTOUTOUT"+"+"&&&
THETHETHETHETHETHETHETHE+++###+++&&+++
THETHETHETHETHETHETHE&&&&&++++++++++#
THETHETHETHEWORDSWORDSWORDSWORDSTHE
####&&"&"&"&WORDSWORDSWORDSWORDS"++

WSB [London] to Allen Ginsberg [New York?]

January 14, 1974
8 Duke Street
St James
London SW1
England

Dear Allen:

[Barry] Miles has conveyed to me your generous offer to make the farm available as a center for advanced studies.[1] The offer is deeply appreciated and I will be in New York in early February so we can discuss the matter further. As you may know owing to your intervention I have been offered a teaching job at New York City College from February through May. As this is only two hours a week that leaves me plenty of time for other projects. I am convinced that America is the place to set up such a center. Any case the more centers the merrier. See you soon

Love
Bill

---

1   Burroughs had been toying with the idea of founding a "Burroughs Center" for studies somewhere in a remote location and on a limited budget.

EDITOR'S NOTE: That winter Burroughs did in fact move to New York City. It was to be the end of a self-imposed twenty-five-year period of living abroad. Once back in the United States, he realized that things had changed drastically during those years, and he found that he had become famous.

WSB [New York] to Billy Burroughs Jr. [Atlanta, Georgia?]
March 18, 1974
452 Broadway
Apt. 3-F
NYC, 10013

Dear Billy,

Have huge loft here and delighted to see you anytime. Did Allen talk to you about possibility of occupying his Cherry Valley farm this summer? I finish here May 21 and after that don't know. Only trouble with Spanish moss and Southern rivers is natives. The more isolated the situation the more curious the nabors. However, Allen seems to have Cherry Valley well cooled.

The sooner you can make it here the better as we have much to discuss. Would rather talk in person than attempt to answer questions raised in your letter — a great letter. Share loft with James Grauerholz, one of your fans who is looking forward to meeting you. See you sooner. All my best to you and Karen.

Love
Bill

SOURCES

(Key to abbreviations: al = autograph letter; als = autograph letter, signed; tl = typed letter; tls = typed letter, signed.)

1959

October 30, 1959. WSB [Paris] to Allen Ginsberg [New York] 2p. tl. Letter found at Columbia University.

November 13, 1959. WSB [Paris] to Kells Elvins [Rome, Italy] Carbon copy. Letter found at New York Public Library.

ca. November 17, 1959. WSB [Paris] to Laura Lee and Mortimer Burroughs [Palm Beach, Florida] Carbon copy. Letter found at New York Public Library.

November 17, 1959. WSB [Paris] to Allen Ginsberg [New York] 3p. tls. Letter found at Columbia University. Four lines deleted.

December 2, 1959. WSB [Paris] to Allen Ginsberg [New York] 1p. tls. Letter found at University of Chicago.

December 7, 1959. WSB [Paris] to Allen Ginsberg [New York] 1p. tls. Letter found at Arizona State University.

December 7, 1959. WSB [Paris] to Paul Bowles [Tangier, Morocco] 1p. tls. Letter found at University of Texas.

ca. December 1959. WSB [Paris] to Laura Lee Burroughs [Palm Beach, Florida] Carbon copy. Letter found at New York Public Library.

ca. December 1959. WSB [Paris] to Billy Burroughs Jr. [Palm Beach, Florida] Carbon copy. Letter found at New York Public Library.

1960

January 4, 1960. WSB [Paris] to Paul Bowles [Tangier, Morocco] 1p. tls.
Letter found at University of Texas.

January 22, 1960. WSB [Paris] to Allen Ginsberg [Concepción, Chile] 1p.
tls. Letter found at Columbia University.

January 24, 1960. WSB [Paris] to Irving Rosenthal [New York] 1p. tls.
Letter found at Stanford University.

January 30, 1960. WSB [Paris] to Paul Bowles [Tangier, Morocco] 1p. tls.
Letter found at University of Texas.

March 2, 1960. WSB [Paris] to Ian Sommerville [Cambridge, England]
Carbon copy. Letter found at New York Public Library.

April 8, 1960. WSB [Paris] to Paul Carroll [Chicago] 2p. tls. Letter found
at University of Chicago.

April 18, 1960. WSB [Paris] to Allen Ginsberg [Lima, Peru] 1p. tls. Letter
found at Columbia University. 8 repetitive lines cut.

April 18, 1960. WSB [Paris] to Paul Bowles [Tangier, Morocco] 1p. tls.
Letter found at University of Texas.

May 3, 1960. WSB [London] to Brion Gysin [Paris] 2p. tls. Letter found
at New York Public Library.

May 16, 1960. WSB [London] to Brion Gysin [Paris] 3p. tls. Letter found
at New York Public Library.

May 20, 1960. WSB [London] to Dave Haselwood [San Francisco] 1p. tls.
Letter found at Northwestern University.

May 26, 1960. WSB [London] to Brion Gysin [Paris] 1p. tls. Letter found
at New York Public Library.

May 26, 1960. WSB [London] to Paul Carroll [Chicago] 1p. tls. Letter
found at University of Chicago.

June 21, 1960. WSB [London] to Allen Ginsberg [Peru] 2p. tls. Letter
found at Stanford University.

June 24, 1960. WSB [London] to Dave Haselwood [San Francisco, Cali-
fornia] 1p. tls. Letter found at University of Kansas.

July 6, 1960. WSB [London] to Bill Belli [Paris?] 1p. tls. Letter found at
Arizona State University.

July 11, 1960. WSB [London] to Dave Haselwood [San Francisco] 1p. tls.
Letter found at University of California, Berkeley.

July 20, 1960. WSB [London] to Irving Rosenthal [New York] Carbon
copy. Letter found at New York Public Library. At least one page of
this letter appears to be missing.

July 24, 1960. WSB [London] to Brion Gysin [Paris?] 1p. tls. Letter found
at New York Public Library.

July 26, 1960. WSB [London] to Paul Bowles [Tangier, Morocco] 1p. tls.
Letter found at University of Texas.

July 26, 1960. WSB [London] to Dave Haselwood [San Francisco] 1p. tls. Letter found at University of California, Berkeley. One line deleted.

July 27, 1960. WSB [London] to John Dent [London] Carbon copy. Letter found at New York Public Library.

August 4, 1960. WSB [London] to Brion Gysin [Paris] 2p. tls. Letter found at New York Public Library. Two lines asking for address deleted.

August 6, 1960. WSB [London] to Brion Gysin [Paris] 1p. tls. Letter found at New York Public Library.

August 15, 1960. WSB [London] to Brion Gysin [Paris] 2p. tls. Letter found at New York Public Library. Six lines deleted sending regards to friends.

September 5, 1960. WSB [London] to Allen Ginsberg [New York] 1p. tls. Letter found at Columbia University.

September 14, 1960. WSB [London] to Brion Gysin [Paris] 1p. tls. Letter found at New York Public Library.

October 1, 1960. WSB [London] to Brion Gysin [Paris] 2p. tls. Letter found at New York Public Library.

October 1, 1960. WSB [London] to Billy Burroughs Jr. [Palm Beach, Florida] Carbon copy. Letter found at New York Public Library.

October 4, 1960. WSB [London] to Ian Sommerville [Cambridge, England] Carbon copy. Letter found at New York Public Library.

October 7, 1960. WSB [London] to Brion Gysin [Paris] 1p. tls. Letter found at New York Public Library.

October 8, 1960. WSB [London] to Charles Henri Ford [Rome] Carbon copy. Letter found at New York Public Library.

October 9, 1960. WSB [London] to Grey Walter [Bristol, England] Carbon copy. Letter found at New York Public Library.

October 21, 1960. WSB [Cambridge, England] to Brion Gysin [Paris] 2p. tls. Letter found at New York Public Library.

October 24, 1960. WSB [Cambridge, England] to Brion Gysin [Paris] 1p. tls. Letter found at New York Public Library. Two lines deleted.

November 1960. WSB [London] to Brion Gysin [Paris] 3p. tl. Letter found at New York Public Library.

November 2, 1960. WSB [London] to Allen Ginsberg [New York] 1p. tls. Letter found at Columbia University.

November 10, 1960. WSB [Cambridge, England] to Allen Ginsberg [New York] 2p. tls. Letter found at Columbia University.

December 30, 1960. WSB [Paris] to Allen Ginsberg [New York] 1p. tls. Letter found at Columbia University.

1961

January 10, 1961. WSB [Paris] to Allen Ginsberg [New York] 1p. tls. Letter found at Columbia University.

January 20, 1961. WSB [Paris] to Timothy Leary [Cambridge, Massachusetts] Carbon copy. Letter found at New York Public Library.

January 23, 1961. WSB [Paris] to Melville Hardiment [London?] 1p. tls. Letter found at University of Kansas.

January 25, 1961. WSB [Paris] to Paul Bowles [Tangier, Morocco] 1p. tls. Letter found at University of Texas.

February 24, 1961. WSB [Paris] to Dave Haselwood [San Francisco] 1p. tls. Letter found at University of California, Berkeley.

March 9, 1961. WSB [Paris] to Allen Ginsberg [New York] 1p. tl. Letter found at New York Public Library.

April 7, 1961. WSB [Tangier, Morocco] to Allen Ginsberg, Gregory Corso, and Peter Orlovsky [Paris] 1p. tls. Letter found at Columbia University.

April 8, 1961. WSB [Tangier, Morocco] to Brion Gysin [Paris] 3p. tls. Letter found at New York Public Library.

April 14, 1961. WSB [Tangier, Morocco] to Allen Ginsberg [Paris] 1p. tls. Letter found at Columbia University.

May 4, 1961. WSB [Tangier, Morocco] to Billy Burroughs Jr. [Palm Beach, Florida] 1p. tls. Letter found at New York Public Library.

May 6, 1961. WSB [Tangier, Morocco] to Brion Gysin [Paris] 1p. tls. Letter found at New York Public Library.

May 6, 1961. WSB [Tangier, Morocco] to Timothy Leary [Cambridge, Massachusetts] Carbon copy. Letter found at New York Public Library.

May 8, 1961. WSB [Tangier, Morocco] to Brion Gysin [Paris] 2p. tls. Letter found at New York Public Library.

May 13, 1961. WSB [Tangier, Morocco] to Brion Gysin [Paris] 1p. tls. Letter found at New York Public Library.

May 16, 1961. WSB [Tangier, Morocco] to Brion Gysin [Paris] 1p. tls. Letter found at New York Public Library.

May 17, 1961. WSB [Tangier, Morocco] to Brion Gysin [Paris] 2p. tls. Letter found at New York Public Library. At least one line appears to be cut off the original letter.

May 28, 1961. WSB [Tangier, Morocco] to Brion Gysin [Paris] 2p. tls. Letter found at New York Public Library. One paragraph fold-in deleted.

June 13, 1961. WSB [Tangier, Morocco] to Don Startin [Vancouver, British Columbia] Carbon copy. Letter found at New York Public Library.

June 14, 1961. WSB [Tangier, Morocco] to Brion Gysin [Paris] 2p. tls. Letter found at New York Public Library.

August 7, 1961. WSB [Tangier, Morocco] to Brion Gysin [Rome] 1p. tls. Letter found at New York Public Library.

August 25, 1961. WSB [Cambridge, Massachusetts] to Brion Gysin [Rome] 2p. tls. Letter found at New York Public Library.

ca. late August or early September 1961. WSB [Newton, Massachusetts] to

Paul Bowles [Tangier, Morocco] 1p. tls. Letter found at University of Texas.

pre-September 28, 1961. WSB [New York] to Brion Gysin [Paris] 1p. tls. Letter found at New York Public Library.

September 28, 1961. WSB [New York] to Brion Gysin [Paris] 1p. tls. Letter found at New York Public Library.

October 24, 1961. WSB [New York] to Brion Gysin [Paris] 2p. tls. Letter found at New York Public Library.

October 25, 1961. WSB [New York] to Brion Gysin [Paris] 1p. tls. Letter found at New York Public Library.

October 26, 1961. WSB [New York] to Allen Ginsberg [Athens, Greece] 1p. tl. Letter found at New York Public Library.

November 1, 1961. WSB [New York] to Brion Gysin [Paris] 1p. tls. Letter found at New York Public Library.

December 12, 1961. WSB [Paris] to Barney Rosset [New York] 1p. tls. Letter found at Syracuse University.

December 18, 1961. WSB [Paris] to Paul Bowles [Tangier, Morocco] 1p. tls. Letter found at Arizona State University.

1962

February 5, 1962. WSB [Paris] to Paul Bowles [Tangier, Morocco] 1p. tls. Letter found at Arizona State University.

February 16, 1962. WSB [London] to Allen Ginsberg [New Delhi, India] 1p. tls. Letter found at Columbia University.

February 16, 1962. WSB [London] to Ian Sommerville [Paris] Carbon copy. Letter found at New York Public Library.

February 20, 1962. WSB [London] to Brion Gysin [Paris] 1p. tls. Letter found at New York Public Library.

February 28, 1962. WSB [London] to Barney Rosset [New York] 1p. tls. Letter found at Syracuse University.

March 1, 1962. WSB [London] to Paul Bowles [Tangier, Morocco] 1p. tls. Letter found at Arizona State University.

March 30, 1962. WSB [London] to Barney Rosset [New York] 1p. tls. Letter found at Syracuse University.

April 2, 1962. WSB [London] to Paul Bowles [Tangier, Morocco] 1p. tls. Letter found at University of Texas.

April 9, 1962. WSB [London] to Brion Gysin [Paris] 1p. tls. Letter found at New York Public Library.

April 20, 1962. WSB [London] to Gregory Corso [New York] 1p. tls. Letter found at University of Texas.

June 4, 1962. WSB [Paris] to Bill Berkson [n.p.] 1p. tls. Letter found at Columbia University. One line deleted.

June 23, 1962. WSB [Paris] to Barney Rosset [New York] 1p. tls. Letter found at Syracuse University.

June 26, 1962. WSB [Paris] to George ? [n.p.] Carbon copy. Letter found at New York Public Library.

July 9, 1962. WSB [Paris] to Paul Bowles [Tangier, Morocco] 2p. tls. Letter found at University of Texas.

August 7, 1962. WSB [Paris] to Barney Rosset [New York] 1p. tls. Letter found at Syracuse University.

August 17, 1962. WSB [Paris] to Paul Bowles [Tangier, Morocco] 1p. tls. Letter found at University of Texas.

August 31, 1962. WSB [Paris] to Howard Schulman [New York] 1p. tls. Letter found at Columbia University.

September 1, 1962. WSB [Paris] to Brion Gysin [n.p.] 1p. tls. Letter found at New York Public Library.

September 17, 1962. WSB [Paris] to Dick Seaver [New York] 1p. tls. Letter found at Syracuse University.

September 20, 1962. WSB [Paris] to Paul Bowles [Tangier, Morocco] 1p. tls. Letter found at University of Texas.

September 24, 1962. WSB [Paris] to Billy Burroughs Jr. [Palm Beach, Florida] Carbon copy. Letter found at New York Public Library.

October 24, 1962. WSB [Paris] to Barney Rosset [New York] Carbon copy. Letter found at New York Public Library.

1963

January 23, 1963. WSB [London] to Brion Gysin [Paris] 1p. tls. Letter found at New York Public Library.

March 15, 1963. WSB [London] to Barney Rosset [New York] 1p. tls. Letter found at Syracuse University.

April 5, 1963. WSB [London] to Paul Bowles [Tangier, Morocco] 1p. tls. Letter found at University of Texas.

May 11, 1963. WSB [London] to Maurice Girodias [Paris] Carbon copy. Letter found at New York Public Library.

May 13, 1963. WSB [London] to Barney Rosset [New York] 1p. tls. Letter found at Syracuse University.

May 21, 1963. WSB [London] to Paul Bowles [Tangier, Morocco] 1p. tls. Letter found at University of Texas.

July 15, 1963. WSB [Tangier, Morocco] to Brion Gysin [Paris?] 1p. tls. Letter found at New York Public Library.

October 24, 1963. WSB [Tangier, Morocco] to Brion Gysin [Paris?] 1p. tls. Letter found at New York Public Library.

November 20, 1963. WSB [Tangier, Morocco] to Allen Ginsberg [San Francisco] 1p. tls. Letter found at New York Public Library.

December 1, 1963. WSB [Tangier, Morocco] to Brion Gysin [Paris?] 3p. tls. Letter found at New York Public Library.

December 17, 1963. WSB [Tangier, Morocco] to Brion Gysin [Paris] 1p. tls. Letter found at New York Public Library.

December 17, 1963. WSB [Tangier, Morocco] to Laura Lee and Mortimer Burroughs [Palm Beach, Florida] Carbon copy. Letter found at New York Public Library.

1964

January 7, 1964. WSB [London] to Ian Sommerville [Tangier, Morocco] 1p. tls. Letter found at New York Public Library.

January 17, 1964. WSB [London] to *Times Literary Supplement* [London] 1p. tls. Letter found at Ohio State University.

February 4, 1964. WSB [Tangier, Morocco] to Brion Gysin [Paris] Carbon copy. Letter found at New York Public Library.

February 5, 1964. WSB [Tangier, Morocco] to Allen Ginsberg [New York] 1p. tls. Letter found at Columbia University.

February 16, 1964. WSB [Tangier, Morocco] to Peter Michelson [Chicago] 1p. tls. Letter found at University of Chicago.

February 27, 1964. WSB [Tangier, Morocco] to Alan Ansen [Athens, Greece] 1p. tl. Letter found at New York Public Library.

March 10, 1964. WSB [Tangier, Morocco] to Dick Seaver [New York] 1p. tls. Letter found at Syracuse University.

March 22, 1964. WSB [Tangier, Morocco] to Antony Balch [London?] Carbon copy. Letter found at New York Public Library.

March 28, 1964. WSB [Tangier, Morocco] to Brion Gysin [Paris] 1p. tls. Letter found at New York Public Library.

March 30, 1964. WSB [Tangier, Morocco] to Jean-Jacques Lebel [Paris] Carbon copy. Letter found at New York Public Library.

April 10, 1964. WSB [Gibraltar] to Brion Gysin [Paris] 2p. als. Letter found at New York Public Library.

April 17, 1964. WSB [Tangier, Morocco] to Brion Gysin [Paris] 1p. tls. Letter found at New York Public Library.

April 20, 1964. WSB [Tangier, Morocco] to David Solomon [n.p.] Carbon copy. Letter found at New York Public Library.

May 3, 1964. WSB [Tangier, Morocco] to Gus Blaisdell [Craig, Colorado] 1p. tls. Letter found at Northwestern University.

May 4, 1964. WSB [Tangier, Morocco] to Laura Lee and Mortimer Burroughs [Palm Beach, Florida] Carbon copy. Letter found at New York Public Library.

May 12, 1964. WSB [Tangier, Morocco] to Alex Trocchi [London] Carbon copy. Letter found at New York Public Library.

May 20, 1964. WSB [Tangier, Morocco] to Allen Ginsberg [New York] 1p. als. Letter found at Columbia University.

June 14, 1964. WSB [Tangier, Morocco] to Mr. Tambimuttu [New York?] Carbon copy. Letter found at New York Public Library.

June 18, 1964. WSB [Tangier, Morocco] to Brion Gysin [Paris] 1p. tls. Letter found at New York Public Library.

June 21, 1964. WSB [Tangier, Morocco] to Laura Lee and Mortimer Burroughs [Palm Beach, Florida] Carbon copy. Letter found at New York Public Library.

June 22, 1964. WSB [Tangier, Morocco] to Brion Gysin [Paris] 1p. tls. Letter found at New York Public Library.

June 30, 1964. WSB [Tangier, Morocco] to Brion Gysin [Venice] 1p. tls. Letter found at New York Public Library.

July 9, 1964. WSB [Tangier, Morocco] to Gus Blaisdell [Craig, Colorado] 1p. tls. Letter found at Northwestern University.

August 26, 1964. WSB [Tangier, Morocco] to Laura Lee and Mortimer Burroughs [Palm Beach, Florida] Carbon copy. Letter found at New York Public Library.

September 10, 1964. WSB [Tangier, Morocco] to Alex Trocchi [London] 1p. tls. Letter found at Arizona State University.

September 28, 1964. WSB [Tangier, Morocco] to Eugene Brooks [Long Island, New York] Carbon copy. Letter found at New York Public Library.

October 11, 1964. WSB [Tangier, Morocco] to Carl Solomon [Bronx, New York] 1p. tls. Letter at New York University.

November 6, 1964. WSB [Tangier, Morocco] to Ian Sommerville [England] Carbon copy. Letter at New York Public Library.

November 9, 1964. WSB [Tangier, Morocco] to Laura Lee and Mortimer Burroughs [Palm Beach, Florida] Carbon copy. Letter found at New York Public Library.

November 9, 1964. WSB [Tangier, Morocco] to [Rives Matthews?] [St. Louis, Missouri?] Carbon copy. Letter found at New York Public Library.

November 17, 1964. WSB [Tangier, Morocco] to Ian Sommerville [England] Carbon copy. Letter found at New York Public Library.

November 18, 1964. WSB [Tangier, Morocco] to John Calder [London] 1p. tls. Letter found at Indiana University.

ca. late November 1964. WSB [Tangier, Morocco] to Barney Rosset [New York] 1p. tls. Letter found at Syracuse University.

December 1, 1964. WSB [on board S.S. *Independence*] to Allen Ginsberg [New York] 1p. als. Letter found at Columbia University.

December 22, 1964. WSB [New York] to Neil Abercrombie [San Rafael, California] Carbon copy. Letter found at New York Public Library.

December 29, 1964. WSB [St. Louis, Missouri] to Jeff Nuttall [London] 1p. tls. Letter found at University of Kansas.

1965

January 17, 1965. WSB [New York] to *Sunday Times* Editor [London] 1p. tls. Letter found at University of Kansas.

February 1, 1965. WSB [New York] to John Calder [London] 1p. tls. Letter found at Indiana University.

February 16, 1965. WSB [New York] to Ian Sommerville [London] Carbon copy. Letter found at New York Public Library.

March 9, 1965. WSB [New York] to Ian Sommerville [England] Carbon copy. Letter found at New York Public Library.

March 22, 1965. WSB [New York] to Ian Sommerville [England] Carbon copy. Letter found at New York Public Library.

April 12, 1965. WSB [New York] to Ian Sommerville [London] Carbon copy. Letter found at New York Public Library.

April 20, 1965. WSB [New York] to Neil Abercrombie [San Rafael, California] Carbon copy. Letter found at New York Public Library.

April 20, 1965. WSB [New York] to John Calder [London] 1p. tls. Letter found at Indiana University.

April 30, 1965. WSB [New York] to Maurice Girodias [Paris] Carbon copy. Letter found at New York Public Library.

May 19, 1965. WSB [New York] to Ian Sommerville [London] Carbon copy. Letter found at New York Public Library.

May 19, 1965. WSB [New York] to Antony Balch [London] Carbon copy. Letter found at New York Public Library.

July 2, 1965. WSB [New York] to Ian Sommerville [London] Carbon copy. Letter found at New York Public Library.

July 2, 1965. WSB [New York] to Antony Balch [London] Carbon copy. Letter found at New York Public Library.

July 24, 1965. WSB [New York] to Mr. Gunsburg [New York?] Carbon copy. Letter found at New York Public Library.

August 12, 1965. WSB [New York] to Alan Ansen [Tangier, Morocco] Carbon copy. Letter found at New York Public Library.

September 8, 1965. WSB [London] to John Berendt [New York] Carbon copy. Letter found at New York Public Library.

October 4, 1965. WSB [London] to Bruce Holbrook [New York] Carbon copy. Letter found at New York Public Library.

October 11, 1965. WSB [London] to David Prentice [New York] Carbon copy. Letter found at New York Public Library.

October 27, 1965. WSB [London] to Mr. Rubin [n.p.] Carbon copy. Letter

found at New York Public Library. At least one additional page of this
letter was missing from the carbon copy.

October 28, 1965. WSB [London] to Brion Gysin [Tangier, Morocco] 1p.
tl. Letter found at New York Public Library.

October 28, 1965. WSB [London] to Paul Bowles [Tangier, Morocco]
1p. tls. Letter found at University of Texas.

December 13, 1965. WSB [Tangier, Morocco] to Antony Balch [England]
Carbon copy. Letter found at New York Public Library. Final page(s) of
carbon copy are missing.

December 17, 1965. WSB [Tangier, Morocco] to Allen Ginsberg [San
Francisco] 1p. tls. Letter found at Columbia University.

December 18, 1965. WSB [Tangier, Morocco] to John Broderick [Ire-
land?] Carbon copy. Letter found at New York Public Library.

1966

February 28, 1966. WSB [London] to Brion Gysin [Tangier, Morocco]
2p. tls. Letter found at New York Public Library.

ca. March 4, 1966. WSB [London] to Editor of the *New Statesman* [Lon-
don] Carbon copy. Letter found at New York Public Library.

March 15, 1966. WSB [London] to Brion Gysin [Tangier, Morocco] 2p.
tls. Letter found at New York Public Library.

April 4, 1966. WSB [London] to Brion Gysin [Tangier, Morocco] 1p. tls.
Letter found at New York Public Library.

April 4, 1966. WSB [London] to Timothy Leary Defense Fund [New
York] Carbon copy. Letter found at New York Public Library.

April 4, 1966. WSB [London] to David Prentice [New York] Carbon copy.
Letter found at New York Public Library.

April 21, 1966. WSB [London] to Carl Weissner [Heidelberg, West Ger-
many] 1p. tls. Letter found at University of Texas.

May 27, 1966. WSB [London] to Brion Gysin [Tangier, Morocco] 1p. tls.
Letter found at New York Public Library.

August 1, 1966. WSB [London] to Brion Gysin [Tangier, Morocco] 2p. tls.
Letter found at New York Public Library. One paragraph deleted.

ca. September 12, 1966. WSB [Tangier, Morocco] to Ian Sommerville
[England] Carbon copy. Letter found at New York Public Library.

September 15, 1966. WSB [Tangier, Morocco] to Ian Sommerville [Lon-
don] Carbon copy. Letter found at New York Public Library.

October 4, 1966. WSB [London] to Allen Ginsberg [New York] 1p. tls.
Letter found at Columbia University.

October 10, 1966. WSB [London] to Dick Seaver [New York] 1p. tls. Letter found at Syracuse University.

October 13, 1966. WSB [London] to Brion Gysin [Tangier, Morocco] 1p.
tls. Letter found at New York Public Library.

November 10, 1966. WSB [London] to Claude Pelieu [New York] 1p. tls. Letter found at University of Kansas.

November 21, 1966. WSB [London] to Laura Lee Burroughs [Palm Beach, Florida] Carbon copy. Letter found at New York Public Library.

November 21, 1966. WSB [London] to Brion Gysin [Tangier, Morocco] 2p. tls. Letter found at New York Public Library.

November 25, 1966. WSB [London] to Laura Lee Burroughs [Palm Beach, Florida] Carbon copy. Letter found at New York Public Library.

December 10, 1966. WSB [London] to Stephen W. Fried [Lewisburg, Pennsylvania] Carbon copy. Letter found at New York Public Library.

December 17, 1966. WSB [London] to Brion Gysin [Tangier, Morocco] 1p. tls. Letter found at New York Public Library.

December 23, 1966. WSB [London] to Brion Gysin [Tangier, Morocco] 3p. tls. Letter found at New York Public Library.

1967

February 5, 1967. WSB [Palm Beach, Florida] to Brion Gysin [Tangier, Morocco] 1p. tls. Letter found at New York Public Library.

February 8, 1967. WSB [Palm Beach, Florida] to Brion Gysin [Tangier, Morocco] 1p. tls. Letter found at New York Public Library.

March 17, 1967. WSB [London] to Brion Gysin [Marrakech, Morocco] 1p. tls. Letter found at New York Public Library.

March 19, 1967. WSB [London] to Hugh Cameron [Chicago, Illinois] Carbon copy. Letter found at New York Public Library.

March 19, 1967. WSB [London] to Peter Elvins [Italy] Carbon copy. Letter found at New York Public Library.

April 20, 1967. WSB [London] to Brion Gysin [Marrakech, Morocco] 1p. tls. Letter found at New York Public Library.

April 20, 1967. WSB [London] to Mr. Hohmann [n.p.] Carbon copy. Letter found at New York Public Library.

April 23, 1967. WSB [London] to Claude Pelieu [San Francisco?] 1p. tls. Letter found at University of Kansas.

July 17, 1967. WSB [London] to Brion Gysin [Tangier, Morocco] 1p. tls. Letter found at New York Public Library.

August 21, 1967. WSB [London] to Brion Gysin [Tangier, Morocco] 1p. tls. Letter found at New York Public Library.

September 7, 1967. WSB [London] to Brion Gysin [Tangier, Morocco] 2p. tls. Letter found at New York Public Library.

October 1, 1967. WSB [London] to Brion Gysin [Tangier, Morocco] 2p. tls. Letter found at New York Public Library.

October 4, 1967. WSB [London] to Billy Burroughs Jr. [Orange City, Florida] Carbon copy. Letter found at New York Public Library.

November 20, 1967. WSB [London] to Norman Mailer [New York?] 1p.
tls. Letter found at University of Texas.

1968

January 23, 1968. WSB [London] to Brion Gysin [Tangier, Morocco] 2p.
tls. Letter found at New York Public Library.

February 11, 1968. WSB [London] to Brion Gysin [Tangier, Morocco] 2p.
tls. Letter found at New York Public Library.

March 8, 1968. WSB [London] to Brion Gysin [Tangier, Morocco] 2p. tls.
Letter found at New York Public Library. Seven lines deleted.

March 9, 1968. WSB [London] to Carl Weissner [New York] 1p. tls. Letter found at University of Texas.

April 15, 1968. WSB [London] to Brion Gysin [Tangier, Morocco] 1p. tls.
Letter found at New York Public Library.

July 1, 1968. WSB [London] to Brion Gysin [Tangier, Morocco] 1p. tls.
Letter found at New York Public Library.

August 19, 1968. WSB [London] to Brion Gysin [Tangier, Morocco] 1p.
tls. Letter found at New York Public Library.

August 23, 1968. WSB [London] to Brion Gysin [Tangier, Morocco] 1p.
tls. Letter found at New York Public Library.

September 9, 1968. WSB [London] to Brion Gysin [Tangier, Morocco] 1p.
tls. Letter found at New York Public Library.

September 10, 1968. WSB [New York] to Antony Balch [London] Carbon
copy. Letter found at New York Public Library.

September 28, 1968. WSB [New York] to Brion Gysin [Tangier, Morocco]
2p. tls. Letter found at New York Public Library.

October 17, 1968. WSB [London] to Brion Gysin [Tangier, Morocco] 1p.
tls. Letter found at New York Public Library.

October 17, 1968. WSB [London] to Joe Gross [New York?] Carbon copy.
Letter found at New York Public Library.

November 5, 1968. WSB [London] to Brion Gysin [Tangier, Morocco] 1p.
tls. Letter found at New York Public Library.

December 6, 1968. WSB [London] to Brion Gysin [Tangier, Morocco] 2p.
tls. Letter found at New York Public Library.

December 8, 1968. WSB [London] to Brion Gysin [Tangier, Morocco]
1p. tls. Letter found at New York Public Library.

1969

January 18, 1969. WSB [London] to Jeff Shero [New York?] 1p. tl. Letter
found at New York Public Library.

March 10, 1969. WSB [London] to Brion Gysin [Tangier, Morocco] 2p.
tls. Letter found at New York Public Library.

March 13, 1969. WSB [London] to Brion Gysin [Tangier, Morocco] 1p. tls. Letter found at New York Public Library.

April 11, 1969. WSB [London] to Mr. Flemming [London?] Carbon copy. Letter found at New York Public Library.

April 30, 1969. WSB [London] to Brion Gysin [Tangier, Morocco] 2p. tls. Letter found at New York Public Library.

May 22, 1969. WSB [London] to John Cooke [Mexico?] Carbon copy. Letter found at New York Public Library.

June 18, 1969. WSB [London] to Brion Gysin [Tangier, Morocco] 4p. tls. Letter found at New York Public Library. Seven lines deleted.

July 22, 1969. WSB [London] to John Cooke [Mexico?] Carbon copy. Letter found at New York Public Library.

August 11–13, 1969. WSB [London] to Brion Gysin [Tangier, Morocco] 4p. tls. Letter found at New York Public Library.

October 6, 1969. WSB [London] to Brion Gysin [Tangier, Morocco] 3p. tls. Letter found at New York Public Library.

November 3, 1969. WSB [London] to Gershom Legman [n.p.] Carbon copy. Letter found at New York Public Library.

November 5, 1969. WSB [London] to Brion Gysin [Tangier, Morocco] 1p. tls. Letter found at New York Public Library.

November 17, 1969. WSB [London] to Brion Gysin [Tangier, Morocco] 1p. tls. Letter found at New York Public Library.

December 4, 1969. WSB [London] to Claude Pelieu and Mary Beach [San Francisco?] Carbon copy. Letter found at New York Public Library.

December 15, 1969. WSB [London] to Brion Gysin [Tangier, Morocco] 2p. tls. Letter found at New York Public Library.

1970

January 2, 1970. WSB [London] to Charles Upton [n.p.] Carbon copy. Letter found at New York Public Library.

January 4, 1969. WSB [London] to Brion Gysin [Tangier, Morocco] 1p. tls. Letter found at New York Public Library.

January 14, 1970. WSB [London] to Billy Burroughs Jr. [n.p.] Carbon copy. Letter found at New York Public Library.

January 21, 1970. WSB [London] to Brion Gysin [Tangier, Morocco] 3p. tls. Letter found at New York Public Library.

February 13, 1970. WSB [London] to Peter Matson [New York] Carbon copy. Letter found at New York Public Library.

April 9, 1970. WSB [London] to Brion Gysin [Tangier, Morocco] 5p. tls. Letter found at New York Public Library.

April 19, 1970. WSB [London] to Brion Gysin [Tangier, Morocco] 3p. tls. Letter found at New York Public Library.

April 20, 1970. WSB [London] to Peter Matson [New York] Carbon copy. Letter found at New York Public Library.

April 21, 1970. WSB [London] to *Los Angeles Free Press* [Los Angeles] Carbon copy. Letter found at New York Public Library. Final page of letter missing.

ca. May 8, 1970. WSB [London] to *Los Angeles Free Press* [Los Angeles] Carbon copy. Letter found at New York Public Library.

May 31, 1970. WSB [London] to Mr. Harr [n.p.] Carbon copy. Letter found at New York Public Library. Two lines deleted.

July 22, 1970. WSB [London] to Brion Gysin [Tangier, Morocco] 2p. tls. Letter found at New York Public Library.

July 23, 1970. WSB [London] to Truman Capote [New York?] Carbon copy. Letter found at New York Public Library. Seven words deleted.

July 24, 1970. WSB [London] to Peter Matson [New York] Carbon copy. Letter found at New York Public Library.

August 9, 1970. WSB [London] to Brion Gysin [Tangier, Morocco] 2p. tls. Letter found at New York Public Library.

August 16, 1970. WSB [London] to Allen Ginsberg [New York] Carbon copy. Letter found at New York Public Library.

August 16, 1970. WSB [London] to Harrison Starr [New York] Carbon copy. Letter found at New York Public Library.

August 30, 1970. WSB [London] to Billy Burroughs Jr. [Orange City, Florida] Carbon copy. Letter found at New York Public Library.

August 30, 1970. WSB [London] to John Cooke [Mexico?] Carbon copy. Letter found at New York Public Library.

September 19, 1970. WSB [London] to Brion Gysin [Tangier, Morocco] 3p. tls. Letter found at New York Public Library.

September 20, 1970. WSB [London] to Peter Matson [New York] Carbon copy. Letter found at New York Public Library. Four repetitious paragraphs deleted.

October 3, 1970. WSB [London] to Billy Burroughs Jr. [Savannah, Georgia?] Carbon copy. Letter found at New York Public Library.

October 15, 1970. WSB [London] to Peter Matson [New York] Carbon copy. Letter found at New York Public Library.

October 26, 1970. WSB [London] to Charles Upton [n.p.] Carbon copy. Letter found at New York Public Library.

November 4, 1970. WSB [London] to Billy Burroughs Jr. [Savannah, Georgia?] Carbon copy. Letter found at New York Public Library.

November 30, 1970. WSB [London] to Barry Miles [New York] 2p. tls. Letter found at Columbia University.

December 1, 1970. WSB [London] to Mike Sissons [London] 1p. tls. Letter found at Indiana University.

January 12, 1971. WSB [London] to Peter Matson [New York]. 2p. tls. Letter found at Columbia University.

1971

February 26, 1971. WSB [London] to Billy Burroughs Jr. [Savannah, Georgia?] Carbon copy. Letter found at Columbia University.

April 1, 1971. WSB [London] to Kevin Roche [n.p.] Carbon copy. Letter found at New York Public Library.

May 4, 1971. WSB [London] to Billy Burroughs Jr. [Savannah, Georgia?] Carbon copy. Letter found at New York Public Library.

May 6, 1971. WSB [London] to Brion Gysin [n.p.] 1p. tl. Letter found at Arizona State University.

May 11, 1971. WSB [London] to Brion Gysin [n.p.] 1p. tls. Letter found at Arizona State University.

May 20, 1971. WSB [London] to Billy Burroughs Jr. [Savannah, Georgia?] Carbon copy. Letter found at New York Public Library.

May 22, 1971. WSB [London] to David Cooper [London?] Carbon copy. Letter found at New York Public Library.

June 2, 1971. WSB [London] to Donald Erickson [New York] Carbon copy. Letter found at New York Public Library.

July 11, 1971. WSB [London] to Billy Burroughs Jr. [Savannah, Georgia?] Carbon copy. Letter found at New York Public Library.

August 23, 1971. WSB [London] to Terry Southern [New York?] Carbon copy. Letter found at New York Public Library.

September 28, 1971. WSB [London] to Billy Burroughs Jr. [Savannah, Georgia?] 1p. tls. Letter found at New York Public Library.

October 10, 1971. WSB [London] to Billy Burroughs Jr. [Savannah, Georgia] Carbon copy. Letter found at New York Public Library.

October 21, 1971. WSB [Haute-Nendaz, Switzerland] to Brion Gysin and Antony Balch [London] Carbon copy. Letter found at New York Public Library.

October 22, 1971. WSB [Haute-Nendaz, Switzerland] to Brion Gysin [London] Carbon copy. Letter found at New York Public Library.

October 24, 1971. WSB [Haute-Nendaz, Switzerland] to Brion Gysin and Antony Balch [London] Carbon copy. Letter found at New York Public Library.

October 25, 1971. WSB [Haute-Nendaz, Switzerland] to John Cooke [Mexico?] Carbon copy. Letter found at New York Public Library.

October 27, 1971. WSB [Haute-Nendaz, Switzerland] to Brion Gysin and Antony Balch [London] 2p. tls. Letter found at New York Public Library.

December 22, 1971. WSB [London] to Brion Gysin [Tangier, Morocco] 1p. tls. Letter found at New York Public Library.

1972

February 15, 1972. WSB [London] to John Brady [San Francisco?] 1p. tl. Letter found at Arizona State University.

February 16, 1972. WSB [London] to Billy Burroughs Jr. [Savannah Beach, Georgia] Carbon copy. Letter found at New York Public Library.

April 17, 1972. WSB [New York] to Brion Gysin [Paris] 3p. tls. Letter found at New York Public Library.

April 23, 1972. WSB [New York] to Brion Gysin [Paris] 2p. tls. Letter found at New York Public Library.

April 28, 1972. WSB [New York] to Paul Bowles [Tangier, Morocco] 1p. tls. Letter found at University of Delaware.

July 9, 1972. WSB [New York] to Billy Burroughs Jr. [Boulder, Colorado] 2p. tl. Letter found at New York Public Library.

October 30, 1972. WSB [London] to Billy Burroughs, Jr. [Boulder, Colorado] 1p. tls. Letter found at New York Public Library.

November 15, 1972. WSB [London] to Fred Halsted [Los Angeles] 1p. tls. Letter found at Arizona State University.

December 9, 1972. WSB [London] to Fred Halsted [Los Angeles] 1p. tl. Letter found at Arizona State University.

December 19, 1972. WSB [London] to Fred Halsted [Los Angeles] 1p. tls. Letter found at Arizona State University.

1973

March 23, 1973. WSB [London] to Allen Ginsberg [Cherry Valley, New York] 3p. tls. Letter found in private collection.

May 1, 1973. WSB [London] to Peter Matson [New York?] Carbon copy. Letter found at Syracuse University.

June 1, 1973. WSB [London] to Liz Strickland [Paris] 2p. tl. Letter found at Arizona State University.

June 8, 1973. WSB [London] to Liz Strickland [Paris] 2p. tl. Letter found at Columbia University.

July 10, 1973. WSB [London] to Billy Burroughs Jr. [Savannah, Georgia?] 2p. tl. Letter found at Arizona State University. One paragraph deleted.

July 16, 1973. WSB [London] to Mack? [n.p.] 1p. tls. Letter found at Arizona State University.

September 6, 1973. WSB [London] to Billy Burroughs Jr. [Savannah, Georgia] 1p. tls. Letter found at Arizona State University.

September 13, 1973. WSB [London] to John Calder [London] 1p. tls. Letter found at Indiana University.

October 30, 1973. WSB [London] to Brion Gysin [Paris?] 1p. tls. Letter found at Arizona State University.

November 14, 1973. WSB [London] to Sanche de Gramont [n.p.] 1p. tls. Letter found at Arizona State University.

November 29, 1973. WSB [London] to John Calder [London] 1p. tls. Letter found at Indiana University.

November 30, 1973. WSB [London] to John Brady [San Francisco] 1p. tls. Letter found at Arizona State University.

December 13, 1973. WSB [London] to Billy Burroughs Jr. [Atlanta, Georgia?] 1p. tls. Letter found at Arizona State University.

December 23, 1973. WSB [London] to Dom Sylvester Houedard [New York?] 1p. tls. Letter found at Arizona State University.

1974

January 14, 1974. WSB [London] to Allen Ginsberg [New York?] 1p. tls. Letter found at Arizona State University.

March 18, 1974. WSB [New York] to Billy Burroughs Jr. [Atlanta, Georgia?] Letter published in *Cursed from Birth*.

INDEX

Barris, Chuck, 386–87
BBC, 38, 323
Beach, Mary, 312–13
Beach Books, 277
Beer, Anthony Stafford, 407–8
Beiles, Sinclair, 28, 34, 82
Belli, Bill, 17, 20, 24, 33–34, 54, 275
Bentham, Jeremy, 345
benzedrine, 236, 293
Berendt, John, 196–97
Berkson, Bill, 90, 105
Berrigan, Ted, 309
Big Table, 8, 10, 11, 18–19, 22
Birch, John, 314
Birnbaum, Peter, 125
Bishop, John, 187, 255
Black Panther Party, 293, 310, 347
Blaisdell, Gus, 154–55, 164–65
Blake, James W., 12
blue movies, 65, 383–85, 387–88
Booker, Bob, 141
Book of the Dead, 337–38
Book of the It (Groddeck), 374
Boston Trial of *Naked Lunch* (1965), 258
Bouthoul, Betty, 232
Bowles, Jane, 12, 97, 125, 230
Bowles, Paul, 81, 125, 160, 230, 284, 296, 298, 349; 1959 letter, 12; 1960 letters, 17, 20, 23–24, 37–38; 1961 letters, 65–66, 85, 93; 1962 letters, 97, 101, 102–3, 108–9, 110, 113–14; 1963 letters, 121–22, 124–25; 1965 letter, 203–4; 1972 letter, 388–89; *A Life Full of Holes*, 173
Boyars, Arthur, 172, 181, 188
Boyars, Marion, 48, 51, 53, 114, 172, 181, 188, 408
Brady, John, 381, 392, 409
British Film Institute, 119
Broderick, John, 207–8
Brooks, Eugene, 167
Broomfield, Peter, 170
Brown, Andreas, 218, 338, 385
Bruce, Lenny, 157
Buckley, William F., Jr., 284

Budd, David, 126–27, 131, 144, 198, 220, 275, 284, 297, 303, 340, 343, 349, 357
Burgess, Anthony, 137, 318
Burroughs, Billy, Jr. (son), 75, 127, 133, 234–39, 251–53; 1961 letter, 71–72; 1962 letter, 114–15; 1967 letter, 265–66; 1970 letters, 320–21, 343–44, 349, 352; 1971 letters, 358, 360, 363–64, 367, 368–70; 1972 letters, 382–83, 389–91; 1973 letters, 402–3, 404–5, 409–10; 1974 letter, 416; drug charges, 141, 229–30, 231, 241, 251–53; grandparents and, 156, 160–61, 165–66, 234–35, 237–39; *Speed*, 299–300, 349, 352, 358, 367
Burroughs, Laura Lee (mother), 6–7, 10–11, 13–14, 251, 352, 389; 1963 letter, 133; 1964 letters, 156, 160–61, 165–66, 169–70; 1966 letters, 234–35, 237–39
Burroughs, Mort (brother), 238, 253
Burroughs, Mortimer (father), 6–7, 389–90; 1963 letter, 133; 1964 letters, 156, 160–61, 165–66, 169–70
Burroughs Archive, xxxii, 389–91, 403, 406, 408
"But is All Back Seat of Dreaming," 10, 22, 30
Byrne, Alfred, 179–80

Cain's Book (Trocchi), 320
Calas, Nicolas, 90
Calder, John, 114, 127, 129, 137, 161, 189, 211, 259, 294–95, 337, 341–42; 1964 letter, 172; 1965 letters, 181, 187–88; 1973 letters, 405, 408
calendar form, 321–23
Cambridge Heretics Society, 67
Cameron, Hugh, 255–56
Cammell, Donald, 362, 363
Cannes Film Festival, 360, 364

Cape, Jonathan, 188, 216, 295, 324, 325, 328, 329, 398
Capote, Truman, 17, 66, 216–17, 252; 1970 letter, 338–39
"Carl Cranbury in Egypt," 211–13
Carr, Lucien, 91, 141–42, 158
Carroll, B.J., 73
Carroll, Paul, 8, 10, 18–19, 22, 30–31
Cassady, Neal, 391
Castaneda, Carlos, 301–2, 310, 320–21, 391
Castro, Fidel, 190, 207–8
Castro, Silvester de, 32
censorship, 109, 112, 115–16, 247, 281, 282
Chamberlain, Wynn, 347
Chappaqua (film), 75, 320
Chelsea Hotel, 173, 190, 195, 353, 371
Cherifa, 12, 93, 125, 376
Chiang Kai-shek, 53–54
Chicago Democratic National Convention (1968), 277, 281, 342, 344
Chicago Review, 8, 18
Chicago Seven, 342, 344
Chomsky, Noam, 304, 309
Chopin, Henri, 398–99
Christie, Agatha, 273
Church, Stuart, 183
CIA, 267, 290, 307–8, 311, 317, 351, 358, 364, 365, 391
Clarke, Arthur, 124
Cleaver, Eldridge, 310–11, 347
Cody, Bob, 115–16
Cohen, Ira, 121, 124, 173, 203, 284, 371
Cole, Tony, 397
Coleman, Ornette, 398
collages (collage method), 76–79, 81–82, 89, 176
Comandante, The (film), 155
Conrad, Joseph, 149
Cooke, John, 225, 304, 305, 322–23, 375–76; 1969 letters, 299, 302–3; 1970 letter, 345–46; 1971 letter, 374–75

Cooke, Mary, 69
Cookson, Jimmy, 51, 226
Cooper, Clarence, 358, 364
Cooper, David, 213–15, 365
Corre, Xavier, 162, 174, 180, 186, 240, 255
Corso, Gregory, xxxii, 4, 11, 45, 58, 108, 110, 128, 149, 275, 402; 1961 letter, 68; 1962 letter, 104
Cowen, Elise, 3
Crawdaddy, 336, 339, 353
Crosby, John, 110
Crowley, Aleister, 13, 336
cut-up method, xxviii, xxx, 3, 10, 19, 22, 26–28, 34–36, 39, 40–41, 43–46, 64, 67, 71, 81–82, 105, 132, 140, 332–35, 337–38
Cyclops, 354

Damianova, Violeta, 46
dating system, xxxii
Dead Fingers Talk, 127, 137, 138–39, 181
Dean, Loomis, 9, 10, 83–84
Death Compass, The (film), 192–93
Decknetell, Bill, 76–77
de Gramont, Sanche, 407–8
de Grazia, Edward, 252, 370–73
de Kooning, Willem, 4
DeLoach, Allen, 309
Deming, Angus, 126
Democratic National Convention (1968), 277, 281, 342, 344
Dent, John Yerby, 25, 28, 36, 48, 52, 179–80, 186–87, 240, 246, 255, 359; 1960 letter, 39–40. See also *Anxiety and Its Treatment*
Descriptive Catalogue of the William S. Burroughs Archive (Miles, ed.), 390
Detective Stories, 51
DiPrima, Diane, 89–90
Disraeli, Benjamin, 5
Domaine Poétique, 127
Doubleday, 272, 287–88, 299, 306, 309–10, 318, 319, 397, 400, 404

Hells Angels, 308
Hemingway, Ernest, 343–44, 401
Herbert, Frank, 376
High Time (movie), 51
Hill, Joe, 8
Hiroshima Mon Amour (film), 85
History of the Occupation, The, 53
Hoffenberg, Mason, 67, 189
Hoffman, Abbie, 344, 358
Hoffman, Julius, 342, 344
Hohmann, Mr., 258
Holbrook, Bruce, 185, 191, 192, 197–98
Hopkins, John, 253, 304, 306, 390
Hopper, Dennis, 369, 382
Houedard, Dom Sylvester, 410–11
Howe, John, 37, 99
Howl (Ginsberg), 59, 168
Hubbard, L. Ron, xxviii, 46, 218, 244–46, 257, 262, 264–65, 266, 271–76, 285–86, 290, 296–97, 299, 302–3, 309, 312, 313, 314, 317–19, 322–23, 330–31, 336, 345, 351, 353, 374–75, 376
Hullis, Billy, 275
Hummel, Odette, 187
Hummel contract/Swiss arrangement, 23, 48, 100, 145, 181, 187–89
Huncke, Herbert, 63, 67, 220
Hustler, The (film), 104
Huxley, Francis, 48, 50, 298

I Am Out (Gysin), 44
ICA (Institute of Contemporary Arts), 121
In Cold Blood (Capote), 216–17, 339
Independence, S.S., 171, 173
indole, 46–47
Ingram-Merrill Foundation, 340–41
International Poetry Incarnation (1965), 193, 194
International Times (IT), 233, 235, 262, 263, 300, 309, 311–12, 318, 325, 328, 329, 339
Ionesco, Eugène, 277

Is London Cracking Up? (TV series), 407, 409

Jagger, Mick, 312, 360–64
Jajouka, Morocco, 125–26
Jeannot, 76–77, 81–82
"Jeff Hawke" (comic), 155
Job, The, 293, 295, 297–98, 309, 327–28, 330, 332, 335, 337, 342, 382
"Johnny's So Long At The Fair," 108, 154
Johns, Jasper, 241
Johnson, Lyndon, 190–91
Jones, Brian, 305
Jones, LeRoi, 89–90
Jordan, Fred, 327
Journeys Out of the Body (Monroe), 397, 400, 404
Julius Caesar (Shakespeare), 283
Junkie, 128, 154, 167, 168, 194, 330
Jurado, Bernabé, 6

Kamiya, Joe, 319, 344, 351
Kasmin, John, 48, 53
Kelly, Peter, 174, 240
Kelly, Richard, 241
Kennedy, John F., 53–54, 151
Kennedy, Robert F. "Bobby," 277
Kentucky Ham (Burroughs Jr.), 358, 402
Kerouac, Jack, 46, 58, 128, 141, 142, 158, 391
Kiki, 25
Klacto, 259
Kluckhohn, Clyde, 164
Knickerbocker, Conrad, 224
Knoebber, Roger, 66, 75, 76, 77, 81–82
Koran, 41
Kramer, 79
Krishnamurti, Jiddu, 345–46
Kubrick, Stanley, 287
Kulchur, 59

Larbi, Mohammed, 70, 73, 75, 349
largactil, 75

Meeker, Marilynn, xxxiv
Meknes, Morocco, poisoning
  (1959), 7, 8
mescaline, 3, 4–5, 9, 11, 41, 53, 58,
  63, 64–65, 87, 89, 215
"Metamorphosis" (Burroughs Jr.),
  114–15, 389
methadone, 359
Metronome, 67, 99
Michelson, Peter, 142–43
Miles, Barry, 325, 329, 337–38,
  342, 352–53, 390, 415
Miller, Karl, 215
Mind Parasites, The (Wilson), 194
Minutes To Go, 30, 32, 34–35, 36,
  38, 39, 44–45, 64, 88, 154, 277
misconceptions about Burroughs,
  xxix–xxx
misspellings, xxxiii–xxxiv
Mistral Bookshop (Paris), 20, 32
Mitchum, Robert, 155
MOB (My Own Business), 313–14,
  317
Mondadori, Fabrizio, 124
Monroe, Robert, 397, 400, 404
Montgomery, John, 66
Morgan, Ted, 17, 25, 407
Mottram, Eric, 325, 328, 329, 342
Moving Times, 148, 155, 157, 166
"Mr Bradly Mr Martin," 25, 30,
  35, 42
Murphy, Doctor, 236
Museum of Modern Art, 108, 314,
  387
mushrooms, 67, 86, 90
Mustain, Gordon, 330–32, 336
"My Love Returned" (Matson), 198
My Own Mag (My Magazine), 148,
  149, 155, 157, 158, 162, 165,
  166, 175, 233

Naked Lunch (book), xxviii, 8,
  17–20, 35–36, 91, 106, 109,
  111, 116, 120–23, 194–95, 334;
  Boston trial, 120, 258; *Chicago
  Review* excerpt, 18; contract
  and financial issues, 23, 48, 100,
  145, 181, 187–89; Grove Press
  and, 37, 81, 92–93, 120–21,
  123, 188–89, 254, 258; obscen-
  ity charges, 258; Olympia Press
  and, 3, 5–6, 35, 80–81, 122–23,
  181
Naked Lunch (script), 360, 363–64,
  367–70, 382, 386–87, 406
Newman, Jerry, 45, 59, 67
Newman, Paul, 104
Newspeak Poetry, xxviii
New Statesman, 213–15, 216, 365
Newsweek, 125–26, 170, 281, 282,
  332
Newton, Massachusetts (1961),
  85–87
New York City College, xxix, 409,
  415
New York Times, 139–40, 194
"Night Before Thinking, The," 101
Nightwood (Barnes), 401
1984 (Orwell), xxviii
Nixon, Richard, 338
Nordenholz, Anastasius, 351, 353
Norse, Harold, 97, 272–73, 276, 371
Nouvelle Revue Française, 21
Nova Express, 83, 97–104, 107, 113,
  115, 120, 124, 154, 164–65,
  169–70, 172, 188, 199–202,
  211–12, 216
November, Sally, 128
Nuttall, Jeff, 155, 157, 158, 165,
  166, 190; 1964 letter, 175–76

Odier, Daniel, 278
O'Hara, Frank, 225
O'Higgins, Patrick, 217
Olmedo, José, 20
Olympia, 88, 99, 100
Olympia Press, 3, 5–6, 23, 35, 74,
  80–81, 122–23, 181
O'Neil, Paul, 9
Open Space Theatre (Chicago), 342
Oregon Shakespeare Festival, 14
orgone box, 21
Orlovsky, Peter, 68, 91, 103, 398
Orwell, George, xxviii